# THE LOWLANDS
## OF
# SCOTLAND

*Edinburgh
and the South*

*Books by Maurice Lindsay*

POETRY

The Enemies of Love
Hurlygush
At the Wood's Edge
Ode for St Andrew's Night and Other Poems
The Exiled Heart
Snow Warning
One Later Day
This Business of Living
Comings and Goings
Selected Poems 1942–1972
The Run From Life: More Poems 1942–1972
Walking Without An Overcoat

PROSE

The Lowlands of Scotland: Glasgow and the North
The Lowlands of Scotland: Edinburgh and the South
The Scottish Renaissance
Robert Burns: the Man: his Work: the Legend
The Burns Encyclopedia
Clyde Waters
By Yon Bonnie Banks
The Discovery of Scotland: Travellers in Scotland from the
    thirteenth to the eighteenth centuries
Environment: a Basic Human Right
The Eye is Delighted: Some Romantic Travellers in Scotland
Portrait of Glasgow
Robin Philipson
History of Scottish Literature

ANTHOLOGIES

Poetry Scotland 1–4 (4 with Hugh MacDiarmid)
No Scottish Twilight (with Fred Urquhart)
Modern Scottish Poetry: an Anthology of the Scottish
    Renaissance
John Davidson: Selected Poems: with a preface by T. S. Eliot
    and an introduction by Hugh MacDiarmid
A Book of Scottish Verse (World Classics)
Scottish Poetry 1–6 (with George Bruce and Edwin Morgan)
Scottish Poetry 7–9 (with Alexander Scott and Roderick Watson)
Scotland: An Anthology

# THE LOWLANDS
## OF
# SCOTLAND

*Edinburgh and the South*

*by*

MAURICE LINDSAY

ROBERT HALE · LONDON ·

First published in *"The Country Books"*
series 1956. This revised edition 1977


ISBN 0 7091 5718 5



Robert Hale Limited
Clerkenwell House
Clerkenwell Green
London EC1R OHT

Printed in Great Britain by
Lowe & Brydone Printers Limited, Thetford, Norfolk

# CONTENTS

FIRTH OF FORTH

EDINBURGH

NORTH SEA

North Berwick

Dunbar

EAST LOTHIAN

Haddington

St Abb's Head

Eyemouth

HIRE

...HIRE

...D LOTHIAN

Tranent

Dalkeith

LAMMERMUIR HILLS

...HILLS

MOORFOOT HILLS

BERWICKSHIRE

Duns

Berwick-on-Tweed

Lauder

Peebles

...BLESSHIRE

Melrose

Coldstream

...on Innerleithen

Kelso

Selkirk

Roxburgh

Yarrow

...uir

SELKIRKSHIRE

Jedburgh

Harwick

ROXBURGHSHIRE

E N G L A N D

...HIRE

...en

Langholm

Ecclefechan

Annan

THE LOWLANDS
OF SCOTLAND
Edinburgh and the South

The higher land
is indicated by
shading
(lowlands counties only)

Scale of Miles
(approximate)

0        10        20

# ILLUSTRATIONS

## PICTURE CREDITS

Hamish Campbell: 1-3; The Scottish Field: 4, 5, 8, 9, 13-15 and 17; the Scottish Tourist Board: 6, 10, 11, 16, 18; the National Trust for Scotland: 7; The Scotsman: 12; and Messrs. Firth Photos Ltd.: 19

# PREFACE TO THE SECOND EDITION

IN the twenty years that have passed since the first version of this book appeared, so many changes have occurred that it is impossible to chronicle all of them. On the personal level, my father, Matthew Lindsay, Mr. George Emslie and Mr. J. M. Reid, all mentioned in the original Preface, are unfortunately no longer alive.

Diesel locomotion and electrification have supplanted steam trains. Edinburgh is linked to Glasgow by a fast double carriageway road, most of it motorway.

The concept of the designation of Conservation Areas—a product of the Civic Amenities Act of 1967—has been strengthened by the Town and Country Amenities Act of 1974, which puts upon planning authorities not only the requirement of designating such areas, but also of drawing up practical plans for their enhancement. The former provisional Listed Building lists have now been made statutory, and the task of their revision is under way. Would-be destroyers of Listed Buildings must now secure positive planning permission to achieve their end, and the Scottish Civic Trust, the Scottish Georgians and local amenity societies be allowed to comment within twenty-one days. A developer out to bring down a Listed Building for profit now has to face the fact that if he is refused permission to demolish, all he can claim, by way of loss of development rights, is the stone-and-mortar value of the building as it stands, and not the site value.

These protective measures stem from a growing awareness among all sections of the community that our man-made heritage is irreplaceable, an awareness reflected in such measures as the successful public insistence that developers should not be allowed to erect a high-rise tower (which would have dominated even Edinburgh Castle) on the site of Haymarket Station, and in the vast voluntary exercise run by The Scottish Civic Trust and Edinburgh Architectural Association whereby, after an eighteen month-long survey by over one hundred and forty professional people freely giving their skills and their time, an international public meeting took place in June 1970 out of which emerged the Edinburgh New Town Conservation Committee, with a former

Lord Provost of Edinburgh as its first chairman and a full-time Director.

The other remarkable physical change of circumstance, however, has been the discovery that oil exists in quantity beneath the North Sea. Grangemouth refinery may not be environmentally particularly pleasing, but it performs a necessary function. The winning of North Sea oil is bound to have a considerable impact on the Forth estuary, though nothing like the environmental impact of the industrialization of the Firth of Clyde (effectively removing from that loveliest of estuaries near a Scottish city its role as a holiday playground for Glaswegians and tourists) or upon the north-east coast.

The decline of public religious observance, in Edinburgh and the south of Scotland, as elsewhere, is placing some fine church buildings at risk. Churches and banks present particularly difficult problems in the search for a viable new use, and we shall have to resign ourselves to the loss of some of them. Support for football, the watching of which is, or should be, a non-participatory pursuit, is, I am told, on the wane. Yet enthusiasm for opera is on the increase, although at the time of writing still not sufficiently powerful to enable Edinburgh to take its courage in both hands and begin building its opera-house on the vacant site long since cleared for it behind the Lyceum Theatre, a cultural gesture which would thus bring the Festival city upsides with Glasgow, whose restored Theatre Royal opened as the permanent home of Scottish Opera in October 1975.

The teaching of Scottish literature has continued slowly to spread through schools during the past two decades, although there is still room for a further extension of this study. The academic pursuit and study of the more recondite aspects of our literature, however, is almost assuming the proportions of a national industry.

The Scottish Tourist Board has turned fully " professional ", in the sense that it is now a Governmental organization so far as finance is concerned, and tourism in Scotland has prospered.

The most important change of all, however, has been the steady strengthening of the Scots sense of nationhood. Re-reading my book in its original form, I was surprised to find how frequently my national bias showed itself. I have always favoured a Scottish Government within some sort of federated United Kingdom framework, and inside the context of a united Europe, of which culturally and economically we are so inevitably a part. Twenty years ago, such a possibility seemed no more than a frustrating dream. Now, the partial collapse of the English economy, disillusion with the old London-controlled two-party system, and the promise which North Sea oil brings to Scotland, have led to an effective rise of support for the Scottish National Party, which makes a particularly strong appeal to the disillusioned young. So, all parties have given assurances that Scotland will have its own Assembly, and the prospect that the distinctive voice of Scotland may soon be heard once more in the concert of Europe's nations becomes a realizable reality. All this is as it should be. The energy crisis of the middle 1970's, if it has taught us anything, should have taught us that bigness is not, as was once supposed, everything: that bigness can, indeed, actually be a disadvantage.

I hope that, together with the revised edition of *The Lowlands of Scotland: Glasgow and the North*, this new and revised edition of *The Lowlands of Scotland: Edinburgh and the South* may increase the enjoyment of those who come to visit the small country that is Scotland, and may further stimulate the curiosity of some of my countrymen to get to know their own heritage more thoroughly than perhaps at present they do.

*11 Great Western Terrace*
*Glasgow.*
*11th January 1976*

To my friend and brother-poet
GEORGE BRUCE
who has Scotland so much at heart

# CHAPTER I

# EDINBURGH: THE OLD TOWN

This city is high seated, in a fruitful soil and wholesome air, and is adorned with many noblemen's towers lying about it, and aboundeth with many springs of sweet waters. At the end towards the east is the King's palace, joining to the monastery of the Holy Cross, which King David the First built, over which in a park of hares, conies, and deer a high mountain hangs, called the Chair of Arthur. . . . From the King's palace at the east, the city still riseth higher and higher towards the west, and consists especially of one broad and very fair street (which is the greatest part and sole ornament thereof) the rest of the side streets and alleys being of poor building, and inhabited with very poor people; and this length from the east to the west is about a mile, whereas the breadth of the city . . . cannot be half a mile. At the farthest end towards the west is a very strong castle, which the Scots hold unexpugnable. . . . And from this castle towards the west is a most steep rock, pointed on the highest top, out of which this castle is cut. . . .

FYNES MORYSON, 1598.

I

" AT least," said the kindly rubicund man who sat opposite me in the railway compartment on a summer's day in 1950, " Edinburgh is still a capital city, where our own kings and queens have lived and loved and died. They can't take *that* away from us anyway."

" Perhaps not," I answered mechanically, wondering how soon this Glasgow train would plunge into the Haymarket tunnel, and set us all reaching with an air of careless leisure for our bags and coats in the racks above our seats, in preparation for that moment when the steam-plumed engine would glide out into the morning sunlight of Princes Street Gardens, slip past the base of the Castle rock, and slide gently to rest alongside one of the more remote platforms of that untidy sprawl which is Waverley, the largest and most imposing of Scottish railway stations.

The station was full of noise and bustle. An artificially constrained voice, whose owner appeared to be striving desperately to suppress her natural accent in favour of the more impressive tones of BBC impersonality, made the atmosphere reverberate with the information that the train for King's Cross was just about to depart from Platform One. The taxis of late-comers raced down the long ramp that is the station's entrance, their flurried

1

inmates leaping out with agility astonishing for their years, and sprinting towards the south-bound train, bags, tartan rugs and overcoats hung all about them.

"They can't take that away from us anyhow." My travelling companion's words sounded on in my mind. Can't they? Haven't they? What, indeed, *have* "they" left us with which, if taken, could possibly have proved profitable? What indeed! How tiresome, I reflected as I emerged from the smoke-charged air of the station, to find these good Edinburgh middle-class folk cherishing the absurd notion that Edinburgh is still a capital city. A capital, indeed, which has to do precisely what it is told by politicians in a metropolis situated four hundred miles away! A capital run to a large extent by people who, for generations, have consciously modelled themselves, almost to the point of caricature, upon the English upper-classes and whose most obvious local characteristic is an acidulation of English ease-of-manner—an acidulation caused, no doubt, as much by the frustration of stagnating beneath long years of impotent make-believe as by the asperities of our northern climate.

"Of course," my rubicund friend would have replied, "you Glaswegians have an inferiority complex, and are therefore not fair judges of Edinburgh's position and status." At that moment, however, I did not think that my judgment was hampered by any such inferiority complex. What I do have is a Glaswegian's impatience with empty talk. Somehow, on this particular morning, Edinburgh seemed to me to be hovering precariously between a state of "having-been" and one of "soon-to-be-again".

Yet in another mood, I should be the first to admit that it is just this "soon-to-be-again" feeling that, in the end, probably justifies my friend's capital claim. However exasperating it may occasionally seem to those of us who become impatient with long-delayed promise, the feeling which for so many difficult years has nourished that claim remains obstinately in the air for all with enough sensitivity to pree it. It is a difficult feeling to track down and analyse. It is not experienced by all Scots. It may even prove, in the end, to have been a delusion. Meanwhile it is there, and must be accounted for; the more so since it is but one, perhaps the ultimate, expression of that sense of re-awakening nationhood which for the past thirty or so years has been stirring the hearts and minds of many of the Scottish people.

How can it be accounted for? How explained? Only by the irresistible accumulation of the past. From the earliest times, Edinburgh has attracted the attention of settlers as a place of safety, a place of pleasing eminence: even in these unrecorded, unimaginable days when the first settlers drifted into the fertile hollows which the shelving ice-masses and the devastating floods of the various glacial epochs had carved and washed out of what later became Mid-Lothian—strange, is it not, to think that the Royal Mile is made up of clay and gravel piled high by the irresistible force of ice-packs grinding round the base of Castle Rock?—Britons, Romans and Picts all made of Edinburgh a place of government. Its Gaelic name, *Dun Eadain*, "Fort of the Hill Slope", indicates the Celt's quick appreciation of its character; and from that name comes Dunedin, later to be Anglicized into Edina by Augustan poets. By a curious linguistic chance, the name of the Saxon king who overthrew the Picts of Dunedin in 617 or 629—historians cannot agree on the exact placing of this important date—was Edwin of Northumbria. From his name, and without too much phonetic violence being wrought upon the original Gaelic, Edinburgh assumed its modern identity.

As Scotland slowly came together to form one nation, Edinburgh, although at various times rivalled by Perth and Stirling, also began to assume her role of Capital City—a role which she held *de facto* until the dark day in 1707 when a handful of bribed cellar-lords signed away their country's independence on conditions now fairly acknowledged to have been as short-sighted as they were unpopular at the time.

But what are a mere two hundred and fifty odd years of bustling white-collar servility when set against vast centuries of stormy independence? Nothing at all. Remembering that, and remembering, too, the quickening temper of the Scottish spirit, Edinburgh's outward refusal to demit her capital gestures and status suddenly becomes, not exasperating, but wholly admirable.

One reason for her self-assurance, her air of "all-will-be-well-in-the-end", may be that her personality is compounded not only out of history, but out of the actual fabric of past ages, much of which is still lovingly preserved. It should be the first task of those who seek to understand her personality to become acquainted with the fascinating disarray of buildings which make up part of Edinburgh's heritage. For Edinburgh literally arises out of stone; stone has therefore remained for her an element of greater significance than it has for most other Scottish—or, indeed, English—towns.

There are the dominating rocks themselves, immovable and immutable, whatever graces and griefs Man may from time to time have wisped across their surfaces. Arthur's Seat, Edinburgh's Fomorian "giant-of-three-heads", which got its present name during the fifteenth century when the Arthurian romances became

3

popular at the Scottish court, and to the summit of which those who still practise primitive rituals ascend every May Day for the sunrise ceremony of rubbing their faces in the dew[1]: Salisbury Crags, steep and forbidding in their urban setting, named, unaccountably, after an Earl of Salisbury who was a commander in the invading army of Edward III[2]; Calton Hill; Blackford Hill, with its stone quarries and its observatory; Corstorphine Hill; and, most prominent of them all, the Castle Rock.

Then there are the ridges; the humph-backit spine of the High Street; the long, lean ridge which carries the New Town across its shoulders. Even the lay mind can conjure up a picture of the convolutions and upheavals which erupted and shaped this raw stuff of the Capital City. To the geologist, indeed, Edinburgh is a compressed textbook of illustrated information.

It has often seemed to me, looking out from the ramparts of the Castle over the indeterminate folds of buildings which sweep down to the Forth, or across the suburban villas and bungalows which surge back to the foot of the Pentland Hills, that Nature and History entered into a singularly well-matched partnership in the matter of Edinburgh's development. Where else in all Scotland could so proper a place be found for the fierce creative and destructive energies of Scottish thought to have seethed and boiled-over into those actions and achievements which, cooled and fixed now, make up the substance of our story?

II

The oldest building in Edinburgh stands high on the summit of the Castle Rock. St. Margaret, the wife of King Malcolm Ceannmór, caused this beautiful little Normanized cell of stone-worship to be erected to the honour and glory of God about the year 1090. Not only does it mark Edinburgh's first memorial of fact over legend and conjectural fancy, but it also remains one of her finest architectural treasures, in spite of various alterations and additions accreted with the years. Over and over again it might have been destroyed; for instance, when in 1313, a few months before Bannockburn, Bruce's nephew the Earl of Moray wrested the Castle from its English garrison and, in the interests of that mediæval strategy which dared not countenance the exis-

---

[1] According to an eye-witness of the 1951 ceremony, which was held in a blizzard of sleet, over five hundred people attended. Presumably, as with more conventional forms of worship, numbers are apt to vary with the weather.
[2] An alternative, though less picturesque, derivation brings the name from the Anglo-Saxon sere, long, and beorgh, a rock.

tence of forts and strongholds at the heart of a besieged country, razed every other building on the rock; or during the Reformation, when the Protestant forces uncharacteristically contented themselves with humiliating its consecrated stones by making it into a gun-store; or at the end of the eighteenth century, when one faction of governmental opinion favoured the destruction of such relics of Scotland's nationality as the castles of Stirling and Edinburgh, ostensibly in the interests of economy. Fortunately, none of these threats materialized, and to-day, the chapel is honoured and preserved, realization of its true worth a guarantee against any future deliberate desecration.

It does not, however, attract anything like the attention which another shrine draws to itself. This, the National War Memorial, stands on the site of an eighteenth-century barracks which in its turn had supplanted a Church of St. Mary. The work of one of Scotland's cleverest twentieth-century architects, Sir Robert Lorimer (1864-1929), the National War Memorial was completed in 1927 at a cost of £150,000 which was raised by public subscription. Its purpose was to render up permanent honour to Scotland's dead of the First World War by housing in a sanctified shrine, wrought upon and jewelled by Scottish craftsmen, a Roll of the Illustrious Dead—a Roll that has since been sadly lengthened with the names of those who fell in the Second World War. Fine masonry, statuary, heraldic symbolism, and the crust of the rock itself rising naked through the floor—these things do combine to make an emotional impact on folk as they pass through the Hall of Honour to the Shrine itself, dominated by the figure of the Archangel Michael. Many people undoubtedly find religious comfort in the jewelled variety of its atmosphere. Many regard it as one of Edinburgh's finest treasures. Some even go so far as to call it Sir Robert's greatest work.

Architecturally, its contrived magnificence seems to me to be so pointlessly artificial that the impression with which I am left is one of spiritual emptiness: and into that emptiness there inevitably surges the strongest resentment that War, almost the worst of all human evils, should indirectly be so glorified. Of course I know very well that it is War's victims and not War itself which the shrine was designed to glorify. But can the one be honoured in this hysterically fulsome way without, indirectly, the other? Is not this strange building merely the Scottish climax of that uneasy public conscience-salving which found expression in an outburst of reckless stone war memorials on every village green during the "twenties"?

It is a relief to turn away from this curious building, and to

5

cross the Palace Yard to the Great Hall built by James IV at the beginning of the sixteenth century. In spite of its fine timbered roof and fancifully-carved stone corbels, it is not as impressive a royal residence as most of the others in Scotland. The earlier Stuart monarchs favoured Stirling, Linlithgow or Falkland, rather than Edinburgh. By the time Edinburgh did take precedence as their place of residence, Holyrood had replaced the Castle as the monarch's dwelling.

The Great Hall is, indeed, the largest, and must once have been the most magnificent, of the rooms which make up the Castle Palace. A solitary chair is all that remains of the once sumptuous furnishings. On occasion, the Great Hall has housed the Scottish Parliament. Now, it is a museum, housing only such relics of the past as that rusty lock of Loch Leven Castle for which young Willie Douglas stole the key to enable Queen Mary to escape: some letters signed by Charles I; and a fairly rich collection of Scottish accoutrements of war.

In the rough security of one of the Palace rooms, its little window turned to the cold east, Mary Queen of Scots gave birth to James VI on June 19th, 1566. That birth took place amidst an agony of political and religious scheming, for this child of a Catholic womb was far from welcome to the turbulent Protestant lords. Much need had the young prince for the prayer painted beneath a badge of the royal coat-of-arms:

> *Lord Jesu Chryst that Crounit was with Thornes,*
> *Preserve the Birth quhais Badgie heir is borne . . .*

The prayer was answered, and James became the first monarch to rule over three kingdoms. His London accession certainly had a devitalizing effect on Edinburgh's upper-class social and intellectual life for many a long year. But it had another, more immediate result.

Once he had tested the way of life of the English court, James VI and I could no longer be content with the domestic standards to which he had been accustomed in Scotland. So, for his much-delayed " hame-coming " of 1617—he went south in 1603, promising to return to Scotland every three years—his Master Mason, who went by the patriotic name of William Wallace, rebuilt the King's Ludging at the eastern end of the Palace, and decorated the window pediments with the royal monograms, a conceit which later offended the dour sight of Oliver Cromwell, who had them erased. The King's bed was conveyed by sea from London, and painted in " all manner of collours ": a special cookhouse was provided for his French chef: and Mons Meg, the fifteenth-century gun which now rests on a replica of its original gun-carriage on a platform by St. Margaret's Chapel[1], was heaved into a place of honour by thirteen stalwart porters. In addition to these earthly comforts, James was regaled with numerous poems, the best being a long effusion by William Drummond of Hawthornden, *Forth Feasting*, in which the king whom we now usually think of as Jamie the Saxt, the wisest fool in Christendom, was hailed as:

> *Eye of our western world, Mars-daunting king,*
> *With whose renown the earth's seven climates ring,*
> *Thy deeds not only claim these diadems,*
> *To which Thames, Liffey, Tay subject their streams*
> *But to thy virtues rare, and gifts, is due,*
> *All that the planets of the year doth view;*
> *Sure if the world above did want a Prince,*
> *The World above to it would take thee hence. . . .*

It would be interesting to know how James reacted to Drummond's rather tactless suggestion of further advancement to come.

Already by that time the Castle had lost much of its military usefulness. But the Half-Moon Bastion, which faces down the High Street and was built by the Regent Morton on the foundations of a tower which King David II had put up in the middle of the fourteenth century on his return from English captivity, still held an intricate maze of gloomy and unhealthy cells and passages ferreted out of the rock. These maintained their usefulness right up to the early nineteenth century, when some of Napoleon's soldiers, including Stevenson's fictional St. Ives, found

---

[1] Mons Meg is a celebrated character in Scottish history. Although she is generally agreed to have been forged in the fifteenth century, no one knows just where. Mons in Flanders is one theory, supported by the similarity between her proportions and those of Mad Marjory of Ghent. Tradition, however, asserts that she was forged in the Castle by one Robert Borthwick, and that her maiden shot was fired in honour of the birth of James V at Linlithgow. Other theories are that one McKim wrought her at Castle Douglas in 1455, for James II to use against Threave Castle, her name, Meg, being that of the gunsmith's wife. Mons is also supposed to relate to Mollance in Galloway, which district also claims her "birth". In any case, she travelled all over Scotland, tossing what Taylor, the Water-Poet (who, in 1618, had crawled up her barrel on his back to see if a child could be "gotten" there), called "balls of wild-fire" against the King's enemies, or up into the air in honour of royal occasions, until finally she burst herself in 1681 firing a salute in honour of James, Duke of York. She was taken prisoner by the English in 1754 as a punishment for the Porteous Riots, but returned in 1829 at the request of Sir Walter Scott, and received back at the Castle with military honours.

7

themselves confined in them.  It is from a platform on the top of the Half-Moon Bastion that, punctually every day at one o'clock, a modern gun roars off its salute.  Visitors to Edinburgh who have not been warned of this amusing barbarity are liable to suffer a severe shock.  Although I myself have stayed in Edinburgh many times, I still experience heart-palpitations when that explosion occurs.  Indeed, it is an excellent means of rendering strangers to the city momentarily conspicuous, for though most incomers either jump or at least look disturbed, the native merely glances at his watch—though whether to check the accuracy of his timepiece or because he is always hopeful of proving the gun incorrect, I have never really been quite sure.

Now, the Castle houses Scotland's military headquarters, while its Esplanade provides the stage for an annual tattoo.  In addition, on occasion the Great Hall is used for a ceremonial banquet, providing a setting which not even the dullest of post-prandial orations could make easily forgettable.  Although it is the movement of the soldiery which gives the grey old buildings their outward air of liveliness, it is the vivid bustle of historical associations that gives them their real, their meaningful life: Bishop Turgot smuggling the body of St. Margaret down the Western Port and across the Forth to Fife under cover of a "providential haar", while the usurping Donald Bane, hot-foot from the Hebrides, besieged the walls: William the Lion tamely surrendering it to the English after his capture at Alnwick, contriving it back again as part of the dowry of his English Queen, Ermengard; Edward Longshanks twice seizing it for the English, in 1291 and in 1296; Wallace recovering it twice over for the Scots; that most daring recovery of them all when Randolph, Earl of Moray, made his successful midnight ascent of the rock-face led by a warrior who, in the heat of his youth, had frequently performed this feat to get to his mistress[1]; Queen Joan fleeing to the shelter of the rock with her young son James II after her poet-husband had been murdered at Perth; the same Queen later rescuing her son from the clutches of an over-ambitious nobleman, Chancellor Crichton, by smuggling the infant outside the walls in a clothes-chest; the ill-advised slaughter of the Douglas heir by the young king a few years later, after a black bull's head had been set down on the table at a feast in the Great Hall; the gallant defence put up on Queen Mary's behalf for three years, long after all practical hope for her cause had gone, by Sir William Kirkcaldy of Grange; James VI and I's ceremonial return;

[1] Sir Walter Scott, as a lame schoolboy at the High School, also scaled the rock-face, an astonishing feat for one suffering from his disability.

Charles I's coronation-banquet in the Great Hall in 1633; Argyle, the persecutor of Montrose, waiting in the State Prison—the Argyle Tower—the moment of his own execution, brought about, not by his unscrupulousness and cruelty, but by his incompetence in ending up on the losing side at the close of the Civil War; the obstinate defence put up by those two tough Hanoverian Generals Guest and Preston, while at the other end of the Royal Mile Prince Charlie was holding his glittering levee in the Palace of Holyrood. These are the major memories. The minor memories, the griefs that once peopled the damp-faced, dingy cells—though many of them have passed unrecorded—contribute their not inconsiderable anonymous share to that atmosphere of stolid strength and gloomy endurance which makes up the Castle's personality.

III

The Old Town of Edinburgh, piled high on its sloping rise, has suggested animal metaphors to many travellers. Carlyle described its " . . . . sloping high street and many steep side-lanes " as " covering like some wrought tissue of stone and mortar, like some rhinoceros skin, with many a gnarled embossment, church steeple, chimney head, Tolbooth and other ornament or indispensability, back and ribs of the slope ". Needless to say, the idea of old Edinburgh as a rhinoceros is not one that has particularly commended itself to the City's panegyrists: as images go, admittedly it is a trifle exotic.

Most late nineteenth and early twentieth-century writers about Edinburgh have been romantics. To-day, when once every year hundreds of authors, broadcasters and journalists descend upon the City during her three flushed and hectic weeks of Festival, she is appraised and described in innumerable tongues. The majority of these appraisals—at any rate those written in English —are almost naïve in their romanticizing. The Old Town becomes " the poop of a stately galleon floating at anchor over the green fields of the Lothians "; the Castle, floodlit in the darkness, is seen as " a fairy edifice, moored in space "; while every little bit of self-conscious processional " revives the colourful pageantry of former days ". Such tushery is not, however, by any means only the work of foreign journalists. It is also the stock-in-trade of civic leaders. Perhaps this hankering after the pretty-pretty, this chaste and delicate falsification of history, represents a guilty stirring of the civic conscience for having destroyed so much of its heritage of stone; perhaps it is merely evidence of a desire, understandable enough in this uncertain age, on the part of a particular writer to project himself backwards into what he imagines to be a less troubled era than his own. In any case, there are more of the qualities of the rhinoceros than the qualities of Technicolor Fairyland about old Edinburgh.

The earliest houses up and down the High Street were made of wood and wattle. Probably they were little more than hovels crouched around the Castle walls. Even in the larger towns, Scotland did not take generally to the use of stone for ordinary domestic buildings until the sixteenth century. Froissart tells us that when the French troops of Sir John de Vienne, who had come hopefully to Scotland in 1383 to assist Robert III in his struggle with the English, were quartered in Edinburgh and the nearby villages, the Edinburgh folk eventually decided that the French were more of a nuisance than the English. The English, the Scots admitted, burned their houses; but then a house could be rebuilt easily in two or three days with six posts and some branches!

A century later, houses with wooden frames and plaster or clay infilling, their gables often turned to the street, and set in gardens sloping down the hillside, lined both sides of what later came to be called the Royal Mile. None of these houses has survived. By the beginning of the next century, the first of the tall lands or tenements were being erected inside the City's walls. These walls—the mediæval perimeter and the lower Flodden Wall which had been hastily piled up on the orders of Archibald "Bell-the-Cat" Douglas, elected Provost after the citizens had received news of that disastrous battle, and of the death of their sovereign and their civic leader—were themselves a prime cause of the development of the land, which was generally adopted by the Scots before it found even partial favour with any other nation in Europe. For safety's sake, no one dared build outside the perimeter. As the streets and wynds filled up, and buildings could no longer be squeezed closer together, there was no alternative but to build higher. In any case, lands of seven, ten or even fourteen storeys brought in more rent-money to the landlord. Most of the highest lands were probably burned down in 1532, the year the High Street was first paved. Because of the fire danger, an order had to be made prohibiting the storing of heather and peat before doors.

An Edinburgh citizen of James IV's time faced a reasonable prospect of having to endure either death by roasting, or death by bubonic plague, which, when it broke out, leapt as easily as fire across the narrow wynds. Even if he did not succumb to either of these extreme menaces, we know from William Dunbar's address *To the Merchants of Edinburgh*, that there were many other offences against both eyes and nose which had to be put up with:

> *Why will ye, merchants of renoun,*
> *Lat Edinburgh, your nobil toun,*
> *For lack of reformatioun*
> *The common profit tine, and fame?*          [lose
> *Think ye not shame,*
> *    That ony other regioun*
> *Sall, with dishonour hurt your name!*

> *May nane pass through your princeful gaits*          [ways
> *For stink of haddocks and of skates,*
> *For crys of carlings and debates,*          [common people
> *For fensum flytings of defame:*          [loud scoldings
> *    Think ye not shame,*
> *Before strangers of all estatis*
> *That sic dishonour hurt your name!*

> *Your stinkand Schule, that standis dirk*
> *Halds the licht fra your parroch kirk;*          [St. Giles
> *Your foirstairs maks your housis mirk,*
> *Like na country bot here at hame:*
> *    Think ye not shame,*
> *Sa little policy to wirk*
> *In hurt and sclander of your name!*

> *At your hie Cross, whar gold and silk*
> *Suld be, there is bot curds and milk;*
> *And at your Tron bot cockle and wilk,*
> *Pansches, puddings of Jock and Jame:*
> *    Think ye not shame,*
> *Sen as the warld sayis that ilk,*
> *In hurt and sclander of your name!* . . .

Some of the evils of which Dunbar complains were remedied by the improvements of 1532. So much so that an English traveller of the later 1530's became quite eloquent in praise of the city.

" There are two spacious streets, of which the principal one, leading from the Palace to the Castle, is paved with square

11

stones. The city itself is not built of bricks, but of square free-stones, and so stately is its appearance that single houses may be compared to palaces. From the abbey to the castle there is a continued street, which on both sides contains a range of excellent houses. . . ."

It is amusing to discover that two of the sights which so annoyed the irascible Dunbar are to be met with more than four hundred years later. Jocks and James are still fond of perambulating; no longer, perhaps, so much at the Mercat Cross as along Leith Walk, and not necessarily in search of puddings. Until a few years ago cockles and wilks were still being sold by an old woman whose place of business was by the High Street causey.

Little else of Dunbar's Edinburgh has come down to us. Less than a year after Mary had been crowned Queen of Scots by Cardinal Beaton at Stirling, and the Scots had declared null and void the Treaty made with England after Solway Moss,[1] Henry VIII began to fancy the infant princess as a politically desirable consort for his son. He chose an odd method of winning her; so odd, indeed, that even in those violent days, it became known as the "rough wooing". On May Day 1544, Henry's brother-in-law the Earl of Hertford led an English fleet into Leith Roads. Leith, Edinburgh, and all that lay between them and the ships, were sacked and burned. Holyrood itself, both the Palace and King David I's Abbey Church of the Holy Rude, were destroyed with the lave.[2] It says much for the native resilience that, by mid-century, Holyrood Palace was being rebuilt, and many of the lands in the Royal Mile had once again reared their towering storeys towards heaven, this time made of good solid stone, though, as Sir William Brereton observed in 1636, a number of the new houses were still "faced with boards". It is strange to think that by 1550, some prosperous citizen had already built the centre part of that noble house in the Lawnmarket acquired about 1620 by a wealthy merchant, Thomas Gladstone, who not only added the piazza (the last original example to survive in Edinburgh), and the Italianate painted fruit-and-flower timber ceilings, but gave the house the name by which we know it to-day. Gladstone's Land was excellently restored by Sir Frank Mears during the 1930s for the Scottish National Trust, and it is now the headquarters of the Saltire Society, a nation-wide company of enthusiasts who have done much to influence contemporary

[1] The disastrous defeat that broke the heart of James V.
[2] The brass eagle lectern was presented by Hertford to the Church of St. Albans, where it still remains.

Scottish life, not least by reminding the people of Scotland how valuable is their heritage from the past.


IV


The Royal Mile, crowned at its summit by the Castle and tipped at its lower end by Holyrood, falls naturally into three sections. Until the late eighteenth century, there were few gaps in the double row of lands to let in light and air from north or south. True, to the south there lay the Grassmarket and a maze of intertwining streets, although these did not venture beyond the Burgh Loch and the edge of the Burgh Muir, which was a favourite haunt for highwaymen. To the north, however, apart from a difficult pedestrian short-cut through Halkerston's Wynd which could only be used in dry weather, the first means of egress from the pent-up city was through Leith Wynd. The main route for wheeled traffic lay lower still, through the burgh of Canongate —so called because it was originally the home of the Holyrood canons—past the Water Gate, the Abbey Hill, Restalrig and thence across the lonely Figgate Whins, where Portobello now sprawls.

Above the Canongate, the High Street stretches up to meet the Lawnmarket: a name derived not, as is sometimes supposed, from the fact that some of the "lawn" or woollen merchants of the eighteenth century lived and traded there, but from a corruption of "landmarket", the place where the landward or country folk were, in earlier days, allowed to set up their stalls. In its turn, the Lawnmarket narrows into the Castlehill, leading directly up to the Castle Esplanade.

Most of the buildings which give the Old Town of Edinburgh its dominant character date from the seventeenth century. On Castlehill, for instance, there is Cannonball House, built by a furrier called Mure in 1630. It gets its name from the cannonball embedded in the wall facing the Castle, and supposed by the credulous to have been propelled there during the Jacobite's siege of the Castle in 1745. Further down, on the south and opposite side of the street, the Outlook Tower can also claim seventeenth-century origin, though it has been badly mutilated and deprived of most of its original character. It was the centre of activity of the supporters of Sir Patrick Geddes, an architect whose advanced ideas on town planning won him an international reputation. It houses the *Camera Obscura*, which provides a reflected view of

Edinburgh no doubt more amusing to a pre-Television age than to ours. Opposite the Outlook Tower stands Boswell's Court, whither "Bozzy" took Dr. Johnson to see his medico relative. The stones still carry the remains of a motto beloved of seventeenth-century builders, "*O Lord in the is al mi trust.*" Lower down, and on the same side of the street, there stood until 1846 one of the most interesting of all Edinburgh's buildings, the Palace of Mary of Lorraine. Here, this strong-minded widowed consort of James V took refuge after the Hertford raid, to be near the safety of the Castle. It is reputed to have contained much fine panelling and several painted ceilings, a few fragments of which have survived in museums. The destruction of the Palace heralded a wave of "improving" vandalism in Edinburgh, and was sanctioned to clear the site for, of all things, the Free Kirk College which now faces dourly down the Mound as part of the Assembly Hall of the Church of Scotland.

Tolbooth St. John's, a good example of the Pointed Gothic revival phase of the nineteenth century, was built in 1842 by James Gillespie Graham, who specialized in this mode of pastiche. It is a former meeting-place of the General Assembly of the Church of Scotland.

Gladstone's Land is the show-piece of the Lawnmarket. Its stone face rises up from its double arcade—it was never "faced with boards"—a forestair climbs up to the main door on the first floor; and, in George Scott-Moncrieff's words, "the whole building suggests a cheerful acceptance of being squeezed up against its western neighbour...." One of the oldest of those houses "faced with boards" was demolished during the present century on the grounds that it was unsafe. It had to be destroyed by dynamite.

Once the gardens attached to the earlier Old Town houses had been sacrificed to the needs of the builders, the construction of courts with pends leading into the main street became a favourite means of preserving a little aristocratic space in front of one's dwelling. Robert Mylne—one of the famous family who were King's Master Masons down seven generations—built Mylne's Court in 1690, part of which has been demolished but the best restored. James's Court, erected in 1725 by a speculative builder, contained, in the western block (which has since been burnt down) the home of David Hume (1711-1776), the philosopher. Here, in his "old house in James's Court, which is very cheerful and elegant, but too small to display my great talent for cookery, the science to which I intend to addict the remaining years of my life", Hume lived both before and after his spell in

Paris as Secretary of the Embassy. And from here, in his old age, he made one of the first flittings to the New Town.

Wardrop's Court contains a noble land which has been admirably restored and modernized by Robert Hurd for the Duke of Hamilton. Restoration by the University and by the Local Authority is also bringing back new life to the Old Town.

These two courts enclose one of the worst Scottish examples of "destoration". Lady Stair's house crouches beneath the towering tenements which surround it, cutting it off from the prospect it once enjoyed when its garden sloped down in terraces to the shore of the Nor' Loch. Eleanor, Lady Stair, was first married to James, Viscount Primrose, from whose refined brutalities she eventually sought shelter with her mother-in-law. On the death of her husband, however, while she was still young and renowned among the drawing-rooms of the wynds and closes for her beauty, the Earl of Stair made her an offer of marriage. Unwilling to embark upon a second doubtful venture, she steadfastly refused his pleadings. Being a man of resource, his lordship thereupon bribed one of her servants to secrete him overnight in her house. He slept alone under the stair; but at seven in the morning, when the city cleaners were brushing aside the slops and refuse that had been dropped over a thousand land window-sills the previous evening, and when the caddies were running their first errands of the day, and men of business were making their way to their dingy cellar shops, his lordship, clad only in his underclothes, showed himself prominently from a conspicuous window. To avoid the scandal, the gentle creature married him, and surprisingly enough, until her death in 1759 found the match a happy one.

Riddle's Court, on the opposite side of the street, contains Hume's first Edinburgh home. It was here that he started to write his *History of England*, a work of which he himself thought highly, but which posterity has awarded little honour. In Hume's day, history had not yet become the highly specialized study it is now; nor was factual accuracy so rigidly and rightly insisted upon by its readers.

Behind the early eighteenth-century houses which face Gladstone's Land, now well restored, and one of them a home of the Scottish Central Library—fragments of older buildings have been incorporated into later structures. The most conspicuous of these is the home of the wealthy Bailie MacMorran, who came to an untimely end in 1595 while trying to mediate in an unofficial strike of High School boys who considered their holidays to be inadequate. Led by young William Sinclair, they barricaded themselves in the school, which was then situated in Blackfriars' Gardens. Persuasion having failed to dislodge them, the magistrates, aided by the Town Officers, launched an attack on the schoolboy stronghold, during which operation Sinclair put a bullet through Bailie MacMorran's head. The incident caused a considerable stir even in those ungentle times, and only the boy's close connection with the Caithness family saved him from unpleasant punishment.

Brodie's Close is named after another Edinburgh worthy, Deacon William Brodie, whose double life provided Stevenson with the *point de départ* for *Dr. Jekyll and Mr. Hyde*. By day, Brodie was a cabinet-maker, well known for his professional skill and his douce sense of civic responsibility. By night, in company with his friend George Smith, Brodie was an equally skilful burglar, entering premises with keys specially forged by his own blacksmith. It was years before he was even suspected. At first, it was thought a little strange that the worthy citizen who had invented the " drop " system of hanging criminals as being a more humane means of dispatch than the old method of turning them off a ladder, should suddenly become addicted to the cruel sport of cock-fighting. But then middle age often afflicts the respectable with strange and unpredictable passions. However, his disappearance after a daring robbery of the Excise Office in Chessel's Court, in 1778, where implicating clues were found, led to his arrest inside a cupboard in Holland, whither he had fled.

One of the most celebrated lawyers of the day, Henry Erskine, defended Brodie, making much play with the sheer improbability of the charge in relation to so well respected a character. But not even Erskine's eloquence could save Brodie. At least he behaved gallantly towards the end. In the condemned cell, he greeted a visitor by singing " 'Tis woman that seduces all mankind " from Gay's *Beggar's Opera*; and when alone, he passed the time by playing chess with himself, his left hand against his right.

On the 1st of October, he was led out to the place of execution —by the old Tolbooth, fornenst St. Giles—the first victim of his own improved gallows. He made a great show of inspecting the apparatus; then, apparently satisfied with its mechanics, he mounted the pedestal and, with a smile on his face, had the rope put round his neck. His last act was to place his hand decorously into the front of his vest. Gallantry on the part of the criminal often inspires strange legends. Brodie's demeanour in the face of death gave rise to the fanciful story that he had persuaded the hangman to let him wear a steel collar, and that immediately the execution was over, he had arranged for his body to be given to a party of friends who would thereupon try to revive him.

The Lawnmarket was always a prosperous part of the Old Town. During the sixteenth century, it was the dwelling-place of ambassadors, and in the seventeenth and eighteenth centuries, of prosperous merchants. The antiquarian Robert Chambers tells us that:

"The Lawnmarket Club was composed chiefly of the woollen-traders of that street, a set of whom met every morning about seven o'clock, and walked down to the Post Office, where they made themselves acquainted with the news of the morning. After a plentiful discussion of the news, they adjourned to a public house, and got a dram of brandy . . . They were always the first persons in the town to have a thorough knowledge of the foreign news; and on Wednesday mornings, when there was no post from London, it was their wont to meet as usual, amuse themselves by the inventions of what was imaginary; and this they made it their business to circulate among the uninitiated acquaintances in the course of the forenoon. Any such unfounded articles of intelligence, on being suspected or discovered, were usually called Lawnmarket Gazettes, in allusion to their roguish originators."

The boundary between the Lawnmarket and the High Street proper is the road known now as George IV Bridge. Between it and St. Mary Street and Jeffrey Street beats the very heart of Edinburgh.

v

The construction of the North Bridge—the first street to breach the close-packed buildings of the Old Town—was brought about by the exertions of George Drummond, the most remarkable of Edinburgh's eighteenth-century provosts. In 1767, he procured the passing of an Act of Parliament which extended the boundaries of the city to take in the fields to the north, and authorized the building of a bridge across the gulley beneath the rock. The South Bridge was added a few years later, to carry the road over the Cowgate. Another bridge, the George IVth, was built between 1827 and 1836. It also spans the Cowgate, and crosses the High Street at the top of the Mound.

The middle sector of the Old Town, bisected by these release-

17

routes, still contains, amongst other buildings, St. Giles, the Tron Kirk, the old Parliament House (which now forms part of the Law Courts), and the restored Mercat Cross. It once also held the Tolbooth and the Luckenbooths. The former Royal Exchange, fronted with a classical façade, is now the City Chambers.

St. Giles's tower probably dominated the mid-Edinburgh sky-scape by the end of the fifteenth century. The Gothic Preston Aisle, a chapel of three bays, went up in 1454 to enshrine the arm-bone of St. Giles, which was presented by one William Preston of Garton.[1] The choir was enlarged in 1462. Five years later, St. Giles was elevated from the status of parish church to that of collegiate church. The lantern spire is said to have been completed in 1495, and in 1646 repaired by John Mylne—one of the seven members of that family who became King's Master Masons—who added the famous crown. But for all the distant, fretted glory of its crowned steeple against a gathering sky, St. Giles itself is an oddly disappointing piece of work. For this disappointment we have largely to thank a Victorian architect, William Burn (1789-1870). Burn certainly has the not unpleasing church of St. John's in Princes Street to his credit. But in his St. Giles "destoration" of 1829, he destroyed irreplaceable Norman and Gothic work and, in the words of George Scott-Moncrieff, brazenly refaced St. Giles "with paving-stones that have no structural meaning, some of them actually resting their points on the windows". Between the years 1872 and 1893, as much as possible of Burn's damage was repaired in the restoration of Dr. William Chambers. In 1911, when the Earl of Leven bequeathed a considerable sum to have restored, in ruined Holyrood, the Chapel of the Order of the Thistle—the premier order of Scot-land—and this was found to be technically impossible, Sir Robert Lorimer designed the Thistle Chapel in St. Giles instead, a noble, if somewhat over-ornate, piece of work.

Apart altogether from the cumulative effects of so much "destoration", part of the reason for the unsatisfactory impression which St. Giles so often makes is undoubtedly due to its change of function. Originally, though only a collegiate church, it was laid out to hold a high altar and side chapels. Presbyterian worship cannot adapt itself to the layout of a Cathedral, the stones of which cry out for a spacious ritual. Little is so depress-ing as the sense of incongruous strain which afflicts a worshipper, striving in vain to catch the gist of a sermon from the far corners of a building intended for praise of a much less intimate and personal nature.

[1] One wonders how he came by it!

18

Mass was sung in St. Giles for the last time in 1560, one year after Knox had preached his first sermon from its pulpit. Thirteen years later, realizing the unsuitability of what was in size if not in status a Cathedral, the early Reformers partitioned the interior of St. Giles into four separate kirks.

It was under Charles I's Episcopacy that St. Giles reached its official status as a Cathedral, a status it only maintained from 1633 to 1638. Thus it came about that when in 1637, acting upon His Majesty's orders, Dean Hannay replaced Knox's Prayer Book with Archbishop Laud's liturgy, a hubbub broke out. Persistent tradition has it that an Edinburgh kail-wife, Jenny Geddes,[1] became so enraged at the enforced change that as soon as the Dean nervously uttered the first few words, she jumped to her feet and hurled her stool at his head, shouting "Dost thou dare say Mass at my lug?" Bishop Lindsay himself could not quell the uproar, and although he managed to make a dignified exit, he was only spared the fury of the mob outside by the fortunate coincidence that at that moment a friend happened to be passing in his coach.

After the signing of the Solemn League and Covenant of 1643, in the Preston Aisle—which has since become known as the Assembly Aisle, because for a time it was the meeting-place of the General Assembly—the fabric of St. Giles was treated with the utmost disrespect. Part of it was used for the storing of gunpowder; part as a public exchange; part as a prison; and even as a kind of unofficial poor-house, where by tradition the workless were not molested. It was in an endeavour to sweep away the physical evidence of these abuses that William Burn did damage of a still more serious nature.

To-day, St. Giles, with its memorials to so many of the great figures in Scotland's story—the rival Marquises of Montrose and Argyll; Hay of Dalgety, one of Montrose's most famous captains who died on the same scaffold as his leader; John Knox; Jenny Geddes and Robert Louis Stevenson among them—is again a Cathedral in name, the centre of Presbyterian ceremonial in the Capital. But compared with the Cathedrals of Kirkwall or even Glasgow, it is still, æsthetically, something of a shorn disappointment.

Near the west door of St. Giles the shape of a heart may be seen picked out in the cobble-stones. This, the Heart of Midlothian, commemorates the Old Tolbooth, whose outline can be traced from setts in the road. Built to replace the original

[1] Her real name was Mrs. Mean according to Wodrow, " Mrs. Hamilton, grandmother to Robert Mein ", according to Kincaid.

Tolbooth which King Richard II destroyed during his sack of Edinburgh in 1385, it stood until 1817. Chambers, who was familiar with the Tolbooth as a boy, left a vivid description of it:

" It stood in a singular situation, occupying half the width of the High Street, elbow to elbow, as it were, with St. Giles Church. Antique in form, gloomy and haggard in aspect, its black stanchioned windows opening through its dingy walls like the apertures of a hearse, it was calculated to impress all beholders with a due and deep sense of what was meant in Scottish law by ' squalor carceris ' . . . It was not merely odorous from the ordinary causes of imperfect drainage, but it had poverty's own smell—the odour of human misery."

In its earliest days. the Tolbooth housed the Parliament of Scotland. Even after it had become a jail, so closely packed was the Old Town that the flat roof of three shops built on to the end of the Tolbooth had to be used as the platform for executions, until the Restoration, when the Grassmarket became the place where criminals made their end. There, " the great Marquis " was turned off in 1650; and there, eleven years later, the evil Argyll, who, in the face of death, also proved himself great, met his end under the blade of the Maiden. In the Tolbooth, too, many famous murderers and political prisoners have languished and sometimes—especially if they were of good family—escaped.

Amongst those whom the old stones felt unwilling to retain was Katherine Nairn, who, in 1765, poisoned her husband, aided by her brother-in-law, with whom she was having an affair. The dead man's brother was duly hanged in the Grassmarket, but Katherine was spared until the murderer's child which she was carrying should be born. It made its appearance on the 27th of January, 1766. A week later, Katherine walked out of the Tol-booth, dressed in the clothes of Mrs. Shiels, her midwife.[1] At least, that is the popular surmise. Historians of such matters later married her alternatively to a Frenchmen and to a " Dutch gentleman ", in both cases crediting her with fertile issue. William Roughead,[2] however, has produced evidence which strongly suggests that she did, in fact, end her days as a penitent convict at Lisle, and that her only child was the wretched infant left behind in the Tolbooth cell, where someone " overlaid " it two months after its birth.

[1] A celebrated member of her profession who was still practising in Edinburgh in 1805.
[2] *Twenty Scottish Trials.*

Those whose only escape from the Tolbooth was through the scaffold, included Major Thomas Weir, a saintly gentleman residing with his sister in the Bowhead, but who, under cover of his unblemished reputation, committed crimes so depraved and horrible that they could only be the work of a madman. He was strangled and burnt as a male witch in 1670. Another inmate executed was Deacon Brodie; and, of course, there was the unfortunate Captain Porteous, murdered by a rioting mob.

Two common smugglers, Wilson and Robertson by name, were arrested, tried and sentenced to death early in 1726, for robbing a collector of revenue taxes. Their first attempt to escape from the Tolbooth was unsuccessful. Accordingly, on the Sunday before the date fixed for their execution, they were taken under guard to St. Giles, so that at least they would face their Maker with Good Words sounding in their ears. Apparently, however, their thoughts were not altogether centred on matters divine, for, at the end of the service, Wilson suddenly attacked three of the four warders in charge of him, while in the ensuing carfuffle, Robertson escaped among the crowd. Wilson could have had no hope of escaping himself, a fact which made him appear something of a hero to the crowd.

In view of this, trouble was anticipated at his subsequent execution in the Grassmarket, and troops were brought in to reinforce the City Guard. As Wilson's body dropped, a surge of indignation swept over the crowd, who thereupon began to attack the soldiers with sticks and bottles. Captain Porteous, the Captain of the City Guard, lost his head in the stress of the emergency, and gave orders for his men to fire. Shots rang out, and people fell dead, amongst them some folk of rank and circumstance who were watching the performance of one of the most popular free spectacles of the eighteenth century from the seclusion of nearby windows. As a result of the affair, Porteous was brought to trial for murder, and sentenced to die on September 8th.

In London, however, Queen Caroline, who was acting as Regent while her husband George II was on a visit to Hanover, granted clemency to Porteous. Her act was interpreted in Edinburgh as a sure indication that she thought the lives of her Scottish lieges of little account.

On the night of September 7th, a great crowd surged up the High Street, overwhelmed the City Guard, and took possession of the Nether Bow. Then they set fire to the gate of the Tolbooth, overcame the terrified jailer, and burst into Captain Porteous's cell. He, by this time, was climbing the chimney, where, unfortunately for him, he stuck against a grating. He was hauled down the chimney by angry hands, and roughly told to prepare to meet his end. On the way to the Grassmarket, the crowd broke into a rope-dealer's shop, selected a suitable piece of hemp, and, with this, strung up the unfortunate commander on a dyer's pole. Justice avenged, they then quietly dispersed to their homes.

Naturally there was an outburst of furious indignation in London when the news of this enterprise reached the Queen and her Government. A bill to penalize Edinburgh severely was drawn up; but fortunately wiser councils prevailed. In the end, all that happened was that the Lord Provost, who had been thrown into the Tolbooth on Government orders, was released after six weeks: that the City had to provide a pension for Porteous's widow; and that Mons Meg was taken away from the Castle.

The Tolbooth's enduring fame, however, bestowed upon it by Scott's novel, based partly on the Porteous riots, *The Heart of Midlothian*, arises out of the confinement there of Effie Deans, a fictitious character symbolical of the many simple folk whom the grim walls of the old buildings broke in spirit and body, for crimes real and imaginary.

Along the length of St. Giles, and hard against the Tolbooth, once stood the Luckenbooths, or closed shops, which, together with the Krames—wooden stalls set up against the buttresses of the Kirk itself—for many centuries formed the fashionable shopping centre of the city. When the Tolbooth was pulled down, the Luckenbooths and the Krames vanished too.

On a first floor at the eastern end of one of the Luckenbooth lands, Allan Ramsay[1] set up his third bookshop, together with Scotland's first circulating library in 1725, beneath what he called the sign of " Hawthornden's and Ben Johnston's [sic] Heads". Thither came such fashionable patrons as the beautiful Lady Eglinton and her seven equally lovely daughters to pree the latest books of the day, to talk with friends, or merely to enjoy the full view down the High Street; a view a later generation also enjoyed from the ground floor of the same building, where Bailie William Creech, the Edinburgh agent and the publisher of Burns, had his bookshop. Needless to say, the Kirk fulminated against the "immoral" novels which Ramsay imported from London. Although the Kirk could do nothing against "the villainous, profane and obscene books and playes printed at London" and "got down by Allan Ramsay, and lent out, for an easy price", Kirk influence led to the closing of Edinburgh's first theatre,

[1] He had previously had premises in Niddry's Wynd (1718 to 1722), and in the High Street "on the South-side of the Cross-well" (1722 to 1725 or 6).

which Ramsay had established in Carruber's Close in 1736.

Edinburgh, and indeed Scotland, owes so much to Honest Allan, as he was affectionately nicknamed, that it is worth while turning aside for a moment to consider the significance of his achievement and influence. By temperament, he was a happy, hard-working little man with a keen eye for the main chance. The majority of his poems are as cheerfully bustling and banal as his conversation must have been. But though his best Scots poems are not of the first order set against the best work of Fergusson and Burns, his talents were by no means as negligible as some writers would have us believe.

He is, in the fullest sense, a purely national writer. By that I mean that he wrote for his ain folk, and for them alone. One of the sad accompaniments to the Union of Scotland and England has been the shifting of critical emphasis to the purely English point of view. Historians and critics of British literature have tended more and more to accord importance—in some cases even mere mention in literary histories—to poets who mean something to English readers. Thus Ramsay, Fergusson and Hogg— except perhaps in the case of the latter's remarkable *Private Memoirs of a Justified Sinner*, to which André Gide affixed the stamp of cosmopolitan approval—are rarely given their due in critical surveys of what purports to be " British " literature.

I am not complaining of this situation; merely drawing attention to it. For like so many other and graver indignities put across upon the Scots with the connivance of their own Westminster-conditioned politicians, the Scots themselves are to blame. Neither a noble tradition nor a virile contemporary national literature could have been long maintained by a country which, for so many years, seemed more anxious to merge all traces of its former distinction in the encompassing way of life of its larger, more successful neighbour.

Generations of English readers have found little satisfaction in Ramsay's pastoral ballad-opera *The Gentle Shepherd*; yet its gracious Lallans verse not only mirrors accurately the rustic Scots manners of the Restoration period, but is descriptively far closer to the actualities of the Scottish Lowland countryside than is any eighteenth-century English pastoral to its native scene. Nor can the English reader be expected to make much of the handful of richly vernacular pieces such as the *Familiar Epistles*, or the *Elegies on Lucky Wood* (an ale-house keeper in the Canongate), *John Cowper, Kirk-Treasurer's Man* (an official paid by the Kirk to " smell " out and bring to Kirk-justice on the stool of repentance those who indulged in intercourse outwith wedlock), or *Lucky*

*Spence's Last Advice* (she being a famous bawd whose brood of lasses functioned nightly in her lodgings near Holyrood). The English, however, cannot be blamed for rejecting these good things. The real tragedy is that too many Scots are nowadays also forced to reject them, wanting the " guid Scots tongue ".

Not only do such stanzas as the following from Ramsay's Third Familiar Epistle to William Hamilton of Gilbertfield express the poet's comfortably easy-going philosophy of life; they also provide the linguistic corner-stones upon which the whole of the eighteenth-century Revival movement was to be built:

> *That bang'ster billy, Cæsar July,*
> *Wha at Pharsalia wan the tooly,*
> *Had better sped, had he mair hooly*
> *    Scamper'd thro' life,*
> *And 'midst his glories sheath'd his gooly,*
> *    And kissed his wife.*
>
> *Had he, like you, as well he cou'd,*
> *Upon burn banks the muses woo'd,*
> *Retir'd betimes frae 'mang the crowd,*
> *    Wha'd been aboon him?*
> *The senate's durks, and faction loud,*
> *    Had ne'er undone him. . . .*
>
> *Ne'er fash about your neist year's state,*
> *Nor with superior pow'rs debate,*
> *Nor cantrapes cast to ken your fate;*
> *    There's ills anew*
> *To cram our days which soon grow late;*
> *    Let's live just now.*
>
> *When northern blasts the ocean snurl,*
> *And gars the heights and hows look gurl,*
> *Then left about the bumper whirl,*
> *    And toom the horn;*        [empty the drinking horn
> *Grip fast the hours which hasty hurl,*
> *    The morn's the morn. . . .*
>
> *Tho I were laird of tenscore acres,*
> *Nodding to jouks of hallenshakers,*        [crowds of atten-
> *Yet crushed wi' humdrums, which*        [dants on a gentle-
> *    the weaker's*                        [man's charity
> *Contentment ruins,*
> *I'd rather roost wi' causey-rakers,*        [street scavengers
> *    And sup cauld sowens*        [cold cabbage-water

*I think, my friend, an fowk can get*
*A doll of rost beef pypin het,*
*And wi' red wine their wyson wet,*       [gizzard
   *And cleathing clean,*
*And be nae sick, or drown'd in debt,*
   *They're no to mean.*

Ramsay's much-vaunted Jacobitism was, characteristically, of the canny sort. He took care to be "out of town" when Prince Charlie entered Edinburgh in 1745. Like most writers confronted with political action, he probably felt that he was not fitted for physical crusading. For him, the all-important thing was the saving of Scottish letters from extinction. The fate of the throne was not the concern of a man of letters.

With the Union of Parliaments in 1707, Edinburgh's role as Capital City, already severely shaken by the departure of James VI for London a hundred and four years earlier, received a blow which might well have proved mortal. The Scots aristocracy flocked south, and mixed in London society. It became the dearest wish of every London Scot to expunge all traces of the national speech from tongue and mind. Thus, even highly intellectual men like Hume and Beattie compiled little lists of betraying Scotticisms for the edification and improvement of themselves and their weaker brethren.

Under such circumstances, Scots as a literary medium lost caste. It became a vulgar tongue, a mark of illiteracy. Ramsay, who loved the Lallans, set himself out to restore it to respectability. He achieved a fair measure of success, mainly through his collection *The Tea-Table Miscellany*, an ingenious compilation of songs by himself and his friends between the covers of which pieces in Augustan English and pieces in guid braid Scots were put cheek by jowl. The *Miscellany* became popular alike with countesses and duchesses and with their serving-maids. It did much to keep the Scots tongue alive for more than a century after its appearance. Ramsay's rather unscholarly attempts to re-edit selections from the poems of the Auld Makars—Dunbar, Henryson, Lyndsay, Alexander Scott and others—in his "Evergreen" collection, also helped to strengthen the Scots literary tradition in another and no less vital way.

I never look up at Ramsay's house—designed by his son, the younger Allan, the portrait painter, and now incorporated in Ramsay Gardens, where the odd shape which led to its being dubbed "The Goosetub" still makes it conspicuous from Princes Street—or pass his statue in Princes Street Gardens, without reflecting upon the importance of the part which "Honest" Allan Ramsay played in helping us to preserve our nationality.

Ramsay, however, has beguiled us some distance way from the Luckenbooths and the Krames. Lord Cockburn (1779-1854), the Scots judge most distinguished in literature if not in law and the author of one of the finest of all Scottish journals,[1] recorded his boyhood recollection of the Krames. . . .

"It was a long narrow arcade of booths, crammed in between the north side of St. Giles's Cathedral and a thin range of buildings that stood parallel to the Cathedral, the eastmost of which, looking down the High Street, was the famous shop of William Creech, the bookseller. Shopless traffickers first began to nestle there about the year 1550 or 1560, and their successors stuck to the spot till 1817 . . . In my boyhood their little stands, each enclosed in a tiny room of its own, and during the day all open to the little foot-path that ran between the two rows of them, and all glittering with attractions, contained everything fascinaing to childhood, but chiefly toys. It was like one of the Arabian Nights' bazaars in Bagdad. Throughout the whole year, it was an enchantment. Let anyone fancy what it was about the New Year, when every child had got its handsel, and every farthing of every handsel was spent there. The Krames was the paradise of childhood."

Not a trace of this "paradise of childhood" remains. Something, though not much, of the nearby Mercat Cross does remain. The original site of Edinburgh's Mercat Cross appears to have been the causeway outside Old Fishmarket Close. It was first put up in the twelfth century, the centre of civic life, here as in all Scottish burghs of the time, and removed to a new site during the preparations for the visit of James VI and I in 1617. It was repaired by Robert Mylne in 1660. Ninety-six years later, by way of "improvement", it was taken down altogether, the pillar being set on the lawn of his house "The Drums" by a Lothian laird. In 1885, the Mercat Cross was reconstructed with the original column incorporated and held together by means of a copper tube inside the stone, the cost being borne by the politician William Ewart Gladstone.

Opposite the Mercat Cross, behind a series of arches and a forecourt, stands the City Chambers, completed in 1761. It was originally the Royal Exchange, built to replace the building of Sir William Bruce which was destroyed in the great fire of 1700,

[1] *Memorials of his Time.*

a fire that ravaged the centre of the Old Town and sent crackling down in flames many of the fourteen- and fifteen-storey lands around Parliament Close. By happy chance, neither in the fire of 1770, nor in the conflagrations of June and November 1824, was Parliament House itself destroyed.

In the centre of Parliament Square or Close, as it was once more accurately called, stands a statue of King Charles II on horseback. When he arrived there in 1685, he was set in his dramatic pose on what was formerly the St. Giles graveyard. So it comes about that, by a deliciously ironic stroke of fortune, the Merry Monarch prances on top of the mortal remains of the Gloomy Reformer, as a plate bearing Knox's initials and the date of his death testifies. Dr. Johnson's famous observation, after he had been looking at some of Knox's "reformations", that the Reformer should have been buried in the public highway, has thus proved to be not so wide of the mark. To and fro over his acrimonious bones pass the legal luminaries of the day, debating matters which have little enough to do with Calvinistic religion.

Parliament House was finished in 1639, its Scottish Jacobean structure having taken seven years in the building. The Scottish Parliament had hitherto met in the Old Tolbooth, sharing the limited accommodation with the Law Courts and the Town Council. There was an imposing ceremony at the opening of the new building, marred only by the fact that Charles I did not see fit to attend in person. There, in the Great Hall, magnificently timbered with arched and trussed oak beams, less than a century later, the debates which led to the Union with England were acrimoniously conducted. English bribes—ranging from the twelve thousand three hundred and twenty five pounds paid to Lord High Commissioner Queensberry, to the sum of eleven pounds two shillings at which Lord Banff rated the price of his humbler conscience—carried the day for incorporating union, against the wise arguments of that great patriot and statesman Andrew Fletcher of Saltoun (1655-1716), who urged federated union. But for the English money, and the contemptible behaviour of many of Scotland's titled leaders, who looked only to their own immediate advancement, Fletcher's logic would almost certainly have prevailed, and a more honourable marriage between the two countries would in due course have been manipulated.

" The end of ane auld sang ", Seafield contemptuously called the fatal document, which had to be signed in a cellar off the High Street so that the signatories could escape the fury of the mob outside; and with which his friend Queensberry stole furtively across the Border by night. It was meant to be the death-warrant of Scotland, the Nation. The execution, however, was not to be a sudden affair; rather a slow course of poison, which, although gradually weakening the patient, allowed frequent intervals when she appeared to be enjoying a hectic revival of flowering health.

One such period was the intellectual flowering of the eighteenth century, centred mainly on Edinburgh, where Scotland, minus her Parliament, looked to her churchmen and her lawyers for intellectual leadership. Another was the sudden expansion of industry centred on Glasgow and the middle west. Both these developments would probably have occurred under either kind of union. In any case, their benefits proved to be transitory.

The Supreme Law Court of Scotland took over Parliament House when the politicians left it, just as the Judges and Writers to the Signet took over patriotic leadership when the aristocracy abandoned the position in their scramble for Londonized status. Most of the leading Scotsmen of Edinburgh's so-called Golden Age were thus either lawyers or churchmen: the great " character " judges like Kames, Monboddo (who was convinced that human beings were all born with tails which conspiring midwives lopped off secretly at birth, thus making him an unwitting predecessor of Darwin), the broad-spoken Hermann (like most of them, renowned for his Herculean potations), and Braxfield the " hanging judge "; authors like the Scottish champion of sensibility Henry Mackenzie (" The Man of Feeling "), Hume (who became librarian to the Advocates), Boswell, Cockburn, Lord Jeffrey (whose criticism of the Lake Poets brought him wide literary notoriety), and Sir Walter Scott himself. Among churchmen, there was that vivid journalist, Dr. Alexander (" Jupiter ") Carlyle, who, by attending an Edinburgh performance of his friend the Reverend John Home's tragedy of *Douglas* in 1756, and thereafter remaining unperturbed by the Church's censure, contributed notably to the abating of its anti-theatre prejudice; Dr Blacklock, the blind poetaster who insisted on writing descriptive verse, but whose kindly interest helped to lure Robert Burns to Edinburgh; and Dr. William Robertson, the most able of Scotland's eighteenth-century historians, a stately wielder of still-enjoyable Johnsonian prose.

Parliament House to-day stands behind the classical façade added by Robert Reid in 1808. Apart from the Great Hall itself, and the Laigh Hall, beneath which Covenanting prisoners were once tried and tortured but which now houses part of the Advocates' Library, much of the original buildings are hidden behind Reid's cooler fronting.

The only other public building of interest in the High Street is Christ's Church at the Tron, started in 1637, on Charles I's orders, to house worshippers ejected from two of the three congregations housed in St. Giles when it was to become an Episcopalian Cathedral. The Tron Church was named after the nearby Tron, or weighing machine, which had occupied its position for so long that it had come to be regarded as a permanency.

Robert Fergusson (1750-1774), the laureate of late eighteenth-century Edinburgh, found the clamour of the old Tron Kirk bell distracting. He had a quick ear, and to many people so gifted, the clashing overtones of a bell-note often become intolerable. But the offending clangour moved him to write one of his liveliest poems:

> Wanwordy, crazy, dinsome thing,
> As e'er was framed to jow or ring,
> What gar'd them sic in steeple hing       [made
>     They ken themsel',
> But weel wat I they coudna bring
>     Waur sounds frae hell . . .

> Fleece merchants may look bald, I trow,
> Sin a' Auld Reekie's childer now,
> Maun stap their lugs wi' teats o' woo'
>     Thy sound to bang,
> And keep it frae gawn thro' and thro'
>     Wi' jarrin' twang.

> Your noisy tongue, there's nae abideint,
> Like scaulding wife's, there is nae guideint:
> When I'm 'bout any bus'ness eident,       [eager
>     It's sair to thole;       [bear
> To deave me, then, ye tak a pride in't
>     Wi' senseless knoll.

> O! war I provost o' the town,
> I swear by a' the pow'rs aboon,
> I'd bring ye wi' a reeshle down;       [crackling noise
>     Nor shud you think
> Sae sair I'd crack and clour your crown       [belabour
>     Again to clink . . . .

The east portion of the church was modified in 1785 when the South Bridge was being constructed. But the seventeenth-century spire, which housed the offending bell, survived until it was destroyed by the fires of 1824. Amongst the onlookers at that conflagration were Sir Walter Scott and Lord Cockburn. Cockburn's description of the fall of the spire is one of the most vivid pieces of reportage in Scottish literature:

"These fires broke out on the evening of Monday, 15th November 1824, on the south side of the High Street, about half-way between the Tron Church and St. Giles Cathedral; and before morning a range of houses six or seven storeys high, with fifteen windows in front, and extending back almost to the Cowgate—as dense a mass of buildings as was perhaps in the world—was a burnt shell. People thought this bad enough; especially as the adjoining ruins of the June fire were still untouched. But about noon next day an alarm was given that the Tron Church was on fire. We ran out from the Court, gowned and wigged, and saw that it was the steeple, an old Dutch thing, composed of wood, iron and lead, and edged all the way up with bits of ornament. Some of the sparks of the preceding night had nestled in it, and had at last blown its dry bones into flame.

There could not be a more beautiful firework; only it was wasted on the day-light. It was one hour's brilliant blaze. The spire was too high and too combustible to admit of any attempt to save it, so we had nothing to do but to admire. And it was certainly beautiful. The fire seized on every projecting point, and played with the fretwork as if it had been all an exhibition. The outer covering boards were soon consumed, and the lead dissolved. This made the strong upright and cross-beams visible; and these stood with the flame lessened, but with the red fire increased, as if it had been a great burning toy. The conflagration was long presided over by a calm and triumphant gilded cock on the top of the spire, which seemed to look on the people, and to listen to the crackling, in disdain. But it was undermined at last, and dived down into the burning gulf, followed by the upper half of the steeple. The lower half held out a little longer, till the very bell being melted, this half came down also with a world of sparks. There was one occurrence which made the gazers start. It was at a quarter before twelve, when the minute hand of the clock stood horizontally. The internal heat—for the clock was untouched outwardly—cracked the machinery, and the hand dropped suddenly and silently down to the perpendicular. When the old time-keeper's function was done, there was an audible sigh over the spectators.

When it was all over, and we were beginning to move back to our clients, Scott, whose father's pew had been in the Tron Church, lingered a moment, and said, with a profound heave, " Eh Sirs! mony a weary, weary sermon hae I heard beneath that steeple! "

A new spire, grosser than the " old Dutch thing ", was put upon the rebuilt Tron, and it played its part in the religious life of the City until 1952, when the last service was held and the congregation skailed to suburban churches. Some Councillors, and the road engineers, immediately urged that it should be pulled down, so that traffic at the High Street cross-road could be speeded up, enabling motorists to " save " some paltry minutes. Five minutes of a motorist's time against a landmark so venerable that around its steeple the crowds of the Old Town once gathered each Hogmanay to bring in successive New Years! Happily, public opinion induced authority to change its mind, and the Tron Kirk survives for Civic use.

Recently, too, there have been other belated changes of heart. The Listed Building regulations and the designation of the Old Town as one of Edinburgh's Conservation Areas ensures that a policy of restoration, where possible, and sympathetic replacement where not, will be carefully enforced.

VI

Over the traffic-lights separating South Bridge and North Bridge, Niddry Street preserves at least the memory of literary glory, for Allan Ramsay announced his first publishing venture " At the Sign of the Moor's Head, opposite Niddry's Wynd ". The timber-fronted land which contained his first shop has gone, as has the nearby shop of Archibald Constable, the publisher-friend of Sir Walter Scott, and joint architect with Scott of their double ruin when, in 1826, Constable's business collapsed.

At the foot of Niddry Street (which leads down to the Cowgate) stands St. Cecilia's Hall, the home of eighteenth-century Edinburgh's most fashionable music-making. It was built in 1762 by Robert Mylne—who modelled his plans on those of the opera house at Parma—for the Musical Society, which consisted of a group of gentlemen who felt that the old, informal music-making which went on at Patie Steil's " Cross Keys " tavern, near Parliament Close—a haunt of the learned Latin poet and medico Dr. Archibald Pitcairn: " *Nunc te clavigeri delectent pocula Stili* ", he proclaimed—no longer adequately met the tastes of a later day. Nor did nearby St. Mary's chapel allow for the expansion of the Society's lists of subscribers which occurred during the '60's and '70's; so a new hall seemed socially essential.

Henry Mackenzie tells us that the music-making which went on within the oval auditorium, crowned with the famous elliptical dome:

> "was styled the *Gentlemen's Concert,* because the original plan was that the orchestra should consist chiefly of amateurs; but the assistance of masters was soon afterwards taken, tho' their salaries were very small, the subscription at that time admitting of a very moderate expense . . . After the building of a new hall at the bottom of the same wynd, which was accomplished by subscription, a number of new members were admitted, which by their annual subscriptions enabled the society to give such salaries as occasionally to procure from London good performers, when by any accident or the capriciousness of the public taste they had no engagement in that city."

That lanky, lugubrious historian of eighteenth-century Edinburgh, Hugo Arnot, tells us that the orchestra consisted of: "A *maestro di capella,* an organist, two violins, two tenors, six or eight *ripienos* (amateurs), a double or *contra* bass and harpsichord; and occasionally two French horns, besides kettledrums, flutes and clarinets." If we may reasonably assume that Arnot merely forgot to mention 'cellos, oboes and trumpets, Edinburgh had at that time a part-professional mid-Haydn period symphony orchestra.

Foreign musicians usually occupied the paid desks. The names of many of them have survived in Edinburgh's musical history. There was Joseph Puppo—" Senior Puppy; First Catgut Scraper " to the caricaturists—a native of Lucca, credited with having said: " Boccherini is the wife of Haydn ", a statement meant, of course, to be interpreted in a purely musical sense.[1]

---

[1] Boccherini also came from Lucca, and probably knew Puppo, whose remark is frequently quoted by those who know little or nothing of the music of Boccherini. But Boccherini's melodic structure, far from being feminine, was often almost aggressively rhythmical, especially after he had come in contact with the folk music of Spain. The real difference between the two composers lay in their attitude to the development of their material. Whereas Haydn continually experimented with unconventional procedures, and from the start allied himself with the development of his thematic material along the lines of the new Sonata Form, Boccherini, being Italian, constantly harked back to the older Suite form favoured by Italian fiddle-composers from Corelli onwards, even when they called their works Sonatas. On the other hand, Boccherini's reflection of Spanish sounds and atmosphere is a unique precursor of nineteenth-century musical nationalism.

Also in the orchestra was Johann Georg Christoff Schetky, the
'cellist, who, besides being present when Brother Burns was
inaugurated as "Poet-Laureate of Lodge Canongate Kilwinning
No. 2" in 1787, spent the evening of January 24th, 1787, in the
company of the poet at a tavern in the Lawnmarket, drinking
heavily, and making the musical setting of "Clarinda, mistress of
my soul". There was Stabalini, who succeeded Puppo as leader
of the orchestra, and who earned the reputation of being a *bon
vivant*. After a concert at which some of Corelli's music had been
played, he was invited to supper. When the meal was over, his
hostess, in the manner of her kind, reverently sought his opinion
on the music he had been playing earlier in the evening. He is
said to have replied:

*A piece av toarkey for a hungree bellee
Is moatch supeerior to Corelli.*

If this be true, it possibly explains why Mackenzie, by then a
Director of the Musical Society, complained that latterly Stabalini
was "indolent and indifferent about the performance except his
own solos".

Other resident foreign musicians who took part in these
strange concerts made up of music by Handel and the Italian
School, C. F. Abel and J. C. Bach, incongruously mixed with
Scots airs—or, as an occasional, daring novelty, an early symphony
of Haydn—were Urbani, Reinagle and Corri. Corri is also
remembered because he owned a famous Concert Room which
bore his name, and which stood on the site of what later became
the Theatre Royal.

Among Scots musicians who performed either in St. Mary's or
St. Cecilia's, there were Adam Craig, James Oswald—Allan Ramsay's friend—William McGibbon and Stephen Clarke, organist of
the Cowgate Chapel and the man responsible for the musical
editing of Johnson's "Scots' Musical Museum". Bustling about
enthusiastically, and taking charge of everybody, was the jolly,
purple-faced Earl of Kellie, who composed charming vapid
minuets and overture-symphonies in the style of his master Johann
Stamitz, but who, according to the severe Dr. Burney, "wanted
application".

Some of those audiences who, on really special occasions, came
to what Lord Cockburn called "the best and most beautiful
concert-room I have ever yet seen . . . gentlemen predominating
with their side-curls and frills and ruffles and silver buckles; and
our stately matrons stiffened in hoops and gorgeous satin, and our

beauties with high-heeled shoes, powdered and pomatoned hair, and lofty composite head-dresses ", did so to hear Dr. Thomas Augustine Arne, performing in company with Tenducci, the favourite London *castrato* of his day; or Michael Kelly, Mozart's Irish friend; or, in 1772, to hear the first Scottish performance of Handel's " Messiah ".

Once the " best people " moved over to the New Town, Niddry's Wynd and the Cowgate quickly became " the last retreat . . . of destitution and disease ", and the music-lovers prepared to transfer their patronage to the Assembly Rooms in George Street. St. Cecilia's Hall then became in succession, a sectarian chapel, a Freemasons' Hall, a school, a warehouse, and latterly a toughly-tatty dance-hall. Now, however, it has been happily restored by the University of Edinburgh for use both as a concert hall and as the home of the splendid Russell Collection of early keyboard instruments. Fittingly, it provided the setting for the culminating ceremony of the Scottish campaign in European Architectural Heritage Year 1975, when the Honorary President of the Scottish Committee, Her Majesty Queen Elizabeth the Queen Mother, presented their award certificates to the Scottish recipients. Scotland secured a high proportion of awards in relation to the United Kingdom.

Quite a number of the closes and lands in the High Street from which the concert-goers must have trooped are still standing. Two are of particular interest. Mowbray House—the town house of the Mowbrays of Barnbougle—with its pleasingly honest vernacular corbelling; and the house which is commonly supposed (on no real evidence whatsoever) to have been that in which John Knox lived, and in which he died. Certainly a Mr. Knox once lived there. The point at issue is whether or not this Mr. Knox was the Reformer. The belief that he was has at any rate led to the preservation of a fine old house. It is the last timber-fronted house to survive in Edinburgh, and although naturally the woodwork has had to be renewed, the original style has been carefully matched. Knox's house is now a museum. Mowbray House may well be one of the few survivors of the Hertford sacking of 1544, and so possibly the oldest domestic dwelling in the High Street. Modern conservation procedures should ensure the survival of what remains. Much of value disappeared around the middle of the century.

In front of these two houses stands one of the six surviving public wells between Castle and Abbey. At the rear of Chalmers Close a passage leads to Mary of Guelders Trinity College Church —or at least to the apse of the 1462 building, pulled down in

1871 from its original site at the end of the Nor' Loch to make way for railway sidings around Waverley, and re-erected from the numbered stones.

At the foot of the High Street, at its junction with Jeffrey Street and St. Mary Street, the site of the old Netherbow Port is tacked out on the road. These two sturdy linked towers were demolished in 1765, having outlasted the last assault against the city, in 1745, when Lochiel, with a following of Camerons, turned the Port by guile, having come prepared to blow it up if necessary.

VII

The Canongate gets its name from the fact that it was originally the "gait" of the Canons Regular of the Order of St. Augustine, who, since 1128, lived out their lives in Holyrood Abbey. The Canongate's status as a separate burgh survived long after the monks had gone, and was not, indeed, finally abolished until 1856. Lying outside the City's ports, the Canongate can hardly have been a safe burgh to live in. Possibly its religious association led to its being spared the full force of English vindictiveness, though it was sacked on more than one occasion.

After the Reformation, nearness to Holyrood kept it fashionable. But it fell from favour soon after the Union, and Allan Ramsay found cause to lament:

> O Canongate! poor elritch hole,
> What loss, what crosses dost thou thole!
> London and Death gars thee look droll,
>     And hing thy heid;
> Wow, but thou hast e'en a cauld coal
>     To blaw indeed.

London had removed the aristocracy, Death the ale-house-keeper Lucky Wood, the virtues of whose house and person were much appreciated by her patrons in their convivial hours.

> She gaed as fait as a new prin,
> And kept her housie snod and bien    [neat with
> Her peuther glanc'd upo' your e'en    everything
>     Like siller plate;    in its place
> She was a donsie wife and clean,
>     Without debate.

35

*She had the gate sae weel to please*                    [way
*With gratis beef, dry fish, or cheese,*
*Which kept our purses ay at ease,*
*And health in tift,*                                                    [trim
*And lent her fresh nine gallon trees*
*A hearty lift.*

Although it was thus the first part of the Old Town to be abandoned to the poorer people, the Canongate has managed to retain more of its old houses than has the High Street. True, many of the lands in the Canongate are now in a derelict state. One of them, Morocco's Land, became so dangerous under the pressure of the heavy snowfull of 1948 that it had to be demolished. But plans have been made, and are in the course of being carried out, to restore some of the old property to habitable condition. White Horse Close and numbers 11 to 15 Canongate are among the most noteworthy of these restorations. Long-range plans also exist on paper for the removal of the unsightly breweries which have settled themselves upon the Canongate's gardens and green spaces. But the brewers dislike the idea of being removed. Their characteristic brewing aroma would certainly be missed.

Meanwhile Shoemakers' Land, built in 1677 (sometimes called Bible Land, because on the shield over the doorway showing the Crown and Paring Knife of King St. Crispin, the patron saint of the shoemakers, or cordiners as they used to call themselves, is also an open Bible), and the surrounding blocks have been restored. The gap left by the demolition of Morocco's Land has been filled in with a new building which does not dishonour its venerable surroundings. Robert Hurd, the architect responsible for this restoration, told me that the rear structure of the old building had become so unsafe that he and his staff were only able to complete their survey at considerable personal risk to life and limb.

Other old buildings have survived in less parlous condition. Golfer's Land is said to have been built by another shoemaker, John Patterson, out of his share of the proceeds when he and the Duke of York (later James VII) together won a foursome. Acheson House, approached through Bakehouse Close, belonged to Sir Archibald Acheson of Glencairney, Secretary of State for Scotland under Charles I. It carries the date 1633, though the main structure is possibly older. It was lived in as a family home as recently as 1948, when the last tenant gave it up because, as he told me, he found it completely impossible to heat the rooms economically in winter. It is now the headquarters of an organization set up to encourage and assist Scottish craftsmen.

Over the pend of Bakehouse Close stands Huntly House, a fine building with two storeys of plastered wood facing, and two further storeys thrusting out of them. It carries the date 1570, and is believed (on no evidence at all) once to have been the town residence of the Marquis of Huntly. It has been well restored as the City Museum, and contains such harmless historical sentimentalities as Sir Walter Scott's Meerschaum and Captain Porteous's sword. It also contains a series of inscribed tablets removed from the outside of the structure. These carry improving aphorisms, which once caused the building to be nicknamed the "Speaking House". The builder, it seems, was sensitive to the jibes of his fellow-citizens about the magnificence of his new home. HODIE MIHI. CRAS TIBI. CUR IGITUR CURAS? —*To-day, I am the happy man; to-morrow, it may be your turn. Why therefore repine?* Next, he quotes the reply of Dictus Tacitus to the charges of Lucius Metellus on the floor of the Roman Senate: UT TU LINGUAE TUAE SIC EGO MEARUM AURIUM? DOMINUS SUM—*As thou of thy tongue, so I am master of my ears.* The other two mottoes abandon arrogance in favour of religious consolation: CONSTANTI PECTORI RES MORTALIUM UMBRA—*To the constant heart temporal things are but a shadow*; and finally: SPES ALTERA VITAE—*Another hope of life.* It would indeed be good to know the name of this builder who first defied the critics of his opulence, then reminded them of the flimsiness of temporal things, and finally held out the hope that at least they might not prove ineligible for a heavenly mansion.

Moray House, its gateway flanked by twin pyramids, was first known as Lady Home's Ludging because Mary, Countess of Home, built it in 1628. It passed to her daughter, the Countess of Moray, and remained in the hands of the Moray family until the middle of the eighteenth century. The eighth Earl of Moray leased it to the British Linen Company in 1753, who partitioned its rich interior into offices and warerooms, and despoiled its famous garden. By 1792 it had become the premises of a paper-maker, from whom it passed to the Free Church of Scotland, who used it as a Training College for Teachers. To-day it performs a similar function for school teachers.

The infamous Marquis of Argyll and his bridegroom son left the gaiety of the wedding-feast to come out on to the balcony of Moray House as a bound prisoner was being carried up the Canongate on horseback. It is said that when the prisoner glanced quickly up at that balcony, Argyll turned away, unable to meet his gaze. It is said, too, that Lady Argyll thereupon graciously spat in the direction of the prisoner's face. The year was 1650, the prisoner the poet-Marquis of Montrose.

Cromwell also knew that balcony, for he slept in the house in 1648, and again in 1650 after the battle of Dunbar, which virtually brought Scotland under his military dictatorship until the Restoration.

The largest of the Canongate mansions, Queensberry House, certainly looks grim to-day. It can never have been a particularly gracious dwelling. The main line of the Queensberry family died out, insanity in their strain. The Earl of March, better known as the eccentric " Old Q " of George III's day, and Wordsworth's " degenerate lord ", sold the place to the Government, who, with a better sense of fitness than Governments usually manifest, turned it into a barracks. Now, it is a home for the elderly.

It was once the scene of a happening so appalling that, to find its parallel, one has to go back to the tragic imaginings of the Ancients. On the day of the ratification of the Treaty of Union, Queensberry had taken his entire household to Parliament House to witness the completion of his triumph. Only a little cook-boy was left behind, to turn on the spit a roast which was being prepared for the return of the victor and his party. The flames of the great fire flickered, flecking the stone floors of the dark kitchen with shadows, and the boy became drowsy. Suddenly the door silently opened, framing the huge bulk of Queensberry's lunatic son, Lord Drumlanrig. He had broken out of his locked room, and tracked the scent of the cooking meat. Eagerly he seized the roast from the spit with both hands, and began to devour it. Then his vacant eyes lighted on the terrified kitchen-boy cowering in a corner. With a terrible chuckle, the monster seized the boy and impaled him on the spit. When Queensberry arrived back in the highest of spirits, he found Drumlanrig gnawing the remains of the roasted child, slavering with idiot satisfaction.

Folk said at the time that this calamity was a judgment on a traitor to his country: a somewhat harsh judgment, surely, on the innocent kitchen-boy!

The Duchess of Queensberry—Prior's Kitty—must have been a more attractive creature than her husband, for it was at her invitation that the poet John Gay came to Scotland when his theatrical projects had been politically frustrated in London. He became friendly with Allan Ramsay, and no doubt the two poets often met to refresh themselves at Jenny Ha's tavern, and discuss the demerits of their contemporaries, as is the manner of men-of-letters of every age.

Between Old Playhouse Close, with its conically-roofed turn-pike stair, and Playhouse Close, there once stood the first of Edinburgh's theatres to survive the anti-theatrical zeal of the more fanatical clergy. It opened in 1747, and before it closed in 1786, Lee, Digges, Mrs. Bellamy and Mrs. Ward had all trodden its candle-lit boards; the thundering iambics of the Reverend John Home's tragedy of *Douglas* had provoked the famous " Whaur's your Wullie Shakespeare noo? " from the darkened gallery; and Home's friend the Reverend " Jupiter " Carlyle had proclaimed his right to attend theatrical performances in the face of censure from the General Assembly of the Church of Scotland. His sensibly courageous stand went a long way towards modifying the Kirk's traditional hostility towards theatre-going.

But it would have taken much more to restore to respectability the art of the drama, which the Reformers had almost entirely suppressed since the last production of *The Three Estatis* in 1554. Consequently *The Three Estatis, The Gentle Shepherd* and *Douglas* are Scotland's only stage " classics ".[1] The anti-theatre instinct—for such it all but became after four centuries of Kirk-inspired inculcation—persisted to the days of my own childhood. The impression existed amongst us youngsters that the theatre was definitely "not nice", and that theatre people, especially women, were a " queer set ". Even to-day, towards the close of the twentieth century, there are plenty of " Wee Free " ministers in the Highlands of Scotland thundering about the alleged sinful ness of an ennobling pleasure they themselves have in many cases never experienced.

In these circumstances, it is perhaps not surprising that in spite of the excellent work done by the late " John Brandane ", " James Bridie ", Robert Maclellan, Robert Kemp, Bill Bryden and others, the native stage should hardly be a hot-bed of genius. Contemporary Scots playwrights have plenty of stage technique, and a real flair for Scots adaptation. But most of them seem somehow to lack original invention. Nevertheless, with repertory companies established in Glasgow, Edinburgh, Perth, Dundee and St. Andrews, support for the drama in Scotland is stronger than ever before, though it is apparently still neither strong nor enthusiastic enough to result in any sustainable, steady outburst of creative brilliance.

Here, too, the political and the artistic state of the nation are

[1] I am not taking into consideration scholars' plays on avowedly foreign models, like the anonymous *Philotus*, or Sydserf's comedies: nor am I considering the roistering adaptations of Scott's novels which flourished early in the nineteenth century: nor the plays of Johanna Baillie and Lord Byron, most of which were never really meant to be acted.

not unrelated. Scotland is divided against herself, in theatrical as well as in political matters. A large number of those who regularly go to the theatre in the bigger Scottish towns, do so only to see London West-end successes or pantomimes. Yet the Traverse Theatre provides Edinburgh with experimental fare, the city-owned Lyceum with a varied diet, and Scottish opera commands large audiences.

At the bottom of the Canongate, just before it branches off into the Watergate and the old road to the south, stands White Horse Close. The Flemish-looking house in the centre of the court was once the White Horse Inn, one of the most famous of eighteenth-century hostelries.[1] It bears the false date of 1523, the real date of its founding being either 1603 or 1623. But very probably a still earlier inn stood on the same site. One Lawrence Ord erected houses and hay-lofts round the close in the seventeenth century and set himself out to cater for incoming travellers. Apparently the ambitious Mr. Ord was also equipped to cater for outgoing travellers, judging by an advertisement of 1707, which gives notice to all " who have occasion for a black herrse, murning-coach, and other coaches, just new, and in good order with good horses well accoutred, that James Mouat, coachmaster in Lawrence Ord's Land at the foot of the Canongate, will serve them thankfully at reasonable rates ".

Twice, the focus of history swung momentarily on White Horse Inn. In 1639, when Charles I found himself faced at Berwick with a stronger army than his own, he invited the Scots nobles to a parley. They met at the White Horse Inn before departing. But the Covenanting ministers were suspicious of the King's intentions, and prevented the nobles setting out, Montrose alone escaping to meet his King. This incident, which caused Charles to turn back to London in a rage and shattered the Truce of Berwick, became known as the " Stoppit Stravaig ". Again, in 1745, tradition has it that many of Prince Charlie's officers lived at the White Horse Inn while their leader held court at the Palace.

The development of the stage-coach and the opening up of the east coast approach to Edinburgh gradually deprived the White Horse Inn of its livelihood. By the end of the century, it had ceased to be an inn. Now it has been restored and converted to provide modern houses. Numbers 11 to 15 Canongate, on the other side of the High Street and of about the same age,

[1] Not, however, the one at which Johnson and Boswell met to set out on their Hebridean Tour. It stood in St. Mary's Wynd, at the head of the Canongate, until the middle of the nineteenth century. Solid, graceless Victorian lands now fill the site.

have also been restored, thanks to the persistance of a group of enthusiasts led by the National Trust for Scotland. It was originally claimed that the buildings lacked a gable end, being supported by a Victorian building due for demolition. Once it had been demonstrated that, hardly surprisingly, the leaning was the other way round, endless wordy vagaries and delaying tactics had to be patiently endured and overcome.

Fortunately, the strength of the conservationist argument is becoming more readily acceptable, and one hopes the affair of 11–15 Canongate was the last feeble kick of now outmoded civic vandalism.

The earlier civic policy of letting such restored houses at cost rents is giving place to the policy of offering them to tenants at subsidized rents with a view to establishing a social "mix": a theory, like comprehensive non-streamed education, yet to be proved effective in practice.

Looking at the restored house, with its seemly newer neighbours on either side, it is easy to see now that it is indeed the key building to the whole charming complex on the curve of the road facing the gates of Holyrood.

Two of Canongate's public buildings are still in hale condition. The Canongate Tolbooth, dated 1592, is an honest piece of vernacular building, though its appearance is slightly marred by the outsize Victorian clock slung about its neck. Canongate Church, which stands back from the Tolbooth and behind a replica of the old Canongate Cross, was built in 1688 to house the congregation displaced by James VII when he turned the Abbey Church into a Chapel Royal. It carries the arms of the burgh— a stag's head with a cross set between the antlers. The church has an outsize organ and a famous pulpit once occupied by Dr. Thomas Chalmers, the "father" of the Disruption of 1843. It was bought from the West Port Kirk when that building was demolished. Amongst the dust that rests in the graveyard is that of Robert Fergusson, over whose grave there stands the head-stone erected at the expense of Robert Burns— it cost him five pounds ten shillings, though the engraver, one Robert Burn, made a mistake in the inscription of the date of Fergusson's death. The stone was restored on the occasion of the bi-centenary of the poet's birth, when many contemporary Scottish writers gathered for an impressive ceremony at Fergusson's graveside. Mrs. Agnes Maclehose, Burns's Clarinda, also lies buried nearby. So does Adam Smith of Kirkcaldy, who had a house in Panmure Close; and James Ballantyne, whose presses in Canongate Close imprinted Scott's pages, and who threw a great banquet at his house, 10 St. John's Street, every time a new novel by "The Great Unknown" was about to be published.

Incidentally, St. John's Street, which leads to the Cowgate, was erected in 1768 as an early attempt at town-planning. Smollett's sister, Mrs. Telfer, lived in the house over the archway of the pend, and there Smollett gathered material for *Humphry Clinker* during his last visit to Scotland. These little houses quickly became fashionable, and the list of residents was once impressive. In numbers 2 and 4 the Earl of Aboyne and Lord Blantyre lived. The houses, alas, have gone, as have the homes of Mrs. Grant of Prestongrange (No. 6), Lord Eskgrove (No. 8), Ballantyne (No. 10), Lord Monboddo (No. 13) and that of Dr. Gregory of laxative powder fame (No. 15)! Incidentally the close, though not the building, of Lodge Canongate Kilwinning No. 2, which appointed Burns its laureate in 1872, survives.

*

## VIII

At the foot of the Royal Mile, the Abbey and Palace of Holyrood mark off the end of Old Edinburgh; and, in another sense, the end of old Scotland too. True, Holyrood House, as it existed in the days of the Jameses, was a very different building from the fine structure which Sir William Bruce built for Charles II. But the present Holyrood House has never really fulfilled its royal purpose, except to serve as a sanctuary for distressed foreign royalty as in the years 1795 and 1830, when it sheltered the exiled Charles X of France; as a Scottish hotel for members of the royal family during brief Edinburgh week-ends; and as the official residence of the Lord High Commissioner of the Church of Scotland during two weeks of the year. As for the Abbey, it is so fragile a ruin that when the 11th Earl of Leven left a legacy to rebuild the Thistle Chapel, the weather-worn piers were found to be too far decayed to be able to bear the weight, so the Chapel was built in St. Giles instead.

The Abbey is, of course, the older building. Legend asserts that Queen Margaret's pious youngest son, David I, somewhat surprisingly broke a holy day—Rude Day, when the Festival of Exaltation of the Cross was observed—to hunt around Salisbury Crags. During these operations, he suddenly found himself menaced by a vicious white hart. He was only saved from death by a mysterious cross or rude which appeared between the beasts's antlers and forced it back. The king thereupon founded the Abbey of the Holy Rude out of gratitude for his salvation.

From what is known of David's character, the more probable though less picturesque story is that he founded the Abbey as a shrine to enclose one piece of the many tons of fragmented timber piously venerated in the Middle Ages as splinters from the True Cross. At any rate, when King David founded Holyrood about the year 1178, he granted the canons the right to establish their own burgh on the mercat land between the Abbey buildings and the burgh of Edinburgh.

Although the lay-out of the original Abbey buildings has been conjectured in studded stones on the ground, all that actually remains standing is the roofless nave of the church; a square Norman tower; and such details as the two soaring Norman doorways which lead, as George Scott-Moncrieff graphically put it, "from daylight to daylight".

The first major destruction was probably that caused to the old fabric during the Earl of Hertford's Abbey-burning excursion of 1544. Thereafter, James V appointed one of his six bastards, the seven-year-old Robert Stewart, to the Abbacy. When Master Stewart came of an age to take an interest in his creature comforts, he built himself a house by the west entrance to the Abbey with stones stripped from the old building.[1]

In 1567, the fanatical followers of the Protestant Earl of Glencairn did a deal of further smashing, and to avoid having to repair the damage, good Master Stewart simply cut off the choir and transepts. But by then he was beginning to lose interest in Holyrood. Two years later he forced Bishop Adam Bothwell of the Orkney and Shetland Islands to change bishoprics with him.

Bothwell's particular lust was for power over people—he married Mary Queen of Scots to the Earl of Bothwell in the Palace, yet turned against her at her trial—whereas Master Stewart's was for fat living. Orkney was for him a safer and a sweeter retreat than Edinburgh, which, on the other hand, held out more glittering promise to Adam Bothwell. Bothwell let the Abbey fall further into decay. It was sufficiently repaired to allow James VI to be married in it; and later, repaired again for the Scottish coronation to which Charles I reluctantly consented. It then became the Parish Kirk for the Canongate. Something more intact than the existing fragments might still have come down to us had not James VII, who took a more genuine interest in Scotland than did his brother, most foolishly decreed that the building was to be converted into a Chapel Royal, with stalls for his revived

---

[1] By this time, of course, the behaviour of many of the upper hierarchy of the Catholic Church in Scotland had become disgraceful, personal gain being their main concern. Naturally, inferiors felt entitled to copy their masters.

Knights of the Thistle. Unfortunately, he had better æsthetic taste than common sense, and when he lost his throne to his Protestant son-in-law, William of Orange, an exultant mob broke into the Chapel, rending and smashing in the name of the Protestant faith. Not even the royal vaults were spared, the coffins of deceased Scottish sovereigns being burst asunder, their remains tossed out or stolen, in a disgusting orgy. Indeed, the royal remains were still exposed in Sir Walter Scott's lifetime, and actually charged for as part of the " show ". The royal vault was finally restored on the orders of Queen Victoria. An eighteenth-century attempt at the restoration of the fabric led to the collapse of a too-heavy roof, which fatally weakened the perpendicular structure.

It was the building monarch James IV who, deciding that the arrangement whereby his forefathers lodged in the Abbey or the Castle when in Edinburgh was no longer good enough, gave orders for the tower to be built in time to receive him and his bride in 1503. Logy, his master mason, did have some of it habitable in time for the royal arrival; but by 1513, when the king was killed at Flodden, it still wanted its top storey. However, further additions were made, one of those having a hand in the building being that flamboyant filibuster Sir James Hamilton of Finart, who finally had to be executed by his employer, James V, for treason.[1]

The only part of James V's Holyrood to survive Hertford's sacking was James IV's original tower. The first rebuilding took place under the auspices of the Commendator of Holyrood, Master Stewart. Having already used some of the Abbey stones to build his own house, he sanctioned a similar, more extensive plundering for the work of making Holyrood Palace fit to receive the young Mary Queen of Scots on her return from France.

Although parts of Mary's Holyrood still survive, the place was again badly damaged when Cromwell's troops, according to their usual practice, caused it accidentally to catch fire. Charles II employed Sir William Bruce to restore the Palace more or less to the state it is in to-day. Bruce, who was really the first great architect to become known as such by name—hitherto, builders in Scotland did most of their own planning—happened also to be an expert in the difficult business of incorporating fragments of an older style into his own plans, at the same time preserving a certain wholesome homogeneity. Thus, James IV's tower is

[1] Lindsay of Pitscottie states that James V actually began the Palace in 1525, but he is probably wrong.

partnered by Bruce's, and the formalizing which Sir William's Renaissant classicism demanded was not too unkind to the earlier remains. It was, however, extremely unkind to the Abbey Church, part of which had to be removed to accommodate a section of the Palace.

The romanticist can still climb up to the second floor of James IV's tower and see Queen Mary's apartments. The coffered oak ceiling of her chamber remains as it was in her day, though Sir William Bruce altered the level of the floor. In her bedroom, the time-worn bed, younger than the Queen by about a century, the shabby-looking mirror, and the faded murals may well remind the less ardent romanticist of Robert Nicol's lines on seeing the dressing-room of Marie-Antoinette, another lovely queen who came to a similar end.

Darnley's apartments, equally shabby now, are on the floor beneath the Queen's rooms. The long gallery still retains upon its walls the images of a hundred and ten Scottish kings, real and imaginary, from Fergus I to Charles II, commissioned by the latter monarch at about two pounds per king from a Dutch painter de Weet (or Wet) who happened at that time to be living in the Canongate. Beneath these faces, lugubrious, pathetic and comic, Prince Charles Edward Stuart held his levee of the White Rose on a glittering evening of seeming triumph in 1745: and past these same royal noses, Butcher Cumberland doubtless stumped a few months later on his customary way to sleep in yet another of Prince Charlie's beds.

The main historical significance of Holyrood Palace, however, is that it was the scene of events which for a time actually united Scotland and France under one sovereign, then shattered for ever the Auld Alliance with France in favour of an English Alliance. Holyrood, indeed, became a sort of symbolic prize for which the leaders of the Catholic and Protestant factions clashed and murdered, often with cruel stupidity and violent passion in no way relatable to the precepts of Christianity, whose differing minor variations they championed.

When James V, sick at the defeat of his army at Solway Moss, turned his head to the wall in his chamber at Falkland Palace, gave "ane little lauchter" and died, the day-old daughter of his second wife, Mary of Guise, became Queen of Scotland. Already, the fires of the Reformation were flickering, and James's widowed second Queen was much too closely connected with a family "zealously addicted to Popery" to be other than a source of displeasure to the Protestants. During Mary of Guise's Regency, the Reformation flamed out into the open. Hertford, in his new

roles of Lord Protector and Duke of Somerset, made his second
Abbey-burning expedition in 1547, sacking Holyrood again, and
on the 4th of September, defeating Mary of Guise's army at Pinkie
Cleugh. The year before, George Wishart had been burned at
St. Andrews, while Cardinal Beaton lolled at a window of the
castle fore-tower enjoying the spectacle. A few months later he
himself was murdered, a new actor destined to become one of
principal protagonists being privy to the deed. In after years,
John Knox declared that he had been a murderer only under
compulsion. But then Knox in his *History of the Reformation*
did his utmost to whitewash all the insalubrious crimes he countenanced or plotted, while he attempted to justify those which
could not thus be glossed over.

The basic technique which Knox and the Reformers employed
aimed at breaking the Scottish people away from their French
allies, and giving them over to their hereditary, though recently
turned Protestant, enemies the English. That they put sectarian
religion before patriotism; that they grew so overweeningly vain
as to suppose that eventually the English themselves must be
brought to worship according to Presbyterian principles, and so
were led into many situations which could only be described as
shameful; that by ceaselessly drumming the absurd doctrine of
predestination into Scottish heads, and by suppressing not only
the Scottish arts but even the normal gaiety of everyday social
companionship, they warped and damaged the Scottish character
in a manner from which it has never really recovered: these
form the gravamen of the charge against Knox and his friends.
The charge against the Catholic faction in Scotland is that it
favoured and supported, or at least failed to reform, clergy who,
from the highest to the lowest, had become lax and corrupt, and
were often little better than an oppressive and lecherous swarm
of blood suckers draining the scanty substance of the poor.[1] Such
thieving and wantonness as is portrayed in *Ane Satire of the Thrie
Estatis* inevitably germinated resistance.

The will to resist the tyranny of the Church was already
expressing itself in certain other parts of Europe in the form of
break-away doctrines. John Calvin of Geneva held out a creed
which both appealed to the extravagant, extremist Celtic element
in the Scots character, and at the same time offered obvious
worldly advantages to the more powerful laymen who might
support the new revolutionary doctrine. The minds of the
common people, chafed by the exactions of their priests, were

[1] See W. Murison's *Sir David Lyndsay: Poet and Satirist of the Old Church
in Scotland* for a detailed account of some of their offences.

easily won over by tight-lipped, licence-condemning public leaders like the four Lords of the Congregation (Argyll, Arran, Glencairn, and James V's most gifted bastard Lord James Stewart, later Earl of Moray) who in 1557 drew up the first Covenant in the quarries of Calton Hill. These men were undoubtedly at least partly actuated by political motives and plain self-interest. Indeed, their ablest member, Lord James Stewart, the infant Queen's half-brother, eventually became a paid tool of Elizabeth of England.

In view of these troubles simmering in Scotland, Mary of Guise not unnaturally decided to send her child-daughter to France to be educated. As the trend of events in Scotland must have made the Queen Regent wonder if there would long be a throne in Scotland for her daughter to fill, Mary of Guise in due course arranged a marriage between her daughter and the sickly boy heir to the throne of France.

For the last six years of her life, though ill with a dropsical complaint, Mary of Guise displayed integrity of purpose and an ability which, in happier times, would have assured her of a more kindly-remembered place in Scottish history than she has in fact been granted. Her central aim was to preserve her throne for her daughter, drawing aid from France to help her in her struggle against the rebel armies of the Protestants. She was an able general. By April 1560, her troops held out in Leith against the combined armies of the Protestants and the English so successfully that the wily Cecil was dispatched from the English court to see what the less expensive alternative of diplomacy could do. Before he arrived, however, Mary of Guise had died in the garrulous and unwanted presence of a Protestant minister, the Reverend Mr. Willcock.

In July 1560, the Lords of the Congregation quite illegally convened a Parliament which the new Queen and her dying consort, François, naturally could not recognize. One of its acts was to establish Protestantism as the religion of Scotland. While Catholicism was being rooted out, and from pulpits up and down the country Knox was inciting hysterical mobs to destroy irreplaceable things of beauty, Lord James Stewart invited his half-sister to come to Scotland.

She arrived unexpectedly at Leith in a thick fog, which Knox, glowering from his window in the High Street upon the cheering crowds, considered a providential omen. Holyrood was not ready for her, so her reception was doubly cheerless. Within a week of her coming, Knox had already thundered against the "one mass" she heard, "more fearful to him, than if ten thousand armed enemies were landed in any part of the realm; of purpose to suppress the whole religion ". The Queen thereupon invited him to wait upon her at Holyrood. He duly presented himself, but after storming against her religion, finally provoked her passionate nature to fury. The Queen said:

> " ' I have borne with you in all your rigorous manner of speaking, both against myself and my uncles, I offered unto you presence and audience, whensoever it pleased you to admonish me, and yet I cannot be quit of you; I vow to God I shall be once revenged.' And with these words scarce could Murdoch, her secret chamberboy, get napkins to hold her eyes dry, for the tears and the howling, besides womanly weeping, stayed her speech."

Knox abided her "fumes", then resumed his wordy attack. It was an attack which was soon to be directed at her from many sides: an attack against her Catholic faith, to which she adhered as sincerely and firmly as her assailants adhered to their breakaway Protestantism. In matters of religious faith, reason and logical argument play little part. But on Mary's side at least there was tolerance, for she conceded the right of the Protestants to worship as they pleased so long as she should be allowed to do the same.

But Mary's position was hopeless from the start. Often, she relied on bad advice; as when her half-brother persuaded her to ride north and accomplish the ruin of the Catholic House of Huntly, an expedition which permanently weakened the support of her Catholic subjects. There was also the strange discovery of the poet Chastelard under her bed at Rossend, which gave Knox and his friends material to insinuate a liaison. Since a similar offence of Chastelard's at St. Andrews had already been pardoned, he must either have been insane, or else forced to stage-manage the second indiscretion by the anti-Marian lords, possibly on promises of safe-conduct—which, in the event, proved false, for he was promptly tried and executed. To complicate the tangled web still further came her unpopular marriage with the Catholic Henry, Lord Darnley (a son of the Earl of Lennox whose lands she had restored). This match apparently gave private satisfaction to Elizabeth of England, though carried through against her suave sisterly council: by this marriage, Mary doubly strengthened her claim to succeed to the English throne. But the match soon proved an unhappy one. Darnley turned out to be an ambitious creature lacking in character—though Mary first saw him as "the loftiest and best proportioned man " that she had ever set eyes upon—whose main intent was to secure the crown matrimonial for his own head.

Darnley provided the culminating evidence of his unworthiness when he signed a conspirator's bond making him a party to the murder of the musician David Rizzio (or Riccio), the Queen's secretary, at a supper party in her rooms on the 9th of March, 1565.

The Queen was far advanced in pregnancy. Ruthven and his accomplices, fully armed, suddenly burst into the supper room, claiming the authority of Darnley for what they were about to do. Rizzio tried to shelter behind Mary's skirts. Ignoring his terrified screams and her furious reproaches and protests, they seized hold of the Italian, and, across her breast, drove home their jewelled daggers.

Darnley's excuses for his conduct—jealous complaints of neglect which would have disgraced an adolescent schoolboy—would have filled any woman's soul with revulsion. After her passionate manner, Mary swore that Darnley would yet have a sorer heart than she had then. What little love may still have been left between them must have been turned to loathing by the Rizzio murder; a loathing which cannot have lessened when, after the birth of her son in Edinburgh Castle, Mary found that she had publicly to counter the sneers of Knox's followers by giving an assurance that her child was in fact Darnley's and not Rizzio's.

Darnley apparently realized that his own life was now in danger, and that he was no match for his wife's cunning. He partly succumbed to her gestures of forgiveness, but he would not so far trust her as to abandon his intention of leaving the country. Before he could take himself off, however, an attack of small-pox laid him seriously ill at Glasgow. He allowed the Queen to nurse him back to health. When she suggested that he should accompany her back to Holyrood to convalesce, doubts again assailed him, and he insisted on lodging in Kirk o' Field, an old, decrepit house familiar already with the sounds of murder.

Mary furbished Kirk o' Field with costly tapestries, and furnished it in keeping with the rank of her husband. Once Darnley had been installed in the house, back at Holyrood Mary flirted with James Hepburn, Earl of Bothwell, a powerful, swash-buckling adventurer possessed of great courage and greater vanity. There, too, she either did—or did not, according to individual interpretation of the highly dubious facts of the case—write the Casket Letters which, if genuine, make her privy to Bothwell's plot to murder Darnley.

On the 9th of February, Mary dined with the Bishop of Argyll. She cut short her visit, however, in order to put in an appearance at a masque which was being performed at Holyrood in honour of a double wedding of two of her attendants. On her way to the Palace, she called in at Kirk o' Field, and stayed with Darnley until eleven o'clock. Then, in company with Bothwell, she showed herself at the festivities.

No one knows exactly what happened during the next few hours. But at two o'clock in the morning, a loud explosion wrecked Kirk o' Field. Darnley's body was later found beneath a nearby tree, scatheless. One of Darnley's servants came out of the affair alive. According to him, his master was suffocated with a vinegar-soaked handkerchief in the presence of the Earl of Bothwell and then strangled.[1]

Darnley was hated by the Queen's subjects while he was alive; murdered, however, his death became a valuable offensive weapon in their hands. The cry went up that his murderers must be brought to trial. At last, very reluctantly, Mary agreed, and Bothwell was " tried " by a court under Argyll, and in a chamber entirely packed with Bothwell's supporters. Not unnaturally, Bothwell was found " not guilty "; not unnaturally, too, the proceedings were regarded as being unsatisfactory by the people of Edinburgh.

Two months later, on April 24th, Mary met up with Bothwell while on her way to Stirling. He took her to Dunbar and there, according to her story, " ravished her . . . against her will ". Had she been all that unwilling, extreme punishment would certainly have been meted out to Bothwell there and then. The true story probably was that Mary had so completely fallen under the spell of this apparently all-powerful man of action, that she was already his mistress, and probably pregnant. Not only because Bothwell was " fair and whitelie ", though " sumthing hingand of shoulder, and yeid sumthing forwart [stooping] with ane gentil and humane countenance ", according to Lindsay of Pitscottie, but because a Queen could hardly produce an illegitimate child (however customary it was for male Stuart monarchs to beget them!), Mary decided to marry. Not only the Protestant nobles, but many Catholics who mistrusted Bothwell personally, warned her clearly that if she married him, they would support her young son in her stead. Yet she made Bothwell her husband at Holyrood on the 15th of May.

The Protestant Lords carried out their threat. A month later, on June 14th, Mary's army was defeated at Carberry Hill. After

---

[1] This man's testimony is unreliable, however, since it alleges that during the course of the evening he and his master sang a psalm together. Darnley was a Catholic, therefore would not sing psalms.

reaching an understanding with Kirkcaldy of Grange (who was later to change his loyalty, and to die for her as the vain defender of Edinburgh Castle, her last stronghold) that she would be received royally by the nobles, the Queen surrendered. But both the nobles and the people of Edinburgh had other intentions. Booed and execrated as she was led through the streets of the capital, she was taken to Loch Leven Castle, and put under the care of her father's former mistress, Margaret Erskine, now Lady Douglas. Her escape from Loch Leven led only to her defeat at Langside, and almost twenty years of weary English imprisonment before Walsingham, Elizabeth of England's number one Gestapo-man, managed to trump up a letter with a forged sentence in it, which offered some sort of justification for Mary's "trial" and execution.[1]

It is these memories of events, sentimental and historical, which keep the stones of Holyrood so interesting to look upon. For it is Mary's Palace. James VI did not use it much; nor did the later Stuarts. The shades that haunt its corridors are the shades of Mary and Knox.

Mary and Knox were the master-pieces on the chessboard which decided the fate of Scotland. Yet the outlook for Mary's foreign policy was hopeless from the start. She had to maintain the alliance with France, upon whom, like her mother before her, she depended for her military strength and much of her personal fortune. Yet she had also somehow to keep the peace with the English, in spite of the fact that their centuries-old aim of annexing Scotland was as rampant as ever. In the end, Mary alienated both France and England, as well as her own people, by her continuing failure to punish the murderers of Darnley. During her last months in power, she must have suffered some sort of inability to accept the inescapable laws of cause and effect; an inability which finally led her tired reason to resign in the face of the urgency of her personal desires.

Both Mary and Knox probably saw the ultimate necessity for some form of union between Scotland and England. Mary, inevitably, could not have countenanced the "annexation" which was virtually the result of the Treaty of Union made a century and a half later. Knox, on the other hand, would have stopped at nothing so long as his own bigoted interpretation of "the Trewth" was accepted by the widest number of people, forcibly or voluntarily.

---

[1] Elizabeth's treatment of Mary was one reason why some historically-minded Scots for a time objected to the numeral incorporation in the present sovereign's title. Elizabeth was never Queen of Scotland.

The heat and passion of that struggle to "break the keys of Rome" fatally sapped the Scottish character, and to this day faint echoes of it are overtoned within our blood. Religious narrowness and intolerance have probably a stronger hold among us, having regard to the size of our population, than amongst the people of almost any other European country. Yet at last it shows signs of dying down. The ecumenical movement may make slow progress, but at least nowadays members of all denominations, except the nearly-extinct "Wee Frees", affirm continuing belief in its ultimate success. Regrettably though, we have bequeathed religious intolerance, through colonization, to the unhappy province of Northern Ireland.

For this surviving sense of bitterness, for the impairment of our tolerance, and for the destruction of so much in our heritage that should have been lovely and gracious, we must, in the final analysis, blame not Mary Queen of Scots, but her adversary Master John Knox. In spite of the undoubted strength and sincerity of his living character, it is a shadow that his influence has thrown across the Scottish centuries: a grim shadow, the occasional awareness of whose presence still throws a sudden chill over the liberalized Scottish spirit; or fires it into a cleansing anger. Today, indeed, a newer dogma, a different intolerance, has taken root in Lowland Scotland, damaging her image in international eyes, and making those who share my own disbelief in ends and absolutes question whether Knox produced Scotland, or Scotland perhaps produced Knox. There is no case, however, for relaxing civilized vigilance "Against the Blasting of Trumpets".*

*John Knox, old thumping beard-and-testament master,*
*who found God's word a thunder-splitting roar*
*that chafed far more than the sweat-smoothed buck of the oar*
*you levered through the splashed and lashed disaster*
*that sucked your middle years; up from the galleys*
*you brought salt's burning and the parch of seas,*
*a chain-ribbed, fiery conscience; and with these*
*to rub your ire, you rabbled bumpkin rallies*
*of fanatic peasants, hurt with feudal wrongs,*
*word-battering till you rang their hearts like gongs.*

* From the author's *Selected Poems 1942-72.*

*Most venerable ranting, randy preacher,*
*women you thought no bible-staining sin;*
*wedded, they stilled the beast's besetting din*
*that troubled even you, haranguing teacher*
*whose tongue bit under blood and germinated*
*its blind, corroding, parasitic kin—*
*Intolerance that breathed no difference in;*
*Power and Force that never need be sated*
*since God sat in your bowels, and through your beard*
*blew forth the single Trewth to be revered.*

*Deforming man who mocked the shape of wonder,*
*(your nightly arms lulled round a lass's waist)*
*who spat forth loveliness like some foul taste,*
*racked fugues and rendered soaring walls asunder;*
*usurping man, who stripped Christ's mythic story*
*of meek forgiveness, up from every land*
*you helped force loose the ultimate staying hand.*
*Popes, Calvins, Marxes share your shabby glory:*
*where men are tortured, riddled freedom falls,*
*hidden in hating hearts your monument tolls.*

CHAPTER II

# EDINBURGH: THE NEW TOWNS

" Here is the capital of an ancient, independent and heroic nation, abounding in buildings ennobled by the memory of illustrious inhabitants in the old times, and illustrious deeds of good and evil; and in others, which hereafter will be reverenced by posterity, for the sake of those that inhabit them now. Above all, here is all the sublimity of situation and scenery—mountains near and afar off—rocks and glens—and the sea itself, almost within hearing of its waves.

JOHN GIBSON LOCKHART, 1819

Edinburgh has but partly abdicated, and still wears, in parody, her metropolitan trappings. Half a capital and half a country town, the whole city leads a double existence; it has long trances of the one and flashes of the other . . . it is half alive and half a monumental marble. . . .

ROBERT LOUIS STEVENSON, 1878.

I

EDINBURGH achieved her European reputation as an intellectual centre about 1760, and maintained it until Scott's death in 1832. From the last decade of the seventeenth century, when an atmosphere free from religious bickering at last gave men time to consider the actualities and the graces of life—time, incidentally, badly needed, for the poverty of the country just before and after the Union was due mainly to the long wasting years of distracting wars and civil turmoils—the life of the Capital increased its colour and bustle.

Prior to 1707, the meetings of Parliament brought a host of noblemen and their families to the City, as a result of which the shopkeepers enjoyed brisk business. After 1707, indeed, there was a period of depression in the City, the Parliamentarians having carried their patronage with them to London. But gradually the Law Lords took the place and the flats of the nobility—heredical jurisdiction having been abolished at the break-up of the clan system in 1746—trade and the arts revived; and Old Edinburgh's vivid, cosy, clarty, mediæval heart pulsed its fullest measure.

Social life maintained a fixed pattern, only affected by minor changes, until about 1760. By seven o'clock in the morning, the shutters were down from the dingy cellar shops: ragged caddies, who ran errands to any part of the town for a penny, were afoot

54

in search of commissions: sewage men were sweeping up the refuse in the open gutters: and men of the world had had their first tipple of the day. Breakfast was commonly eaten at eight. It was a substantial meal consisting of a main meat course washed down with ale, sack, claret, brandy or—after 1730—tea.

At half-past eleven, shops were shut again for the " meridian "— another tipple of brandy or ale. Next came dinner—one o'clock, until after the '45, when it gradually got moved back to, in some cases, as late an hour as four o'clock. This again was a substantial meal, extending to two or more courses as the century went on. Four o'clock was the tea-hour of the ladies, who, for lack of other accommodation, often entertained in their bedrooms. Supper-time was commonly at eight o'clock. For that, many women and most men repaired to the taverns—dingy, candle-lit cellars where you could enjoy oysters:

> *A crum o' tripe, ham, dish o' pease,*
> *An egg, or cauler frae the seas,*
> *A fluke or whitin',*
> *A nice beefsteak; or ye may get*
> *A guid buffed herring, reisted skite*
> *An' ingans, an' (though past its date)*
> *A cut o' veal.*

Once the ladies had finished their repast, and had been escorted back to the turnpike stairs of their homes, the men returned to their taverns for serious drinking, which officially was meant to end at the sound of the ten o'clock drum, but often went on long after. Those who obeyed the drum and set out homewards, had to dodge the contents of many a slop-pail falling on them from a fourteenth storey; for at that hour, to the cry of " Gardy loo ", the accumulated slops of the day, including the latrine slops, were tilted down into the street to await the attentions of the early-morning scavengers.

For recreation, the men had their clubs, to which the cramped nature of their homes made them eager to escape. For in the lands, Law Lords' studies not infrequently became their children's dormitories by night, while servants had frequently to sleep in pulled-out drawers. Married women had their tea-parties, while the young had their assemblies of promiscuous dancing, formalized to such an extent that the promiscuity was reduced to the stepping out together of a minuet or a gavotte, and the exchanges of a few hurried whispers. In less exalted circles, however, promiscuity flourished; for while theft was almost unheard of and murder was a comparatively rare occurrence, fornication throve healthily, in spite of the fine-seeking nose of the Kirk Treasurer's Man.

It was only natural that so cramped a city, where rich men and poor had to share the same turnpike stairs, would sooner or later expand itself somehow. Natural physical difficulties in the way of lateral expansion preserved Edinburgh's mediæval condition for an abnormally long time. But in the 1760s, the first serious attempts to relieve the pressure were made at last. James Brown laid out George Square (which he named after his brother) to the south of the town in 1766.[1] Though regarded at first as a suburb, it quickly became popular. Only the graceful west side has survived the pressures of an expanding University.

In spite of such extensions towards the south (where, since 1628, had stood George Heriot's Hospital, one of Edinburgh's many famous schools[2]—a magnificently flamboyant Renaissance building well worthy of " Jinglin' Geordie ", the goldsmith and banker who accompanied his royal master Jamie the Saxt to London— and William Adam's fine new Infirmary, founded in 1738 but now no more), the obvious direction for expansion was clearly across the Nor' Loch. James VII, when Duke of York, had reached this conclusion; but nothing was done in a practical way until the energetic Lord Provost, George Drummond, started to agitate for the building of a North Bridge—on the official grounds that it would improve the terrible road to Leith!

The North Bridge was eventually begun in 1763. Five years later, Parliament empowered an extension to the Royalty over the fields where George Street and Princes Street now lie. A prize was offered for the best plan for the New Town, and it was won by James Craig (1740-95). The foundation stone was laid in Rose Court on October 26th, 1767, and building began in earnest. There were two initial set-backs. One was the unfortunate collapse, with some loss of life, of the North Bridge in 1769, its piers having been planted on unsettled carried earth: the other was the reluctance of many folk to leave the comfortable fug of the Old Town for the muddy, wind-swept barrenness of the New.[3]

---

[1] Two tiny squares, long since vanished, were actually built earlier: Argyll Square about 1746, and Alison Square in 1750.

[2] George Watson's, Fettes, Daniel Stewart's, Merchiston, and Loretto are some of the others. All are nowadays more or less modelled on Dr. Arnold's Rugby. They give an English education, with its emphasis on leadership in sport and militarism. If any boy still emerges a Scotsman, then that is a remarkable tribute to the native strength of his personality!

[3] One of the first to move, incidentally, was David Hume, after whom St. David's Street was named in jest by his friend, Nancy Orde.

Even after the physical soundness of the rebuilt North Bridge had been established beyond doubt, the chilling experience of crossing it during a winter gale was for long still a matter for comment. The most amusing comment perhaps came from Captain Edward Topham, who spent six months of the season 1774-5 as a member of the Castle garrison, and whose *Letters from Edinburgh* give us an intelligent Englishman's observation on Scottish manners. Of the passage across the North Bridge, Topham wrote:

" The most peculiar effect which I find is the winds, which here reign in all their violence, and seem indeed to claim the country as their own. A person who has passed all his time in England cannot be said to know what a wind is. He has zephyrs and breezes and gales, but nothing more; at least they appear so to me after having felt the hurricanes of Scotland.

As this town is situated on the banks of the sea, and surrounded by hills of an immense height, the currents of air are carried down between them with a rapidity which nothing can resist . . . The chief scene where these winds exert their influence is the New Bridge, which by being thrown over a long valley that is open at both ends, and particularly from being ballustraded on each side, admits the wind in the most charming manner imaginable, and you receive it with the same force as you would do were it conveyed to you through a pair of bellows. It is far from entertaining for a man to pass over this bridge on a tempestuous day. In walking over it this morning I had the pleasure of adjusting a lady's petticoats, which had blown almost entirely over her head, and which prevented her disengaging herself from the situation she was in, while one poor gentleman who unfortunately forgot his hat and wig, had them lifted up by an unpremeditated puff and entirely carried away."

Though modern fashions ensure that the diversions are less entertaining, the behaviour of the wind has altered little with the years.

Craig's plan envisaged George Street as the centre-piece of the New Town, the pattern finished at either end with Charlotte Square and St. Andrew's Square: Queen Street, one-sided and overlooking the blue coast of Fife: and Princes Street, also one-sided, overlooking the Castle Rock. Between these main streets there were to be " meaner " streets for " shopkeepers and mechanicals "; and, of course, mews.

Craig died before his New Town could be completed, and it fell to Robert Adam (1728-1792) to design Charlotte Square. In it, he made use for the first time in Edinburgh of houses treated as architectural blocks. Unfortunately, Adam also died before his plans were fully realized, and an inferior church in the wrong style of Doric replaced his conception: but one of several instances where later, less talented, architects have tinkered unsuccessfully with work greater than their own.[1] The restored church now forms an extension to Register House.

Whilst this activity was going on, minor suburbs such as Nicholson Square were being added to the south, in the vicinity of the University; but they were not part of any wider plan.

At the turn of the century, a second New Town was begun to the north of Queen Street Gardens. The architect responsible for much of this plan was Robert Reid (1776-1856), aided by William Sibbald, the City's Superintendent of Works. Once again, the conception was that of a wide street running from east to west, with open spaces at either end. Great King Street forms the centre-piece of this second New Town, with Heriot Row and the gracefully-curved façade of Abercrombie Place, balanced by Fettes Row and Royal Crescent. In one sense the overall conception of the second New Town, not having the advantage of a crest for its centre-piece to rest upon, is less easy to comprehend than that of Craig's Town. Broadly speaking, however, Reid followed Adam's example, and treated whole blocks of houses architecturally.

Unfortunately, the effect of many New Town buildings has been spoiled by the removal of the astragals which picked up the pointed stone motif, and their replacement by gaping plate-glass windows. The establishment of the New Town Conservation Committee with a full-time architect as director, and Government and Local Authority support, augurs well for continuing restoration.

While all this home-building was being carried through, public building was not being neglected either. Robert Adam's best Edinburgh work, Register House, was started in 1774, though again it was not completed at the time of his death. Here, the officious Robert Reid saw fit to alter the plans for the rear of the building.

The Assembly Rooms in George Street were built between 1784 and 1787 to plans by one John Henderson, though in 1843

---

[1] Worst of all, however, was Playfair's interference with Adam's plans for the University, begun in 1789. Adam intended two courts. Playfair not only scrapped one, but rather pointlessly lowered the level of the surviving court. The dome, of course, was a late-Victorian addition of 1884.

William Burn, the desecrator of St. Giles, added both the Tuscan portice in front, and the Music Hall behind.

At least two New Town churches are remarkable. St. Andrew's Church in George Street, was begun in 1785, to the prize-winning plans of a Major Frazer of the Royal Engineers. The steeple was added in 1789. This graceful, oval-shaped building still contains its original pulpit and galleries, and some of its first pews. St. Stephen's Church also attracts attention, because it stands at the foot of Frederick Street, causing the road to divide and enriching one of the most exciting of the many Fife-coast vistas to be glimpsed from George Street. St. Stephen's has a tower as its main axis, behind which stands the square body of the church, set, however, diagonally to the tower. The interior is octagonal, and as a further surprise, the main entrance sweeps up to the gallery. St. Stephen's was the work of William Henry Playfair (1789-1857), who was also the builder of the Royal Institution on the Mound, the National Gallery (in 1850), and the Grecian memorial on Calton Hill to Dugald Stewart, umquhile Professor of Moral Philosophy at Edinburgh University.

Calton Hill itself is an impressive monument to an hallucination which beset the good folk of Edinburgh about this time. For they chose to think of their city as a modern Athens; the Athens of the North. Beginning with the gentle classicism of the Adam brothers, the Greek influence had gradually become more and more intense. So in spite of the fact that the Nelson Monument put up near the summit in 1807 was more than a little romantic in style, Calton Hill was conceived as a sort of Acropolis. Playfair replaced Craig's Observatory with an elaborate four-portico affair near the Dugald Stewart Memorial: Thomas Hamilton (1784-1858), designer of the magnificent Royal High School, added his variation of the choragic Monument to Lysicrates, in a memorial to Robert Burns:[1] while on the summit, Playfair began in 1822 his full-sized reproduction of the Parthenon, as an intended church monument to the Napoleonic Wars.[2] After the first twelve columns were built, however, the money ran out. The "ruined" Scottish Parthenon is to this day a reminder of Scotland's Grecian folly. As Douglas Young puts it:

> These chill pillars of fluted stone
> shine back the lustre of the leaden sky,

---

[1] He also designed the much-criticized Burns Monument at Alloway, along similar lines.

[2] Pity the poor congregation who might have had to climb twice daily to the top of the hill!

*stiff columns clustered on a dolerite hill*
*in solemn order, an unperfected vision*
*dimly gleaming. Not at random thrown*
*like old Greek temples that abandoned lie*
*with earthquake-riven drums. Rigid and chill*
*this still-born ruin stands for our derision.*

*A fine fantasy of the Whig literati*
*to build a modern Athens in our frore islands,*
*those elegant oligarchs of the Regency period,*
*Philhellenic nabobs and the Scots nobility.*
*As soon expect to meet a bearded Gujerati*
*stravaiging in a kilt through the uttermost Highlands,*
*or in Princes Street gardens a coy and blushing Nereid.*
*Athens proved incapable of such mobility.*[1]

Whilst Playfair and Hamilton were thus unleashing their Greek
enthusiasm, and Archibald Elliot (1761-1823) was laying out his
highly-castellated (but now demolished) Calton Jail—the Governor's House of which still stands perched on a rock above the
railway—a third New Town was being planned. This was to
bring into Grecian conformity the Glasgow approach. Melville
Street was to be the main axis, with Atholl Crescent and Coates
Crescent traversing it. Beyond that, the scheme was not carried
through, and when further houses were added eighty years later,
they were in the coarse style of late-Victorian jumblery. Gaps in
the plans of the three New Towns were also filled in while the
craze for Grecian planning still persisted.

When it became clear that Edinburgh's urge for expansion was
something which would not easily be contained, a commercially-
minded Earl of Moray bought a stretch of land between the
second New Town and the Water of Leith—the glorified burn
which is Edinburgh's only native river. This corner was built
to the plans of James Gillespie Graham (1777-1855), who had been
born without the "Graham" in the Perthshire village of Dunblane, but who was wise enough to marry a wealthy Graham heiress. Gillespie Graham had a certain grossness of taste, and a
fondness for mock-baronial turevettings, which make him a link
between the Georgian architects and the later Victorians. Moray
Place and Albyn Place represent his best work.

Gillespie Graham's scheme surged round, but did not entirely
obliterate, the charming Dean Village, over which the engineer
Thomas Telford (1756-1834) threw a bridge in the year of his

[1] *Auntran Blads* by Douglas Young.

death, linking the Learmonth estates with those of Moray. Another village to be encompassed was Stockbridge, also on the Water of Leith. This ground was feued by Sir Henry Raeburn, the portrait painter, and the charming Ann Street, named after his wife, was started in 1816. St. Bernard's Crescent suffers from the fact that only one side of it was completed to the original design. In Stockbridge, too, may be seen that delightful landscape toy, St. Bernard's Well, product of the fancy of the painter Alexander Nasmyth (1758-1840), who built it in 1789. Once, the waters it pumped were supposed to have medicinal properties. Nowadays, the properties of the Water of Leith are certainly far from medicinal, whatever else may be said of them.

It is quite impossible to mention all the Georgian or Georgian-pattern streets in Edinburgh, for so many have survived. But the massive terraces on the lower slopes of Calton Hill, which were originally meant to link up Edinburgh with Leith, must be mentioned. On earthen terracings engineered by Robert Louis Stevenson's grandfather, Calton Terrace, Regent Terrace, and Royal Terrace were built up. Royal Terrace sweeps rounds its uninterrupted façade for over a quarter of a mile, high above the Forth. (It became the home of many a merchant who could watch for the arrival of his ships from his drawing-room window, and so was once nicknamed "Whisky Row".) Unfortunately, most of the lower terraces were never built, Playfair's plans being abandoned because of the usual lack of money.

Just as the mediæval life of Old Edinburgh persisted long after it had been swept away elsewhere, so Edinburgh's Georgian phase outlived the Georges. Georgian-style building was continued in the Capital until the 1880s. As the Victorian era advanced elevations deteriorated, and the stylistic slide towards jumblery gathered rapid momentum.

One reason for the ultimate abandonment of the building of gracious houses in favour of humbler dwellings was that, apart from Craig, all the later planners had failed to consider the needs of "shopkeepers and others". The poorer folk huddled themselves closer into the fug of the Old Town, as people of rank and position abandoned it. Others—from the country, from Ireland, and even from the Highlands—also began to crowd into Old Edinburgh in search of work. Scotland's nineteenth-century industrial expansion certainly reserved its worst social effects for Glasgow; but Edinburgh felt a little of the human shock. She also experienced the disrupting arrival of the railways.

Even in 1819, when Robert Southey set out from Edinburgh in company with Thomas Telford on a journey round Scotland, the wynds of the Old Town were places " down which an English eye may look, but into which no English nose would willingly venture, for stinks older than the union are to be found there ".

Southey was but one of several men of sensibility who were curiously critical of the New Town. He alleged that the Edinburgh people had begun " to be ashamed of their mound of which they formerly boasted and to wish that they had made a bridge instead. A single wall is built along this mound, with a pavement on both sides; it is for the sake of shelter from the wind whether it blows east or west. The good sense of this makes one wonder the more at the enormous length of the streets in the New Town, where there is neither protection nor escape from the severe winds to which Edinburgh is exposed."

Ruskin indulged in an ungenerous and flowery onslaught upon almost every aspect of the New Town, finding it " coarse, without soul ", and " inconvenient ". Even Stevenson had his complaints. He lamented the " draughty parallelograms ": but then he, poor man, never enjoyed robust Scottish health. He also found fault on quite other grounds:

" It cannot be denied that the original design was faulty and short-sighted, and did not fully profit by the capabilities of the situation. The architect was essentially a town-bird, and he laid out the modern city with a view to street scenery, and street scenery alone. The country did not enter into his plan . . . If he had so chosen, every street upon the northern slope might have been a noble terrace and commemorated an extensive and beautiful view."

To my mind, and in spite of Stevenson, there are two delights about the New Towns of Edinburgh. One is the street scenery, which, at its best, is surely superb. Only a person with no sense of the beauty of well-disposed stone could have written as disparagingly of it as did Stevenson. The other delight is the many sudden glimpses which one may catch, in the course of ordinary business, of the distant Forth and the yellow coast of Fife beyond, framed between elegant Georgian angles. The essential quality is in the contrast.

Stevenson's architectural demands reach quite impossible proportions when he regrets that you may not pause " in some business perplexity, in the midst of the city traffic, and perhaps catch the eye of the shepherd as he sat down to breathe upon a heathery shoulder of the Pentlands; or perhaps some urchin, clambering in a country elm, would put aside the leaves and show you his flushed and rustic visage; or a fisher racing seawards, with the tiller under his elbow, and the sail sounding in the wind, would fling you a salutation from between Ans'ter and the May ".

All of which is mighty pretty writing, but little else besides. Anyone who wishes to have an uninterrupted pastoral view needs only to move out into the country.

II

What sort of social life did the New Towns produce? A gracious expansion which the enforced intimacies and the cribbed nature of the Old Town could not allow.

Mrs. Andrew Fletcher, a Yorkshire woman who married a Scottish Whig solicitor and lived much of her life in Edinburgh, recorded her impressions in 1811:

A little before this time the forms of social meeting had somewhat changed . . . Large dinner-parties[1] were less frequent, and supper-parties—I mean hot suppers—were generally discarded. In their place came large evening parties (sometimes larger than the rooms could conveniently hold) where card-playing generally gave place to music or conversation. The company met at nine, and parted at twelve o'clock. Tea and coffee were handed about at nine, and the guests sat down to some light cold refreshment later in the evening. People did not in these parties meet to eat, but to talk and listen."

There was certainly plenty of good talk which must have been well worth hearing. For even if architecturally the "Athens of the North" whim was little more than a folly, there was at least a solid enough basis of intellectual achievement centred on the Capital to justify native pride.

At fashionable parties, groups of people would cluster round the Reverend Sydney Smith (1771-1845), the begetter, and Francis Jeffrey (1773-1850), the editor of the *Edinburgh Review*, which, since 1802, had become the leading European periodical written in English. Jeffrey, a fearless and often a fierce critic, examined the poetry of his day with the aim of assessing its moral tendencies. His was therefore ethical criticism—a kind of criticism with which the twentieth century has little enough patience. As he took the

[1] They became customary in the New Town towards the close of the eighteenth century.

view that the Romanticism of the Lake Poets was ethically a retrogressive rather than a progressive development, he opposed many of their innovations, though he praised their work when he considered it to be free of excessive individualism. As Jeffrey was a willing and witty talker, he was much sought after in the drawing-rooms of the New Town.

So, too, was Walter Scott, whose novel *Waverley* provoked a literary sensation in 1814, though it was not until his financial collapse in 1826 that Scott publicly owned himself to be "the Author of Waverley". By this time, *Blackwood's Magazine* was challenging the *Edinburgh Review* in fierceness and superficiality of criticism. It provided the young Lockhart with a testing-ground for his *Scorpion* satire. There was also genial old Henry Mackenzie, "The Man of Feeling", who had outlived the age in which the work of his youth had won its tearful popularity. He, too, was an excellent talker.

Amongst the older school of able men whose fame has necessarily been more ephemeral, was Professor John Playfair, who, with Dugald Stewart, gave Edinburgh University a reputation for learning enhanced by Stewart's successor Dr. Thomas Brown. There was also the medico Dr. John Russell, whose carefully-planned parties at 30, Abercrombie Place were amongst the most popular in the city.

From 1803 until 1815, the year of Waterloo, there was a dash of military glamour to enliven social life. The Napoleonic Wars kept alive the persistent fear of invasion. So, as Lord Cockburn put it: "We were all soldiers, one way or other. Professors wheeled in the College area; the side arms and the uniform peeped from behind the gown at the Bar, and even on the Bench; and the parade and the review formed the staple of men's talks and thoughts." Even the lame Walter Scott was an officer in the Midlothian Yeomanry Cavalry.

But after the signing of the Treaty of Paris, there was no further need for such Home Guard activities.

"War was over," another brilliant diarist, Mrs. Elizabeth Grant[1] (1797-1885) recorded; "all its anxieties, all its sorrows had passed away, and though there must have been many sad homes made for ever, in a degree, desolate, these individual griefs did not affect the surface of our cheerful world. The bitterness of party still prevailed too much in the town, estranging many who would have been improved by mixing more with one another. Also it was a bad system that divided us all into small coteries; the

---

[1] *Memoirs of a Highland Lady* is one of the most delightful of all Scottish journals, full of piquant, womanly observation.

bounds were not strictly defined, and far from strictly kept; still, the various little sections were all there, apart, each small set over-valuing itself and under-valuing its neighbours."

She goes on to enumerate " the fashionable set . . . seeming to live for crowds at home or abroad ", an " exclusive set ", a " card-playing set ", a " quiet country-gentlemen set ", a " literary set including college professors, authors and others pleased so to represent themselves ", a " clever set with Mrs. Fletcher "[1], the " law set; strangers and inferiors ". " All shook up together ", she adds, " they would have done very well . . ." but " when primmed up, each phalanx apart, on two sides of the turbulent stream of politics, arrayed as if for battle, there was really some fear of a clash at times ".

Politics had been made a " turbulent stream " by the manipulation of the Tory Government, vastly strengthened in its anti-reform attitude by the events of 1791 in France, and by the subsequent Napoleonic threat. This threat of invasion, indeed, was used as an excuse to suppress opposition. " There was no free, and consequently, no discussing, press," Cockburn tells us. " Nor was the absence of a free public press compensated by any freedom of public speech. Public *political* meetings could not arise, for the elements did not exist . . . Nothing was viewed with such horror as any political congregation not friendly to existing power. No one could have taken a part in the business without making up his mind to be a doomed man."

The shameful example made by the gross judge Lord Braxfield —" Let them bring me prisoners and I'll find them law "—of the young advocate Thomas Muir of Huntershill, sentenced to fourteen years transportation in Botany Bay, for being a delegate of the newly-formed " Society of the Friends of the People " in 1792, was still fresh in men's minds. Whigs found the greatest difficulty in getting fair treatment even in private society, while " every official gate was shut against them ". Mrs. Fletcher's lawyer husband, for instance, had to endure years of near starvation because his Whig reputation kept away clients.

But the humble and the progressive people could not be permanently suppressed. Even Sir Walter Scott, one of the most popular men in Scotland, was given an angry reception when in the last year of his life, broken and ill, he struggled into Jedburgh to speak against the Reform Bill. In 1832, the Scottish Reform Bill was at last passed, in a public atmosphere which could easily have been heated into revolution had the measure been talked or voted out. No wonder, therefore, that Cockburn, the most

[1] The diarist quoted on page 63.

eloquent Whig of his day, recorded his feelings on the 6th of August; a great whoop of joy.

" Our Reform Bill has become law. Much follows from this one fact. Nobody who did not see it could believe the orderly joy with which the people have received their emancipation. They[1] are preparing to exercise their franchise for the first time and under forms to which they are strangers, with great zeal."

Cockburn then added a judgment (typically shrewd) which has come to pass, and the underlying principles of which still operate.

" The Tory Party, as such, is extinguished. They are fighting, and obstinately, for their favourite object of resisting change and keeping down the people. But though those ends are in their hearts, they feel that they are untenable, and that the people themselves are henceforth to be the chief avenues by which power is to be reached. Accordingly, every Tory candidate, without exception, is professing popular opinions. In a few years, the Whigs will be Tories and the Radicals the Whigs. It is between these two that the struggle will henceforth be."

The struggle to-day is between violent change inspired by prejudice, and sensible piecemeal "social engineering".

Lord Cockburn lived to see other manifestations of the growing power of the workers, arising out of the unemployment of many weavers in the West: Chartist riots, and marches of hunger strikers. In fact, through the periods of his maturity and old age, the social climate altered its Scottish Georgian character, and assumed many of the grosser qualities of British Victorianism.

He recorded significant happenings which illustrated this general change: the founding of *The Scotsman* in 1817; the disbanding of the City Guard, now rendered unnecessary by the more efficient police in 1817; and a few years later, the abolition of the Corps of Water Caddies, whose services were superseded by the introduction of piped water. In 1818, too, there was the excitement caused by the rediscovery of the Honours of Scotland; and the establishment of concerts open to the general public, in place of the Gentlemen's Subscription Concerts which flourished during the latter half of the preceding century.

The theatre also flourished in Georgian Edinburgh. The old Theatre Royal had been built by Lord Provost Drummond in 1769 on the site opposite the Register House where the Post Office

[1] Occupiers of houses or owners of land valued at £10 a year, or over.

now stands, and "Bozzy" had written a Prologue for the opening night. Mozart's Irish friend Michael Kelly appeared in a piece called *Love in a Village* in 1802. *The Duenna*, by another of Mozart's friends, Thomas Linley, came to the Royal in 1806, followed by *The Beggar's Opera* in 1807. It is strange to read the names of the long since forgotten operas that charmed the citizens of the New Towns in the second decade of the century—Sir Henry Bishop's *Knight of Snowdoun* in 1811; the same composer's *The Miller and His Men* in 1813; and in the same year, Kelly's *Royal Oak*. To-day, we remember Bishop by the gentle, faded sentimentality of his most popular song, *Home, Sweet Home*, and by the bird-imitation of his *Lo! Here the Gentle Lark*, beloved of coloratura sopranos.[1]

After this outburst of English opera, there came a long run of dramatized or operatic versions of Scott's novels. Of these, the only one to survive, more as a curiosity than anything else, is *Rob Roy* (1826). For this, as for most of the others, the music was arranged by the ubiquitous Bishop. A few years ago, I saw a revival of the piece in a Scottish town. Unfortunately, when that part in the overture was reached where the principal 'cellist has to make a plaintive solo appearance with the air *Mary of Argyll* (who had, of course, nothing whatever to do with the noble cateran!), the lady presented herself half a tone lower than she should have done. Her unfortunate entry was very soon noticed by the audience. When at last it became apparent to the conductor, the orchestra shuffled into a ragged silence, out of which an angry voice from the rostrum whispered audibly: " E flat, damn you—not D ! "

Needless to say, the music is an absurd hotch-potch of badly-arranged Scots airs and mawkish original numbers, amply deserving the opprobrium which Scott himself registered in his *Journal* after attending one of the earliest performances. However, the New Athenians loved these pieces, and under the copyright laws of the day, Scott could do little to control the arrangers.

Interlaced with melodramaticized Scott, the Edinburghians were also able to see Rossini's *The Barber of Seville* in 1824, suitably "arranged" by Bishop: *La Gaza Ladra* in 1827: Balfe's *Bohemian Girl* in 1849: and, three years before the Theatre Royal was closed in 1859, Verdi's *Il Trovatore*.

In 1809, Corri's Concert Rooms were redecorated and opened as the New Theatre Royal, a title which was later changed to

---

[1] A happier bird-association is Linley's charming little song *Still the Lark Finds Repose*, which seems recently to have been " re-discovered ".

the Caledonian Theatre. There, the New Towners first saw Weber's *Oberon* in 1826. In 1830, they were offered not only Mozart's *Figaro*, and *Don Giovanni* and Weber's *Der Freischutz*, but also a revival of Arne's *Artaxerxes*, for the first Edinburgh performance of which, in the Old Town, poor Robert Fergusson had written some extra songs for Tenducci to sing.

Corri's site seems not to have been conducive to theatrical permanence. On it, the Adelphi Theatre was burned down in 1853. On it, too, the Queen's Theatre and Opera House met the same fate in 1905. And on it the latest Theatre Royal was finally burned down during the Second World War. This time, the planners decreed that the phœnix to arise out of the ashes should be the monstrous St. James complex.

A different kind of entertainment was provided for the New Towners when in 1822, George IV—a pleasant rotund man in his sixties—paid his first visit to the Capital of his Scottish kingdom. He disembarked from his yacht at Leith, and on the 15th of August first set foot on Scottish soil. There was a tremendous outburst of pageantry, the culminating glory of which was the appearance of the Monarch himself at his first levee in Holyrood Palace, amply attired " in complete Highland costume made of the Royal Stewart tartan ". He dined to the strains of Nathaniel Gow's " celebrated band ", after the meal addressing himself in such flattering terms to the overawed fiddler that Gow could only gasp " I'm perfectly content to dee noo ". But Gow's interest in living revived after his Majesty had sent over a copious supply of Atholl Brose for the musicians. Going home later to the surrounding villages where they had their homes, it was reported that these fiddlers " astonished the slumbering rustics along the whole way ".

Another Scot who derived the greatest satisfaction from the pomp and circumstance of it all was Sir Walter Scott who, indeed, was one of the principal stage-managers of the affair. Mrs. Fletcher went with her three daughters: " to a window above Trotter's shop in Princes Street, to see the royal cavalcade come down St. Andrew Square to cross the Calton Hill to Holyrood. It was certainly a most imposing and gorgeous sight; but it was not the gilded coach or the fat gentleman within it which made it an affecting one: it was the vast multitude assembled . . . animated by one feeling of national pride and pleasure in testifying their loyalty to their sovereign. Sir Walter Scott had so admirably arranged the reception, that the poorest and humblest of his subjects had an opportunity afforded them of bowing to their King."

*Edinburgh: Princes Street from the Castle*

Another diary entry—this time by Mrs. Grant—confirms that not all of Edinburgh's society folk took the event as seriously as Sir Walter. Commenting on the King's appearance in Highland Dress, she tells us that it " gave occasion for a laugh at one of Lady Saltoun's witty speeches. Some were objecting to this dress, particularly on so large a man. ' Nay,' she said, ' we should take it very kind of him; since his stay will be short, the more we see of him the better '."

Unfortunately, there are no such human records of Queen Victoria's visit in 1842, though she surely gave equal grounds for gentle merriment by solemnly professing herself a Jacobite. But by then the citizens of Edinburgh had become too self-consciously sentimental to see the humorous aspect of outbursts of pageantry which had long since outgrown any real meaning.

### III

Edinburgh did not entirely escape the effects of the Victorian Industrial expansion. Pleasing houses were put up as far out as Newington about the middle of the century. But by 1878, when Stevenson wrote his *Picturesque Notes*, speculative building of what then seemed the worst sort had already disfigured the outer fringes.

" Day by day, one new villa, one new object of offence, is added to another; all around Newington and Morningside, the dismallest structures keep springing up like mushrooms; the pleasant hills are loaded with them, each impudently squatted in its garden, each roofed and carrying chimneys like a house. And yet a glance of an eye discovers their true character. They are not houses; for they were not designed with a view to human habitation, and the internal arrangements are, as they tell me, fantastically unsuited to the needs of man. They are not buildings; for you can scarcely say a thing is built where every measurement is in clament dispro- portion with its neighbour. They belong to no style of art, only to a form of business much to be regretted."

These are hard words. Yet the offending villas have one factor in their favour. They at least possess solid masonry. What, I wonder, would Stevenson have written about later develop- ments like the between-the-wars Niddry Estate, an abortive attempt at slum clearance doomed to visual failure from the start?

*Edinburgh's New Town:* above *Moray Place* below *Heriot Row*

Or about much of the still less imaginative immediately post-Second War council housing?

Certainly, in the late 1940's and throughout the 50's, there were many pressures other than aesthetic ones. Broadly speaking, a community gets the environment it deserves. At least Edinburgh has been spared any unfortunate despoilation of its sky-scape with the screaming punctuation marks of high rise towers!

In Edinburgh, as elsewhere, there has been a steady improvement in the overall design quality of council housing estates. In spite of rigorous cost control, architects have striven to defeat monotony, and their success has increasingly been recognized by the Saltire Society annual award scheme, and by the tri-annual award scheme organized by the Civic Trust. As in Stevenson's day, though on a level of monotony which now make his unfortunate villas look like architectural masterpieces, private housing estates have sprung up with " off-the-peg " models set down side by side, sometimes not even architect-designed.

Disappointing as is the spoilation of the approaches to Edinburgh, the City has still much for which to be thankful. The industries which became closely associated with her were mostly light and clean—the manufacture of flour and meal; the weaving of yarn; and the processing of tobacco. She also became the Scottish centre of banking and insurance, which added substantially to the numbers of her professional classes, already numerous because of her position as the main repository of Scots Law. With the transfer of routine Scottish administration from Whitehall to the uncompromisingly bleak-looking St. Andrew's House, the work of Thomas Tait (1882-1954), a large number of civil servants made their homes in Edinburgh. With the establishment of a Scottish Assembly, Edinburgh should regain something of the *de facto* Capital status which for more than two centuries it has sadly lacked, having had to rely on a sustaining climate of the mind.

The Victorian era brought about the eclipse of Edinburgh as a literary centre. Exept for Robert Louis Stevenson who, in one mood, saw himself as a sort of reincarnated Robert Fergusson, she produced no outstanding writer during the latter half of the nineteenth century. Stevenson found the physical climate too severe for his frail body. He also found the spiritual climate so hostile to a man of imagination that only after he had settled in Samoa did Scotland come in to, what was for him, true focus. " O my sighings after romance," he complained, " and O the weary age which will not produce it." In one of .his early poems, he placed his adolescent dilemma in everyday terms.

*I walk the street smoking my pipe*
*And I love the dallying shop-girl*
*That leans with rounded stern to look at fashions;*
*And I hate the bustling citizen,*
*The eager and hurrying man of affairs, I hate,*
*Because he bears his intolerance writ on his face*
*And every movement and word of him tells me how much*
    *he hates me.*

*I love the night in the city,*
*The lighted streets and the swinging gait of harlots.*
*I love cool pale morning,*
*With only here and there a female figure,*
*A slavey with lifted dress and the key in her hand,*
*A girl or two at play in a corner of waste-land*
*Tumbling and showing her legs and crying out to me loosely.*

For a time, escape was to be found in the pose of velvet jacket Bohemianism: until at last he discovered "the romance of the bright picturesque image". The Stevenson of *Weir of Hermiston* had no need for romantic devices of escape. He had discovered how to see Scotland whole, and had come to artistic terms with her.

Some Victorian writers made their homes in Edinburgh and left a little of the impact of their personalities upon her. One of these visitors was Stevenson's early friend, W. E. Henley, the crippled roaring-boy editor of the *Scots Observer*. Another was Alexander Smith, who, while Secretary to Edinburgh University, wrote *A Summer in Skye*, which contains one of the most vivid of all Edinburgh descriptions.

"The quick life of to-day sounding around the relics of antiquity, and overshadowed by the august traditions of a Kingdom, makes residence in Edinburgh more impressive than residence in any other British city . . . What a poem is that Princes Street! The puppets of the busy, many-coloured hour move about on its pavements, while across the ravine Time has piled up the Old Town, ridge on ridge, gray as a rocky coast washed and worn by the foam of centuries; peaked and jagged by gable and roof; windowed from basement to cope; the whole surmounted by St. Giles's airy crown. The New is there looking at the Old. Two Times are brought face to face and are yet separated by a thousand years. Wonderful on winter nights, when the gully is filled with darkness, and out of it rises, against the sombre blue and the frosty stars, that mass and bulwark of gloom, pierced and quivering with innumerable lights."

With the dimming of her fame as a literary centre, Edinburgh lost her reputation as a place where good talk could always be heard. It was left to the doctors and scientists to build up for her a different kind of reputation. Sir James Young Simpson's practical application of chloroform was a major contribution towards the alleviation of human suffering. Clerk Maxwell, who discovered the wireless ray, and Graham Bell, who was closely connected with the practical development of the telephone, added further lustre to the youngest of the four Scottish Universities. Later still, Sir Donald Francis Tovey's delightful combination of literary wit and musical erudition won for Edinburgh a borrowed musical reputation which, on more general grounds, she hardly deserved.

Just as Georgian Edinburgh gradually abandoned the sedan chair in favour of the coach, so Victorian Edinburgh developed the horse-tram, and Edwardian Edinburgh the cable-tram. It, in turn, gave place to the electric tram, which in Edinburgh took the form of an uncomfortable box the progress of which forced the occupants to undergo the maximum amount of pitching, rolling and jolting which the human frame would reasonably be expected to endure. The atomic age has no patience for such primitive forms of torture, however, so Edinburgh's tramcars were sent to the scrap-heap: some would say, with hindsight, a regrettable decision, in view of the energy shortage.

By the beginning of the Edwardian era, Edinburgh had at last come to appreciate the merit of her New Towns. Certainly, much damage had been wrought on them by then. Princes Street had already begun to assume the jumble of clashing elevations and styles which characterize it to-day. The grace of George Street had also been marred in the interests of commerce, and gaps were soon to be torn out to accommodate those ornate vulgarities which banks and insurance companies deem necessary to impress their customers. Across the expanding city, hotels and tea-rooms, halls and churches (adorned with meaningless towers, turrets and tarradiddles) sprang up, conceived in the prosperous heat of Capitalism's Indian summer. The big houses in the eloquent terraces and crescents were still homes for single families. The cold manners produced by an Anglicized education, the overwhelming preponderance of the professional classes, and that illusion of immunity from the contaminating bustle of the outside world which these Georgian façades so easily confer earned Edinburgh its reputation for chilly inhospitality.

IV

Just before the beginning of the Second World War, I was shown over an old land in the High Street. The smell of cramped poverty which each twist of the turnpike stair intensified turned my stomach over upon itself. Up until then, I had been, so to speak, strictly an outside viewer; one of these who volubly urged the preservation of old buildings regardless of their worth as setting for lives yet to be lived. That visit cured me of all sympathy with any such romantically false approach to the problem of how our heritage of stone may be preserved.

*Warriston's Close, Halkerston's Wynd!*
*Crookit and cramped, dim, drauky, blind.*   [damp; draughty

*Juttan tenements, lair on lair,*
*cuttan the lift tae a narrow gair;*                   [sky; strip

*glaur mair auld nor the stanes themsels,*            [mud
*gether't in dubs roun court-yaird wells;*          [puddles

*bailies and lawyers scurryan doun*
*the Castle grounds tae the newer toun;*

*rattle o buses, clatter o caurs*
*hurlan shoppers hame frae bazaars;*

*howfs packit oot wi waly dugs*            [china dog ornaments
*grandfaither clocks, maps, brooches, jugs;*

*pubs whaur a rauchle, frienly stour*
*swirls thru the bricht-lit steaman door;*

*auld wives skreichan at shilpit weans,*              [shrunken
*rickets and history in their banes;*

*the fierce-like edge o wir Lallans leid*            [Scots speech
*flicked roun a flytit guid-man's heid;*          [scolded husband

*wemen, aulder nor their years,*
*loungan on hopeless, worn-oot leers;*

73

*Ramsay, Fergusson, Mary, Knox*
*thocht less o noo than fear o the pox;*

*ilk gutter fu o floatan grime,*
*the nameless fitsteps rinsed frae Time.*

*Warriston's Close, Halkerston's Wynd!*
*Crookit and cramped, dim, drauky, blind. . .*

*Fegs, and you're gey romantic places*
*for thae wha ainly pree your faces.*                    [experience

Fortunately, it is unnecessary to preserve the smells; and there
is a better solution than the destruction favoured by the
Victorian City Fathers; drastic restoration which, while preserving the shell of an old building, brings its interior arrangements
up to twentieth-century standards of hygiene and comfort. The
City Fathers belatedly realized that the Old Town is still the heart
of modern Edinburgh. Victorian destructiveness can hardly be
made good; but already much that might still have been destroyed
under less enlightened guidance has been saved, and much more
has been scheduled for ultimate restoration. The Old Town, like
the New, is now protected by the laws relating to Conservation
Areas, and the requirement put the Local Authority to draw up
plans of enhancement. There are thus good grounds for feeling
confidence that even at this late stage, there should be fewer further
losses through neglect, or for private or municipal profit.

In spite of the jumbled elevations which characterise the built-
up side of Princes Street—a jumble which began to be inflicted
upon it quite soon after its completion—it remains one of the
most spectacular highways in Europe, with its view over the
chasm of the railway-line to the Castle rock and the spine of
the Old Town. It is a view which changes constantly with the
weather and the slanting of the sun. I have never ceased to marvel
at the clarity of our northern light which, even at such a distance, can enable the eye to pick out the coloured dresses
of the girls lying sunning with their lovers on the banks of the
green valley, and to absorb the shaded grey contrasts of the
gnarled rock itself. The visual exhilaration which the sharp
dawns of spring, and the long, lingering evenings of autumn
provide is not, of course, peculiar to Edinburgh. It may be
experienced in Scotland wherever mountains and water come
together; wherever gentle slopes bend down towards the sea-
bound horizon. But it is not normally so noticeable in her

towns. In Glasgow, the influx of clear light is quickly broken and sullied against the jumbled heights and pseudo-Gothic details of that city's many styleless buildings, sending the sensitive eye hurriedly down towards the ground again. But in Edinburgh, the northern light plays about the Old Town and humanizes the New; it flashes blue glints of the Forth up hilly streets, and carries the fair gold fringe of Fife to the very crown of George Street.

The Old Town may now have its share of dour Victorian tenements, shining forth dully, like badly stopped teeth; the north side of Princes Street may, indeed, present one of the most horrifying rows of jumblery to be met with in all Europe; George Street may have been scarred and pitted by ornate flights of nineteenth-century fancy, and plastic shop-fronts; classical terraces and crescents may here and there have been split too obviously into the cosy convenience of divided flats and flatlets: but the spirit of Edinburgh's long centuries still remains about her stones. For all the cold artificiality of her phoney-English upper classes; for all her Festival whigmaleeries and her occasional outbursts of irritating and apparently pointless arrogance, she alone among Scotland's cities could again assume the real role of a Capital if, as now seems a decided possibility, the Scottish people should ever wish their affairs to take such a turn.

To-day, she is associated in the minds of many people the world over with the arts because of her International Festival of Music and Drama, held annually since 1947.

Various claims have been made as to who first thought up the idea. In any case, the first practical move towards the foundation of the Festival seems to have been made by Mr. Rudolph Bing, a professional impresario, who sold the idea to a group of Edinburgh citizens.

Much has been said about the courage and faith needed to launch such an enterprise. Courage and faith are, of course, essential for the launching of any commercial venture in which money has been risked.

Nevertheless, that East-Windy West-Endy Edinburgh—where, according to Glaswegians, sex are what the coalman uses to deliver fuel in—should have managed to promote and sustain for more than quarter of a century the most ambitious and artistically wide-ranging of all post-Second War Festivals, is a considerable tribute both to its succession of talented Directors, and to the men and Women, Councillors and " laymen ", who have borne the responsibility for its practical management.

At first, it was undoubtedly regarded with deep suspicion. The tartan-and-haggis brigade protested loudly that what tourists really wanted to see and to hear was the native product, not imported opera or orchestras they could hear in other European cities. The East-Windy West-Endy set announced loudly that they wouldn't *dream* of remaining in their City while its buses and restaurants were overcrowded with foreigners.

I freely admit that originally I was one of the doubters, though not on any of those grounds I have outlined. I simply felt that a festival without geographical roots had little chance of attracting customers. Salzburg has Mozart, Bayreuth Wagner, Munich Richard Strauss. Edinburgh has only its post-Athens of the North century of retiring, genteel philistinism, and its nineteenth-century hypocritical and absurd licensing laws. These ensure that Sunday visitors to its elegant Festival Club in the George Street Assembly Rooms must content themselves with Coco-Cola, while the good burghers regale themselves in their own homes with more agreeable spiritous or vinous potions. The licensing laws remain absurd, and a disincentive to tourism. The hypocrisy of a late Lord Provost with whom I was politely arguing the case for change when a guest in his own home, epitomized the curious Scots double-think which has selected the Edinburgh upper middle-class mind as its last redoubt. " When in Rome, do as the Romans do, " he said, cheerfully handing me a glass of sherry in his Sunday dining-room. " Besides, the Church of Scotland would never agree to any relaxation. " Since the Romans practice no such absurdity, and the Church of Scotland's steadily declining influence now extends over no more than about a third of the adult population of the country, this particular City Father's argument was much less convincing than his taste in sherry.

Gastronomically, the Festival has resulted in the sweeping away of the starchy, traditional Scots High Tea, and its replacement with a wide choice of meals from speciality restaurants. Little about the city has changed more dramatically than the Edinburgh way of public eating. For that improvement, credit must go to " thae Festival furreners ", as I once heard a bus conductor describe the annual influx of visitors (a not inconsiderable proportion of whom venture no further than the forty-six miles separating Glasgow from the Capital).

Financially, the Festival is supposed to lose money. So, of course, it does, if you place Government and Local Authority grants against box-office takings, and look to find a profit. So do our educational system, our health services and our public libraries. So, what? An American study undertaken as part of a master-plan for a Philadelphian Festival of 1976 to mark the two hundredth anniversary of American Independence, revealed some startling facts and figures. On what we laughingly call in these islands a "conservative" estimate, a certain Harry Putsch, Executive Director of the Greater Philadelphia Cultural Alliance, and his colleagues, calculated that the economic impact of the three-week event on the region was no less than fifteen million pounds annually. Of the one hundred and fifty thousand visitors to the Festival in 1974, the year the study was undertaken, fifty per cent of the visitors were from furth of Scotland, twenty-five per cent from Edinburgh and its environs. For the benefit of those who find such statistics meaningful, let me add that the Festival achieves an average annual press coverage of fifteen thousand, eight hundred and fifty column inches: which, for those who are interested, means that, laid end to end, there would be a continuous litter problem from the foot of the Mound to Register House.

But Scottish publicity, like the proverbial Yorkshire muck, means money. The report concludes: "As a result, Edinburgh has become a leading international tourist attraction, and its annual tourist season has increased from three to six months in duration. The economic benefits of the Festival provide significant direct and indirect economic benefits for a majority of citizens of the region."

Having done what would naturally be expected of me as a Scot, and dealt with food and finance before coming to the less tangible benefits the Festival affords (for those who can afford them), let me simply say that in three decades, many Scots have been able to see more great pictures, enjoy a wider range of operas and plays, and hear an incomparably enriched selection of noble music presented "live" than they could otherwise have achieved in half-a-lifetime's globe-trotting.

Robert Kemp's and Tyrone Guthrie's successful revival of Sir David Lyndsay's pre-Reformation "morality", "Ane Satire of the Three Estates", with Cedric Thorpe Davie's music, has been revived successfully on several occasions. We have had the gentler experience of watching in gracious surroundings a revival of the first British ballad-opera, Allan Ramsay's "The Gentle Shepherd", and of realizing, after a revival of John Home's "Douglas", that any answer to that famous eighteenth-century gallery-shout, "Whaur's your Wullie Shakespeare noo?", is scarcely likely to disturb the Swan of Avon's Elysian serenity.

Some of the finest plays of Jonson, Shakespeare, Schiller, Synge, Brecht and Thornton Wilder have been brought vividly alive

77

before us. The later plays of Eliot were specially written for Edinburgh. Sydney Goodsir Smith's "Wallace" had its patriotic airing. That year, a devoted old-style Scottish Nationalist (one of the breed who could still afford to indulge in extravagant gestures because political power then seemed forever an impossibility,) attended every night to leap to her feet at the conclusion of each performance, and set the rafters of the Assembly Hall ringing with a communal rendering of "Scots Wha Hae". Unfortunately, either the majority of the audience was unable to remember the words beyond the first verse, or felt no burning desire to lay any proud seat-paying usurper low, whatever his or her nationality.

One remembers incomparable Glyndebourne/Mozart productions in the earlier years—a "Marriage of Figaro" and a "Cosi" too delectable for words to describe: Hamburg presentations of "Fidelio" and "Mathis der Mahler": the Swedes in their own version, dramatically so much more acceptable, of Verdi's "Ballo in Maschera" and Blomdahl's "Aniara": Milan's chuckling presentation of Rossini's "Il Turco in Italia" and Cimarosa's "Il Matrimonio Segreto": Scottish Opera's "Alceste", and much else besides.

In music, the Festival played a notable part in first introducing the symphonies of Carl Nielson to the British public (and, incidentally, in helping to prove right the present writer who – at a time when older critics were still sneering at Mahler's alleged long-winded ineptitudes – as the still-youthful critic of a since vanished Scottish daily, suggested that his *angst* would speak with immense appeal to the younger generation. And so it does).

There are, of course, those who still attack the Festival. It is a common enough reaction for people to attack what they cannot understand. Nowadays, there are the levellers who, equating socialism with selfishness, seek to bring everything down to their own dreary plain of envious dissatisfaction. There are also the circus-for-the-people brigade, who attack the Festival because it does not make adequate provision for "Pop" fans, boxing devotees, variety vultures, model train enthusiasts, or cat-fanciers. Admirable as these pursuits may be in themselves, other provision is made for their supporters. Art is elitist to the extent that only by withdrawing from the clamour of the community into his own lonely solitude can the artist create anything. Like nature itself, the creative spirit is not egalitarian, and political attempts to make it so are as relevant as pretending that human love can be levelled to the basic requirements of whoredom.

Not the least pleasing aspect of the Festival is the magnet it proves to companies made up of students, professionals on a free enterprise fling, or gifted amateurs. They set up their stages by the dozen in dowdy back-street halls, often achieving astonishing effects, and sometimes presenting talents which emerge from this shadowy beginning to take the footlights of full-scale professionalism. The Festival apart, Edinburgh has always nourished many painters, grouped around its Royal Scottish Academy. As with Scottish poetry, colour has always been an important ingredient in Scottish painting.

Above all, however, it is poetry that is the supreme Scottish art. Throughout the ages, the Scots have resorted to verse to edge their satire, proclaim their passions, or celebrate their joy or dismay in their surroundings. Edinburgh has had her share of admirable poets in the "Scottish Renaissance", not least among them those who use the Scots tongue; most notably, Robert Garioch and Sydney Goodsir Smith, whose love elegy *Under the Eildon Tree* is a highly sophisticated masterpiece tinged with a detached irony, as a brief extract must suffice to show:

> *The lums o the reikan toun*
> *Spreid aa ablow, and round*
> *As far as ye coud leuk*
> *The yalla squares o winnocks*
> *Lit ilkane by a nakit yalla sterne*
> *Blenkan, aff, syne on again,*
> *Out and in and out again*
> *As the thrang mercat throve,*
> > *The haill toun at it*
> *Aa the lichts pip-poppan.*
> > *In and out and in again*
>
> *I' the buts and bens*
> *And single ends,*
> > *The banks and braes*
> *O' the toueran cliffs o lands,*
> *Hail tenements, wards and burghs, counties,*
> > *Regalities and jurisdictiouns,*
> > > *Continents and empires*
> > > *Gien ower entire*
> *Til the joukerie-poukerie!*
> *Hech, sirs, whatna feck of fockerie!*
> *Shades o Knox, the houchmagandie!*
> > *My bonie Edinburrie,*
> > > *Auld Skulduggerie!*

*Flat on her back sevin nichts o the week,*
*Earnan her breid wi her hurdies' sweit.*

*—And Dian's siller chastitie*
*Muved owre the reikan lums,*
*Biggan a ferlie toun o jet and ivorie*
*That was but blackened stane*
*Whar Bothwell rade and Huntly*
*And fair Montrose and aa the lave*
*Wi silken leddies doun til the grave.*
  *—The hoofs strak siller on the causie!*
  *And I mysel in cramasie!*

Another writer, the Aberdonian-born Alexander Scott, sees in the crowd of shoppers and shop-gazers walking about Princes Street in one of those haars which from time to time come creeping in from the North Sea, a symbol of the present " lost " plight of the individual in the modern world, against which the Castle Rock becomes a symbol of an abiding past.

*The heich o the biggins is happit in rauchens o haar,*
    *The statues alane*
  *Stand clearlie, heid til fit in stane,*
*And lour frae then and thonder at hencefurth and here.*

*The past on pedestals, girnan frae ilka feature,*
    *Wi granite frouns*
  *They glower at the present's feckless loons,*
*Its gangrels tint i the haar that fankles the future.*

*The fowk o flesh, stravaigan wha kens whither,*
    *And come frae whar,*
  *Hudder lik ghaists i the gastrous haar,*
*Forfochten and wae i the smochteran smore o the weather.*

*They swaver and flirn i the freeth lik straes i the sea,*
    *An airtless swither,*
  *Steeran awa the t'ane frae t'ither,*
*Alane, and lawlie aye tae be lanesome sae.*

*But heich i the lift (whar the haar is skailan fairlie*
    *In blufferts o wind)*
  *And blacker nor nicht whan starns are blind,*
*The Castle looms, a fell, a fabulous ferlie.*

> Dragonish, darksome, dourlie grapplan the Rock
>   Wi claws o stane
> That scart wir historie bare til the bane,
> It braks lik Fate throu Time's wanchancy reek.

Yet another Edinburgh poet, Norman McCaig, has captured, in fine flying words, a feeling which often assails one in the Capital: that the past is somehow less remote than five minutes ago.

> Here's where to make a winter fire of stories
> and burn dead heroes to keep our shinbones warm,
> bracing the door against the jackboot storm,
> with an old king or two, stuffing the glories
> of rancid martyrs with their flesh on fire
> into the broken pane that looks beyond Fife
> where Alexander died and a vain desire,
> hatched in Macbeth, sat whittling at his life.
>
> Across this gulf where skeins of duck once clattered
> round the black Rock and now a tall ghost wails
> over a shuddering train, how many tales
> have come from the hungry North, of armies shattered
> an ill cause won, a useless battle lost,
> a head rolled like an apple on the ground;
> and Spanish warships staggering west and tossed
> on frothing skerries; and a king come to be crowned.
>
> Look out into this brown November night
> that smells of herrings from the Forth and frost;
> the voices humming in the air have crossed
> more than the Grampians; East and West unite,
> in dragonish swirlings over the city park,
> their tales of death and treacheries, and where
> a tall dissolving ghost shrieks in the dark
> old history greets you with a Bedlam stare.
>
> He talks more tongues than English now.  He fetches
> the unimagined corners of the world
> to ride his smoky sky, and in the curled ˉ
> autumnal fog his phantoms move.  He stretches
> his frozen arm across three continents
> to blur this window.  Look out from it.  Look out
> from your November.  Tombs and monuments
> pile in the air and invisible armies shout.

Throughout most of the year, however, Edinburgh cultural life is still less rich than that of Glasgow, where both Scottish Opera and Scottish National Orchestra have their homes. Yet in its Royal Lyceum theatre company Edinburgh possess a company of players devoted not only to an international repertoire, but employing a large proportion of Scots actors and actresses, and eager to foster Scottish writing talent.

Edinburgh has long since lost her dominating position as the United Kingdom home of fine printing and of magazine publishing. Most of her publishing firms have vanished, and few of her recent cultural magazines have exceeded their infancy. The Scottish author nowadays has to seek a London publisher for his work. If he is a poet, he must perforce rely on small firms whose means of distribution are limited, or on non-profit-making academic presses whose efficiency often lacks credibility.

Yet in spite of such shortcomings and deficiencies, life in late-twentieth-century Edinburgh has still a snell tang of its own. The overtones of her history; the contrasts of her stones; the light which plays upon them; above all else, that illusive feeling of "soon-to-be-again"—these are what give the Edinburgh scene its mildly stimulating flavour.

So in the end, I find myself back in imagination where I started; back in the carriage of that Glasgow train listening to my rubicund friend telling me, in his kindly, fluted tones: "At least Edinburgh is still a capital city, where our own kings and queens have lived and loved and died. They can't take *that* away from us . . ." Perhaps, after all, they can't!

# Chapter III

# THE LOTHIANS

*From Berwick to Dombarre twenty miles it is,*
*And twelve miles forward unto Haddyntoune,*
*And twelve miles from these to Edinburgh I wisse,*
*To Lithko twelve, and so Northwest to Bowne,*
*Twelve miles it is unto Sterlyng toune,*
*Besouth Forth, that river principall,*
*Of right faire waye, and plentiful at all.*

JOHN HARDYNG (whose mileages are, of course, inaccurate), *circa* 1420.

I

THE land of Lothian is said once to have stretched along the east coast from the Forth to the Tweed. The country was called *Loidis* in the seventh century, *Lothene* in the twelfth, *Laadinia* in the thirteenth, and *Lawdien* in the seventeenth. Legend avers that it took its name from King Loth, reported to be the father of Thenew, whom he cast out when she naïvely allowed herself to be seduced by a prince whom she had already refused to marry, surviving to bear his child, St. Kentigern or Mungo. *Lothian* and *Loth* possibly derive from the Gaelic *Lathach*, clay or mire.

At the time of the coming of the Romans, Lothian was inhabited by the Otadini or Votadini and the Galeni or Gadeni,[1] possibly northern branches of the Brigantes of Bernicia, whose territory would thus range upwards from the Midlands of England to the Forth. Very little is known about them. Probably they collaborated with the Romans, flourished on their own for a while, after the Romans had withdrawn, but by the sixth century A.D. had almost certainly been supplanted by the Picts.

Early in the seventh century A.D., Pictish overlordship of the Lothians was replaced by Anglian. Throughout the tenth century, the English held sway, until 1006, when, according to an Anglian record, the pre-Danish Earl Adulf of Northumbria

---

[1] Some copies of the map of the ancient geographer Ptolemy, who flourished during the second half of the second century, showed them as Ladeni. But only copies of Ptolemy's maps have come to us, so that this may well be a mere error, and the similarity to the modern Lothian accidental.

voluntarily relinquished the Lothians to King Malcolm II (1005-1034) in the vain hope that the Scottish monarch would thus be dissuaded from invading Northumbria to avenge his defeat at the hands of Earl Adulf's brother earlier in the year. Malcolm, however, eventually marched, and defeated the Earl's army at Carham in 1018.

This battle had several far-reaching consequences. It led to a peace-treaty of some kind with King Canute, out of which Canute may or may not have tried (unsuccessfully) to make Malcolm his liege. Since Saxo Grammaticus, the twelfth-century Danish extoller of Canute's conquests, did not mention Scotland in his list of kingdoms which his hero had subjugated, it is probable that the story of Canute's overlordship was invented by Edward I in 1301 as part of his attempt to strengthen his case when writing to the Pope to claim Scottish overlordship for himself.

More important, Carham also produced a Gaelic Scotland united for the first time under one king. Malcolm may even have expelled many of the Anglian settlers from the Lothians, giving their lands to Gaels instead; for the late Professor Watson has shown conclusively[1] that from about the middle of the tenth century, Gaelic became a widely-spoken language in the Lothians.

Thereafter, the Lothians flourished with the rest of the Scottish Kingdom, until the untimely death of Alexander III at Kinghorn ended a long stretch of comparatively peaceful years. During the long and bloody struggle for independence which lasted throughout the fourteenth century and much of the fifteenth, the Lothians, because of their nearness to the Border, were often ravished by raiding sorties or invading armies. In common with most other parts of Scotland, they knew the fierce fury of the Reformation. The Covenanters fought one of their least hopeful battles on Lothian soil. Mary Queen of Scots played out several of the most dramatic moments of her career within their boundaries. And Prince Charles Edward Stuart won his first victory on a Lothian battleground.

Since the middle of the eighteenth century, the story of the Lothians has been less spectacular. Their territory contains some of the most fertile agricultural land in Scotland as well as rich mineral deposits. Industry has taken its toll on the fair face of the countryside. Yet its ill-effects have so far been marvellously limited. Happily, many of the great houses of the seventeenth and eighteenth centuries have been preserved; not, as is so often the case, in a state of neglected near-ruin, or as barrack-like rest-homes for overworked trade-unionists; but in

[1] *Celtic Place-names of Scotland.*

*Midlothian: Hawthornden, home of the poet William Drummond*

much their original magnificent condition, though now accessible to the public.

II

West Lothian—or Linlithgowshire as it once called itself—is the smallest of the Lothian counties, having a surface of just over one hundred and twenty square miles. Its hills compensate in charm for what they lack in height. Some have descriptive names, like Cuckold le Roi (now corrupted to Cocklerue, a mere 916 feet in height), which lies between Linlithgow and Bathgate; or Glower-o'er-'em, which raises its far from aggressive 516 feet to the north of Linlithgow. On the highest of these West Lothian hills, Cairnpapple (1,010 feet), between Bathgate and Torphichen, evidence of habitation in the ages of pre-history has been uncovered—a Neolithic sanctuary remodelled in the early Bronze Age (*circa* 1800 B.C.) as a "monumental open-air temple in the form of a stone circle with enclosing ditch: later (*c.* 1500 B.C.) despoiled and built over by a Bronze Age cairn, considerably enlarged several centuries later."[1]

It is hard for us to reconstruct in imagination the damp, fierce, draughty uncertainty which must have been the way of life of our pre-historic ancestors: much easier to visualize the efficient and uncompromising military way of life of the Romans, whose Antonine Wall rested its eastern flank at Carriden, in West Lothian. Thereafter, the Wall ran through the grounds of Kinneil House, crossing the River Avon and the county boundary with Stirlingshire near Inveravon. There was once a Roman station at Cramond, which was linked with Carriden by a coastal road: Blackness is said to have been a Roman fort: and at Bridgeness, near Bo'ness, one of the best preserved and most interesting legionary tablets was found in 1868.[2] On one side of it, a Roman soldier rides triumphantly over defeated Britons; on the other there is a representation of a sacrificial ceremony. The inscription records that the Augustan legion—who had made 4,652 Roman paces of the wall's 39,726—set up and dedicated the stone to the Emperor Cæsar Titus Antoninus.

During the Dark Ages, in common with Mid-Lothian and East Lothian, West Lothian changed hands several times—or perhaps more accurately, suffered several ethnical changes—until the fall of the Northumbrian kingdom, when it became once and for all

[1] *Ancient Monuments of Scotland*: 1952.
[2] Now in the Scottish National Museum of Antiquities, Edinburgh.

*West Lothian: the Royal Palace, Linlithgow*

a part of "modern" Scotland. From the time of David I, West Lothian was, at any rate nominally, a sheriffdom, until Robert the Bruce put it under a constable. James III made it a sheriffdom again, the office becoming hereditary, first in 1600 to a branch of the Hamilton family, and after the Restoration to the family of the Hopes of Hopetoun, who held sway until hereditary jurisdictions were abolished throughout Scotland.

The county falls naturally into two divisions: the coastal area, bounded roughly by Torphichen, the Forth Bridge, and Bo'ness, which, in spite of an industrial concentration at the latter place and some lesser mining eruptions here and there, is primarily agrarian in economy: and the hinterland, the home of the shale oil industry. The richest farming land is thus around the coast, though just before the war about two-thirds of the county's acreage was under cultivation.

Until quite recently, I never had cause to explore West Lothian. It was a county one passed through travelling between Edinburgh and Stirling. But, as I have discovered, it has much to commend it. It has, for instance, its county town, Linlithgow, situated in the middle of the pastoral division. The etymology of this name is uncertain—it possibly derives from the Brythonic Linlideu, meaning *dear broad lake*—but for many centuries Linlithgow was a royal residence. The Romans may have had a station there. On the site where the ruins of the Palace and the Church of St. Michael now stand, there was first a chapel of some sort, and then a peel. Edward I made Linlithgow his invasion headquarters during the winter of 1301-2, building on to the existing peel. When he went home to London, he left behind him an English garrison, who cultivated the awkward habit of sallying forth and interfering with Scots folk travelling on their lawful occasions between Edinburgh and Stirling. According to the poet John Barbour, a local farmer, William Binnock (or Bunnock), during the summer of 1313—the year before Bannockburn—put an end to this nuisance by a simple ruse that has paid handsome dividends to conquering rustic heroes and opera librettists "since Virgil wrought and Homer sang".

It was Binnock's duty to supply the garrison with hay. One day he filled his waggon, not with its legitimate cargo, but with six armed men, who were hidden under a covering of hay. Outside the portals he secreted as many of his armed friends as would join in the enterprise. Binnock drove the cart himself, having for his mate a stout carl with a handily-concealed axe. As soon as they were half-way through the portcullis, the axe-man snapped the yokes of the cart, so that the gate could neither be lowered nor the portcullis shut. At the same time, Binnock attacked the porter, while the armed men leaped from the cart, crying " Call all; call all ", the pre-arranged sign for their companions outside to join the fray. In a very short time, Binnock and his men made themselves masters of the castle. Robert the Bruce rewarded the patriotic farmer with a grant of land, and caused the castle to be destroyed. However, it seems to have been rebuilt again by 1334, for in that year Edward Balliol, the son of Bruce's old rival, John, paid for Edward III's assistance towards his brief usurpation by presenting the English monarch with the constabulary, town and castle of Linlithgow.

The oldest part of the present Palace—which is almost square in plan—dates from the earliest years of the fifteenth century. The Stewarts were fond of it, James I laying the ground plan, James III adding part of the surviving west side, James IV adding more to the west, and James V, who was born within its walls, building the south and east sides, and bringing it to its highest degree of magnificence. It became the royal custom for Stewart kings to settle Linlithgow upon their brides. Thus, Mary Queen of Scots was born there while her father lay dying of a broken heart at Falkland. And it was at Linlithgow that the first performance of Sir David Lyndsay's *Ane Satire of the Thrie Estatis* took place before the assembled court, probably in 1535.

By this time, the Reformation was about to burst upon Scotland, bringing with it a wave of vindictive and stupid destruction. One of its leading protagonists, the Regent of Scotland, Queen Mary's bastard half-brother James Stewart, Earl of Moray, died in Linlithgow Palace on the 20th of January, 1569, two years after the Battle of Langside.

He was travelling from Stirling to Edinburgh and had to pass through the town. Hamilton of Bothwellhaugh, a laird whose property the Regent had caused to be forfeited, and whose wife had gone out of her mind as a result of the inhumane treatment she received at the hands of the Regent's men during the seizure, secreted himself on a balcony of the house of his uncle, Archibald Hamilton, which fronted the main street. The town was decorated in honour of the approaching visitor, so the comfort-loving murderer was able to conceal a feather-bed behind the bunting. As the Regent passed the house, Hamilton fired at him with a hackbut. The bullet passed between Moray's waist and thigh, and he was carried, mortally wounded, to the Palace. Meanwhile, Hamilton escaped, his horse having been kept ready at the back of the house. He fled to France and eluded justice. Not so his uncle's house, however, which, according to a contemporary *Diurnal of Occurants*, was shortly afterwards mysteriously "all utterlie burnt with fyre". The County Court Buildings now occupy the site, and a plaque designed by the Scottish Pre-Raphaelite artist Sir Noel Paton commemorates the event.

After James VI's departure for London in 1603, the Palace served mainly as the occasional residence of its keepers, the Earls of Linlithgow, though the hall of the Palace was sometimes used as a meeting-place for the Scots Parliament. It was used thus for the last time in 1646, when a plague was ravaging Edinburgh. It had one last moment of royal glory, however, in 1617, when James VI[1] made his return visit to Scotland. He came to Linlithgow, where he encountered the plaster figure of a lion, within which was concealed the local schoolmaster, one James Wiseman. As the king approached, the voice of Wiseman welcomed his sovereign from the lion's bowels.

> *Thrice royal sir, here do I you beseech,*
> *Who art a lion, to hear a lion's speech;*
> *A miracle, for since the days of Aesop*
> *No lion, till those days, a voice dared raise up*
> *To such a majesty! Then, king of men,*
> *The king of beasts speaks to thee from his den,*
> *Who, though he now enclosed be in plaster,*
> *When he was free, was Lithgow's wise schoolmaster*

No doubt the king appreciated the pedagogue's sentiment, if not the quality of his verse!

Charles I spent a single night in the Palace in July 1633. Between 1651 and 1659, Cromwell's men lived in it, and since some of his letters are dated from Linlithgow, it is possible that their leader also slept beneath its now vanished roof.

Roof, rafter and plenishings were all destroyed in 1746. Its keeper at this time was a Jacobite lady, Mrs. Glen Gordon, who, when Prince Charles Edward Stewart was on his way to Edinburgh in 1745, had provided him with as near an imitation of an erstwhile royal reception as her limited resources allowed. After the defeat of General Hawley's dragoons at Falkirk in 1746—the Prince's last victorious battle—the English troops fell back on Linlithgow, quartering themselves in the Palace. According to tradition, so large were the fires heaped up in the hearths that Mrs. Gordon drew Hawley's attention to the danger they created. Newly-defeated generals, however, have usually more

---

[1] He caused the north side to be rebuilt in 1619-20.

to occupy their minds than consideration towards the domestics of the victorious opposing commander; so General Hawley told the good lady to be about her business. "A-weel," she threw back at him, as she abandoned the Palace to its fate, "I can rin frae fire as fast an ony general in the King's Army."

Time has worked further damage on the injuries wrought by the dragoons in February 1746. It has several times been proposed that the Palace should be roofed and turned into a Museum for Scottish Antiquities.

Looking at the damaged fountain in the quadrangle—a fountain that once ran with wine—or wandering round the cold stone corridors, it is hard to imagine the Palace as it must have been when it was a home of kings. Then, tapestries hung from the walls and rushes were strewn on the floors. The records still exist to show that five shillings was paid to one Haw for supplying new reeds on the occasion of a visit from foreign ambassadors in the days of James V. Indeed, at the height of its glory Sir David Lyndsay called it a "palace of pleasure", which "micht be ane pattern in Portugall or France".

When Sir William Brereton, a journalizing English traveller with Puritanical leanings, arrived in Linlithgow in the summer of 1636, he records that he found it "a fair, ancient town and well built, some part of it of stone. Here is a fair church and a dainty conduit in the middle of the street. Here the king hath a very fair palace, built castle-wise, well seated, so as it may command the whole town. . . ." The Palace still "commands" the whole town. Its domination may be felt, and its massive presence glimpsed through gaps in the main street. It stands beside a little loch where swans have arched their elegant necks since first the fortress was the delight of Scotland's kings.

I have always supported the traditional Scottish view that the swan is, by nature, a royal creature. The behaviour of the Linlithgow swans during the occupancy of Cromwell's troops provides pleasing confirmation. According to the *Mercurius Caledonius* of 8th January, 1661, whose unbiased veracity I am sure no reader would question, the royal swans flew away the day the Roundheads arrived, and stayed away until the very day Charles II was crowned at Scone. Furthermore, two English birds, which might reasonably have been supposed to be suitably inculcated with Parliamentary sympathies before being dispatched from the south, refused to settle.

The "conduit in the middle of the street" which pleased Sir William Brereton was the Cross Well, originally erected about 1535. Cromwell's soldiers amused themselves by knocking it down, so it had to be rebuilt after they left, and again, as a result of more natural destruction, in 1807. Fulfilling the celebration of the old jingle " Glasgow for bells, Lithgow for wells ", there are at least three other "conduits" in the town. The most interesting of the old wells is St. Michael's, which supports the information that " St. Michael is kind to strangers ", and is appropriately topped by his figure, which was taken from one of the older Cross Wells. St. Michael is the town's patron saint.

The "fair church", which stands just south of the Palace, is also dedicated to St. Michael, and is very old. A Church of St. Michael apparently stood on the same site in the reign of David I. Its successor, a Gothic edifice with an embattled tower, was put up in 1242 by Bishop David de Kernham, when Alexander II was on the Scottish throne. In 1384, Robert II contributed the odd sum of twenty-six shillings and eighteen pence towards the cost of repairing the tower; but tower and church were both seriously damaged in a fire which nearly wiped out the whole of the wooden town in 1424.

Much of the present structure dates from the reign of James III, including its open-work crown, similar to that of St. Giles. That building monarch James V made substantial alterations. The steeple tower was uncrowned in 1820 because it was thought to be unsafe. By that time the fabric had suffered much desecration.[1] The Lords of the Congregation, who " broke churches and burnt fugues" in the name of the Protestant faith, reached Linlithgow on the 29th of June, 1559, during their southward march from Perth. They destroyed all the altar statues in St. Michael's, except that of St. Michael himself, which still survives, saved perhaps by the sudden stirrings of Popish superstition in one obstinate Protestant bosom!

In 1646 partitions were put up inside the Kirk, and it was turned into classrooms for the students of Edinburgh University who had been evacuated from the Capital to avoid the same plague that drove Parliament into the nearby Palace. 1812 saw the old building considerably repaired, the "repairs" being designed to bring it more into conformity with the nineteenth-century notion of a place of Protestant worship. The oak roof was torn down and replaced by an unctuous plaster ceiling, while galleries were squeezed in between the pillars, destroying the gracious proportion of the main aisle. Since then, however, there have been several restorations, most notably in 1894. The galleries have been taken out again, and the building has been

[1] An inappropriate gilt construction, added to the tower after the 1939-45 war, is, fortunately, removable.

reinvested[1] with some of its original dignity. Since 1942, the 700th anniversary of the founding of the church, the Friends of St. Michael have been planning further extensive restoration, including the rebuilding of the roof at its original level.

One of the three bells in the tower—"Blessed Mary"—declares that she was made "in the time of the august Lord James IV in the year 1490". It is one of the three oldest bells in Scotland. It was not old, however, when it had to echo a knell which sounded all over Scotland—the knell for Flodden Field.

Urged on by "ane love lettre" from the Queen of France, "ane ring aff her finger, with fyfteine thousand French crounes", and a plea that he should help her in her struggles against the English forces of Henry VIII by raising an army and coming "thrie fute on Inglis ground", James, against the advice of his nobles and the pleadings of his own Queen, an Englishwoman, marched south to meet defeat and death at Flodden on September 9th, 1513, in the twenty-fifth year of his reign. The historian Robert Lindsay of Pitscottie tells us that according to report, "the ladie Foord being ane bewtiful woman, the king melled [mingled] with hir, and the bischope of St. Androis with hir dochter, quhilk was agains the ardour of all guid captanes of warre to begine at whoredome and harlottrie, befoir ony guid succes battell or victorie"—counsel which particularly applies when the "bewtiful woman" is on the side of your enemy! In any case, the king seems to have betrayed the positions of his army to the Lady Ford, who promptly passed on the information of the aged English general, the Earl of Surrey. As a result, Surrey's army not only roundly defeated the Scots, but killed the king and the flower of the Scottish nobility.

One of those who did not attend the king at Flodden was the poet Sir David Lyndsay. He remained behind, probably because he was the guardian of the young prince who that day became James V. Lyndsay also disapproved of the English excursion, and may well have staged the appearance of the famous "apparition". While the king prayed for success in Katherine's Aisle of St. Michael's church at Linlithgow, a mysterious apparition appeared beside him and urged him not to march.[2] Lindsay of Pitscottie—who, incidentally, was not directly related to Sir David—related the incident as he heard it from his kinsman.

[1] Its comparatively recent stained glass windows include one by Burne-Jones, and one in memory of Sir Charles Wyville Thomson (1830-1882) of Bonnyside, the scientific director of the *Challenger* Expedition.

[2] Sir Walter Scott uses the incident in Sir David Lyndsay's tale in *Marmion*.

" . . . Thair[1] cam ane man clad in ane blew gowne, belted about him with ane roll of linen and ane pair of Brottikines [sandals] on his feet, and all ither things conforming thairto. But he had nothing on his head, but side hair to his shoulders, and bald before. He seemed to be ane man of fifty years, and cam fast forwards, crying among the lords, and speciallie for the king, saying that he desired to speak with him, while at the last he cam to the desk where the king was at his prayers.

But when he saw the king, he gave him no due reverence nor salutatioun, but leaned him down gruflings upon the desk, and said: 'Sir king, my mother has sent me to thee, desiring thee not to go where thou art purposed, whilk if thou do, thou sall not fare weill in thy journey, nor none that is with thee. Fardded, scho forbade thee, not to mell nor use the counsel of women, whilk if thou doe, thou will be confoundit and brought to shame!' Be [by the time] this man had spoken thir words to the king, the evin song was neir done; and the king paused on thir words, studying to give him ane answer. But in the meantime, befoir the king's eyes and in presence of the whole lords that were about him for the time, this man vanished away, and wuld be no more seen.

I heard Sir David Lyndsay and John Inglis . . . thought to have taken this man that they might have speired [asked] farther tydings at him: but they could not touch him."

Which, in the circumstances, is perhaps hardly surprising. In any case, this dramatic performance failed to impress the king. He went ahead with the plans that brought him disaster; and in vain did Queen Margaret watch from her turret in the north-west corner of the Palace for her consort's return.

The old High Street of Linlithgow has been seriously despoiled by the demolition of part of the north side, and the destruction of the west side of the central square. Several houses owned and restored by The National Trust for Scotland were bulldozed away in order to allow a developing architect achieve a larger unified scheme. The result, which might have been commendable enough in a New Town or even on an unimportant site, is here an inappropriate visual disaster; one of the most serious of post-1946 blotches on the battered environmental escutcheon of Scotland's historic towns. A motorway on the far side of the loch, however, has been well adapted to the lie of the land, and is practically invisible from the town itself, a pleasing visual distraction, however, for car passengers.

[1] The spelling is slightly modernized in the interest of intelligibility.

Until mid-sixteenth century, Linlithgow, under the privileges of its charter[1] as a Royal Burgh, engaged in vigorous trading through its harbour at Blackness, and later through the port of Grange at Borrowstounness. Thus in 1309, the customs at Linlithgow yielded more than those of any Scottish town except Edinburgh: and, by an Act of the Scots Parliament passed in 1618, the measure of weight for all Scotland was established as being that in use at Linlithgow. During the seventeenth century, the development of Queensferry and Borrowstounness, both on the Firth of Forth, gradually superseded it. In the eighteenth century, however, it found a new means of livelihood, for Daniel Defoe recorded in 1703 that "the people look here as if they were busy and had something to do . . . The whole green, fronting the Lough or Lake was covered with Linnen-Cloth, it being the bleaching season, and I believe a Thousand Women and Children, and not less, tending and managing the bleaching business."

Now, bleaching and cloth-making are as extinct in the town as is its ancient trade of making arrow-glue. Glue for less dangerous purposes is still made in Linlithgow, however, as are chemicals, paper, soap and whisky. The town also numbers a tannery among its industries.

When Cromwell's Excise Inspector, Thomas Tucker, arrived in West Lothian in 1655, he found Blackness, the port of Linlithgow, "now nothing more than three or foure pittifull houses and a piece of an old castle". By that time, the superior harbour facilities of Borrowstounness (or Bo'ness, to give it its modern contraction), had probably already forced Blackness into a decline. But the "piece of an old castle" still survives, sometimes known as the "Ship Castle" because it stands on a spit of land like a prow, has one tower that suggests a mast, and another which resembles a stern and battery. The date of its construction is unknown, although in the earlier part of the fifteenth century it was apparently strong and of importance in the defence of the realm. Douglases, Livingstones, Crichtons and Forresters fought over it, and about 1443 set it alight. The English burned it again in 1481. James III used it in 1480 as a meeting-place between himself and his rebellious nobles, who were later to overthrow him at Sauchieburn. It played its part in the religious struggles of the sixteenth century, being occupied by a French force in 1548: and about a hundred years later, it served as a prison for captured Covenanters. Although at one time during the nineteenth century it became the central

[1] The oldest to survive is dated 1389.

ammunition depot for Scotland, it is still in a good state of preservation, and in use as a hotel.

Not long after Blackness Castle had become a repository for explosives, the secret passage was destroyed which linked it with the old mansion of the Binns, three quarters of a mile back from the banks of the Forth.

The Binns, built in 1623 and much enlarged about 1820, has been, and still is, the home of the Dalzells [pronounced Dee-ell], though it is now the responsibility of the National Trust for Scotland.

Its most famous occupant was Sir Thomas Dalzell (1599?-1685), better known as General Tam Dalzell or the "Bluidie Muscovite", a royalist soldier who was captured at Worcester by Cromwell's troops. Though lodged in the Tower of London, General Tam escaped and fled to the Continent. He made his way to Russia, where he entered the service of the Czar. There, he learned many refined barbarities which he was able to put into practice when Charles II recalled him after the Restoration. He raised the Scots Greys to hunt down the Covenanters, and achieved his most distinguished success in November 1666. With a force of three thousand soldiers, he defeated an ill-armed rabble of nine hundred Covenanters at Rullion Green, in the Pentlands. It slightly lightens his dark record that, although he spared no men, when he heard that the captured women and children he had sent to Edinburgh had been shot, he resigned his commission and retired to the Binns, where he redecorated the house and adorned the grounds with avenues and parks.

Traditions of an unpleasant nature have gathered thickly about his reputation. His favourite game is said to have been called Hell. The rules were simple. After a good dinner with plenty of wine, he and his guests retired to a locked and darkened room, each armed with a whip. Everyone lashed out at everyone else until the victor alone was left standing. No wonder an effective threat of Lothian mothers to their naughty children was: "If ye're no guid, Tam Dalzell'll get ye!"

Much of the neighbouring parish of Abercorn is taken up by the grounds of Hopetoun House, once the seat of the Earls of Hopetoun and now of the Marquis of Linlithgow. The village of Abercorn itself lies by the Hopetoun walls. Its most interesting possession is its ancient church, refitted in 1579, just after the Reformation. A Norman doorway was turned into a window either then or at its second restoration in 1838. The stone cross of the seventh-century Bishop Trumuini (who in A.D. 675 made St. Wilfed's Monastery of Aebbercurnig the site of Scotland's first bishopric) was retrieved from its long use as a lintel at the later restoration. Round about the church, tomb-stones marking the burial-place of invading Danes have also been discovered. The Hopetoun pew, which has a richly-painted ceiling, is a relic of the time, not entirely past, when in the eyes of God a laird was deemed to merit superior comfort. Another interesting Abercorn survival is the set of three public coffins, used to give an outward resemblance of decency to the funerals of the poor. The Dalzell vault is officially said to contain the mortal remains of General Tam, though these are popularly supposed to have been long since removed to more appropriate quarters by the Devil himself.

Hopetoun House is probably the best-preserved of all Scottish mansions in the grand style. The centre-piece was built by Sir William Bruce of Kinross in 1699. William Adam planned the extra storey and the two wings with their domed octagonal towers, though the work was actually completed by his most famous son, Robert. Since he finished these additions, however, the house has not been further added to, and so has been spared the usual accretions of Victorian bad taste.

Inside, it is sumptuously furnished. The Yellow Drawing Room has walls lined with damask, and houses several master-pieces—Rembrandt's portrait of his mother, Van Dyck's "Marquis de Sperda", Titian's "Emperor Charles Vth", as well as pictures by Reubens, Janssen, Backhuysen, Canaletto, Teniers and Koenig. The Red Drawing Room is lined with silk which came from the Hague in 1760. It also contains several famous pictures—including an "Ecce Homo" of Van Dyck, a Cuyp, and a Viviano. It was the setting in which a great Scottish artist was once honoured. In 1824, shortly before he embarked for England on the royal yacht at Port Edgar on the Forth, George IV dined, wined, and knighted Sir Henry Raeburn in Hopetoun's Red Drawing Room. The gracious furniture in the State Rooms was specially made for them by Thomas Chippendale.

Hopetoun House is set in formal gardens modelled on those of Versailles. Beyond the gardens, one vista opens out upon the Forth, and takes in the flattened peak of distant Ben Lomond. Other views lead the eye down the widening Firth.

On the Hopetoun Estate there still stands, barely intact, Midhope Castle, a Scots keep which was once the country house of the earlier Earls of Linlithgow, the Livingstones. It must be hoped that oil industry activities nearby will not produce the spread of environmental havoc oil refining has caused further up the Forth, at Grangemouth.

Having thus come back again to the shores of the Firth, it is inevitable that we should pass through South Queensferry. Many places which exist upon a main trunk road have suffered grievous damage to their ancient fabrics since the coming of the motor car; none more so than the Royal Burgh of South Queensferry.

It got its name and fame from the fact that it was used by Margaret, wife of Malcolm Ceannmór, as one of the ports from which she crossed between Dunfermline and Edinburgh, towards the end of the eleventh century. Her great-grandson, Malcolm IV, granted the right to operate a ferry to the monks of Dunfermline, while David II granted the burgh regality jurisdiction, a right which was renewed by subsequent sovereigns until Charles I raised it into a Royal Burgh shortly before 1641. In that year, an Act of Parliament also made it a separate parish from Linlithgow, the worthies of that place, it seems, having shown some resentment at the growing importance of their sister town more advantageously placed to trade along the coast.

But South Queensferry's real importance has always been as a port of arrival or departure. For many centuries, it managed to exercise this function discreetly and without retarding its natural development as a small herring-fishing port. Its old houses perch along the rocky coastline, dominated by the steep hill behind, and by the looming nearness of the Carmelite Priory built and endowed by Sir George Dundas in 1547. The Priory was dissolved in 1564; the chancel remained the Dundas family burial-ground; and, until 1633 when the Presbyterian Church was put up, the nave did duty as the parish kirk. Thereafter, it fell into ruin, though the square tower became a stable and a shop. Then in 1890, what was left by Time and secular desecration was bought by the Scottish Episcopal Church and restored as a mission station. It is still in use as a church.

Though many of the relics of South Queensferry's ancient character have been "improved" out of recognition, there are still some interesting vernacular houses left, like Black Castle, built in 1626, and its near contemporary Plewlands, once threatened with demolition but restored as modern flats. The Forth Road Bridge sweeps across the estuary up-river from the impressive tubular girder-work of its Victorian companion, the railway bridge. The Road Bridge, supported by woven wire ropes two feet by seven thousand feet long, took six years to build, and is of particularly elegant construction. Opened in 1964, it was designed by Sir Giles Gilbert Scott, and is similar to the road bridge over the Severn. It replaced paddle-steamer car-ferries.

At the east side of the village, and now close under the huge girders of the Forth Railway Bridge, the old Hawes Inn crouches. There was space enough around it when it went up in 1683: when, in *The Antiquary*, Scott dined Jonathan Oldbuck and Lovell there together; and later, when Stevenson made it the scene of the place where those unsavoury characters Captain Hoseason and Ebenezer Balfour arranged that kidnapping of young David which gives *Kidnapped* its title. Stevenson's personal association is with Room 13, above the entrance, where he is said to have begun writing the novel.

Queensferry has one further peculiar civic distinction. Apparently it became bankrupt in 1881, only obtaining its discharge the following year by increasing the local rates.

Moving up across West Lothian's agricultural area, we pass through the village of Gateside, and come, though by no such direct route as I have taken, to Torphichen (or in Gaelic *torr-fithichean: the ravens' hill*), which stands in its own parish, the hilliest in the county. The village itself slopes steeply, but it is interesting mainly because of the nearby remains of the hospital and preceptory of Torphichen, which in 1153 was the founding-place of the Scottish order of the Knights of Saint John of Jerusalem. I made my first visit to the " quier "—a tower and vaulted transept are all that remain of the old building, on the site of the nave of which a pleasing little kirk was built in 1753— on the occasion of the celebration of the octo-centenary of the founding of the Scottish branch of the Order. On a sunny winter Saturday afternoon the Knights of the revived Order assembled in the " quier ", and marched in procession round the kirk, where they held a service of commemoration. A handful of urchins gathered round the gates. Perched among old tombs, press photographers crouched. And on a square stone which looks like a milestone but is actually a remarkable relic containing both a pre-Christian cup-mark and a carved Cross, stood a television camera man. There seems to be something unnatural about the revival of ancient feudal pageantry in our modern class-levelling times. Both actors and audience nearly always sense, and show, a sort of defiant embarrassment at the incongruity of it all.

Torphichen must once have been a proud and important little place, for relics of buildings of considerable dimensions lie scattered around the village. Relics of a still older civilization were uncovered by Professor Stuart Piggott's excavators on Cairnpapple in 1947. It is strange to think of human worship and burial being conducted on Cairnpapple in 2000 B.C., and of its despoliation about 1500 B.C. to make way for the remains of an Early Bronze Age chieftain. The mind reels in humiliation before such reminders that man lived, loved, begot, fought and died on our Scottish soil so very long ago.

From another hill, Cockleroy, it is possible to view Ben Lomond, Dumyat in the Ochils, and the lower Highland foot-hills. In Stevenson's droll poem " The Scotsman's Return from Abroad ", Mr. Thomson reminds Mr. Johnstone of the view they once enjoyed together from the top of that eminence.

> *In many a foreign pairt I've been,*
> *An' mony an unco ferlie seen,*
> *Since, Mr. Johnstone, you and I*
> *Last walkit upon Cocklerye . . .*
> *Wi' whatna joy I hailed them a'—*
> *The hilltaps standin' raw by raw,*
> *The public house, the Hielan' birks,*
> *And a' the bonny U.P. kirks! . . .*

Except to the eyes of such a dour Secession Burgher as Mr. Thomson seems to have been, "bonny" is about the least apt adjective which could reasonably be applied to the places of worship of the United Presbyterian Church. However, there are still less pleasant sights to catch the eye now—the red shale bings of West Lothian's industrial division, and the steamy mist which, in cold dank weather, breathes thickly over its towns and villages.

The valley of the River Almond traverses not only the hinter-land of West Lothian, but also a substantial area of Mid-lothian. Up until the middle of the nineteenth century, most of the industrial towns were mere rural villages. There are, of course, substantial mineral deposits in the area: but it was the invention of shale oil, or paraffin as it is still called in Scotland, which brought prosperity and ensured the blotching of the fair face of the countryside.

Dr. James Young (1811-1883)—or " Paraffin " Young as he was called after 1850, when he obtained his patent for producing paraffin oil—was born in Glasgow's Drygate, a son of poor parents, who educated himself in his evenings under Thomas Graham at the Andersonian University, eventually becoming a chemistry lecturer there himself. On December 3rd, 1847, Lynan Playfair, a former student colleague, wrote to Young from

London describing a petroleum spring in Reddings Colliery at Alpreton, Derbyshire, which belonged to his brother-in-law. Young was at this time employed at Manchester by Charles Tennant and Company, a firm of chemical manufacturers. He tried to interest Messrs. Tennant in the development of the petroleum spring, but they deemed its yield of three hundred gallons a day "too small a matter" for their attention. So Young went into partnership with one Edward Meldrum, and from 1848 to 1851, they exploited the Alpreton spring until it ran dry.

By this time, however, Young had discovered a means of producing paraffin from the dry distillation of shale. So, during the summer of 1853, he, Meldrum and one Binney went into partnership and founded the firm of E. W. Binney and Co. in Bathgate, where the shale coal offered a high yield. It was not until 1856, however, that paraffin oil as we know it to-day came on the market.

Young's invention enabled folk to exchange their flickering candles for the soft, steady light of the paraffin lamp. His name is still blessed in many a corner of the Highlands too remote even to be within reach of the North of Scotland Hydro-Electric Board's schemes. Young himself acquired Kelly House near Wemyss Bay. On the death of his close friend David Livingstone, Young brought to Kelly the two bearers who had borne the explorer's body to the coast: and in the grounds of Kelly, they built a replica of the hut in which Livingstone had died.

Young's other inventions included a means of preventing iron ships from rusting, and the establishment of some of the principles of producing light from electricity. But it is with paraffin and with the country of the Calders that his name is most firmly associated.

Since the establishment of the first shale mine at West Calder, the shale oil industry has spread widely over the area of the Calders, barren red bings rising sheerly out of the green fields. At present the greater part of Europe's shale oil is produced in this "county of the red mountains". But shale deposits exist in many parts of the world, those in New South Wales being richer than any in Europe. The discovery of petroleum has limited the exploration of the shale deposits. While it is possible that some by-product of atomic energy will eventually replace oil products, escalating petroleum costs may, in the short term, lead to a renewal of interest in the potential of shale oil.

From Armadale to Broxburn, and from Fauldhouse almost to Ratho, industry has left huge scars upon the countryside. Most of the towns and villages in this area are cramped and ugly, having been rapidly expanded at a time when anything was considered good enough to house a working man. Our mid-twentieth-century toy brick suburbs, with their identical houses and severely geometrical squares and crescents, at least let in light and air.

Here and there, however, even amidst the industrial sprawl, a few interesting relics of the past survive—notably the sixteenth-century church of Midcalder, and Calder House itself, seat of the Torphichen family whose great hall is one of several places claiming to have been the scene of John Knox's first Protestant Communion ceremony in 1556:[1] the church at Uphall, most of it rebuilt in the seventeenth century, but still possessing fragments of its twelfth-century origin: Houston House, near Broxburn (the burn of the brock, or badger), tall and severe, built by Sir John Shairp in 1601, its hillscape outlook still marvellously intact: and the farm of Kirkhill, where the eccentric eleventh Earl of Buchan, who founded the Society of Antiquaries of Scotland in 1780, and regarded himself as a patron of Robert Burns, had a mansion and built a model solar system in the grounds 12,183 and 28 hundredths miles to one inch in scale, only a solitary solar stone of which now survives.

These relics of a peaceful pre-industrial age have to be sought out. The average traveller passing the country of the Calders, around the boundary between West and Midlothian, is usually most likely to notice the development of the car industry near Bathgate, an industry in Scotland bedevilled by bad industrial relations and a poor production record.

III

To Edinburgh folk the Pentland Hills, which form the spine of Midlothian, are, in Stevenson's phrase, "the hills of home". To a man from the West Country, accustomed to his rugged peaks, they may well seem mere mountains in miniature. No one knows certainly the origin of the name, though the view most generally accepted is that "Pent" has become corrupted from "Picts" or "Pects" land. To know the Pentlands intimately, it is necessary to have wandered through the lonely passes that lead between their gentle heights. But most people are content to make their acquaintance by road.

[1] Sir David Wilkie's unfinished picture depicting this event hangs in the Scottish National Gallery.

It leads out through the former village of Colinton, now a suburb of the Capital. Though Colinton has long since lost its independent status, it has not lost its literary memories. Here that " Man-of-Feeling ", Henry Mackenzie, had a thatched cottage to which he regularly retired during the summer. He had an interest in gardening, recording that:

" The science of gardening seems to have been successfully cultivated in the county of Edinburgh long ago. I forget at what period (I believe about the close of the seventeenth century) a treatise on gardening was published by the gardener at Colintoun . . . which I have seen, and was thought to be a very sensible performance."

This must have been one of the earliest Scottish gardening books to be published.

Here, too, Stevenson's grandfather, Lewis Balfour, ministered in the parish kirk on the banks of the Water of Leith. His thirteenth child became the novelist's mother. And here, R. L. S. himself came on holiday as a boy.

Now, Colinton lives the life of suburbia, the blue blazers of the boys of nearby Merchiston Castle School adding occasional colour to its streets. For the school is no longer housed in the sixteenth-century castle where once lived John Napier, inventor of the logarithm, and dubbed by David Hume " the person to whom the title of a great man is more justly due than to any other whom this country ever produced ". The castle forms part of the Heriot-Watt University.

A few miles south-east of Colinton stands Bonaly Castle, originally a peel tower and from 1811 until his death the seat of the judge Lord Cockburn (1779-1854). There he was so happy, he tells us, that he feared the blows Fate must surely have in store for him. Cockburn may not have left any notable imprint on Scots Law, but he was by far the most brilliant of Scotland's diarists, his *Memorials of his Time* and *Circuit Journeys* chronicling the close of the eighteenth-century revival, Edinburgh in her "Athens of the North " phase, and the gathering strains of militant industrialism with a poet's eye for significant detail. Nearby once stood the seventeenth-century Dreghorn Castle, owned at one time by the Home family, but blown up in the late 1940's. In 1720, their tutor, the shiftless David Malloch who changed his name to Mallet when he moved to London to make it easier for the English to pronounce it, wrote his one famous poem, the pseudo-ballad *William and Margaret*.

From Colinton, the road follows a parallel course to the Water of Leith, which rises in Torweaning Hill: past the sturdy ruins of Lennox Castle, once owned by the Earls of Lennox, a favourite hunting seat of James VI and the passing residence of Mary, Queen of Scots; past the Cauldstaneslap, across the North Medwin river, to Carnwath in Lanarkshire. To the left of this road, known as the Lang Whang, the Pentland Hills loom, seeming larger by proximity than they really are.

The road up the eastern side of the Pentlands is by far the more interesting. As far as Medwinbank, it follows the direction of the South Medwin. Dunsyre—"Dun Seer", the hill of the prophet—had an old church claimed by tradition to stand on the site of a Druidical temple. Agricola's Romans are said to have marched through Dunsyre, along the Garvald Valley, on their way from Tweeddale to Cleghorn Camp. And on the church wall the "jougs" from the old castle of Dunsyre are still preserved.

Dunsyre's strongest historical associations, however, are with the Covenanters. In the rugged glens above Dunsyre, many a manly psalm rang out defiantly against the echoing rock-face. One of their number, the Reverend Donald Cargill, held his last conventicle on Dunsyre Common. Soon afterwards he was captured at Covington Mill, and strapped, back down, upon his horse to be carried to Edinburgh. He was but one of many "Sons-of-the-Lord" hanged in the Grassmarket in 1681.

Another famous and more fortunate Covenanter also knew Dunsyre. William Veitch safely eluded capture by hiding in a barn, while, just over a mile away, dragoons ransacked his house. Later, when assisting the Covenanting Earl of Argyll to escape from a trap, Veitch disguised himself so well that he was able in perfect safety to hold the reins of the dragoon's horses while they carried out their search. Eventually, however, Veitch was captured and prosecuted by the Scottish Government. He was defended by Sir Gilbert Elliot of Minto, a pastoral poet whose best-remembered production was his spinster daughter Jean, authoress of the earlier of the two versions of "The Flowers o' the Forest". The defence was spectacularly successful. Years later, when Sir Gilbert had become Lord Minto, the two men met by chance in Dumfries, where Veitch was then ministering.

"Had it no been for me, my lord," Veitch is said to have boasted, "ye'd been writing papers yet at a plack a page."

"Had it no been for me, Willie," Minto promptly replied, "the pyets wad hae pecked your pow on the Netherbow Port."

Newholm was once owned by the gallant Major Learmont (1605-93), who commanded the Covenanters' horse at the rout of Rullion Green in 1666. A secret passage ran from the banks of the South Medwin up to a subterranean refuge-room beneath the house. Many a preacher, fleeing for his life, owed its preservation to Major Learmont's secret passage. He lies buried in the kirkyard of Dolphinton.

The jewel which inspired Scott's novel *The Talisman* is still to be seen at Newholm. The Lee Penny belongs to the Lockharts of Lee and Carnwath.[1] Sir Simon Lockhart, who accompanied Sir James Douglas on his mission to carry Robert the Bruce's heart against the Saracens, survived his companion and fought the enemy. While Sir Simon was watching the wife of a distinguished Saracen prisoner counting out her husband's ransom, he noticed her suddenly try to hide a dark jewel shaped like a heart in the folds of her drapes. The prisoner's demobilization was thereupon interrupted until the Christian knight had succeeded in wresting away the heathen lady's most treasured possession, together with its magic secret. The stone, now mounted in an Edward I shilling, is supposed to have healing properties. When the story of the Lee Penny's curing abilities was re-publicized in the mid-1940's, a surprising number of people, dissatisfied, apparently, with the National Health Service, sought to make use of them.

At Dolphinton, the modern road to West Linton strikes out to the right of the Old Biggar Road, now a mere track, but once the bustling inspiration of a swinging fiddle tune "The High Road to Linton", the happy amateur work of one Dickson of Medwinbank, an eighteenth-century millwright.

It may have occurred to some at least of my Scottish readers that although this chapter is avowedly about the Lothians, I have traigled over the boundaries of Lanarkshire, and am now, indeed, trespassing into Peeblesshire. If their sense of precision be offended, alas! it cannot be helped. There is no other route round the Pentlands: and no law of trespass in Scotland! Having once come thus far, who would want to hurry by, merely in order to satisfy literary propriety?

West Linton, on the Lyne Water, used to bear the more impressive name of Linton Roderick. Romanticists attribute the old name—spelt, amongst other ways, in mediæval times "Lyntunruderic"—to Rhydderch Hael, or Roderick the Liberal, an early Christian king of Strathclyde and a supporter of St. Mungo, who died in the same year as the saint, A.D. 603. More

---

[1] Kinsfolk of John Gibson Lockhart, Scott's son-in-law and biographer.

likely, this name-providing Roderick was just a powerful local chieftain. But, chieftain or king, his commemoration has long since been abandoned in favour of the modern nomenclature.

West Linton still retains an individual charm. Apart from its old houses, set down with an attractive disregard for regularity which would gar any modern town-planner grue, its most interesting relic of former times is the statue of a woman. This reposes in a niche in the clock-tower which has been built over the village well. The lady was once the wife of a West Linton laird, James Gifford; a man with a strong thirst for immortality, and some talent for stone masonry. In order to celebrate the memory of his spouse and their four children, Gifford placed statues of them upon the village cross, when he designed it in 1606; Mrs. Gifford in an attitude of devotion, supported by the effigies of her progeny. What could be a more natural grouping? But Nature chose to play the laird a trick! Long after there was reason to expect such a happening, Mrs. Gifford bore her husband a fifth child. The idea of his youngest infant having to go uncommemorated was more than Laird Gifford could contemplate. So he pummelled his muse for a solution. Eventually, the effigy of the fifth child was placed upon the only part of the monument where there was a vacant space—on the top of his wife's head. Now, Time has played yet another trick on Laird Gifford. Four of the children's effigies have been lost, while a fifth, amputated, survives in Spitalhaugh House. Mrs. Gifford alone remains, a benign monument to connubial fertility.

Two curious literary characters came from estates around West Linton. The medico Alexander Pennecuik (1652-1722) lived at Romanno House. In 1715 he published an interesting account of the locality, *A Geographical and Historical Description of the Shire of Tweeddale, with a Miscellany and Curious Collection of Select Scottish Poems.* In spite of some amorous pieces written in youth, he was a moral man, this West Linton medico, and in one of his poems is much concerned because worshippers, newly come from church, could find no place for Truth at their dinner tables.

> *When kirk was skailed and preaching done*  [dispersed
> *And men and women baith hame,*
> *Nae man call'd Truth to his disjeun,*  [breakfast[1]
> *Albeit he was of noble fame.*
> *There was not one that kept a craim,*  [merchant's booth

[1] But eaten at the time we would now take our Sunday lunch.

*But they had bacon, beef and ale,*
  *Yet no acquaintance Truth could claim,*
*To wish him worth a dish of kail.*

*Except pastors or judges sought him,*                    [unless
  *I trow his dinner was but cauld;*
*For advocates much skaith they wrought him*              [injury
  *He makes their gowns so bare and auld;*
  *And merchant men, that bought and sauld,*
*For sindrie things could not abide him,*
  *And poor craftsmen, albeit they wald*    [even if they would
*They had no portion to provide him.*

What Pennecuik said of the Protestants, Sir David Lyndsay
had been saying of the Catholics seventy years before. Truly,
the times are never what they were.

The other curious poetaster who also left valuable papers on
local matters was the advocate Robert Dunmoor Crawford
Brown of Newhall. He founded the present village of Carlops
in 1784. His best poem, " Carlops Green, or Equality Realized ",
was written in 1793. An Edinburgh dealer called James—a
Friend of the People—comes to Carlops to buy Farmer John's
cow. James, filled with that self-righteous zeal which so often
loudly animates theorists of any extreme, takes the opportunity,
when sealing his bargain, of lecturing poor honest John on the
principles of Equality.

> *" I'm for Equality," cries he,*
>   *" I've read all Thomas Payne,*
> *And, lest a word I should forget,*
>   *I'll read him o'er again:*
>
> *" What right have those they call the rich—*
>   *Come, here's to you, Friend John—*
> *What right have they to more than we?*
>   *I answer, surely nane! "*
>
> *" What would you do, then, tell me James? "*
>   *" Oh, by all means divide!*
> *I'd like, if 'twere but from mere spite,*
>   *In Croesus coach to ride . . . "*
>
> *" Your equal purse would soon be gone,*
>   *All would be as before;*
> *Some would pick up what you had lost,*
>   *And add it to their store.*

*" Ere lang, this sure would be the case,*
*    And what would you do then? "*
*" Why what else would I do," says James*
*" But just divide again? "*

Farmer John defends the British Constitution, but James's advocacy of French principles grows more heated. A little crowd gathers round them. Presently, two sailors, who have been listening to James's arguments, decided to put them into practice. They slip outside and make off with his newly-bought cow. When the theft is discovered, James is not at all consoled by the thought that he still has many other cows.

*Quoth John to James, " What think you now?*
*    Is't this you call Equality? "*
*Quoth James to John, " It surely is,*
*    Though it won't do in Reality."*

Newhall provided the setting for one of the most pleasant poems in the Scots tongue: Allan Ramsay's pastoral ballad-opera *The Gentle Shepherd*. In Ramsay's day, Newhall was owned by the advocate John Forbes, whose father, Sir David Forbes, provided Ramsay with the prototype for his character of Sir William Worthy. Newhall was also the summer meeting-place of " The Worthy Club ", a group of Edinburgh literati dedicated to the celebration of Ramsay's memory. It was from the scenes around Newhall[1] that Ramsay drew such poetic pictures as that with which Peggy entices Jenny to bathe.

*Go farer up the burn to " Habby's Howe ",*
*Where a' the sweets of spring and summer grow;*
*Between two birks, out o'er a little linn*
*The water fa's, and makes a singin' din;*
*A pool breast-deep beneath, as clear as glass,*
*Kisses with easy whirls the bord'ring grass;*
*We'll end our washing while the morning's cool,*
*And when the day grows het, we'll to the pool . . .*

The Clackmannanshire artist David Allan (nicknamed the " Scottish Hogarth ") sought out Ramsay's scenes, and illustrated an edition of the poem in 1808; an edition for which, incidentally, Laird Brown of Newhall wrote the notes.

---

[1] The rival claims of Logan Valley and Woodhouselee are undoubtedly both spurious.

This, then, is Ramsay country. At Ninemileburn—nine Scots miles, though nearly twelve English miles from Edinburgh—the architect George Meikle Kemp (1795-1846) was born. His father was a shepherd on Newhall Estate, and for the first fourteen years of the boy's life, the family lived in:

> *A snug thack house, before the door a green;*
> *Hens on the midden, ducks in dubs are seen;*
> *On this side stands a barn, on that a byre;*
> *A peat-stack joins, an' forms the rural square.*
> *The house is Glaud's. . . .*

Glaud is, of course, a character in *The Gentle Shepherd*.

Kemp's main claim to fame is the Scott Monument in Edinburgh's Princes Street. Begun in 1840, its designer died by falling into a canal basin at night two and half years before its completion.[1] To-day, its Gothic extravagance makes us smile. But Kemp meant it sincerely, for he reverenced the man whom it honours, though his only two meetings with " the Shirra " were both fleeting social occasions.

After Ninemileburn, the road leaves the hills, coming close to them again as it passes the highest hill in the Pentland Range, Scald Law (1,898 feet), and Carnethy. The countryside about Glencorse is martyrs' ground, for on Rullion Green the Covenanters suffered their cruellest defeat at the hands of General Dalzell of the Binns on 28th November, 1666.

A great deal of sentimental nonsense is written about the Covenanters nowadays. They are depicted as gallant men who fought only for the right to worship as they pleased. That may have been the motive which inspired the more moderate among them. The real Covenanters wished to impose Presbyterianism by force upon England and Ireland, as well as upon Scotland. Nor were the brutalities practised against the Covenanters any more disgraceful than those which they themselves perpetrated on royalist victims who fell into their power.

At Rullion Green, however, nine hundred tired, ill-equipped Covenanters—some of whom had marched from Galloway—under a gallant Colonel Wallace, faced up to Dalzell's three thousand well-armed regulars. By nightfall, the Covenanting ranks had broken. Those who could not escape were savagely hacked by

---

[1] Hugh Miller, who thought Kemp a genius, tells of the attempts made to secure his burial in the Scott monument, and described the funeral, in a leading " Witness " article, now to be found in Mackenzie's *Selections from the Writings of Hugh Miller*.

Dalzell's men, while some of those who did escape were sucked to a still more terrifying death by the Pentland bogs. Many who were taken prisoner subsequently suffered death in the Grassmarket by hanging.

A fenced stone on the lower slopes of Carnethy Hill commemorates the battle. It reads:

"Here and near to this Palace lyes the Reverend Mr. John Crookshanks and Mr. Andrew McCormack Ministers of the Gospel and about Fifty other True Covenanted Presbyterians who were killed in this Place in their own Innocent Self-Defence of the Covenanted Work of Reformation by Thomas Dalzell of Bins upon the 28th November 1666 . . . Erected Sept 28, 1723."

The Edinburgh road leads past Flotterstone, whose surrounding fields have squelched and trembled not only to the army of the Covenanters on their luckless way to Rullion Green, but to the much more impetuous hoof-beats of the Scottish army of 1302 which, under Sir Simon Fraser and Sir John Comyn, defeated an English army more than three times its size near Roslin. Through this same countryside, part of Prince Charlie's army moved on their southward march.

On the left, beneath Castlelaw Hill, lies Woodhouselee, for nearly two centuries the home of the literary-minded Tytler family. Woodhouselee was acquired by an Edinburgh Writer to the Signet, William Tytler, in 1748. His son, Alexander Fraser-Tytler, elevated to the bench with the judicial title of Lord Woodhouselee, became a leader of Edinburgh's literary circle, and is remembered as the person who wisely urged Burns to write more in the vein of "Tam o' Shanter": advice which Burns apparently intended to follow, but was never able to do. Many were the literary house-parties held at Woodhouselee. Scott, "Man-of-Feeling" Mackenzie, the Lakers' critic Lord Jeffrey, John Leyden, poet and antiquarian, the philosopher Dugald Stewart, and the once-popular novelist Elizabeth Hamilton were often among the guests there. So firmly did Lord Woodhouselee make up his mind that the scene of Ramsay's *Gentle Shepherd* must be within his grounds, that he caused a memorial to the poet to be erected on the estate. His fourth son, Patrick Fraser-Tytler, became the author of *A History of Scotland* which took him twenty years to write, and is still by no means valueless.

After Woodhouselee, the main road joins the suburbs of

Edinburgh at Fairmilehead, beneath the Braid Hills, where golf
has been played since the seventeenth century. But between
Hillend and Bowbridge, a track strikes off to the left, leading to
the village of Swanston. Here, a museum now, preserved in that
artificially-fixed, musty-smelling hush in which people not interested in living literature pickle the relics of dead authors, is the
cottage "in a green fold in the lap of the Pentlands" which
Stevenson's parents bought when he was seventeen—tall, velvet-
jacketed, and affecting an adolescent Bohemianism—and to which
he came back, again and again, for fourteen years.

Stevenson loved Swanston. Not only did he make fictional use
of it—the cottage appears in St. Ives; and Hunter's Tryst, so
called because it was once the meeting-place of Edinburgh's
sporting Six-Foot Club, is depicted in its original status as an
inn—but he also left descriptions of the place in many of its moods,
all illuminated by a poet's observation, and couched in prose
exquisitely jewelled, yet through which the sights and sounds
rise fresh to the senses. There, on the slopes of Halkerside, the
Pentland shepherd John Todd taught Stevenson all he knew
about what he called "that hillside business". Up the beds of
the hill burns the young man wandered, listening to the silver
sound of the falling water, and dreaming the young heart's
dreams. Later in life he remembered:

"That nameless trickle that springs in the green bosom of
Allermuir, and is fed from Halkerside with a perennial tea-
cupful, and threads the moss under the Shearer's Knowe, and
makes one pool there, overhung by a rock, where I loved to sit
and make bad verses."

The cottage and its garden, quiet before they were exposed to
the attentions of his admirers, also inspired affectionate description.

"The gardens below my windows are steeped in diffused
sunlight, and every tree seems standing on tip-toe, strained and
silent as though to get its head above its neighbours and listen.
I wish I could make you feel the hush that is over everything.
Only made the more perfect by rare interruptions and the rich
placid light and the still autumnal foliage."

Shortly before the final stroke that he carried within him had
nearly reached its disintegrating moment in far-away Vailima, the
Pentland scene came vividly before his eyes.

*The tropics vanish, and meseems that I,*
*From Halkerside, from topmost Allermuir,*
*Or steep Caerketton, dreaming gaze again.*
*Far set in fields and woods, the town I see*
*Spring gallant from the shallows of her smoke,*
*Cragged, spired, and turreted, her virgin fort*
*Beflagged. About, on seaward-drooping hills,*
*New folds of city glitter. Last, the Forth*
*Wheels ample waters set with sacred isles,*
*And populous Fife smokes with a score of towns.*

The shores of " populous Fife ", on sunny days happed in a soft blue haze, are visible from many points along the descending road towards Edinburgh; through suburbs by the Braid Hills that were once independent villages. Liberton has no celebrated associations, but Colinton, to which the Pentland circle returns us, contributed nearly as much as, later on, Swanston did to Stevenson in his childhood.

Much about the place has changed now beyond what Stevenson might have regarded as recognition, though between the thick trees of Colinton glen, the Water of Leith begins that part of its course which carries it meandering across the back-gardens of Edinburgh. But for Stevenson, Colinton was:

" . . . a place in that time like no other: the garden cut into provinces by a great hedge of beech, and overlooked by the church and the terrace of the churchyard, where the tombstones were thick, and after nightfall 'spunkies' might be seen to dance, at least by children: flower-pots lying warm in sunshine; laurels and the great yew making elsewhere a pleasing horror of shade; the smell of water rising from all round, with an added tang of paper-mills; the sound of water everywhere, and the sound of mills—the wheel and the dam singing their alternate strain; the birds on every bush and from every corner of the overhanging woods pealing out their notes until the air throbbed with them; and in the midst of this, the manse."

Here, in a " dark and cold room, with a library of bloodless books ", his grandfather, Lewis Balfour, wrote his sermons.

As our journey round the Pentlands has brought us back to the rapidly spreading outer-feelers of Edinburgh, let us by-pass the city now, and make for the places along the coast of Midlothian, some of which the Capital has long since annexed. The most important of these places is, of course, Leith.

Glasgow cherishes her seaport right at her heart. Edinburgh, characteristically, has developed hers at a discreet distance—about one and a half miles from her heart, to be precise, and so escaped the roughness of dockside civilization. For long enough, of course, the connection between port and city was commercial rather than civic, and Leith was not tied to the Capital by any political and administrative strings as it is now.

Its strategic importance as a seaport may be traced through its long history of burnings. The English set fire to the ships in Leith harbour in 1313, and again in 1410. In 1544, the Earl of Hertford seized the port, made it the beachhead for his expedition of destruction through the Lothians and the Borders, and finally withdrew from it leaving its tinder houses in flames. As Protector Somerset, he repeated his combined operation three years later, this time also capturing thirty-five vessels which were sheltering in the harbour.

The following year, Leith was turned into a fortified town by Mary of Guise. In her struggle with the Lords of the Congregation, she found it not only a vital port through which men and supplies from France could reach her, but also a useful emergency exit from Scotland should it ever be necessary for her to leave the country in a hurry. In 1559, ten years after the first fortifications went up, Mary of Guise's Leith successfully withstood the siege of Arran, Argyll, Ruthven and the other Protestant Lords; withstood them, indeed, until the spring of 1560, when the Regent moved up into Edinburgh Castle for her greater personal security.

In shipping parlance, there have been many famous arrivals at Leith: most important, Mary Queen of Scots from France in August 1561. There are two views on that event. According to the imaginings of Scott:

> *After a youth by woes o'ercast,*
> *After a thousand sorrows past,*
> *The lovely Mary once again*
> *Sets foot upon her native plain;*
> *Kneel'd on the pier with modest grace,*
> *And turned to heaven her beauteous face,*

A rather different view was taken by John Knox, who tells us: "Never was a more dolourous face of the heavens than was at her arrival . . . the mist so thick and dark that the sun was not seen to shine two days before nor two days after." To his charitable sense of judgment, that haar seemed a "fore warning God gave unto us, but alas, the most part were blind".

Less auspicious, and under less unfavourable conditions, came George IV in 1822, and Queen Victoria in 1842.

Leith has also had its due share of famous arrivals and departures of the more basic sort. John Home (1722-1808), whose verse-tragedies *Douglas* and *Agis* won him a high contemporary reputation, was born in a house in Quality Street, and now lies in the graveyard of the much-restored fifteenth-century church of St. Mary. Hugo Arnot (1749-86), the learned eccentric "lean as a dried haddock", whose *History of Edinburgh* still retains vivid period interest, was another son of Leith. So, too, was the father of William Ewart Gladstone, the Liberal politician and Victorian Prime Minister.

Of those who have died in Leith, the most notorious must surely be the sinister Secretary Maitland of Lethington who, to escape execution, poisoned himself in 1573 while lodged in the Old Tolbooth.

Among those having Leith connections which did not extend to either of life's terminal points, have been John Kay (1742-1826), whose stiff-looking semi-caricatured *Edinburgh Portraits* form a valuable pictorial comment on the days of the Capital's intellectual supremacy: Robert Nicoll (1814-37), a minor poet who did not live long enough to find an individual voice; and that unscrupulous literary hack and plagiarizer of the work of Michael Bruce, the Reverend John Logan (1748-88).

Leith also figures in Scotland's marine story. At or near Leith, James V's spectacular but useless battleship the *Great Michael* was built. (It proved to be totally unmanœuvrable, and was finally disposed of to the French, who doubtless did not notice this drawback.) And on July 26th, 1698, the Darien expedition of five frigates with " 1200 men and "—nice distinction—" 300 gentlemen " aboard sailed proudly out from Leith Roads, carrying the good wishes and much of the monetary capital of Scotland with them.

Leith has preserved several links with its past. The most obvious is its harbour, though the original single quay has grown into a complicated system of docks covering many acres of sea. A modern lock system makes Leith the second seaport in Scotland. Leith Links still survive, where Scotland's kings once golfed. So, too, do the sands, though the Races celebrated so vigorously in verse by Robert Fergusson are no longer held on them. Of stone and mortar survivals there is Trinity House, which dates from 1816; the " Old Ship Hotel " and the " King's Wark "—the " King " being James IV—a seventeenth-century house; and, most interesting of all, Andrew Lamb's house in the Water Close, a sixteenth-century mansion such as was inhabited by the merchants of Leith before they moved up the hill, early in the nineteenth century, to Royal Terrace—nicknamed "Whisky Row", because the merchants could watch the arrival and departure of their ships over a decanter of whisky from their leather armchairs by their windows.

To-day, Leith is a bustling place, occupied with the manufacture of things as diverse in quality as paint and gin, ham and leather. My first visit to the port was in the early summer of 1934. I was on my way to join the steamer *St. Rognvald*, bound for the Orkney Isles. She sailed on a Sunday afternoon. I drove down from Edinburgh in a taxi, claimed my berth aboard ship, and, as I had an hour or two to put in before sailing time, set out to wander about the town. I had always been given to understand that Leith was a very wicked place, like all ports, though the nature of its "wickedness" had never been vouchsafed to me. So on that warm July afternoon, I hoped very much to come upon some of Leith's unspecified "wickedness". Fortunately, perhaps, I found none. The streets were thinly-peopled. All that was to be seen were a few lounging jersey-clad seamen, sending slow puffs of pipe-smoke drifting about the corners of shut buildings; and two or three groups of girls hurrying into a missionary gathering from which the tuneless sounds of lusty hymn-singing presently floated forth. So my fifteen-year-old interest soon turned from its search after wickedness to an enjoyment of the gleaming copper lamps and brass compasses which signalled their presence from the blindless windows of the shops of the ship-chandlers.

Aboard the *St. Rognvald* again, I remember watching the afternoon trippers clamber down the steep paddle-box stairs of the ancient paddle-steamer, *Fair Maid of Perth*, which was getting ready to set out on an excursion up the Forth. It was a disappointment to me that the *St. Rognvald* cast her ropes first, and I was thus deprived of the pleasure of watching the venerable virgin manœuvring, stern-first, out of what seemed to be an unusually narrow berth.

The quay behind us, Leith blurred quickly into the background, and the sea spread out its impersonal expansiveness. If a man should have to leave Scotland for ever, I would recommend him to sail from the Forth rather than from the Clyde: for the lingering loveliness of the Clyde's estuary will tear at his heart-strings intolerably, while the Forth quickly opens out its land-arms, as if striving to push him and his ship the sooner towards the ocean.

This open aspect of the coastline has been the governing factor in the development of Portobello, Edinburgh's seaside playground, where the accents of Glasgow often predominate over those of the Capital. Its name is evidence of a complicated kind of Scottish romanticism. Just as many of the inhabitants of Scots suburbia to-day name their bungalows in accordance with what might be called the Bellevue Code, so also once did their masters name their lands and houses after foreign ports or battles temporarily in the news. Thus, what is now Edinburgh's seaside playground owes its name to the capture of Portobello by Admiral Vernon in 1739. By 1765, it was still only a small village in which a brick works was being erected. Gradually, houses spread outwards, many of them built with brick, until Portobello had become a small town. From this period of its development, too, came its charming little porcelain figures, now no longer made, and valued as collectors' pieces. In the early part of the nineteenth century, the good folk of Edinburgh discovered its sands. By 1870[1] when its promenade was built, it was a highly fashionable residential resort.

Then, inexplicably, after the first World War, fashion deserted it. Now, it is unashamedly a popular playground, with ponies on the sands, a fun-fair and amusement park, a bathing pool, and innumerable cafés and boarding-houses. As in so many other places, the mock-baronial houses of the rich of a former era stand, awkward-looking and neglected.

Two writers have had connections with Portobello. On the Portobello sands, Sir Walter Scott, then unknighted, an officer in the Midlothian Yeomanry Cavalry, received a kick of a horse which confined him for three days to his lodgings, during which time he finished the first canto of *The Lay of the Last Minstrel*. In the study of his house in Tower Street on Christmas Eve, 1856, Hugh Miller—that northern Scottish master of vivid prose—worn out with overwork and haunted by Apocalyptic visions, scribbled a desperate note of farewell to his wife, pulled up his heavy blue jersey, and shot himself through the heart.

Though Musselburgh—once Eskmouth, used as a port by the Romans, and said to derive its modern name from a profitable mussel-bank in the estuary of the Esk river—nominally still has its independence, it has already been pawed by the creeping tentacles of the Capital. But it is proud of its traditions. Does not an old jingle run?

---

[1] In which year, incidentally, the Scots comedian, Sir Harry Lauder, was born there.

*Musselburgh was a burgh*
*When Edinburgh was nane,*
*And Musselburgh'll be a burgh*
*When Edinburgh is gane.*

True, there are learned cynics who point out that " burgh " is a pun on " brogh " or " brugh ", the Scots word for a mussel-bed. But every lad in the Honest Toun firmly rejects any such interpretation. The town's motto, *Honesty,* commemorates the death of Bruce's friend and ally, Randolph, Earl of Moray. His last hours were spent in a house in the High Street, and until he died —on July 20th, 1332—the inhabitants formed a guard round about it. The Earl of Mar, who succeeded Moray as Regent, praised the " honest fellows " who had made this gesture of patriotic love, and backed up his praise with unspecified privileges. Ever since, Musselburgh has claimed to be an " Honest Toun ".

Yet its honesty has been no shield. For Musselburgh has had its share of battles and burning. The Chapel of Our Lady of Loretto, founded in 1533 by a hermit, Thomas Douchtie, who named it after the Church of Loretto in Italy (an early example of the Scot's fondness for borrowing foreign nomenclature), flourished for only a decade before it was burned in the English sack of 1544. The remains of the chapel were used by the citizens in 1590 for the building of their Tolbooth, an act of sacrilege which brought them under sentence of Papal excommunication for two hundred years.

Three years after the affair of 1544, the Battle of Pinkie was fought on the outskirts of the town. Cannon-fire from the English ships at the mouth of the river killed Montrose's eldest son, Lord Graham, and his followers. In 1548, the victorious English commander razed both Musselburgh and Dalkeith. Pinkie House itself, clustered around an ancient tower, has a Painted Gallery adorned with heraldic ornaments in bright colours. It also boasts a King's Room, wherein Prince Charles slept after his victory at Prestonpans on 21st September, 1745.

Douchtie's Chapel has given its Italian name to Loretto School, which stands almost at the edge of Musselburgh Links, famous for golf since the eighteenth century. The Golf Club, founded in 1774, offered a special prize of " a creel and a shawl " to the best of the fisher-wife golfers. It is interesting to find eighteenth-century Scotswomen on a golf course. But then the women of Musselburgh were uncommonly sturdy. One of them, who fell foul of the law, was hanged in the Grassmarket of Edinburgh in 1728. Duly cut down, in her kisted condition she set out on her last journey to Musselburgh to be buried. On the way, however, the jolting of the waggon over the cobbles brought her back to life. Unkisted, she recovered, married and bore many children. The story of her ordeal has been picturesquely elaborated in *The Merry Wives of Musselburgh's Welcome to Maggie Dickson* by Alexander Pennecuik (?-1730), an eighteenth-century poet whose pieces, set mostly in the Lothians, were unfortunately compounded too much of topicality and bawdry to survive.[1]

At the beginning of the poem, we are introduced to three witches, seen huddled together; "three clav'ring carlings o'er their pot", discussing the sad fate of their fellow-witch, Maggie:

*The auldest cummer o' the three*         [gossip
*(Born when the English took Dundee)*
*Cry'd, "Shame light on that lown-like tree*     [quiet
  *Plays sic foul tricks;*
*De'il nor it were hewn down for me*
  *To puddin' pricks*     [sticks for stirring porridge

*"What's come of a' our witches now,*
*I'm sure we ha' a gey large crew,*
  *Last Hallow-e'en,*
*And made my skin baith black and blue,*
  *Fell'd titty Jean.*         [sister

*"They say Auld Nick commands the air*
*When drunken Maggie's hanging there,*
*And for to help her were unfair;*
  *Pox tak such deils,*
*To let Dalgleish,[2] O dole and care,*     [sorrow
  *Pu' down her heels.*

*Had a' the wives that carry creels,*
*Gutsters, and we wha spin on wheels,*
*At brake o' day made souple heels,*
  *Ta'en her awa*
*Fra' the cheese-lest, near to St. Giles*
  *We'd birk the law.*

---

[1] According to the Dictionary of National Biography, this Pennecuik is said to have been the nephew of the Alexander Pennecuik referred to on page 104.
[2] Dalgleish was the executioner.

*" But now, 'tis e'en o'er late I think,*
*Besides, I've gat nine draps o' drink;*
*I'm fitter for to tak a wink*
  *O' sleep, I trow;*
*And Bessie, ye hae gat a blink—*
  *Confess ye're fou."*

Bessie was certainly fou, but not too fou to be able to devise a plan for Maggie's rescue.

*" Ken ye the Shetlan-cockle-shell?*     [Shetland fishing-boat
*I mind I brought it hame mysel,*
*Gi'en by the Auld Guid-Man in Hell;*
  *(He's kind to me!)*
*Frae a' the boats it bears the bell,*     [It's the best boat going
  *E'er crost the sea."*

Of course, they all " ken " the Devil's present to Bessie. So she proposes that she and Grissie should hasten by aerial means to the Grassmarket. There, to:

*" . . . dance upon the ladder top*
*When Hangie put Meg in the rope,*
*To his design we'll put a stop*
  *And glamer cast;*     [spell
*That she's cauld deid the carle will hope,*     [fellow
  *And breath'd her last.*

*" And when Dalgleish cuts Maggie down,*
*My boat shall bear her thro' the town,*
*To the wind-mill, and there we'll soon*
  *Stairt up a cart;*
*My boat will neither brak nor drown,*
  *I ha' sic art."*

This plan is enthusiastically agreed upon, particularly by Lucky, whose role is to stay at home and be ready to receive the rescued witch. Bessie and Grissie get up from the fire.

*Syne baith evanis'd in the air,*
*And Lucky saw their face nae mair,*
*But heard their arses ga' sic a rair,*
  *Blow thro' the links,*     [golf course
*The blast turn'd a' the pewter-ware*
  *Down frae the binks.*     [kitchen dresser

117

In due course, Bessie and Grissie return with their cargo, and Lucky goes out to meet them. As she opens the door, however, she falls over the coffin:

> *" O dole," she cries, " I hae nae pith*   [energy
> *I've dung my thigh-bane out o' lith;*  [knocked, position
> *The meikle Deevil tak her with;*
>  *His cloven feet. . . ."*

But Lucky soon recovers her poise. Though:

> *". . . when she saw the milk-white ghaist,*
> *She gathered up her heels in haste,*
> *Fell in a gutter to the waste,*
>  *There lay again;*
> *Que she; " Was ever ane sae taist*   [tried
>  *I scarce dow grain."*

The welcome ceremonies at last safely over, the ladies promptly settled down to hear Maggie's version of the affair.

> *Maggie said, and she spak nae joke;*
> *" Cummers, I think my heart's half-broke.*
>  *This day I've been wi' fashious folk*
> *They brought me in an unco lock*
> *Wae worth them a'.*   [woe be to them all
>
> *" They sang kirk-tunes, and gart me dance*
> *(Fean nor they were a' sent to France)* [The devil take them
> *Until I fell into a trance,*   all to France
>  *Cauld be their cast;*   [bad luck to them
> *I cannot tell you how to scance*
>  *On a' that's past. . . .*
>
> *" They bade me ay make clear confession,*
> *And tauld me of my great transgression;*
> *It was an unco kind of session,*   [queer
>  *Sib to Auld Nick;*
> *I never met wi sic opression*
>  *Sin I was quick. . . .*   [living
>
> *" To clim yon stair is nae sma' talk*  [task
> *As high's the wirk of Inneraik.*   [Inveresk
> *And o'er my face they drew a maik*  [mask
>  *I cou'd nae see,*
> *And then the beadle cam to aik*   [ask
>  *' You'll pardon me!' "*

Next, the dempster, or executioner, tried to turn her off the ladder, pulling at her arms and legs. But at this point, Bessie and Grissie went to work with their "glamer". The ladder suddenly shakes: the dempster is seized with panic, and, in the general confusion, Maggie slips through the noose and falls unconscious to the ground. Thus is she brought home.

Her tale told, the witches suggest a bumper tipple, and Maggie finishes her tale with an apt apology:

> "When folks half-hang'd, wha can them blame
> To rin away?"

The eastern hinterland of Midlothian is traversed by the roads from Edinburgh to Selkirk, and from Musselburgh to the Lammermuirs; the first a main highway, the second a minor village-linking meander.

The main Border road passes by Craigmillar Castle, where Mary, Queen of Scots spent some of her time, including one sorry week of December 1566, when she lay sick, wishing she were dead. For it was here that the so-called "Conference of Craigmillar" took place, at which Moray, Lethington, Bothwell, Argyll and Huntly put it to her that she should divorce Darnley; and where they probably first laid plans for his murder. The hamlet which housed Mary's staff is still called Little France.

Before Mary's time, in its pre-Hertford state, Craigmillar housed the young James V with his tutor, Gavin Dunbar, and at a still earlier date, James III used Craigmillar keep as a prison for his rebellious brother, the Earl of Mar.

Apart from Craigmillar, Duddingston attracts interest not only because of the charm of the little loch, but because two painters have caught some of that charm in their work. Scotland's first landscape painter of distinction, the Reverend John Thomson of Duddingston (1778-1840), a native of Dailly in Ayrshire, painted and ministered there for the greater part of his life. In spite of his eccentricities, he was both loved for himself, and admired for his work by his parishioners, who forgave him his unmade pastoral visitations because of the fame which reflected on their village.

The companion in later years of his second wife, who was for a time a member of the household at Duddingston, provides us with an account of the division of his days.

"After breakfast he would go to his studio, as other men might go to business, and there he would remain working on his pictures until four o'clock, when we all dined together. This spell of painting was sometimes relieved by a stroll in the garden, and he had a light luncheon about mid-day in the studio. His full time at the easel was determined by the quality of the light and by the season. . . . Five days of the week were occupied by him in this manner, but Saturday he reserved for the preparation of his sermon."

Stories of what were then regarded as marks of his eccentricity abound. Once, he gave a needy girl some money, with the remark that it would more probably prove more effective than his prayers. And:

"Once, during divine service, a thunderstorm of unusual grandeur suddenly broke over the district. It is said that Thomson, who was in the middle of his sermon, hurriedly brought the service to a close, and, hastening to his studio, seized brush and palette and began to paint the striking spectacle."[1]

It is a pity that the quality of his pigment has caused many of his pictures to darken, and raised doubts as to their prospects of survival: for there is a spontaneous vigour and a fresh directness about Thomson's Scottish landscape which few other eighteenth-century Scottish artists captured, and which is not to be found in the romantic landscapes of the nineteenth century. In one of the *Noctes Ambrosianæ*, Thomson's qualities are aptly summed up by North and the Shepherd (Professor John Wilson and James Hogg).

NORTH. Mr. Thomson of Duddingston is now our greatest landscape painter. In what sullen skies he sometimes shrouds the solitary moors!

SHEPHERD. And wi' what blinks o' beauty he aften brings out frae beneath the clouds the spine o' some pastoral parish kirk, till you feel it is the Sabbath.

NORTH. Time and decay crumbling his earth seems to be coming against the very living rock—and we feel their endurance in their desolation.

[1] Robert Inglis: *John Thomson of Duddingston.*

SHEPHERD. I never look at his roarin' rivers wi' a' their pre-
cipes, without thinkin', somehoo or ither, o' Sir William
Wallace. They seem to belang to an unconquerable country.

"Pleasant Dalkeith" is now a busy little town producing
amongst other things, carpets and beer. David Moir (1798-1851)—
"Delta" of the Blackwood Group—its best known literary son[1]
who thus described the place, is remembered more for his novel
*Mansie Wauch*, the life-story of the genial tailor of Dalkeith,
which, though its pawkiness foreshadowed the Kailyard school,
has enough Galtian pith to preserve it as a minor Scottish classic,
than for his highly-polished verses which somehow never warm
into poetry, but which won him his high literary reputation (he
was a physician in Musselburgh) during his lifetime.

The streets of Dalkeith maintain their ancient narrowness so
that traffic has to follow a one-way circular route. The town's
eastern limits are marked off by a high stone wall which shuts off
the grounds of the Palace, the property of the Buccleuch family.
The Palace was built early in the eighteenth century by the
versatile Restoration dramatist Sir John Vanbrugh (1664-1726),
who modelled it on the neo-Grecian Loo Palace in the Nether-
lands. Made of reddish stone, it wears a slightly formidable
look. But it pleased Queen Victoria when she stayed in it in
1842, for she recorded in her journal that it was:

"A large house constructed of reddish stone . . . The house
has three fronts, with the entrance on the left as you drive
up . . . The park is very extensive, with a beautiful view of
Arthur's Seat and the Pentland Hills; and there is a pretty
drive over-hanging a deep valley . . . The pleasure-grounds
seem very extensive and beautiful, wild and hilly. . . ."

That Duchess of Monmouth who features in *The Lay of the
Last Minstrel*, and whose unfortunate husband was executed in
1685 for organizing an abortive rising against James II and VII,
was responsible for Vanbrugh's transformation of the old castle
to the new Palace. Earlier, Froissart recorded that he was "full of
fifteen days resident with William, Earl of Douglas at his castle
of Dalkeith". The Douglases, indeed, heired Dalkeith by
marriage from a de Graham who, about 1128, first received it
from David I. James II made James Douglas of Dalkeith Earl of
Morton in 1658. Thus the castle came into the hands of the

---

[1] The only rival would be the poetic medico Archibald Pitcairne (1652-
1750), who, however, chose to write mainly in Latin.

sinister Regent Morton, who rebuilt it about 1575, and furbished it richly, though it was known locally as the "Lion's Den". It passed to the Buccleuch family in 1642, the second Earl of Buccleuch buying it from the ninth Earl of Morton.

There are many interesting or historic houses round about Dalkeith. There is Melville Castle, the mansion which Henry Dundas, Viscount Melville, once "uncrowned king of Scotland", commissioned James Playfair to build for him on the banks of the North Esk in 1778.

> O! Willie's gane to Melville Castle,
> Boots and spurs an' a',
> To bid the leddies a' farewell
> Before he gaed awa'

runs the old song. Now, other folk can gae, faced with no such perplexing task as frightened the ungallant and unmarrying Willie; for to-day the place is a delightful hotel.

To the north-east is Gilmerton Grange, formerly Burnsdale, where Scott set his early ballad The Gray Brother. And, as well as "Roslin's rocky glen . . . and classic Hawthornden" mentioned in that poem, there are also Newbattle and Dalhousie Castle.

Newbattle was originally a Cistercian monastery founded for a colony of monks from Montrose by David I in 1140. Its story does not differ from that of most of the Lothian and Border religious houses; for Richard II burned it in 1385—it took about forty years to rebuild!—and Hertford repeated the operation in 1544. Mark Ker, the last Abbot of Newbattle, turned Protestant, and became the first commendator of Newbattle. His son, also Mark, persuaded James VI to grant him a temporal barony of Newbattle in 1587, and five years later, to make him Lord Newbattle. Advancement was rapid in these days for a favourite of King Jamie, and in 1606, Lord Newbattle became Earl of Lothian. The Abbey thus came into the family of the present Marquis of Lothian. Apart from the stone-vaulted rooms in the basement, little of the original Abbey has survived the building operations of the Lothians during the eighteenth and nineteenth centuries, though the plan of the church built by the monks is traced out on the ground. The house is now a college for adult education. One of its previous principals was the Scottish poet Edwin Muir.

Dalhousie Castle, ancient seat of the Ramsays, goes back in parts to the twelfth century, but has been so much altered and added to that little outward trace of antiquity remains. Queen Victoria found it:

" . . . a real old Scottish castle of reddish stone . . . from the windows you see a beautifully wooded valley, and a peep of the distant hills."

The house of the Laird of Cockpen, whose matrimonial manœuvres Lady Nairne celebrated in song, stood a little to the east of the castle, on the banks of the Esk.

But the Esk has more tangible literary associations than those of the song-celebrated, unsuccessful laird.[1] Near Polton Station stands de Quincey Cottage, where Thomas de Quincey lived from 1840 until his death in 1859. It was to Lasswade that Walter Scott brought his bride in 1798. And it was in Lasswade Cottage, which was his home until 1804, that he laid the foundations of his literary career with his *Gray Brother* ballad, and his translation of *Goetz von Berlichingen*.

So it happened that on Saturday, September 17th, 1803, Dorothy and William Wordsworth:

"Arrived at Lasswade before Mr. and Mrs. Scott had risen, and waited some time in a large sitting-room. Breakfasted with them, and stayed till two o'clock. . . ."

In her diary, Dorothy recorded her impression of this part of the Esk valley:

"Roslin Castle stands upon a woody bank above a stream, the North Esk: too large, I think, to be called a brook, yet an inconsiderable river. We looked down upon the ruins from higher ground. Near it stands the Chapel, a most elegant building, a ruin, though the walls and roof are entire. I never passed through a more pleasant dell than the glen of Roslin, though the water of the stream is dingy and muddy. The banks are rocky on either side, and hung with pine wood. About a mile from the Castle, on the contrary side of the water, upon the edge of a very steep bank, stands Hawthornden, the house of Drummond the poet, whither Ben Jonson came on foot from London to visit his friend . . . After

---

[1] Made " successful ", though without issue, by the novelist Susan Ferrier (1782-1854), who added to the song a verse in dubious taste.

Hawthornden, the glen widens, ceases to be rocky, and spreads out into a rich vale, scattered over with gentlemen's seats."

The Castle to which Dorothy refers probably had its foundations laid in the twelfth century. But the ruined western walls, now its oldest part, date only from the fifteenth century. The eastern block belongs to the sixteenth century, though the upper stones were probably added early in the seventeenth century. It was a stronghold of the powerful St. Clair family. William St. Clair, third Earl of Orkney, who was waited on by lesser lords and whose wife had a staff of seventy-five gentlewomen, aspired to leave a spiritual monument which, in size and splendour, would reflect his temporal estate. So in the year 1401, he set about building a collegiate church which was to be dedicated to St. Matthew. But Lord St. Clair died when only the choir, the Lady Chapel and the beginning of the transepts had been completed. His son abandoned the plan, and walled in the fragment against the weather.

It is fortunate for us that he did so, for what has come down to us is a vaulted barrel roof and a series of carved pillars so richly ornamented with storied biblical detail that the eye is oppressed with the constriction of it all. Had the whole church been completed in the same style, it would surely have been one of the most remarkable mediæval buildings in Europe. Even the fragment is remarkable, though more as a technical achievement than as an overall work of art. The impression which Roslin makes is of a piously vulgar display of wealth. It reminds us that vulgarity, after all, is not peculiarly a vice of the twentieth century.

There is nothing of vulgarity about Hawthornden, the home of William Drummond (1585-1649), which perches on a rock above the gully, and from whose windows there is a higher drop down sheer rock-face than from the windows of the Castle.

Hawthornden was originally owned by the Abernethy family, from whom it passed to the Douglases. But Sir John Drummond, the father of the poet, acquired it during the latter half of the sixteenth century, and it is still in the possession of his descendants. The old fifteenth-century Abernethy tower is ruined, but the attached seventeenth-century house has been little altered since the poet's time. When I paid a visit there at the time of the tri-centenary of the poet's death, the present laird, Sir James Williams-Drummond, showed me the "Poet's Room", which tradition avers to have been Drummond's study.

Drummond lived a strangely sheltered life in this romantic castle. Tragically bereft of his intended bride by her sudden, fatal illness; out of sympathy with the prevailing cause of the anti-royalist Covenanters; and a scholar whose inquiring mind ranged freely over the literature of Europe—sometimes rather too freely, as we may discover from an analysis of his poetic borrowings—he was the first Scottish poet whose work in English stands comparison with the work of his English contemporaries.

As I stood in his little study with its later iron dog-grate, I pictured him brooding over his elegiac lines until they shone with that grave polish which is their peculiar beauty.

> Dear wood, and you, sweet solitary place,
> Where from the vulgar I estranged live,
> Contented more with what your shades me give,
> Than if I had what Thetis doth embrace:
> What snaky eye, grown jealous of my peace,
> Now from your silent horrors would me drive,
> When sun, progressing in his glorious race
> Beyond the Twins, doth near our pole arrive?
> What sweet delight a quiet life affords,
> And what is it to be of bondage free,
> Far from the madding worldling's hoarse discords,
> Sweet flow'ry place I first did learn of thee:
>   Ah! if I were mine own, your dear resorts
>   I would not change with princes' stately courts.

There is perhaps some poetic justice in the fact that from one who himself borrowed many phrases from Sidney, Tasso, Du Bartas and others, Thomas Gray should borrow a phrase which was in turn to be borrowed again by Thomas Hardy to title one of his most powerful novels.

But Drummond would not have worried. His borrowings were probably innocent, gleaned by his subconscious mind from his wide reading. In any case, his muse so metamorphosed the thoughts of others that in the end the result is always a music of solemn dignity recognizably his own.

"If thou dost complaine, that there shall bee a time in the which thou shalt not bee, why dost thou not too grieve, that there was a time in the which thou wast not, and so that thou art not as old as that enlifening Planet of Time? For, not to have been a thousand yeeres before this moment, is as much to be deplored as not to bee a thousand after it, the effect of them both being one . . . Our children's children have that same reason to murmure that they were not young men in our dayes, which wee have, to complaine that wee shall not be old in theirs. The Violets have their time, though they empurple not the Winter, and the Roses keepe their season, though they disclose not their beauty in the Spring."[1]

To-day the waters of the Esk are even dingier and muddier than they were when Dorothy Wordsworth saw them, for the valley contains both a paper-mill and a gunpowder factory.

Down the "rich vale, scattered with gentlemen's seats" lies Inveresk. Extensive Roman remains have been unearthed in the parish, particularly in the grounds of Inveresk House, where urns, coins and the remains of a hypocaust have been found.

Inveresk itself seems somehow still to retain the quiet atmosphere which its Georgian houses evoke. But that quiet was disturbed by an unholy theatrical row when, in the latter part of the eighteenth century, Dr. Alexander Carlyle (1722-1805) was the parish minister. Carlyle, dubbed " Jupiter" because of his imposing visage, and the "grandest old demi-god" that young Walter Scott ever saw, not only defended the right of his colleague the Reverend John Home of Athelstaneford (1742-1808) to write plays, but he actually attended the first performance of Home's *Douglas* in Edinburgh in 1756. Summoned to appear before the General Assembly, Carlyle defended his action with such force and dignity that the Kirk's attitude of condemnation to the theatre was thereafter gradually modified.

As a young student, Carlyle had watched the Battle of Prestonpans from the window of his father's manse. In his uncompleted but vivid *Autobiography* he left an eye-witness account of the proceedings. On the eve of the battle so great was the press of people in the Manse that he had to sleep at a nearby farm.

"I directed the maid to awake me the moment the battle began, and fell into a profound sleep in an instant. I had no need to be awaked, though the maid was punctual, for I heard the first cannon that was fired, and started to my clothes; which, as I neither buckled nor gartered, were on in a moment, and immediately went to my father's, not a hundred yards off. All the strangers were gone, and my father had been up before daylight, and had resorted to the steeple. While I was con-

[1] *A Cypress Grove.*

versing wth my mother, he returned to the house, and assured
me of what I had guessed before, that we were completely
defeated. I ran into the garden where there was a mount
in the south-east corner, from which one could see the
fields almost to the verge of that part where the battle was
fought. Even at that time, which could hardly be more than
ten or fifteen minutes after firing the first cannon, the whole
prospect was filled with runaways, and Highlanders pursuing
them. Many had their coats turned as prisoners but were still
trying to reach the town in hopes of escaping. The pursuing
Highlanders, when they could not overtake, fired at them, and
I saw two fall in the glebe."

Carlyle was, of course, firmly on the Hanoverian side: which
perhaps explains the severity of his verdict against the men who
made up the Highland army.

" In general they were of low stature and dirty, and of a contemptible appearance. The officers with whom I mixed were
gentleman-like, and very civil to me, as I was on an errand of
humanity . . . This view I had of the rebel army confirmed
me in the prepossession that nothing but the weakest and most
unaccountable bad conduct on our part could have possibly
given them the victory."

But we have been carried by the tide of battle out of Midlothian and into East Lothian, which lies between the Lammermuir Hills and the sea.

IV

East Lothian may best be explored by following three axis-
routes, and branching down side-roads to left and right. The
first of these axis-routes winds round the hinterland of the
county from Tranent, passing through the villages of Ormiston,
Pencaitland, East Saltoun and Gifford, making a loop to take in
Garvald, passing through Stenton, Pitcox and Spott, and rejoin-
ing the coast road south of Dunbar. The second route, the A1
highway to the south, by-passes Haddington and East Linton,
and carries fast-moving traffic to and from the English border.
The third route meanders pleasantly along the coast, through
industrial villages and former fishing ports like Cockenzie and
Port Seton, and delightful sand-duned places like Gullane, North

Berwick and Dunbar, whose principal justification and means of livelihood is that they exist to give holiday pleasure. Let us explore the three routes in the order in which I have set them down.

Tranent, where coal was first worked in Scotland as long ago as 1210, has twice looked out across a field of battle. On the eve of Prestonpans, Prince Charlie's men camped around in the neighbourhood, and it was to the Manse of Tranent, recently destroyed by fire ʻas it was about to be restored, that one of his most gallant opponents, Colonel Gardiner of Gardiner's Dragoons, was brought wounded and dying. Earlier still, in 1547, Tranent was the scene of military activity when the Battle of Pinkie gave Protector Somerset a victory over the Scots army.

Two miles south of Tranent is Elphinstone Tower, where Cardinal Beaton waited gloatingly for the reforming preacher George Wishart, captured near Ormiston, to be brought before him in 1545. Neglected and cracked now by the tunnelling of mines, it was built in the fifteenth century by Sir Gilbert Johnstone, who had married an Elphinstone heiress. From the hill on which the tower stands there is a good prospect not only of the Firth of Forth, but also of the surrounding hinter area, now blighted by the too-rapid and thoughtless exploitation of the coal beneath the fields.

Not until Gifford is reached does the countryside become free and fertile again. In the grounds of the Marquis of Tweeddale's seat, Yester House, stands the underground chamber known as Goblin-Ha', where Scott's Marmion sought the elfin warrior, who, centuries earlier, had fought with Alexander III. It was the workshop or study—whichever magicians favour!—of Sir Hugo de Gifford, the thirteenth-century wizard of Yester.

Like Gifford, Garvald is also cradled in a fold of the gentle Lammermuirs. It is now the scene of an occupation strangely out of tune with the discordant fears and stresses of the twentieth century: for behind the grounds of Nunraw House a new abbey has been built. There were once eleven Cistercian abbeys in Scotland, the eldest of which was Melrose. There were also thirteen Cistercian convents, one of which was at Haddington. All were closed down at the Reformation, or destroyed shortly beforehand by the English invasions of 1544 and 1548.

In January 1946 a little group of monks set out from Mount St. Joseph Abbey in Ireland to found the first Cistercian abbey in Scotland to be built since the Reformation. They turned the old mansion house of Nunraw into a temporary monastery, and shortly afterwards began work upon the building of the new abbey, the Sancta Maria, on a field on the foothills of the Lammermuirs, about seven miles from Haddington. The very name Nunraw, the Nuns' Row, is a reminder of the time when the place was used as a grange for nuns who could not be accommodated at the convent in Haddington itself.

The first sod of the Abbey Sancta Maria was cut on Easter Monday 1952. The abbey has been designed by an Edinburgh architect, Peter Whiston. His plan is, naturally, dominated by the church, but the abbey also contains a sacristy, cloister-garth, refectory, guest house, and all the traditional appurtenances and offices. Mr. Whiston's design translates the ideas behind the great Cistercian building tradition into modern architectural terms. When I visited the site, some years ago, some of the monks were at work on the new building. There were then in all fifty-seven members of this community, but as the Cistercians are self-supporting, and have in this case 1,000 acres to farm, only a proportion of them worked on the new abbey. Those who did were assisted by holidaymakers and by voluntary helpers from nearby villages. The stone quarried by the monks and transported by them in a lorry came from the nearby Rattlebak quarry. It is a hard trachyte stone, which wears well. The building work was interrupted during the worst months of the winter, when the monks, instead of being in the fields, were in their stone-mason's shed, cutting and facing the huge blocks to be placed in position in the spring.

I watched some of the shifts, in their monks' garbs, mixing cement, in silence, for Cistercians do not speak to each other. Others were placing stones, others dressing them. All worked with a fervour and energy which would have astonished the average brick-counting trade-unionist. The autumn sun was shining down brightly on the scene. The outline of some of the abbey buildings were already shaping three or four feet above the ground. There was absolute silence, but for the sound of shovelled sand and tools on the face of stone. Somehow it all seemed timeless, as if the monks were simply beginning again, where, 400 years ago, their predecessors had to leave off.

The pastoral villages of Whittinghame and Stenton (with its excellently preserved mediæval Road-Well) need not detain us here, although their charms certainly detained me when I drove through them. Near Stenton stands the house of Ruchlaw, which " James Bridie " (Dr. O. H. Mavor) bought early in 1951, though he died before he was able to move into it from his home at Craigendoran. To the south-west of Stenton lies Pressmennan Lake, formed in 1819 by the erection of an earthen dam across the end of the ravine, and once stocked with Loch Leven trout. The idea was to make of it a cultivated fishing-ground, but it has also the distinction of having robbed the Lake of Mentieth, in Perthshire, of its claim to be Scotland's only *lake*![1]

The name of the village of Spott has its place in the history of Scottish crime, for in the year of grace 1570 the first Protestant incumbent of its parish, the Reverend John Kello, so far succumbed to the temptations of Satan as to strangle his wife by putting a towel over her mouth while she was kneeling at her devotions. He had come to feel that a richer wife would carry him further forward in the press of the world's affairs. Like so many murderers, however, he was foolish enough to elaborate upon his crime.

After she was dead, he strung her up on a hook in the rafters, locked the front door of the manse on the inside, and left by a back door rarely used. He then mounted his pulpit and preached a sermon, after which he asked several of the elders back to meet his wife. The pantomime of husbandly grief to which they were thereafter treated following the " discovery " of the suicide's body may easily be imagined.

Poor Margaret Thompsone, his spouse, was given a suicide's burial, and the matter was forgotten; forgotten, at least, until the loquacious Reverend John started discussing the theological implications of the event with his colleague, the Reverend Andrew Simpson of Dunbar. Simpson became suspicious, and told Kello of a prophetic vision which had come to him, and in which the Reverend John would be " carried be ane grym man befoir the face of ane terrible Judge, and to escaip his furie ye did precipitate your self in ane deip river, when his angelis and messengers did follow you with two-edge swordes. . . ."

Mr. Kello did not at once take any action over this vision. But he gradually became convinced that his colleague of Dunbar spoke with the voice of God. Kello thereupon went to Edinburgh and confessed before " the Judge criminale ". As a result, he was sentenced on 4th October " to be hangit to the deid, and thairafter his body to be cassin in ane fyre and brint in assis ", all of which appears to have been expeditiously carried through the same day.

The middle route through East Lothian—the highway to the south—brings us to Haddington, the county town. It is one of the pleasantest towns on the East coast of Scotland, and—though not on the sea, and lacking a University—has an atmosphere in

[1] A fact I overlooked when writing the first volume of *The Lowlands of Scotland*, as some readers may have noticed.

some way comparable to the well-preserved calm after a stormy history which characterizes St. Andrews.

Haddington's first recorded appearance in history is its mention as a burgh in David I's charter of confirmation to Dunfermline Abbey, made in 1130. It went to the king's son in 1139 as a dower to his bride, Ada, daughter of the Earl of Surrey; when she died in 1178, it came back to the crown. Thus in its palace, William the Lion's son Alexander II was born in 1198.

Like most other Lowland towns, its wooden houses were often burned: in 1216 by King John of England: in 1244, by English marauders: and in 1355-6 by Edward III of England, whilst avenging the Siege of Berwick.[1] In April 1548, the year after the Battle of Pinkie, English troops under Sir James Wilford garrisoned the town, and held it in the face of siege for over a year, until the Earl of Rutland marched over the Border, relieved the garrison, and conducted them in safety to Berwick. Haddington's final burning—in 1598—was apparently caused by domestic carelessness. Tradition avers that a maidservant put a clothes-horse too near an open fire. In any case, the magistrates decreed that the town-crier should give public warning of the fire danger on winter nights. One of the verses of this "Coal an' Can'le" ceremony, as it was picturesquely known, has come down to us.

> A' guid man's servants where'er ye be,
> Keep coal an' can'le for charitie!
> Baith in your kitchen an' you ha',
> Keep weel your fires whate'er befa'!
> In bakehouse, brewhouse, barn and byre,
> I warn ye a' keep weel your fire!
> For oftentimes a little spark
> Brings mony hands to meikle wark!
> Ye nourrices that hae bairns to keep,
> See that ye fa' nae o'er sound asleep,
> For losing o' your guid renoun,
> An' banishing o' this barrous toun
> 'Tis, for your sakes that I do cry:
> Tak warning by your neighbours bye!

If the poetry is scarcely noteworthy, at least the point is firmly driven home.

Having got over its fire difficulties (more by the construction of stone houses than by the effects of "Coal an' Can'le" crying)

[1] Described in Chapter IV.

Haddington found itself faced with another kind of scourge—flooding by the River Tyne, on whose banks it stands. The earliest recorded flood swelled up in 1358, but floods still pour water into the homes of those who live along the banks of the placid-looking river, and set afloat the leaden coffin of that seventeenth-century Duke of Lauderdale who was deemed by one with no Covenanting sympathies to have been the "learnedest and powerfullest Minister for his age". A plate on a house in the High Street records the impressive level to which the flood waters rose "on the Fourth Day of October 1775 . . . at three o'clock afternoon". The plate itself was submerged in the floods of 1948.

In spite of fire and flood, however, Haddington has preserved many of its older buildings. The royal palace has gone, its remains giving place in 1833 to the County Buildings designed for the town by William Burn, the desecrator of the Cathedrals of Dornoch and St. Giles. In the centre of the High Street stands the Town House, put up by William Adam in 1748, the steeple being added by Gillespie Graham in 1831. Bothwell's Castle, an old town house of the Earls of Bothwell, still survives in Hardgate Street.[1] The house which claims to have contained the birth of John Knox stands in the Giffordgate, though neither it nor any man can prove its claim or disprove the rival claim of the village of Gifford.

In the High Street is the house of Dr. Welsh to which Thomas Carlyle came in June 1821, succeeding Edward Irving, the future preacher and secession leader, as tutor to the doctor's literary-minded daughter, Jane. She married Carlyle, on her own confession, out of ambition. But his love for her during their forty years together was to some extent locked in the hidden recesses of this gruff heart. It was only when she died that the lock re-opened, and he made his yearly pilgrimage to her tomb in the grass-covered choir floor of St. Mary's, which bears his own inscription:

"In her bright existence she had more sorrows than are common; but also a soft invincibility, a clearness of discernment, and a noble loyalty of heart, which are rare. For forty years she was the true and loving helpmate of her husband; and, by act and word, unweariedly forwarded him, as none else could, in all of worthy that he did or attempted. She died in London, 21st April 1866, suddenly snatched from him, and the light of his life as if gone out."

[1] Pulled down after this was written.

*East Lothian: the Bass Rock, from the coast at North Berwick*

St. Mary's Kirk, on the banks of the Tyne a little out from the town, dates from the fifteenth century, and must once have been one of the largest and noblest buildings of its kind: so much so that it was known as *Lucerna Loudoniæ*[1], the lamp of Lothian. It suffered much during the siege of Haddington of 1548, and was finally all but snuffed out by the forces of neglect and decay. The nave is still used as the parish church. It has recently had its roof completed, the restored portion serving communal needs and interests, as in medieval times.

Others who sleep within its stones are the Maitlands, earls of Lauderdale; and John Gray of Haddington (1646-1717), sometime minister of Aberlady, who bequeathed to his native town a magnificent library of nine hundred books from all the leading printing-presses in the Europe of the late seventeenth century.

The twelfth-century ruined nave of St. Martin's stands east of the Nungate.

The Tyne, which flows through Haddington, is spanned by five bridges, two of them mediæval. The oldest is the Abbey Bridge, a mile to the east of the town; the most striking is the Nungate Bridge, which throws three arches over the water and two smaller arches over the Giffordgate. The Waterloo Bridge, which spans the river south of the town was, as might be guessed, built in 1817. The Stevenson Bridge dates from the latter part of the nineteenth century.

Haddington lies on the road to East Linton, where the finest of the county's old water-powered mills still operates. Its conical pantiled roof makes it a favourite subject for artists and photographers. Charming as is the village, its main sources of interest to the wayfarer lie about a mile respectively to the south-west and to the west—Traprain Law and Hailes Castle. Traprain Law, by virtue of its dominating influence over what are now flowering fields, but which once must have been tangled scrub and golden gorse, was an obvious choice for a fortified site in the Dark Ages, when self-preservation depended on constant alertness. The "Treasure of Traprain", unearthed from the Law in 1919, consists of silver ornaments dating from the fifth century, and Roman coins, in all, a hundred and sixty pieces of silver weighing nearly 800 ounces, Troy weight. The silver dishes, worn thin by the action of sulphur in the soil, were crushed and broken, as if they had been hurriedly buried. Teutonic relics in the hoard suggested that the silver was brought by Saxon

[1] Some say that *Lucerna Loudoniæ* was really the Franciscan monastery, founded by Ada, Prince Henry's widow, in 1178, and totally destroyed by Edward II in 1355.

*East Lothian: Preston Mill*

pirates from Gaul, and hurriedly buried before an imminent attack in which, presumably, the defenders were vanquished.

Having skirted the sheep-farming foothills of the Lammer-muirs, and journeyed through the farming heart of East Lothian, let us turn now to the coast: to the sand beaches where children play in the summer, the nesting bays of wild birds, the dunes, with their spray-swept golf courses, and those few fragmented castles which once contained some of the pivot-movements of Scottish history within their cleanly-preserved shells.

Apart from giving its name to the scene of the first Jacobite victory in the 'forty-five, Prestonpans has other smaller claims to fame. Eight centuries ago, the monks built salt-pans in its bay, and its now derelict port of Morrisonhaven was used for the export of that commodity. In Prestonpans itself, there stands the jagged ruin of Preston Tower, built in the fifteenth century[1] by a branch of the family of Hamilton. It suffered the usual fate of burning under Hertford in 1544 and Cromwell in 1650. In 1663, not long after it was rebuilt, it caught fire again, and has remained unoccupied ever since.

Not so the charming Hamilton Dower House at the top of the West Loan, a seventeenth-century dwelling now owned by the National Trust for Scotland, and in use as a home.

The Mercat Cross of Prestonpans, which was probably erected by the Hamiltons in 1617 after they obtained the right to hold an annual fair, is the oldest one in Scotland which still stands unaltered on the site where it was originally built.

Cockenzie is still a fishing port where smaller craft are built. Cockenzie House, where Prince Charlie's men found Sir John Cope's military chest containing two thousand pounds, was once the seat of the Cadell family who had publishing connections with Scott, and, but for their own dilatoriness, might also have had an interest in the second edition of Burns's poems.

Back from Port Seton stands Seton Castle, and within its grounds a church which, though since both burned and restored, has a fabric dating in part from the fourteenth century. Seton Castle itself is a castellated affair erected supposedly " after a design by Adam " and dating from the end of the eighteenth century. Its predecessor figured in history, most notably when the Castle was the home of George, fifth Lord Seton, who was one of Queen Mary's most zealous supporters. It was to Seton that the Queen and Darnley rode on that dark night in March, 1566, after Rizzio had been murdered in Holyrood. Lord Seton fought beneath Mary's standard at Carberry Hill, helped in her

---

[1] Above the parapet are the remains of a seventeenth-century addition.

escape from Loch Leven, and took her to his castle at Niddry, in Linlithgowshire—that noble pile now cracked by underground mining and dwarfed by an unsightly bing—after the escape was successfully accomplished.

Aberlady reminds us of the Gaelicizing of the Lothians under Ceannmór, for its name derives probably from *abhir—liobhaite*, the *confluence of the smooth place*. Though once the port for Haddington, when the smoothness of the waters of its bay would no doubt be valued, it is now a part of that holiday playground which forms the remaining stretch of the Lothian coast.

Gullane rivals North Berwick in sandy popularity. My own first memories of Gullane go back to the 'thirties. My brother was a pupil at an Edinburgh boarding school. Once a month, my parents used to visit him, and take him out. I was sometimes included in these excursions. There would be lunch in an Edinburgh hotel, and then an afternoon trip down to Gullane or North Berwick, both of them wind-swept and what is euphemistically termed bracing during the off-season. Then back we would come to the starchy delights of a Scots high tea in a Princes Street Café-Restaurant.

In later years, I have found myself much more attracted by the inland village of Dirleton, where, across the English-looking village green from a hostelry of more than ordinary comfort, stands the great shell of the Castle. Its Drum Tower was built by a de Vaux in the thirteenth century; taken, but only after a fierce struggle, by Edward I's military cleric, Beck, Bishop of Durham; and badly pounded by Cromwell's General Monk, when some Mosstroopers held out against him.

Dunbar, the "fort on the point" stands, in Carlyle's words:

" . . . high and windy, looking down over its herring boats, over its grim old Castle now much honey-combed—on one of these projecting rock-promontories with which that shore is niched and vandyked, as far as the eye can reach. A beautiful sea; good land too, now that the plougher understands his trade; a grim nicked barrier of whinstone sheltering it from the shiftings and tumblings of the big blue German Ocean. . . ."

The "plougher", it may be noted in passing, learned his trade in East Lothian earlier than in most Scottish counties; for among the eighteenth-century Scottish pioneering farmers was George Rennie, who named his house Phantassie.

Dunbar's recorded history goes back to the seventh century.

Here, St. Wilfrid, Bishop of York, was imprisoned in 678 by Ecgfrid, and, according to legend, burned at the stake in 849. Here, in 1072, Gospatric, ex-Earl of the Northumbrians, got from his royal kinsman Malcolm Ceannmór the town and its environs. His descendants, the Earls of Dunbar and March, lived in Dunbar Castle; until the fifteenth century, the town's story centres mainly on their actions.

It was to Patrick, the seventh Earl, and one of the leaders of the pro-English faction, that on March 11th, 1286, True Thomas of Ercildoune (now Earlston) made a famous prophecy. Arriving at the Castle of Dunbar, the prophet found himself being teased by the Earl, and mockingly asked if the next day would bring forth any remarkable event. Mediæval prophets, like all persons whose reputation and livelihood depends upon the perpetuation of superstitious beliefs, evidently disliked raillery inferring disbelief. So Thomas loosened upon the sceptical Earl a flood of vehement prophecy.

" That on the morrow, afore noon, will blow the gretest wind that evir was hard afore in Scotland.[1]

On the morrow, when it was neir noon, the lift [sky] appeiring lowne [calm], but [without] ony din or tempest, the Earle sent for this propheit, and reprevit him.

This Thomas made litil answer, but said: " Noon is not yet gane." And, incontinent [thereupon], ane man come to the yett [gate], schawing that the King was slaine. Then said the propheit: " Yon is the wind that sall blow, to the greit calamitie and truble of all Scotland."

" Black Beard ", the eighth Earl of Dunbar and the first also to carry the title March (Merse), was one of the ten claimants to the Scottish throne left vacant by Alexander III's death, and " Black Beard" rode with Edward I's invading army in 1296. His Countess, however, was of a more patriotic disposition, and delivered the Castle over to the Scottish army, although Edward later forced the native garrison to capitulate.

When Wallace had undertaken to deliver his country from the English menace, Earl Patrick refused to attend a meeting of the Estates convened at Perth. Wallace thereupon met the " quisling " Earl at Innerwick and defeated him and his vassals. Earl Patrick then fled into Northumberland, to rouse up an English army under Bishop Beck. Wallace and the Earl came face to face

[1] First told by Walter Bower (d. 1449), the continuer of Fordun's *Scotichronicon*.

in combat, but the results were inconclusive, the English—Bruce among their number—fleeing across the Tweed at Norham. Wallace and his men thereupon, in Blind Harry's words:

> Passit with mony awful men,
> On Patrick's land, and waistit wonder fast,
> Tuk out guids, and places doun thai cast;
> His steidis sevin, that Mete Hamys was call'd,
> Wallace gert break the burly biggins bauld,
> Baith in the Merse, and als in Lothaine,
> Except Dunbar, standand he levit nane.

The ninth Earl received at Dunbar Edward II, fleeing from his defeat at Bannockburn in 1314, and helped the English king to "coast" in a fishing boat to Bamburgh. It was now politic for the Earl to make peace with the victor, which he did, though after the Scots defeat at Halidon Hill, in 1333, the treacherous Earl again swore allegiance to Edward.

In 1337, however, the Castle, rebuilt after its razing to the ground a few years earlier, was again in the service of the Scottish king, when the Earls of Arundel and Salisbury advanced to take it at the head of an English host. The Earl being absent in the north, its defence fell to his lady, who, because of her swarthy countenance, was known as "Black Agnes". John Barbour has preserved picturesque stories of her hurling from the walls insulting rhymes at her besiegers. For five months, until her supplies were done, she kept the English at bay. Then Ramsay of Dalhousie ran the English blockade one night, and brought in fresh supplies. Next morning, "Black Agnes" got in another shot; she sent a gift of white bread and wine to Salisbury, who was himself short of supplies. Thereafter, he withdrew from the sturdy, sea-washed walls of her Castle.

The Countess's brother, the Earl of Moray, falling in battle at Durham in 1346, she heired extensive estates, and brought her husband the Moray title. Her son, the tenth Earl, was thus one of the most powerful nobles in Scotland. But the size of the family possessions finally proved their undoing. The eleventh Earl was arrested and stripped of his possessions by the young James I after his return to Scotland, and, as part of the royal policy of curbing the barons' power, James II bestowed the Earldom on his second son. During the reign of the next three Jameses, Dunbar Castle formed a sort of diplomatic counter, and changed hands several times; till Hertford, returning from his first burning expedition, camped near Dunbar on 26th of May,

1544. Thereafter, in the words of one Patten, a member of the expedition, they:

". . . burnt a fine town of the Earle of Bothwell's called Haddington, with a great nunnery and a house of friars. The next night after we encamped beside Dunbar, and there the Scots gave a small alarm to our camp . . . That night they looked for us to have burnt the town of Dunbar, which we deferred till the morning at the dislodging of our camp, which we executed by 500 of our hackbutters being backed with 500 horsemen. And by reason we took them in the morning, who, having watched all night for our coming, and perceiving our army to dislodge and depart, thought themselves safe of us, were newly gone to their beds; and in their first sleeps, closed in with fire, men, women and children were suffocated and burnt."

Dunbar played its part in Queen Mary's story. After Rizzio's murder, she and Darnley came from Seton Castle to Dunbar Castle. But on the return journey, Mary bitterly upbraided Darnley for his complicity and conduct over the affair, comparing it unfavourably with that of the Earl of Bothwell, whom she rewarded with the Captaincy of Dunbar.

Thus, ten weeks after the Kirk o' Field murder, it was to Dunbar that Bothwell brought Mary "full gently", after his almost certainly pre-arranged armed meeting with her train at Fountainbridge. They remained ten days at Dunbar "with no great distance between the Queen's chamber and Bothwell's", George Buchanan tells us, until they thought it expedient to return to Edinburgh. Mary's last visit to Dunbar with Bothwell was on 13th June, the night before the Battle of Carberry Hill.

Dunbar's next major appearance in Scottish history was as the scene of the defeat of the Scottish army of General Leslie at the hands of the Protector Cromwell. Cromwell's aim was to make himself Dictator of Scotland, as he had already made himself Dictator of England. The Scots had befriended Charles II, which made them Cromwell's enemies, but they had successfully scunnered their monarch with their theological bigotry. And it was this bigotry which led to the destruction of the Scots army on 3rd September, 1650.

Twenty-two thousand Scotsmen were overthrown by an army half their size; an army, moreover, tired, sick and dispirited.

Shortly before the battle was joined, the Scots Covenanting

ministers—whose functions were apparently not dissimilar to those of political commissars in the Russian army of to-day—had caused three thousand experienced officers to be sacked because they were not theologically sound. These same ministers, with their bigoted nagging, forced Leslie, against his judgment, to forsake entrenched positions on the side of the Dun Hill, and charge the enemy. The result was that the Scots army (with its motto "The Covenant") was made by "The Lord of Hosts" (the motto of Cromwell's army) "as stubble to their swords". Cromwell recorded that at the conclusion of the engagement:

"The best of the enemy's horse being broken through and through in less than an hour's dispute, their whole army being put into confusion, it became a total rout; our men having the chase and execution of them near eight miles. We believe that upon the place and near about it were about three thousand slain. Prisoners taken; of their officers, you have the enclosed list; of private soldiers, near 10,000 . . . I do not believe we have lost 20 men."

The more enthusiastically patriotic of these "private soldiers" would seem to have had a rough time in captivity, if the testimony of John Nicoll, a contemporary Writer to the Signet, is to be believed. For, he relates:

"They . . . tuik sum of the Scottis men prissoneris, amongis whom ane simple sodger, whois eyes they hokit [dug] out of his heid, becaus uponc his bak their wes drawn with whyte calk [chalk] thir words, I AM FOR KING CHARLES, stryped him naked of his cloathes, and sent him back."

The defeat at Dunbar left Scotland south of the Forth open to Cromwell's army, and led to his victory at Inverkeithing, which resulted in a long and harsh dictatorship under the rule of military "gauleiters".

A century later, it was at Dunbar that Sir John Cope landed those troops which, a week after, were to be so easily defeated by the Jacobites at Prestonpans.

Dunbar was twice visited by privateers. In 1779, Paul Jones's ships lay off the town, but did no damage: and two years later, that same Captain Fall who so charmingly threatened Arbroath[1] also made threatening gestures at Dunbar; gestures, however,

[1] See The Lowlands of Scotland: (Glasgow and the North).

which were not implemented when it became obvious that the town meant to resist his attack.

The townsfolk's own leader at that time was, by a curious coincidence, Robert Fall, a member of a powerful local family whose ancestors sprang from the Gypsy Faas of Kirk-Yetholm.

It was this Provost Fall—"an eminent merchant and most respectable character, but undescribable as he exhibits no marked traits"—who entertained Robert Burns when, on May 21st, 1787, he arrived at this "neat little town", accompanied by a nameless lady who insisted on riding with him:

"... by way of making a parade of me as a sweetheart of hers among her relations.—She mounts an old cart horse, as huge and as lean as a house; a rusty old side saddle without girth or stirrup, but fastened on with an old pillion girth—Herself as fine as hands could make her, in cream-coloured riding clothes, hat and feather etc. I, ashamed of my situation, ride like the devil, and almost shake her to pieces on old Jolly—Get rid of her by refusing to call at her uncle's with her."

The Fall's seventeenth-century red sandstone house at which Burns was entertained stands at the end of the High Street. Above it is set a large couchant sphinx. From the Fall family this house passed by purchase to the Earl of Lauderdale, who in turn sold it to the Government in 1859, since when it has been a barracks. The seventeenth-century Town House has a charming hexagonal tower. Beside it stands the remains of the town's Mercat Cross.

Through the openings and side-walks of Dunbar's High Street, the North Sea glints. It is over the fringe of that sea that those who wish to visit the Bass Rock must pass.

I sailed round the Rock in a motor-boat from North Berwick, on an afternoon in late summer. At first, more interesting than the growing shape of the Rock itself, was the sight of Tantallon Castle from its seaward approach. This fortress of the Douglases, which several Stewart kings tried unsuccessfully to "ding doun" —"As lief ding doun Tantallon as bigg a brig tae the Bass", ran an old proverb of impossibilities—is still excellently preserved, and from the landward approach its sturdy battlements offer a dizzying view of jutting rock and precipice. Seen from the sea, its ancient impregnability may be the more fully appreciated. But as the boat beat over the heavy swell, the Bass Rock attracted my interest.

According to the geologist Hugh Miller, the Bass Rock is

probably "a mass of lava moulded in a tubular crater, and from around which, after it cooled and hardened, all the more yielding rocks were swept away". Long after these violent processes had settled, the Bass gave shelter to the hermit St. Baldred, who founded the monastery of Tyningham, and died on the Rock in 756. From the fourteenth to the middle of the seventeenth centuries, it was owned by the Lauder family, who sold it to the Laird of Waughton. From him, it passed to Sir Andrew Ramsay, who in 1671, sold it for £4,000 to the Government. Thereafter, it became a state prison for recalcitrant Covenanters, amongst whom at one time were the leaders Blackadder, Traill and Peden. The Yorkshire traveller Thomas Kirke visited the Rock in 1679, "taking boat", as he put it, at the farm of Castleton, near Tantallon Castle, "a ruinous thing". There were:

". . . about twenty of us in the boat; the sea being very rough, we thought she was overladen . . . The Island is two miles from shore; it is very steep on every side, except that towards the land, whereon is built a block-house. There is but one place to land at, and that very dangerous to climb up the rock; the place is impregnable, the rocks on every side, but this one place, being above a hundred yards in perpendicular height, and from the edges on every side of it still ascends up to the middle point, like the mounting of a sharp hay-cock.

Here were five or six prisoners, Presbyterians, parsons and others, for stirring up the people to rebellion in their conventicles. Before we landed we were asked if we came to see the prisoners, for they will admit no visitants to them. After we had passed the guards, the Governor inquired what we were, and our business; and understanding we were travellers, he ordered some to walk about Island with us."

On the return journey, Kirke tells us, "some of the company were sea-sick, but more were land-sick with looking down the steep rock".

A few years later the Bass Rock became a prison for Catholic supporters of the exiled James VII and II. On June 15th, 1691, four of these Jacobites managed to shut the gates of the fort against its garrison, whose members were down in the rocks unloading coal. Thereupon sixteen men in all, periodically supplied by sloops of the French Government, held the rock for King James until April 1694, when they capitulated on honourable terms. To prevent a recurrence of this success, the fort was demolished by the Government in 1701.

To-day, the Rock is a breeding ground for sea-birds. Once, the solan geese, or gannets, were a source of profit to the owners of the Bass, their eggs a delicacy. In 1618, for instance, John Taylor, the Water-Poet, found that the flesh of the "soleand geese" was a great delicacy.

"It is very good flesh, but it is eaten in the forme as we [the English] eate oysters, standing at a side-board, a little before dinner, unsanctified without grace; and after it is eaten, it must be well liquored with two or three good rowses of sherrie or Canarie sack."

Taylor estimated that the owner of the Bass Rock profited by the sale of solan geese to the extent of two hundred pounds a year; an estimate confirmed eighteen years later by another traveller, Sir William Brereton. The naturalist John Ray further tells us that in 1662, the young birds, "esteemed a choice dish in Scotland", were "sold very dear (1s. 8d. plucked)".

To-day, however, recipe and price quotations are both only of academic interest, because gannet flesh is too strong for the modern palate. In any case, though we still have side-boards to stand against, we no longer regularly drink "good rowses of sherrie or Canarie sack".

The culminating moment of most visits to the Bass, however, is still the threshed press of air which accompanies the mass upsurge of birds from the rock at the sound of a sudden hand-clap or the blowing of a klaxon.

"Delta" Moir described such a scene in verse a century ago: not very good verse, it must be admitted. But if his verse might be improved upon, the scene which he describes could not.

*The rower with his boat-hook struck the mast,*
*and lo! the myriad wings, that like a sheet*
*Of snow, o'erspread the crannies—all were up!*
*The gannet, guillemot, and kittiwake,*
*Marrot and plover, snaipe and eider-duck,*
*The puffin and the falcon, and the gull—*
*Thousands on thousands, an innumerous throng*
*Darkening the noontide with their winnowing plumes,*
*A cloud of animation! the wide air*
*Tempesting with their mingled cries uncouth!*

# CHAPTER IV

# BERWICKSHIRE

*At Tweidis mouth thee stands ane noble toun,*
*Whair many lordis hes bene of great renoune,*
*Whair mony a lady bene fair of face,*
*And mony ane fresche lusty galand was.*
*Into this toun, the whilk is callit Berwik,*
*Apoun the sea, thair standis nane it lyke,*
*For it is wallit weill about with stane,*
*And noble stankis cast in mony ane,*
*And syne the castell is so strang and wicht,*
*With staillie towrs, and turrets hie on hicht.*
*The wallis wrocht craftilie with all;*
*The portculis most subtellie to fall,*
*When that thame list to draw thanae upon hicht,*
*That it may be into na maner of micht,*
*To win that hous by craft or subtiltie,*
*Whairfore it is maist gud alluterlie;*
*Into my tyme, whairever I have been,*
*Most fair, most gudelie, most pleasand to be seen.*

ATTRIBUTED, MOST IMPROBABLY, TO WILLIAM DUNBAR.

I

DURING the early weeks of the second world war, it pleased the military powers-that-were to elect that the formation in which I was a very junior officer should be uprooted from its native haunts around Glasgow and transported to the Borders. Thus by chance, and under Government arrangement, I paid my first visit to Scotland's Border counties. Although I was stationed at Hawick, such activities as route-marching and field-exercises carried me across many painful Border miles. Much to my disappointment, I was never able to get as far afield as Berwick-upon-Tweed.

This was a disappointment because of a fascinating paragraph about the place I had come upon in my Border guide book. Writing about Berwick railway station, the writer declared that on stormy nights " when the last train has rumbled southwards into the darkness and the station is deserted, there may, perchance, be glimpsed the gaunt apparition of Edward Plantagenet pacing to and fro ": further opining, " It is fitting that his ghost should wander here."

Although not a member of the Psychical Research Society, I found myself fascinated by the hardihood of any ghost—even the ghost of a gallant tyrant like Bloody Edward—who chose to haunt so draughty a site as a railway-station platform. Such a hardy spectre, indeed, obviously ought to qualify for consideration as the Patron Saint of the Society of Dissatisfied Railway Travellers, whose members are always numerous.

But alas! Edward I had little interest in either comfort or discomfort. My guide-book mentor thought it fitting that his ghost should haunt Berwick station merely because the remains of the old castle that he had once fought for and gained, had been knocked down in order to make way for main line and sidings.

By the time the railway builders accomplished their act of vandalism, little enough remained to destroy, because the town's eighteenth-century barracks and a number of nearby houses had already been built with castle stones. Still, the traveller with a due sense of the proprieties can sympathize with the ghost's sense of loss: for one of the first things which occur to the inquiring tourist is the incongruity of a walled city with no castle at its heart to defend. However, Berwick may be forgiven if it showed no concern over the preservation of the symbol of its dungeon days. For, until comparatively modern times, it has been a pivot-point of violent struggle.

Even in the dark side of the Middle Ages, Berwick must have been an important town, for legend makes it the *Garde Joyeuse* of King Arthur's most famous knight, Lancelot.[1] About 1018, when the Tweed was definitely recognized as the boundary between Scotland and England, Berwick assumed importance as the largest town on the frontier. Under Alexander I, it became one of the four oldest Royal Burghs in Scotland. Its importance, in the centuries ahead, was to prove its undoing.

When Alexander III died, and Edward I of England nominated himself as mediator in the ensuing disputes on the right of succession, his decision in favour of Balliol was made in the Great Hall of the Castle on 17th November, 1292. This, together with the acknowledgment of England's superiority, which was implied when Balliol swore allegiance to Edward three days later at Norham, did not unduly upset the Scottish nobility, who were, in any case, mostly foreigners—Normans and Anglo-Saxons brought north by Malcolm Ceannmór and his Saxon wife

[1] Rival legend makes a similar claim for Bamburgh Castle in Northumberland.

Margaret and their successors.[1]  The natives, however, were not willing to accept any such humiliating condition.

In time, the overbearing demeanour of the English proved more than even the Scottish nobles could stomach, so that when Edward found himself in trouble with Wales and France, the Scots took the opportunity of renouncing all fealty and allegiance to England.  An alliance was formed with Norway and another with France—the beginning of that " auld Alliance " the preservation of which was to be a recurrent aim of Scottish foreign policy for the next three centuries—and an unsuccessful but necessary nuisance raid was made into England.  Edward thereupon decided to end even the pretence of a Scottish king. In the spring of 1302 he marched north and, as the anonymous author of the contemporary *Voyage of Kinge Edward into Scotland, with all his Lodgyings Briefly Expressed* tells us, crossed " the forenoon the River Twede with five thousand horse and thirty thousand footmen, and lay that night in Scotland at the Priory of Coldstream; and the Thursday at Hatton; and the Friday took the town of Barwyk-upon-Twede by force of arms without tarrying ".  So little, indeed, did he tarry that he is credited with being the first to win the outer dyke, mounted on his war-horse Bayard.  The numbers of those slain in the sack of the city, including a colony of Flemish traders, has been variously given at eight thousand, and at seventeen thousand. Whatever the figure, clearly it was a bloody day.

While Edward was marching as far north as Stracathro, in whose churchyard the wretched Balliol had to do penance for his " insubordination ", and Scone, from which the English king removed the Stone of Destiny, his masons were busily constructing the first of Berwick's great walls.  Thereafter, the English used Berwick as an arsenal during their unsuccessful but determined campaign to subdue Scotland.

Bruce, however, did recapture Berwick.  Contrary to his usual custom of razing to the ground forts that could all too easily become enemy strongholds, he garrisoned it with troops under his son-in-law, the High Steward of Scotland.  But Edward II was not the man meekly to accept such an affront to his military strength.  So, in the late summer of 1319, he sent a fleet north from Newcastle to blockade Berwick, while he himself marched over the Border with his army.  His assault upon the city failed. Edward then had brought up a heavy movable shelter nicknamed the " Sow ", under cover of whose armoured flanks his sappers

[1] Some of the Norman-sounding Scottish nobles may, of course, merely have Normanized their names to keep in fashion and favour.

were to undermine the rampart walls. But John Craib, the Flemish engineer who was on the side of the Scots, quickly devised two cranes on the principle of the Roman catapult. When the "Sow" was positioned, these cranes dropped large stones on it, the third of which shattered it to fragments. The result of this defensive action was that Berwick remained a Scots town for the next fourteen years.

With the accession of the boy king David II to the Scottish throne in 1332, Edward III, keeping up the Scot-taming efforts of his forbears, also laid siege to Berwick, but failed to take possession of it, even although Edward Balliol, the latest "quisling" Scots king, had already given it to him in a present. But Seton the Governor, baulked of the support of a French relieving force which had been destroyed at Dundee, and embarrassed by delays in the arrival of the Scots army, was in the end forced to agree that unless he were relieved within a specified number of days, he would render up the town to its besiegers. Inside the time-limit, the Regent Douglas and the Scots army arrived within sight of the town; but Edward held that mere arrival did not constitute relief. Seton still refused to open the Gates, so Edward hanged the Scots hostages, including Seton's younger son.

In the end, however, the Governor's gallantry was vain. Edward brought the Scots to battle at Halidon Hill, two miles from Berwick, on July 19th, 1333. Douglas sent his light cavalry across a bog and up the hill under heavy English archer fire. As the Scots had hardly any archers of their own, they could not reply. The result was a massacre. Douglas himself died, and Edward murdered all the Scots prisoners before he entered Berwick.

Once again, however, the town returned to Scots hands when, in 1355, the Earl of Angus captured it by escalade from the sea while Edward was warring in France. So great was the destruction wrought by the English king when he marched to avenge this loss, that his invasion became known as the raid of Bloody Candlemass.

While sheltering from the victorious Yorkists in 1461, Henry VI of England gave Berwick back to the Scots in return for a promise of Scots help. But in 1482, Gloucester, in support of the Scots pretender Albany, took the town from James III's weakened garrison. It has remained English ever since.

Queen Elizabeth of England was aware of its value to her. She built new fortifications round the city similar to those which once girdled Antwerp, Lucca, and Verona. The Berwick ramparts alone survive, and are thus of the greatest interest. An

Elizabethan traveller who visited Berwick, the Cambridge man Fynes Moryson, was able to report that life within the fortified city was not without its advantages.

"Myself upon the occasion of business in the month of Aprill and the yeer 1598 took a journey . . . to Barwick, a Towne then very strongly fortified by the English, to restrain the sudden incursions of the Scots, and abounding with all things necessary for food; yea, with many dainties, as salmon and all kinds of shell fish, so plentifully, as they were sold for very small price."

The accession of James VI of Scotland to the English throne in 1603 did away with the urgent need for Berwick's military preparedness, and by 1636, when Sir William Brereton inspected the ramparts, he found them "something in decay". In 1688, however, the walls were once again strengthened, and the garrison manned against a possible French or Spanish invasion, and further strengthened towards the close of the eighteenth century.

The ramparts include three bastions, and two demi-bastions; Meg's Mount, facing the Tweed; the Middle Mount; the Brass Mount, named after its brass cannon; the King's Mount, facing what is now a cricket field; Cumberland's Mount; and facing the sea, the Windmill Mount. The only tower to survive more or less structurally intact is the octagonal Bell Tower, though fragments of another, Lord Soulis's Tower, may also be seen. Only one of Berwick's four original gates survives in its original form, that of the Cowport. Other reminders of former glories are the Governor's House in the Palace Yard, and the oldest of the bridges, a structure of fifteen arches begun in 1611 and opened about 1624. It forms a noble contrast with the high-up Royal Border Bridge of twenty-eight arches, opened in 1850 to carry the railway.

The bridge and the fruitfulness of the Tweed particularly impressed Brereton as he arrived in the town at five o'clock on a late June day.

"We passed a very fair stately bridge over Tweede, consisting of fifteen arches, which was built by King James, and, as it is said, cost £17,000. This river, most infinitely stored with salmon, one hundred or two hundred salmon at one draught, but much more was reported by our host, which is almost incredible, that there were two thousand salmon taken since Sunday last."

The splenetic Yorkshire traveller and journalist Thomas Kirke, who arrived at Berwick in May 1777, *en route* for Orkney, tells us that he walked:

" to the middle of a long bridge of fifteen arches; the greatest arch is the next arch but one to the town, and is a very large one; the rest from the town diminish orderly till they come to the other side; there are no buildings on it, but a plain straight bridge. Here, in the middle arch, we took leave of one of our company, who returned southward again. We drenched him in sack, and the Governor of the town, Captain Sterling, and another officer, came to us, and assisted us in the combat; he fired his pistols and departed."

This, of course, is characteristic of that exuberant schoolboyishness which English travellers have so often manifested in colonial and foreign lands since Kirke's day.

Until fairly recently, it used to be customary in acts of Parliament for Berwick-upon-Tweed to be mentioned specially after Wales, a custom still sometimes continued in proclamations. This was because Berwick formed a special territory known as Berwick Bounds, which took in Spittal and Tweedmouth and until 1881 returned two members to Parliament.

But although Berwick is now administered by the county authorities of Northumberland, physically and spiritually it is still very much Scottish. Its vernacular grey stone houses in the older part of the town have the red pantiled roofs commonly met with in Fife and the Lothians. Though naturally there are now many English residents in the town, the Scots accent is frequently heard.

The boundary between Scotland and England is at Lamberton, once an important toll-point. Thereafter, the coast road branches off from the main highway between the two countries. A fork descends steeply to the half-deserted harbour of Burnmouth, whose houses crouch on a rocky ledge beneath high cliffs, and whose main street, except for a few fishing-sheds, fronts the sea.

In the next valley along this cliffy coast, astride the mouth of the Eye water, is Eyemouth. Its harbour is protected by a jagged ridge of rocks called the Hurkers, and is still used by a few fishing-boats. Once, Eyemouth was an important place, for not only was it Scotland's most southerly seaport, but it was also the port for the Priory of Coldinghame, of which it was a dependancy. Smugglers made much use of it and the caves nearby along the

*Berwickshire: Wolf's Crag*

coast. The village itself smacks of the vernacular, with its rubble houses, it twisting wynds and its narrow alleyways.

It has achieved two appearances in history. The rather ugly-looking eighteenth-century mansion of Gunsgreen was built (complete with all the latest smugglers' conveniences) near the site of an older house of the same name, by the Logans of Restalrig. After the death of one of its owners, John Logan, two letters written at Gunsgreen in July 1600 to the Earl of Gowrie, revealed that Logan was involved in the Gowrie Conspiracy, whose parti-cipants planned to capture James VI at Perth, and ship him from the bottom of the garden of Gowrie House, on the Tay, to Fast Castle, then another of Logan's Berwickshire possessions. There, he was to have been kept to await disposal by Elizabeth of England, or by the conspirators themselves. The incriminating letters had been stolen from one John Bour, to whom Logan had entrusted them, by a notary public called Sprott. It proved to be a disastrous theft for him, however, because he was tried and executed. Although Logan was by then nine years dead, he, too, was tried for high treason, his bones being brought into the court to receive their sentence.

Eyemouth's other claim to fame is of a more peaceful nature. In May 1787, Robert Burns and his friend Robert Ainslie (whose father owned Berrywell, near Duns) made their Border Tour. The poet kept a Journal. Berwick struck him as " an idle town, rudely picturesque ". He was more impressed with the fact that while walking round the walls he met Lord Errol, and his lord-ship took " flattering notice " of him.

At Eyemouth, both Burns and Ainslie were made Royal Arch Masons, Burns being admitted gratis on account of his " remark-able poetic genius ", though Ainslie had to pay one guinea ad-mission dues.

Three miles back from the coast, between Eyemouth and St. Abbs, lies the delightful village of Coldinghame. It climbs up a little hill, shoots out a few turning side-street, and tumbles down the other side again. On the top of the hill stand the remains of the once mighty Priory of Coldinghame. It was founded in 1096 by King Edgar, son of Malcolm Ceannmór, after he had won back his throne from the usurper Donald. He fought under the banner of St. Cuthbert, so to St. Cuthbert, St. Mary and the local St. Ebba he consecrated this Priory, granting it to St. Cuthbert's canons regular of Durham. Thus it came about that a religious building on Scottish soil was for long under the control of the English Church. Their Priory having been burned in 1216 and again in 1430, the inmates eventually had to

*Berwickshire: Dryburgh Abbey*

appeal to the local Douglases for protection against raiding parties from both sides of the Border. Coldinghame was rich, and no doubt the Douglases were well paid for this insurance. The Douglases' connection with the place led to James III's attempt to suppress it in 1488, and so to his death at Sauchieburn in the ensuing Douglas-inspired rising of the nobles. Thereafter, it came into the possession of another Border family, the Homes, (or, phonetically, Humes), until it was annexed to the crown by an Act of Parliament in 1504. Coldinghame suffered its third burning in 1545, and was further destroyed at the Reformation. In 1834, the choir was reroofed and patched up to form the local parish church. The result is singularly unbeautiful.

St. Abbs also has religious origins, being named after St. Ebba, who founded a nunnery there. She was the daughter of Ethelfrid, a seventh-century king of Northumbria, and half-sister of those other kings Oswald and Oswy. She fled seawards from her father's court to escape the attentions of the pagan King of Mercia, Penda. Her ship was driven ashore, or (since tradition nearly always supplies alternatives) landed her by choice on the Colding-hame Sands. She was so hospitably received by the inhabitants that she founded her monastery of *Urbs Coludi* on the nearby St. Abbs cliffs, ruling as its Abbess until her death in 683. It was unusual in that it was a double monastery, the distinct male and female communities being under her single rule. Amongst her visitors were St. Cuthbert in 661 and in 671 Ethelreda, the founder of Ely. Shortly before its destruction in 679, Adamnan also came, prophesying fire from heaven as a punishment for the sins of the house; sins left unspecified, but which may reasonably be guessed.

It was rebuilt as a nunnery. Tradition tells us of a later Abbess who, in A.D. 870, on hearing that Norse invaders were approaching the shore, ordered her nuns to cut off their noses and their upper lips to avoid the fate worse than death, she herself setting the example. However, the Norsemen are reputed to have burned the nunnery with the mutilated ladies inside it.

The rugged coastline of Berwickshire throws out two great shoulders against the North Sea. On St. Abbs Head, there stands a lighthouse: on Fast Head, the ruins of Fast Castle, immortalized by Scott as "Wolf's Crag" in *The Bride of Lammermoor*. The stumpy remains of a castle which was once extraordinarily powerful and much fought over, do indeed, look like a decayed fang.

John Logan, whose connection with the Gowrie conspiracy has already been noted, made a curious bargain with Napier of

Merchiston, the inventor of the logarithm, over Fast Castle. Their contract dated July 1594, reads:

> "Forasmuch as there were old reports and appearances that a sum of money was hid within John Logan's houses of Fast Castle, John Napier should do his utmost to find out the same, and by the grace of God, shall either find out the same, or make it sure that no such thing has been there."

Napier's reward, if successful, was to be a third of whatever was found: if unsuccessful, whatever Logan might chose to give him. There is no evidence to show that Napier, in spite of his bargain, ever implemented its one-sided conditions.

The road winds back a little from the coast, passes Grant's House, a former inn, crosses Pease Bridge, a hundred feet above a wooded gully, and comes to Cockburnspath, the scene of many an ambush when the narrow gully was the only roadway from north to south.

Away from the coast, Berwickshire is divided into two regions—the Lammermuirs, and the Merse or March, which was, indeed, the ancient name for a much larger area taking in parts of Teviotdale. The Merse is the largest flat lowland basin in Scotland, and contains some of the richest farming soil. It rolls down to the banks of the Tweed. Lauderdale forms the eastern rib of the county, and carries the road to the Borders, surmounting the gently-rounded Lammermuirs at Soutra Hill. Let us first move down Lauderdale.

From Soutra summit, it is possible on a clear day to see the Sidlaws in Angus, and the three paps of the Eildons. Torphichen Law, Berwick Law, and Arthur's Seat may also be seen. The eye is delighted by the expansive prospect.

Lauder itself is a douce little town with a pleasing middle-of-the-street tolbooth, some good houses, and a church which is reputed to be the work of Sir William Bruce. Lauder Water joins the Tweed just outside a curve of the country boundary in Roxburghshire. But Dryburgh Abbey is in Berwickshire.

Dryburgh, on the banks of the Tweed, is the most beautiful of the ruined Border Abbeys. Built probably on the foundations of earlier religious buildings, it came into use in 1152, when the pious David I was on the throne of Scotland. Tradition has it that the White Friars were a little premature in ringing the bells to celebrate the retreat of Edward II in 1322; so that monarch, irritated by their rejoicing, came back and burned down the place. Robert the Bruce encouraged its repair; but its proximity to the Border kept it an always tempting prey to hostile invaders. It was burned by Richard II of England in 1385, and again in 1544 and 1545. In 1587, after the Reformation, Dryburgh was annexed to the Crown, but granted by charter in 1604 to the Earl of Mar. The land changed hands several times, being once owned by a grand-uncle of Sir Walter Scott, before coming into the hands of the Earls of Buchan, from whose descendants it was eventually gifted to the nation by Lord Glenconner.

Of the conventual buildings—all in the Transition style, Romanesque to First Pointed—the most perfect is the chapter house, which still has its barrel-vaulted roof. St. Mary's Aisle, a fragment of choir and north transept, contains not only the bodies of the brothers Erskine, who headed Scotland's first secession church, but also those of Sir Walter Scott, and his wife; of John Gibson Lockhart, his son-in-law, who lies at his feet; and of Field Marshal Earl Haig, and his ancestors from nearby Bemersyde.

> *Tyde what may betyde,*
> *Haig shall be Haig of Bemersyde.*

was said to be the prophecy of True Thomas of Ercildoune at the end of the thirteenth or the beginning of the fourteenth century. He uttered it to the fifth of the Haigs, Johannes de Haga, and so far it has proved true. The other great mediæval Border families—the de Marvilles, the Avenals, the Maxwells, the De Viponts and the De Vescis—have all disappeared from Tweedside, but the descendants of the original Petrus de Haga still flourish. Bemersyde itself goes back at least to 1150. The peel tower is not unlike nearby Smailholm, and was in existence early in the sixteenth century. Hertford set it on fire, but it was restored in 1581. The eighteenth-century east wing, though not in keeping with the style of the central tower, is much less offensive than the Victorian west wing, built by a tenant of Bemersyde, one Lord Jerviswood, in 1859.

Scott's connection with the Haigs is of some interest, since it is by virtue of Margaret Haig's marriage to James Haliburton, in 1542, that the "Wizard of the North" came to rest in the Haig burial ground at Dryburgh. For the eldest son of this marriage, Thomas Haliburton, was the great grandfather of the wife of Robert Scott of Sandyknowe, who was in turn Sir Walter's grandfather.

Along the banks of the noble Tweed, Scottish and English villages face each other. When I first visited Coldstream, it was during the second World War—I remember crossing the Tweed over a Bailey bridge in the middle of a cold spring night, as part of an attacking Blueland force. My sympathies on this occasion were entirely with the defending Redlanders. But of course British army manœuvres are—or at any rate were during the second World War—always so arranged that the invading force won.

I next visited Coldstream on a peaceful early summer morning. White and pink blossom flounced over garden walls, and the fast-flowing Tweed glittered like silver in the sunlight. The "silver Tweed" is a commonplace. indeed; but it also happens to be a factual description under frequently prevailing conditions of sunlight.

Coldstream once had a Cistercian Priory, built in 1143 by Cospatrick, Earl of March. Nothing remains but a few stones of a vault. It does, however, still possess Smeaton's noble bridge, thrown over the Tweed in 1766, replacing the age-old invasion ford. To most people, however, Coldstream is the place where in 1650 General Monk recruited the regiment of foot-guards which has since proudly carried the name on many a foreign field. Though the actual house at the east end of the market in which the Coldstream Guards was founded has been demolished, a plaque has been built into the walls of its successor.

The fertile farmland of the Merse of Berwickshire is peopled with villages, most of which have known destruction many times over, for even stone was not secure along the Border across which two hostile kingdoms fronted one another. Two of these villages have grown into little towns.

The history of the present Greenlaw, set in wooded country, does not go back further than the seventeenth century, when it replaced the older village that stood on the nearby law or hill. It still has its seventeenth-century church, the Mercat Cross of the older village, and an early nineteenth-century Grecian-style court house.

With the removal of what should be the county town from the county, the place of the county capital has been taken by Duns.[1] It, too, has a history of burning and sacking. It was on Duns Law that General Leslie set up his camp in 1639, with so imposing an army that Charles I signed the Pacification of Berwick on June 18th—a false peace, as it proved to be. Duns is also credited with the honour of being the birthplace of the mediæval schoolman philosopher Duns Scotus (1265-1308), second only to Thomas Aquinas in the learning of his age. In the grounds of

[1] Greenlaw once shared some of the county town's functions with Duns.

the nineteenth-century Duns Castle there are still to be seen the remains of a tower built soon after Bannockburn by Bruce's friend and fellow-champion Sir Thomas Randolph, Earl of Moray.

Duns itself is a pleasing Lowland town, but lacking a little in character and distinction. The return to Scotland of what should by rights be the country town is mooted and discussed from time to time: but the good folk of Duns are not over-anxious to lose their pride of civic place, while the good folk of Berwick still do not wholly trust the Scots. Logic suggests a readjustment of the boundary line between Scotland and England so that it should follow the Tweed. But when have our English partners and neighbours ever been famed for their logic?

# CHAPTER V

## ROXBURGHSHIRE AND SELKIRKSHIRE

*Three crests against the saffron sky,*
*Beyond the purple plain,*
*The kind remembered melody*
*Of Tweed once more again.*

*Wan water from the Border hills,*
*Dear voice from the old years,*
*Thy distant music lulls and stills*
*And moves to quiet tears.*

*Like a loved ghost thy fabled flood*
*Fleets through the dusky land;*
*Where Scott, come home to die, has stood,*
*My feet returning stand.*

*A mist of memory broods and floats,*
*The Border water flow;*
*The air is full of ballad notes*
*Borne out of long ago. . . .*

ANDREW LANG.

1

ROXBURGH is in many ways the most characteristic of the Border counties. Wherever you may go within its boundaries, it is hard to stray far from a river, or at least from a brattling burn. The Teviot is its central artery, and into it flow the Ale and the Borthwick, Slitrig Water, Rule Water, Kale Water and the gentle Jed. Thus reinforced, the Teviot itself merges majestically with the Tweed, which, for two of its twenty-six Roxburghshire miles, forms the boundary of the county with Selkirkshire.

The rivers, the lonely moors where these waters have their source, and the commanding hills, have shaped the civilization of Roxburghshire for centuries. For the dales whose folded loneliness promised security, also offered secrecy of approach to the invader: the rivers whose waters filled castle moats, and whose courses were ramparts of defence, could all too easily turn into traps preventing manœuvre or escape. The history of this county is one of human uncertainty and violence, breeding courage, foresight, and energy.

Standing stones at Plenderleath, between the Kale and Oxnam,

155

and at Midshiels on the Teviot, still commemorate the Pictish inhabitants. Near Hermitage Castle, and at Whisgill, later stones are said to mark the defeat of the Britons of Strathclyde by Ethelfrith, King of Bernicia, at Deganstane (or Dawstane) in 603. On the most easterly of the three Eildons, too, there are the remains of the largest hill fort of its kind in Scotland. Part of the mysterious forty-eight mile long Catrail, or Pictish Dyke, its double ramparts now smoored to the level of the surrounding earth in many places, runs through the county before vanishing on Peel Fell, in the Cheviots.

Roman remains are also plentiful. Apart from an occasional hillside scar, little trace survives now either of Dere Street, which ran from Brownhart Law on the Border, over the Kale, Oxnam, Jed and Teviot, to Newstead, near Melrose; or of the Wheel Causey, said to be a continuation of the Maiden Way from Lancashire and Cumberland. Much of these Roman roads subsequently formed the basis of the roads which have come down to us to-day.

But evidence of numerous Roman camps has survived, the main ones apparently having been at Capuck, south-east of Jedburgh; and near Newstead, at the foot of the Eildons—sometimes claimed to have been the town of Trimontium. After the Roman occupation, Roxburghshire was at first divided between the Britons of Strathclyde in the west, and the Bernicians in the east. Like the Lothians, it was then conquered by the Northumbrians in the eighth century, and, with those other counties, ceded back to Scotland in 1018.

The shire was constituted by David I, and for many centuries played a part of leading importance in Scottish affairs. For the old town of Roxburgh formed one of the Court of Four Burghs, and its castle was a favourite residence of David I, Malcolm IV, William the Lion, Alexander II, and Alexander III, as well as a bastion of Border defence. The fact that old Roxburgh, which stood on the peninsula formed by the meeting of Teviot with Tweed, has been utterly razed (but for a few crumbled walls of the second castle[1] destroyed by the English in 1640, yet strong even in decay) is memorial enough to that violence which, from the end of the Dark Ages to the Union of the Crowns in 1603, Borderland had to withstand.

[1] The first castle was besieged by James II in 1460, after he had already captured the town. On 3rd August standing too near a cannon called " The Lion ", he was fatally wounded when the weapon burst. His widow, Queen Mary, with the infant James III, inspired the Scots army to complete the capture. They razed the castle, which was rebuilt by Protector Somerset in 1547.

It is easy to be carried away by facile romanticism when thinking or writing of Border warfare and—especially after 1603, when
the English were no longer legitimate objects of raiding
attention—Border feuding; easy to overstress the glamour of the
bale-fire's warning; of the stirring in every peel as its menfolk
scrambled for their armour and saddled their horses; and of the
reckless defiance which animated the clash of spears on steel. But
the ballads survive to remind us that cruelty and sudden death
were constant attendants on those whose lives were lived out in
the Border Marches; that life in "Brave Borderland" was, on
the whole, a dirty business. Still, an aura of romance persists;
a sublimated regret for vanished independence. As John Leyden
puts it:

> On these fair banks thine ancient bards no more,
> Enchanting stream! their melting numbers pour;
> But still their viewless harps, on poplars hung,
> Sigh the soft airs they learn'd when time was young:
> And those who tread with holy feet the ground,
> At lonely midnight, hear their silver sound;
> When river breezes wave their dewy wings,
> And lightly stir the wild enchanted strings.

Roxburgh is not an easy county to explore. I spent some
months in Hawick during the winter of 1939-40; long enough
for me to feel the storied impact of the past, and so to learn why
Borderers feel so passionately attached to their homeland. But
my discovery of most of the county had to wait until I was free
to make deliberate excursions of exploration, or when some
necessary business brought me within driving distance of a particular vicinity. I am still conscious, however, that, so far as the
Borders are concerned, the newcomer—be he traveller or tourist,
and however enthusiastic—must to some extent remain an out-
sider. These grim ruins of castles and peels preserved in song
or ballad may thrill him, the rolling freedom of the countryside
delight his eye: but so strong is the personality of Borderland,
even to-day with its feuds half-forgotten and its glens slowly
emptying, that Highlander and Lowlander alike must feel to
some extent a stranger in a strange land, albeit now a friendly,
and æsthetically a rewarding one. He may come to comfortable
enough terms with the Present; but he is not likely to be able to
come to full terms with the Past.

A peninsula of the county juts northwards, and on the narrow
neck of this peninsula, upon the River Tweed, stands Melrose.

For more than three centuries there had been a Columban religious establishment nearby before David founded the first Melrose Abbey in 1136. His Abbey became the mother foundation for the Cistercian Order in Scotland. It took a hundred and ten years of faith and loving energy to build, before it was dedicated to the Virgin Mary on July 28, 1246. It took a considerably lesser number of hours for the soldiers of England's Edward II to burn it down in 1321. Robert the Bruce, however, gave a substantial royal grant to help in its rebuilding, and ordered his son to bury his heart beneath its gracious red stones. His son David I renewed his father's grant. Surprisingly, too, the English king Edward III ordered the restoration of the Abbey lands forfeited to his father. But Richard II, after spending a night of frustration in the Abbey during his raiding incursion of 1385, peremptorily ordered the place to be burned again, an act of sacrilege which later seems very properly to have troubled his conscience. Nevertheless, Melrose Abbey was once more restored and during the fifteenth century it reached the height of at least its material glory. But it was set alight during the English raid of 1544, and more thoroughly destroyed during the following year by the English soldiery under Sir Ralph Evers and Sir Bryan Latoun. Riled that these invaders should have wantonly defaced the tomb of his Douglas ancestors, the Earl of Angus, aided by Scott of Buccleuch, came upon the retiring English host— about five thousand of them—on Ancrum Moor, and utterly routed the desecrators. As the Teviotdale poet John Leyden put it:

> When Scott and Douglas led the Border spears,
> The mountain streams were bridg'd with English dead;
> Dark Ancrum's heath was dyed with deeper red;
> The ravag'd Abbey rang the funeral knell,
> Where fierce Latoun and savage Evers fell.

But there was no time now for further reconstruction, for the Reformation was at hand; its purpose, so far as noble buildings were concerned, differing little from that of the Latouns and the Everses sent against them by the English. Just before the Reformation, Melrose had been given by James V to his illegitimate son, James Stewart, who became its Commendator. Thereafter, it passed through the hands of James, Earl of Bothwell, James Douglas (second son of William Douglas of Loch Leven, Queen Mary's former jailer), Sir John Ramsay, Sir Thomas (" Tam o' the Cowgate ") Hamilton and successive generations of the Buccleuchs, before finally coming under the care of the Ministry of Works. All that has survived for us to enjoy is the ruined shell of the church, fifteenth-century Scottish Decorated work of a fine and delicate order. The Commendator's House is of sixteenth-century origin. The carved figures of the Abbey are reckoned to be the loveliest of their kind in Scotland.

The town of Melrose—the Kennaquhair of *The Abbot* and *The Monastery*—suffered along with its Abbey and fell into a state of decay after the Reformation. It owes much of its later fame and tourist prosperity to Sir Walter Scott. Since the beginning of the nineteenth century, it has also developed as a residential town where, in the words of a Victorian guide book, " people of substance take up their dwelling"; or, more accurately nowadays, a place to which wealthier folk retire.

Scott built his own home two miles to the west of Melrose. He bought the farm of Cartley Hole in 1811, adding to his estate by further purchases in 1813 and 1817. He built first a cottage, to which he removed from Ashiesteel in May 1812. Then he set about the exterior of the extraordinary edifice which he called Abbotsford, and which is a romantic blend of many styles, incorporating features copied from historical buildings as diverse as the old Tolbooth of Edinburgh, Linlithgow Palace and Roslin Chapel. To-day, there may still be seen at Abbotsford Scott's library, his fine collection of armour, the writing desk presented to him by George III, the silver urn which was a gift from his poetic rival Byron, the little room in which Scott wrote, and the adjacent rooms in which he and, later, his son-in-law, John Gibson Lockhart, died.

I made my first visit to Abbotsford in the late summer of 1952. The P.E.N. International Congress was in session at Edinburgh, and the delegates were transported to Abbotsford in three motor coaches. On the outward journey, I had the Irish poet Austin Clarke as my travelling companion. We talked of Yeats, whom he had, of course, known well; and of contemporary literary prospects in both Ireland and Scotland. So much Yeats-adulation is now practised in English University circles that it was refreshing to hear first-hand word-pictures of the poet's idiosyncrasies and mannerisms. Indeed, I found Austin Clarke's rough-tweed recollections more of an aid to the richer understanding of Yeats's work than those learned rival expositions of his symbolism which academic persons so regularly produce.

The press of authors thronging Abbotsford became so exhausting that I spent most of my time wandering around the gardens. There, I was eagerly set upon by a Pakistani poet who, with the shrill persistence of the Oriental, insisted upon giving me a descriptive outline of his country's literature: an outline which only our arrival back in Edinburgh eventually terminated.

I wondered afterwards what Scott would have thought of this mass literary descent. Probably it would have amused him. Certainly, the professional coming-together of any group of people sharing a common means of livelihood never fails to upset me. Temporarily, the counter-balancing checks of the civilization of which a man is a part, are loosened when he turns himself into a conferring specialist. He becomes de-humanized. His speciality looms over-large upon his consciousness—larger than life ever allows it to be in practice—and he expends much energy in proclaiming, supporting or approving resolutions designed to prove to his fellow-men that they grievously undervalue him. Probably there is little to choose between a gathering of Trade Unionists, a get-together of school-teachers, or a clamjamphrey of authors, except that the two latter groups perhaps talk less loudly and more literately. But all are concerned primarily with the problem of how to increase their store of worldly gear: just as, I suppose, I am myself by writing this book!

Two pictures of Melrose have been preserved for us by travellers: one revealing a glimpse of it at the height of its glory, the other showing it at its most decayed, when a mean parish kirk had been put up in the middle of the ruins.

The first is by Peder Swave, a Swede, who came to Scotland in 1535 to persuade James V to help the Scandinavian king Christian II reassert his authority over the rebellious citizens of Lubeck. The translation from Swave's Latin was made by the historian P. Hume Brown.[1] Says Swave:

"On the 12th of May I was conducted to the king who was then at a monastery, very richly endowed, by name Jemoers [Melrose]. Its abbot is said to have an annual income of 1500 crowns. When mass was over, I paid my respects to the king, whom I found standing not far from the altar. I presented my letters, and was ordered to defer my business till the king should be able to summon his councillors . . . I returned to John Campbell, to Jeduart . . . Master Campbell told me that, in the Abbey of Jemoers, in which I paid my respects to the king, on the approaching death of a monk, a few days before his death, the brethren hear the ringing of a bell in their cells, whereupon they hasten to confession, uncertain which of their number death now makes his prey."

[1] *Early Travellers in Scotland.*

Dorothy Wordsworth came to Melrose on September 19th, 1803, having set out before breakfast from Clovenfords, six miles away.

"At Melrose the vale opens out wide; but the hills are high all round—single distinct risings. After breakfast we went out, intending to go to the Abbey, and in the street met Mr. Scott, who gave us a cordial greeting, and conducted us thither himself. He was here on his own ground, for he is familiar with all that is known of the authentic history of Melrose and the popular tales connected with it. He pointed out many pieces of beautiful sculpture in obscure corners which would have escaped our notice.

The Abbey has been built of a pale red stone; that part which was first erected of a very durable kind, the sculptured flowers and leaves and other minute ornaments being as perfect in many places as when first wrought. The ruin is of considerable extent, but unfortunately it is almost surrounded by insignificant houses, so that when you are close to it you see it entirely separated from many rural objects, and even when viewed from a distance the situation does not seem to be particularly happy, for the vale is broken and disturbed, and the Abbey at a distance from the river, so that you do not look upon them as companions of each other.

And surely this is a national barbarism: within these beautiful walls is the ugliest church that was ever beheld—if it had been hewn out of the side of a hill it could not have been more dismal; there was no neatness, nor even decency, and it appeared to be so damp, and so completely excluded from fresh air, that it must be dangerous to sit in it . . . What a contrast to the beautiful and graceful order apparent in every part of the ancient design and workmanship! "

The damp church has long since been pulled down: but Melrose Abbey remains hemmed in by the near presence of industry, in spite of the removal of some of the more "insignificant" of the neighbouring houses.

The road from Melrose to Kelso along the southern banks of the Tweed is one of the loveliest in Scotland. The full enchantment of the Tweed's course is perhaps best enjoyed from the hillside on which Bemersyde stands, just over the county border. But the road itself has its own characteristic pastoral vistas. It passes through the village of St. Boswells (once called Lessudden, or Lesseduin, "the manor-place of Edwin") which lies about a fair green common. In the eighteenth and early nineteenth centuries this common was the scene of the largest annual fair in the south of Scotland. Lambs, cattle, horses and wool went to the highest bidder. Many of the bidders were itinerant Border gypsies or potters. The gypsies have largely vanished now, but St. Boswells still holds the most important sheep and lamb sales in the Borders.

Near St. Boswells stands Lessudden House, a charming late sixteenth-century home with a seventeenth-century wing. It is still (1954) in the possession of the family who were its builders, the Scotts of Raeburn.

On the 9th of May, 1787, Robert Burns entered in the Journal of his Border Tour: "Breakfast at Kelso; charming situation; fine bridge over the Tweed, enchanting views and prospects on both sides of the river. . . ." Scott also recorded his delight in Kelso and its surroundings.

"The meeting of two superb rivers, the Tweed and the Teviot, both renowned in song—the ruins of an ancient abbey —the more distant vestiges of Roxburgh Castle—the modern mansion of Floors, which is so situated as to combine the ideas of ancient baronial grandeur with those of modern taste—are in themselves objects of the first class, yet are so mixed, united and melted among a thousand other beauties of a less prominent description, that they harmonize into one general picture, and please rather by unison than by concord."

John Leyden, whose best poem *Scenes of Infancy* contains a warmth of local patriotism and observation which goes some way towards melting the static frigidity of his Augustan vocabulary, also enthused over Kelso:

> *Teviot, farewell! for now thy silver tide*
> *Commix'd with Tweed's pellucid stream shall glide;*
> *But all thy green and pastoral beauties fail*
> *To match the softness of thy parting vale.*
> *Bosom'd in woods, where mighty rivers run,*
> *Kelso's fair vale expands before the sun:*
> *Its rising downs in vernal beauty swell,*
> *And, fringed with hazel, winds each flowery dell;*
> *Green spangled plains to dimpling lawns succeed,*
> *And Tempe rises on the banks of Tweed.*
> *Blue o'er the river Kelso's shadow lies,*
> *And copse-clad isles amid the waters rise;*
> *Where Tweed her silent way majestic holds,*
> *Float the thin gales in more transparent folds.*

The bridge which so took Robert Burns's fancy has disappeared, swept away by the great Border flood of October 26th, 1797; and the " modern taste " of Floors, the seat of the Duke of Roxburghe, may excite less rapture in a twentieth-century bosom than it did in Scott's: but Kelso is still a beautiful place, the fairest of all the Border towns, and the least despoiled by pseudo-Gothic Victorian building. Rennie's five-arched bridge, which sweeps across the river below the railway station, went up between 1800 and 1803, and was later used by the same architect as his model for London's Waterloo Bridge.

Kelso was the home of the Victorian poet Thomas Tod Stoddart (1810-1880) from 1836, the year of his marriage, until his death. An advocate who had no need to practise his profession, he was also a keen angler who knew every mood of the Tweed. He is the author of what I, who do not fish, take to be the best poem ever written about the art of the " Compleat Angler ".

> *A birr! A whirr! a salmon's on,*
> *A goodly fish! A thumper!*
> *Bring up, bring up, the ready gaff,*
> *And if we land him, we will quaff*
> *Another glorious bumper!*
> *Hark! 'tis the music of the reel,*
> *The strong, the quick, the steady;*
> *The line darts from the active wheel,*
> *Have all things right and ready.*
>
> *A birr! A whirr! the salmon's out,*
> *Far on the rushing river;*
> *Onward he holds with sudden leap,*
> *Or plunges through the whirlpool deep,*
> *A desperate endeavour!*
> *Hark to the music of the reel,*
> *The fitful and the grating;*
> *It pants along the breathless wheel,*
> *Now hurried—now abating . . .*
>
> *A birr! A whirr! the salmon's in,*
> *Upon the bank extended;*
> *The princely fish is gasping slow,*
> *His brilliant colours come and go,*
> *All beautifully blended.*
> *Hark to the music of the reel!*
> *It murmurs and it closes;*
> *Silence is on the conquering wheel,*
> *Its wearied line reposes.*

In mediæval times, Kelso was divided into two parts. Wester Kelso, which extended into what are now the grounds of Floors Castle, was a kind of suburb to Roxburgh and had its own market cross. Easter Kelso grew up around the Abbey, and after Roxburgh's destruction in 1460, inherited that more ancient town's trade and influence.

Modern Kelso has an eighteenth-century atmosphere, with its large square gathering together the roads into the town, and its spacious main street.

One of the earliest local newspapers in Scotland, the *Chronicle*, was first published in the town in 1783. Scott's friend James Ballantyne had his printing works at Kelso, and it was from them that the first two volumes of *The Minstrelsy of the Scottish Border* came.

The chief glory of Kelso is, of course, its Abbey, another of David I's foundations, dating from 1128. The monks of Kelso were of the Tironesian Order. All the pre-Reformation Stewart monarchs were generous to Kelso Abbey, and it amassed considerable wealth. James III was crowned within its walls.

The last Abbot of Kelso was another of James V's bastard sons, James.[1] By this time, however, the Abbey itself had been destroyed. The Duke of Norfolk despoiled it in 1542, and Hertford set it on fire three years later. The monks on this occasion are reputed to have put up a stout, though vain, defence. The work of destruction was completed in 1560 by the Reformers, who expelled the remaining members of the brotherhood.

As usual, stones stolen from the Abbey were used throughout the eighteenth century for secular purposes. The eastern transept was roughly thatched over in 1649, and made to do duty as the parish kirk, until it collapsed during a service in 1771. What was then left of the Abbey was cleaned up and repaired in 1866 by the Duke of Roxburghe, and is now owned by the nation.

The architecture of Kelso Abbey is almost wholly Norman and Transitional. Originally, the Abbey had western as well as eastern transepts, with a tower over both crossings, and in this respect was unique in Scotland.

Every year in the autumn, a horse and pony sale is held at Kelso, in a big field crooked by the river. Buying a pony or a horse is, of course, an event of some significance in a man's life: of much greater significance, for instance, than buying a motor car. While it is important to be sure that both are working properly in the purely mechanical sense, there the comparison

[1] Could it have been the mothers of these royal bastards who were responsible for their offspring bearing their father's name?

ends. For however affectionately a man may come to regard his car, he does not expect it to respond. Nor does he have to stroke it under the nearside front wing, whispering gently into its bonnet, in order to ensure that it does not buck, or sidle in evasive circles, as he tries to establish himself in a position of control. Horse-buying is therefore a business which creates considerable anticipatory excitement.

We set out early in the morning from Loch Lomondside and arrived at Kelso about half-past nine. Already, so many cars had filed through the gate into the field that was doing duty as a parking-place that the single-tracked, wooden-posted pass was a phutter of mud, through which wheels whirred and squelched unsteadily. But, miraculously, no car stuck in the mud-churn, and we soon joined the long lines of tightly-packed vehicles inside.

Horses and ponies stood tethered round the perimeter of the show-ground. Here, a hunter was being put through his paces; there, a prospective buyer was venturing a timid canter. In the centre of the field stood a wooden grandstand overlooking the main ring, in which finely-groomed horses of blood and breeding were being shown. A little to the right there was roped off a smaller ring, without a grandstand. Here, less fashionably over-looked, sturdy little ponies were proving their points, many of them ridden by children. Both these performances had their clusters of admirers; but the biggest crowd—the kind of crowd that drifts from one focal-point of interest to another—had newly knotted itself around the long racks containing second-hand saddlery and equipment, which an auctioneer was putting up for sale in a patter of ceaseless rapidity. We joined this central crowd.

Twice before I had ventured into an auction sale. On neither occasion had I found the experience a pleasant one. Once, on the island of Stronsay, in Orkney, curiosity had persuaded me to become part of a press of stolid fish-buyers. On the quayside round about lay boxes of fish-samples culled from the newly-arrived drifters, whose catches flashed up from the darkness of their open holds. The auctioneer stood on an upturned barrel, banging one hand with a roll of paper wielded ceaselessly by the other, pittering through an upward creep of prices per cran. His dialect was beyond my comprehension, but apparently it was fully understood by the smoking, deliberately-spitting buyers and fishermen who were his regular customers. A lizard-flick of a lazy eye seemed enough to send this vocal purchase-barometer up another few points. Suddenly at the other end of the harbour,

I saw a friend. Unthinkingly I raised my head to attract his attention. Almost instantly—or so it seemed to me then—the mechanism of the price barometer seized up, and I was the centre of a circular stare of disapproval, while a broad Aberdeenshire accent told me curtly that if my bidding was not meant to be regarded, I had better take myself elsewhere. Horrified at the thought of what I had apparently so nearly done, I slunk quietly away.

My second auction sale took place in a Glasgow house which was being displenished because of the death of the elderly owner. I arrived at what had been optimistically described in the announcing poster as viewing-time. It was, however, quite impossible to view anything, because the viewers themselves formed a solid human phalanx entirely blocking both passage-way and stair. By chance, however, I found myself in the very room where the set of Georgian fire-arms, in which I was interested, was being sold. I had to wait about an hour while tightly-compressed people outbid each other for articles of worth-less Victorian furniture. At last the fire-arms were held up. "Lot 169," the auctioneer announced. "Five pounds for this beautiful and interesting lot."

A fat red-faced woman wedged sweatingly against my right elbow muttered something vaguely improper. The auctioneer ignored her. "Four pounds ten, then, for this really beautiful lot? Four pounds? Nobody give four pounds? Come on now. The frames alone are worth that money."

The fat woman suggested a possible use to which the auctioneer himself might put the frames; a proposal which drew from him a venomous glare.

"Three pounds? Two? One?"

The auctioneer mopped his brow, and the fat woman made an unpleasant indescribable sound.

"Any bid at all, then?" the auctioneer asked in a burst of renewed desperation.

"Five shillings," I said nervously.

No one added anything, except the fat woman, who snorted.

And so after the usual procedure of gradual departure, "this really beautiful lot" changed hands at the knock of the auction-eer's hammer.

A further two hours elapsed before the crowd thinned out enough for it to be possible for me to get near my " lot " to inspect it. I saw at once that the Georgian fire-arms had been made during the reign of a later George than the monarch commonly implied among antique-dealers. I saw also that I had become the owner of about twenty heavy gilt frames. These encompassed a variety of objects which ranged in interest from a hand-painted text reminding me that VIRTUE IS ITS OWN REWARD—cold enough comfort, to be sure!—to the soot-blackened portrait of an elderly gentleman with side-whiskers and an expression of severe disapproval, whom I took to be the late owner's grandfather.

For a moment or two, I experienced a sentimental qualm at the thought of committing someone else's grandparent to the flames. But I could think of no other satisfactory method of disposal. So after a sordid argument with a barrowman lurking hopefully outside, to whom I stressed the remarkable value of the frames, I handed over ten shillings to be relieved of my recently-acquired responsibilities.

At least there was no fear of finding myself the owner of an unwanted grandfather at Kelso; but with *Esther Waters* in mind, and other more dimly-remembered stories of double-dealing horse vendors, I felt reluctant to risk a bid. As a result of my reticence, I shortly found myself the possessor of two animals with no saddlery to equip them.

I had only meant to buy one animal; a pony for one of my daughters. A two-year-old Shetland gelding called Snip seemed exactly the sort of pony we were after. (The name may have derived from a fondness for chewing buttons, but as with so many problems of etymology, this solution is open to doubt.) He had a late number in the catalogue. Once we had decided that Snip's reference, qualities and appearance were satisfactory, there only remained the question of his price.

In due course, he was led into the ring. A bid was made: I topped it: another was made: I topped it again. Suddenly I felt full of a curious exhilaration. The fact that every lift of my catalogue meant parting with an extra guinea ceased to have any real meaning for me. I wanted Snip, and I meant to have him. Fortunately my rival's resolve slackened after another bid, and I acquired my first pony at a still reasonable price.

But the sense of exhilaration persisted. The next pony came into the ring—a four-month-old Exmoor called Bruntsie. (He had been bred on Edinburgh's Bruntsfield links). Bruntsie had a soft nose, a shaggy mane, and big, appealing eyes. He also carried a prize-winner's ticket. Once again the bidding started. Once again I raised my catalogue: more discreetly now, because I noticed that my wife had joined the crowd, and was standing at the other side of the ring.

"Knocked down to the gentleman in the kilt," declaimed the

auctioneer in stentorian tones. At this, my wife's eyes searched me out, a look of horror draining away her previous expression of interested amiability.

However, "facts are chiels that winna ding". In spite of wifely recriminations, there was really little to be said; the only problem now was how to get two ponies from Kelso to Loch Lomondside. I was astonished and relieved to discover that British Railways had anticipated my requirements, and had in fact laid on a horse-box which could work the ponies' transformation overnight.

I was thus more experienced the following year when I went back to Kelso to buy a horse for myself. Two of the beasts I fancied quickly soared into price-realms where no amount of exhilaration could possibly support me. Another turned out to be a shambling stumbler. A fourth had all the virtues, so far as I or my friend the Expert could discover, but had been withdrawn from the ring because he had failed to make his reserved price. I was frightened out of buying him privately by the blarney of the broguing Irishman rolling out the beast's merits. Finally, I bought a staid Highland garron, whom I promptly christened Cimarosa, but who refused, and with Highland dourness still refuses, to answer to any other name than Mousie. With Mousie I made my way once more up to the station.

A huge blood stallion was about to be put into a waiting horse-box. When the horse-box was made ready, the stallion decided upon a policy of non-co-operation. But after a deal of pulling, pushing, coaxing and sweating, the reluctant stallion was at last safely embarked. The whole performance filled me with superior amusement. I glanced at my garron's shaggy mane and solemn eye, and remarked to my friend the Expert that a horse as difficult to handle as the stallion must be an insufferable nuisance to its owner. The Expert only smiled.

Another horse-box was made ready. I led Cimarosa/Mousie to the foot of the ramp. In an instant, he reached a verdict similar to the stallion's: only his resistance was more prolonged and, perhaps because of his Highland blood, more doggedly determined. Twice as much pulling, pushing, coaxing and sweating were called forth before our object was achieved. I could not conceal my embarrassment from my friend the Expert. The Expert only smiled.

If one were to write about every part or feature of interest in Roxburghshire, one would need to have a book-length's worth of print-space at one's disposal. But I, indeed, do not pretend to have done more than explore the places which particularly aroused my active curiosity. Thus, from Kelso I went to Yetholm and nearby Kirk-Yetholm; not because there are pre-historical camps on the summits of Yetholm Law and Camp Hill; not even to see the kirkyard at Yetholm, where some of the dead of Flodden are reputedly buried: but because I wanted to see Gypsy Row, at Kirk-Yetholm, where the Border gypsies once had their head-quarters, their "palace" and their king. Leyden pictured them vividly in the late eighteenth century.

> On Yeta's banks the vagrant gypsies place
> Their turf-built cots: a sun-burn'd swarthy race!
> From Nubian realms their tawny line they bring.
> And their brown chieftain vaunts the name of king:
> With loitering steps, from town to town they pass,
> Their lazy dames rock'd on the panniered ass.
> From pilfered roots, or nauseous carrion, fed,
> By hedge-rows green they strew the leafy bed,
> While scarce the cloak of tawdry red conceals
> The fine-turn'd limbs, which every breeze reveals:
> Their bright black eyes through silken lashes shine,
> Around their necks their raven tresses twine;
> But chilling damps, and dews of night impair
> Its soft sleek gloss, and tan the bosom bare. . . .

Gypsies first arrived in Europe, probably from Asia, in the fourteenth century, though when they first reached Scotland is uncertain. The Faa family were in the ascendancy at Yetholm for many generations, the most famous of the "kings", Willie Faa, having had twenty children. Another of the former gypsy inhabitants was Madge Gordon, who was also prolific, and who provided Scott with the prototype for his Meg Merrilees.

Passing through the ominously-named village of Morebattle, I drove down three winding miles of narrow Border road to see the ruined keep of Cessford. Cessford was once the stronghold of one of the Ker brothers, both of whom founded noble families. The descendants of Ralph Ker of Ferniehurst became Marquesses of Lothian. Robert's ancestors became Dukes of Roxburghe. Cessford was, until 1660, the home of this branch of the Kers from about 1446, when they acquired it through the crown from the Mowbrays, who had become involved in a conspiracy with Lord de Soulis of Hermitage against Robert the Bruce. It is now a grim ruin.

The Kers of Cessford entangled themselves in a bitter family feud with the Scotts of Buccleuch in 1526. It came to a head in

1552 when Sir Walter Scott of Buccleuch, Governor-General and Justiciar of all Liddesdale and Warden of the Middle Marches, was set upon by a party of Kers in the High Street of Edinburgh and murdered. Both branches of the Kers were outlawed for this exploit. Faced with starvation, they successfully petitioned the king to withdraw his sentence on those not actually implicated. The feud was made up a few years later when Sir Thomas Ker of Ferniehurst married Buccleuch's sister Janet Scott.

Cessford itself was besieged by the Earl of Surrey in 1545. The defendants held him at bay until its absent laird came suddenly over the hill and, making a false appreciation of the military situation, bargained the lives of the faithful defenders of his castle against his property. The feelings of those thus unnecessarily saved may well be imagined, for Surrey himself recorded later that the place could never have been taken had " the assailed been able to go on defending".

I drove down the valley of the Kale, re-joining the main Berwick-Carlisle road near Eckford. This village was once surrounded by several peel towers, mostly destroyed by the English under Lord Dacre in 1523, and Hertford in 1545. None now remains. Eckford has an old church which, though much maltreated in later "destorations", dates from 1662. Its jougs still hang by the eastern doorway.

Passing through Crailing—where the ministerial historian David Calderwood settled in 1604, and across the river from Nisbet, where the eloquent Samuel Rutherford was born—I turned up Roman Watling Street at Jedfoot Bridge, marvelling again that the very proper Roman principle of making roads straight should subsequently have been overlooked for the best part of seventeen hundred years. Then I drove round to Jedburgh, built upon the eastern spur of Dunian Hill, the Hill of St. John.

Jedburgh's name is thought by the fanciful to derive from Gadburgh, " the town of the Gadeni ", the tribe who once occupied the territory between the Northumberland Tyne and the Teviot. This overlooks the fact that in the middle ages mention of the town not infrequently appeared in charters as Jedwarth, "town on the Jed ". In any case, the local folk call their town "Jeddart"; it is a royal burgh and the county town.

The oldest streets of the town take the form of a cross, the High Street and the Castlegate being intersected by the Canongate and Exchange Street. Prince Charles Edward Stewart lodged in the Castlegate in 1745, Burns at No. 27 the Canongate in 1787, and Wordsworth at 5 Abbey Close in 1803. The house in which Queen Mary lodged in October 1566, when she arrived to open the Justice Eyres, and from which she made her ride of sixty miles across the moors to visit her wounded lover Bothwell at Hermitage, is now a museum. That ride gave her a fever which nearly cost her her life. In her later days of unhappiness, she was heard more than once to remark that she wished she could have died at Jedburgh.

The modern town has spread considerably and has reached right down the slope of the hill, and across the river. The whole town, however, is still dominated by the square castellated crown of the former county prison. Now converted into a museum, this prison was built in 1823 on the site of the ancient castle.

That castle, of which not a trace remains, at one time brought Jedburgh its power and prosperity. It was built during the twelfth century, and was a favourite residence of these Border-conscious monarchs who also favoured Roxburgh with their presence. The nearness of Jedburgh to the Borderline made the castle a frequent object of struggle during the Wars of Succession, and it changed hands several times. In 1409, the men of Teviotdale, wearied with the latest English occupation which had lasted sixty-three years, ejected the enemy garrison and destroyed the castle at the Regent Albany's expense. (A sensible proposal to levy a twopenny tax to pay for the work of demolition was overruled by Albany: one of the several popular vote-catching manœuvres, as we would call them nowadays, which he employed to maintain himself in power, and prevent the people of Scotland pressing him too closely to take action for the release of the young James I from his English captivity in the Tower of London.) The six peel towers which were subsequently erected to defend the town have also disappeared.

As with Melrose and Kelso, the glory of Jedburgh is its Abbey. Like the other three great Border Abbeys, it also was founded by David I—in 1118—as a priory for Augustan canons regular from Beauvais, in France. In 1147 its status was raised to that of an Abbey. In 1285, Alexander III married his beautiful second wife Iolande, daughter of the Count de Dreux. It was at the wedding-feast held later in the castle that some misguided master of the revels allowed a figure representing Death to appear in the banquet-hall: an incident which sent a shudder of horror through the guests, and which the superstitious subsequently took to have been an omen presaging the king's tragic death at Kinghorn the following year.

From 1297 until 1300, the Abbey was so badly damaged by the English that the monks were unable to live in it. Repaired again, however, a period of relative peace and considerable prosperity allowed Jedburgh to flourish during the fourteenth century. Thereafter, the sad story of English vandalism monotonously repeats itself. The Abbey was damaged in 1410, 1416, 1464, and finally, after a struggle, captured by the Earl of Surrey on 23rd September, 1523. He caused it to be stripped of everything of value, then set it on fire. Force was used against what remained of it; in 1544 by Sir Ralph Evers, who, as we have seen, at least paid for his sacrilege with his life; and in 1545 by the Earl of Hertford.

The Reformers suppressed the Abbey in 1559, and the wily James VI appropriated its revenues. In the eighteenth century, a low roof was erected across the noble walls to make part of the nave usable as a parish kirk. But in 1875 the Marquis of Lothian had this later excrescence removed.

To-day, although only the church itself survives, Jedburgh is the most complete of the Border Abbeys. The central tower is entire: and though roofless, also standing are the centre of the nave, the northern transept and the two western bays of the choir. The styles are Norman and Transitional, and particularly notable is the arcading of the choir. The Abbey is now also in the care of the Ministry of Works.

A distinguished son of Hawick, the Reverend Thomas Somerville (1741-1830), was presented with the living of Jedburgh by George II in 1771, where he remained until his death. In his autobiography, *My Own Life and Times*, he tells of what must have been the only time the fields around Jedburgh bore tobacco:

" From the time of my settlement at Jedburgh, I rented a field of few acres, which, together with the glebe, occupied the attention of my leisure hours, and afforded me recreation and amusement. I even acquired the reputation of being a skilful farmer, to which I had not the slightest pretensions. The only speculation in farming, or indeed of any kind into which I had ever entered, was an attempt to profit by raising a crop of tobacco in the year 1782. Of the occasion and circumstances of this speculation I shall give some details, because at that time they excited great interest among agriculturalists in this and the adjacent counties. After the commencement of the American War, the price of tobacco had been gradually advancing, and in the year 1781 it reached the unprecedented rate of two shillings per pound. Dr. Jackson, a gentleman who possessed a small estate in the vicinity of Kelso, had, for two years preceding, laid out a few acres in the culture of tobacco, which he perfectly understood, having resided several years in America, and given particular attention to that branch of agriculture. If I rightly recollect, he mentioned to me his having sold the whole of his crop at the rate of two shillings and six pence per pound. His example and accredited success communicated the rage of speculation to all the neighbouring farmers. There was not, perhaps, a single farmer within the counties of Roxburgh, the Merse, and Selkirkshire, who did not devote a considerable part of his arable ground to this adventurous speculation, and many thousand acres were planted with tobacco in the spring of 1782. I did not escape the epidemical mania, and in partnership with Dr. Lindsay and Mr. Fair, two of my intimate acquaintances, I set apart five acres of the glebe for a tobacco plantation. By a combination of circumstances, unforeseen and unexpected, our industry was rendered unavailing. The weather, during the whole of the spring and summer 1782, was the most unfavourable that had occurred within the memory of any person then living . . . If such was the fate of our indigenous plants, the complete failure of tobacco, and the disappointment of the planters, could not be matter of surprise. A very small portion of it, perhaps not one acre out of twenty that had been planted, produced a mature crop, or such as was fit to enter the market . . . But, independent of natural causes, every hope of profit was frustrated by another ontoward event, which had never entered into the computation of the farmers. The tax on tobacco had been lately augmented, I believe, to the amount of one shilling and fourpence per pound. The dealers in American tobacco, and particularly the Glasgow merchants, who had their warehouses crammed with immense stores of it, and were selling it at an exhorbitant price. ignorant of the insignificance of the home crop, became jealous of its encroachment on their profits, and were suspected of communicating to the servants of the Government magnified estimates of its values, and of its operation to the detriment of the public revenue. The Crown lawyers, both in England and Scotland, were consulted, and, after mature deliberation, agreed in opinion that the Colonial laws of England were equally binding on both kingdoms, from the period of the Union, when all the privileges of Colonial trade were imparted to Scotland, and that all the growers of tobacco were strictly liable to the penalties enacted by the statute of the twelfth of Charles II. Though the advisers of the ministry admitted that unavoidable ignorance was a cogent and justifi-

able reason for remitting the heavy fines incurred by the trans-
gressors of the law, they judged it unwarrantable to indulge
them in an exemption from the duties imposed on the tobacco
of foreign growth.  In the end, after much correspondence, the
Government came to the resolution of instructing the Commis-
sioners of the Customs at Edinburgh to examine competent
witnesses for ascertaining the average value of the home grown
tobacco, and authorizing them to purchase it from the planters
at the price fixed upon (which was not more than fourpence per
pound), upon the condition of its being carried to Leith, where
it was to be weighed and consigned to the flames."

From Jedburgh, I drove out to Southdean, or Souden, above
the gate of whose ruined kirk a plaque reads:

" Here, in the year 1338, James, Earl of Douglas and the other
Scottish leaders assembled their forces, matured their plans and
began the invasion of England which culminated in the battle
of Otterburn. 'Where the dead Douglas won the field.'"

Ten days after James Thomson (1700-1748) was born at Ednam,
near Kelso, his father moved into the manse of Southdean, where
the young poet was brought up.  Much of the poet's descriptive
power lavished later in "The Seasons" must thus have been
gleaned from the countryside around Southdean.

I then turned and drove back through the mighty pass of Note
o' the Gate, past Carter Fell and the Larriston Fells, down
Liddesdale.  From Castleton Church, I drove up to lonely Hermitage.  Hermitage is in the centre of what was once the most lawless
part of the Borders, for at Larriston were the Elliots, at Mangerton
the Armstrongs, and, nearby, was the Debatable Land.

The oldest part of Hermitage Castle was built by Nicholas de
Sules, or Soulis, early in the thirteenth century.  His construc-
tional activities annoyed Henry III of England, who claimed that
the Castle menaced his side of the Border, though the "menace"
was further removed than his own castles of Norham and Wark,
on the Tweed!  However, King Henry was only looking for a
reason justifying invasion, and the building of Hermitage was
as good a one as any.

The Castle remained in the de Soulis family until 1320, when
Lord William de Soulis conspired against Robert the Bruce in
an attempt to get the crown for himself, on the grounds that he
was descended from an illegitimate daughter of Alexander II.  The
plot was discovered, however, and de Soulis ended his days a

prisoner in Dumbarton Castle, while Hermitage went to a natural son of the king.

As a reward for having driven the English out of Teviotdale, in 1358, Sir William Douglas received Hermitage from the king. Except for brief periods of English possession, it remained in the keeping of various branches of the Douglas family until 1491, when Douglas treachery led to its forfeiture, and subsequent bestowal upon the Earl of Bothwell. When the Bothwells in their turn were disgraced, the castle was given by James VI to the Buccleuchs, who retained it until it passed to the nation.

My tour of Roxburghshire finished at Hawick, the birthplace in 1880 of Scotland's most distinguished composer, Francis George Scott. During my wartime stay in Hawick, I looked distantly on Branxholme, one of the earliest homes of the Buccleuchs, the scene of Scott's *Lay of the Last Minstrel*, and of Allan Ramsay's song "The Bonnie Lass of Branksome": on Harden, famous as the home of the Scotts; on Cavers, once owned by the Douglases of Liddesdale; and on Stobs Castle, home of the Elliots.

The only building in Hawick itself which equals these old castles in years, is part of what is now the Tower Hotel. The original tower, owned by the Douglases of Drumlanrig, somehow escaped destruction at the hands of the Earl of Sussex in 1570, and a century later became the home of Anne Scott, later Countess of Buccleuch, who became Duchess of Buccleuch and Monmouth when she married Charles II's eldest natural son. It was already an inn in 1803, when, on September 27th, Sir Walter Scott, William and Dorothy Wordsworth dined and spent the night within its "walls above a yard thick".

Older antiquity is represented by the mote, which overlooks the main street. It is an artificial circular earthen mound constructed at the beginning of the Dark Ages for some purpose which we cannot now even guess at.

The church of St. Mary's, though in its present form no older than 1880, in which year a fire destroyed much of the structure put up in 1763, stands on the site of the original church of 1214. It was from this St. Mary's that Sir Alexander Ramsay of Dalhousie was captured while holding a court of justice on June 20th, by the men of Sir William Douglas of Hermitage, euphemistically dubbed the "Flower of Chivalry", in whose dungeons Dalhousie was subsequently starved to death.

As in most other Border towns, Hawick's industries were founded almost two centuries ago. The making of stockings on the stocking-frame was begun in 1771. Carpets, rugs and inkle tapes were also made in Hawick at this time, though by 1830 these industries had largely given place to the manufacture of twilled clothes, or tweels—later corrupted to tweeds. To-day, Hawick's tweeds and woollen goods are known the world over, and local agriculture prospers about the town. But the population of Hawick, like the populations of Selkirk and Galashiels, is being dangerously thinned by emigration to the central industrial belt, or to lands overseas.

Most of the Border towns have revived their ancient ceremonies of inspection. On the day of Hawick's Common Riding, the Cornet and his men ride round the municipal lands bearing the replica of a flag they captured from a group of English soldiers after Flodden.

II

My first visit to Selkirkshire[1] was made ignominiously on the back of a lorry in 1940. An army general had had the happy idea of toughening his very young troops, most of whom had never before walked more than ten consecutive miles, by making them march from Glasgow to the Borders—a distance of about 85 miles—in three consecutive days, bivouacking on the way. It should be unnecessary to explain further how I came to be driven up the hilly approach to Selkirk, my feet so blistered that I could hardly stand on them. This experience so scunnered me at the place—I still feel my feet twitching as I drive myself up the Selkirk braes—that for more than a decade I avoided visiting the county, accepting Wordsworth's verdict when, in "Yarrow Unvisited" he sang:

> '*What's Yarrow but a river bare,*
> *That glides the dark hills under?*
> *There are a thousand such elsewhere,*
> *As worthy of your wonder.*'

Like Wordsworth, I, too, was to feel a very different emotion the first time I drove down Yarrow. It was a clear spring afternoon, the hills and the trees flushed with that intense crisp green brilliance that so soon dulls beneath the flagging heat of the dog-days. I thought I had never seen any river course so beautiful. And it is not only the physical loveliness of Yarrow—or, indeed, of the whole of the county—which makes such an impact on the traveller; for, intermingled with his first impressions, come

[1] Formerly the Forest of Ettrick.

flooding in memories of the past: not only of the literary hey-day of the Borders, when Scott and Hogg, Lockhart and Leyden, wandered among its rivers and hills, and the jaunting Lakers came to enjoy and celebrate the charms of Sir Walter Scott's own countryside: but also of the earlier times, after the Union of the Crowns in the seventeenth century, when terrible punishments were wrought on the Borderers to cure them of their reiving habits; and of those times earlier still when raids across the marches were often either a political or a judicial necessity.

There are no Roman remains in Selkirkshire,[1] though there was probably a Roman station across the county border at Newstead, near the Eildons. Nor has any evidence of early "British" camps been found on the upper or middle reaches of the two principal rivers of the county, the Yarrow and the Ettrick. Prehistoric remains have, however, been found in Galashiels parish, at Rink Hill; and from Rin Hill or Torwoodlee, two miles northwest of the town of Galashiels, there runs the curious Pictish barrier, the Catrail, which—still a puzzle to archæologists—crosses the county as far south-west as Yarrow Church, and then passes into Roxburghshire.

Before becoming a part of Scotland about the year 1016, Selkirkshire was first part of the British kingdom of Strathclyde, and then of Northumbria. It was apparently almost entirely wooded—the Ettrick Forest was part of the old Caledonian Forest—and even in the days of the later Stewarts was a favourite royal hunting ground. Selechirche or Seles Chirche, the oldest forms of its name, probably means "the church among the hunter's huts or shiclings".

It was, indeed, the founding of the great Border churches that lit up the lights of history for us, after the silence of the Dark Ages. Apart from the Tironesian Abbey which David I, when still Earl David, founded in 1173 at Selkirk, but which proved to be too near Kelso, most of them lie outwith the boundaries of this county, though their near-presence no doubt made its influence felt during the outburst of religious fervour which surged through the thirteenth and fourteenth centuries. The monks were also farmers, physicians, and, in many other ways, the most important civilizers of their day.

The town of Selkirk itself once had a royal castle, which was also built by David I. Scottish kings from David I to Alexander III apparently spent a considerable part of their time in their

---

[1] Since writing the above, I learn that an archæological foray made in 1949 uncovered conclusive evidence that Roman occupation of the old Forest of Ettrick must have been considerable.

Border castles, though Roxburgh, both on strategic grounds and probably also because it was a castle of greater size, seems to have enjoyed a greater degree of the royal favour than Selkirk.

One of the earliest travellers to visit Selkirk, Sir Christopher Lowther, found evidence of careless good living when he arrived in the town on November 7th, 1629. " The inhabitants of Selkrig are a drunken kind of people," he declared. " Here had we a smoky chamber; and drunken unruly company thrust in upon us called for wine and ale, and left it in our score." Naturally, to have to pay for the drinks of strangers, especially "drunken unruly" strangers, does not put an itinerant diarist in the best of moods.

Like the other Border counties, Selkirkshire found itself repeatedly involved in the wars of succession which followed Alexander III's death. The list of the Selkirk contingent who signed Edward I's Ragman's Roll on submission at Berwick in 1296 provide for us a link with the Norman names of the nobles of the great mediæval Border families—de Witton, de Ailmer, de fiz Aruad, Crocelyn, de Crake, and many others now equally unknown, either because they have died out, or because, for political reasons, their owners adopted names with a more patriotic ring during the wars of succession.

While it cannot be said with absolute certainty that either the church of St. Mary at Selkirk, or that of St. Mary of the Lowes, was the scene of William Wallace's election as Guardian of Scotland after his Stirling Bridge adventure, Blind Harry declares:

*At Forrest kirk, a metyang ordaned he;*
*Thai chesd Wallace Scott's wardand to be.*[1]     [chose

At any rate, Selkirkshire frequently figured in the struggle for liberation, by providing bowmen and other forces. The thickly-wooded nature of her territory no doubt saved her from becoming a major battle-ground; in any case, Roxburgh was the key to the defence of the Middle Marches. But, like the other Border counties, Selkirkshire also knew periods of temporary defeat under the rule of the English.

During the fourteenth and fifteenth centuries, the Borders formed a sort of buffer, extending in both directions, between Scotland and England. Between raids and counter-raids, there were arranged truces, during which it was possible to attend to matters agricultural. But in common with all Scotland, Selkirkshire suffered grievously in 1513 at Flodden. Of the eighty

[1] Carluke is a rival claimant.

inhabitants of the town itself who went forth to fight, one alone returned—the town clerk, William Brydone, who was knighted by James V for his courage. It was from the memory of this local disaster, with its national implications, that Jean Elliot (1727-1805), daughter of Sir Gilbert Elliot of Minto, produced the first and finer version of " The Flowers of the Forest " in 1756.

> *We'll hear nae mair liltin' at the ewe milking,*
> *Women and bairns are heartless and wae;*
> *Sighin' and moanin' on ilka green loaning,*
> *The Flowers of the Forest are a' wede away.*

Like too many fine Scots songs, " The Flowers o' the Forest " was divorced from its beautiful old modal tune in the early nineteenth century, and forced into an outwardly gayer union with a much inferior tune. But many twentieth-century singers are striving to annul this second marriage, and to woo again the original air.

As a result of the weakness of the Scots after Flodden, the pressure of English raids increased. There were other immediate stimuli to the terrible raids of 1544 and 1548: but they made the cultivation of crops seem to many Borderers a precarious waste of time. So instead they cultivated their inclination (perhaps part of their turbulent Northumbrian racial inheritance) to live by reiving English cattle. Thus, when raiders threatened, folk would drive in their cattle to the barmkyn, or fortified enclosure, of the nearest peel tower, which would itself shelter them. The peel towers were, at one time, the characteristic Border fortifications. James V, indeed, ordered all major landlords in the Border counties to erect peel towers for the defence of the realm. Many of them are larochs now, visible only as mounds of stone to the walker over the lonely hillsides: others fret the skyline in gaunt ruin, the strength of their thick walls alone defying the elements. Perhaps because of their size, a surprising number of the smaller peel castles are still inhabited, though fewer have survived in Selkirkshire than in Roxburghshire.

The most famous of Selkirkshire's ruined fortalices is Newark, in Yarrow. Newark, or the " New Werke ", was probably already standing by 1429. It was first owned by the powerful Douglas family, until their downfall in 1455, when it was annexed to the crown. " Outlaw Murray " of the ballad—Murray of Hanginshaw—had it for a short time thereafter while he was sheriff of Ettrick Forest. But he was slain by Sir Walter Scott of

Buccleuch—"Wicked Wat"—who got himself made Keeper of Newark by James IV as a reward for his assistance in suppressing a Douglas rebellion. Later, a grant of the Castle of Newark was given to the Buccleuch's in perpetuity. It was burned by the English troops of Lord Grey in 1548.

Newark made its last flourish in history in 1645. Opposite the confluence of the Ettrick and the Yarrow lies the moor of Philiphaugh. On September 13th, the Parliamentarian Army of General Leslie surprised the Royalists of Montrose and defeated them in the battle that broke the Great Marquis. He, it seems, had withdrawn with his troopers to the town of Selkirk, possibly believing that his previous six battles had destroyed all effective armed resistance to the king in Scotland. But Leslie had marched up from Hereford, where he had brought about the royalist defeat at Marston Moor. And now, in spite of Montrose's strenuous efforts to rally his split and surprised troops, Leslie won the day. Tradition avers that, after the battle, a large detachment of royalist troops were marched to Newark Castle where, in a field still called "The Slain Men's Lea", they were peremptorily shot.

A ruin of a very different kind faces Newark, by the roadside across the water. It is the cottage where Mungo Park, the African explorer and friend of Sir Walter Scott, was born in 1771.

Another Yarrow peel is Dryhope, now only a sturdy stump. Once it was owned by a branch of the Scott family. Mary, a daughter of the house, known as "The Flower of Yarrow", became the bride of the most famous of all the Walter Scotts of Harden. It was from their grandson "Wattie Wudspurs" that the novelist Sir Walter Scott claimed descent.

It is possible to re-create with some degree of certainty the life-stories of the local chieftains and clansmen whose homes were in these peels; for out of the hand-on-sword violence of Border conflict grew a localized ballad literature, of which Scotland's store is infinitely richer than England's. Often, these old anonymous balladists reported on disasters and triumphs in so vivid a manner as to suggest that they themselves were actually eye-witnesses of the events they described. One of the finest of the many ballads having a connection with Yarrow, and indeed one of the best ballads relating to duels and combats, is "The Dowie Dens o' Yarrow". In 1609, a duel took place between a Scott of Tushielaw, and a Scott of Thirlestane. Seven years later, Walter Scott of Tushielaw secretly married Grace Scott of Thirlestane, without the knowledge of her family. As a result, a Scott of Thirlestane—perhaps one of Grace's brothers—and some

accomplices, murdered Tushielaw. Successive generations by whom the ballad-maker's words were polished and passed on, may have lightened a highlight here, or deepened a detail there; but the stark story still carries to us in words of uncompromising simplicity, which even its late eighteenth-century collector did not dare smooth over.

The permanent precariousness of Border life is vividly depicted in the opening stanza:

> *Late at e'en, drinking the wine,*
> *And ere they paid the lawing,*
> *They set a combat them between,*
> *To fight it in the dawing.*

In the morning, Scott's wife tried unsuccessfully to persuade her husband to " stay at hame "; but honour must be satisfied. Her lord fared forth, until in the appointed places " on the dowie houms of Yarrow ", he came upon nine armed men, and knew then that his foes meant dishonourable treachery. After wounding four of his enemies fatally, and killing five others outright, Scott himself was stabbed from behind. His lady found ten dead men on the field, though she had eyes for only one.

> *She kiss'd his cheek, she kaim'd his hair,*
> *She search'd his wounds all thorough;*
> *She kiss'd them till her lips grew red,*
> *On the dowie houms of Yarrow.*

For that ballad, in its present collected form, we are indebted to Sir Walter Scott. Aided by James Hogg, and to a lesser extent by John Leyden, Scott caught and preserved much of the Border literature when the advance of industrial civilization was just beginning to force it into oblivion. In one sense, the braes of Yarrow and of Ettrick are Scott's country: but they are even more truly the country of James Hogg (1770-1835), the Ettrick shepherd.

Hogg, a descendant of the Hoggs of Fauldhope, was born in a cottage, now demolished, near Ettrick Hall. His ancestors had held Fauldhope from the Scotts of Harden for centuries, and the Scotts held nearby Oakwood Tower—a peel now used as a grain store, but at least kept safe against the elements. Hogg himself shepherded first for the Laidlaws in Yarrow, with whom Scott found him. Thereafter, Scott helped Hogg to get his first book, *The Mountain Daisy*, published in 1807. On the proceeds which he received from its sale, together with the proceeds from the sale

*Roxburghshire: Abbotsford, home of Scott*

of a once highly-regarded technical book on the treatment of sheep's diseases, Hogg made a disastrous excursion into farming on his own account in Dumfriesshire. He next tried the literary life in Edinburgh, editing a short-lived periodical *The Spy*. Then, in 1817, the Duke of Buccleuch installed him in the farm of Altrive, where he lived until his death at the age of sixty-four. He was buried in Ettrick: but it is with Yarrow that he is most strongly associated. Altrive, which stands about two miles to the north-east of St. Mary's Loch, is a larger building to-day than it was in Hogg's time; but the place remembers his name. On a grassy hillock above the strip of land which separates St. Mary's Loch and the Loch o' the Lowes, and contains Tibbie Shiel's Inn—a favourite meeting-place of Hogg, Scott, "Christopher North", Leyden and Allan Cunningham—there is now a monument of the poet. From the top of a pedestal, his dog at his feet, the Ettrick Shepherd looks over the waters and the inn, towards the Ettrick hills. Beneath the figure is inscribed: "He taught the wandering winds to sing"—the last line of his first sustained poetic enterprise, "The Queen's Wake".

The angling poet Thomas Tod Stoddart was another of those who frequented Tibbie's inn.

"My introduction to this snug retreat," he recorded, "dates from the 28th of July, 1828. It was recommended to me by the Ettrick Shepherd, with whom I had previously become acquainted, and who at that time lived at Mount Berger, a farm lying along the banks of the Yarrow . . . Consequent on my first visit to Tibbie's inn, I was in the habit for a number of years of spending several weeks at St. Mary's Loch."

Hogg's description of the place is much more fanciful.

"A wren's nest is roond, and theekit wi' moss—sae is Tibbie's; a wren's nest has a wee bit canny hole in the side for the birdies to hap in and out o', aiblins wi' a bit hangin' leaf to hide and fend by way o' door—and sae has Tibbie's; a wren's nest's aye dry on the inside, though drappin' on the out wi' dew or rain—and sae is Tibbie's; a wren's nest for ordinar biggit in a retired spot, yet within hearin' o' the hum o' men as weel's o' water, be it linn or lake—and sae is Tibbie's: a wren's nest's no easy fund, yet when ye happen to keek on't, ye wunner hoo ye never saw the happit housie afore; therefore, sirs, for sic reasons, and a thousand mair, I observed, a cosie bield this o' Tibbie's—jist like a bit wren's nest."

In spite of the banter he gave her, Tibbie said of the Shepherd:

"Ay, for a' the nonsense that he wrat, Hogg was a gey sensible man—in some things! " And Stoddart described Tibbie as " one of the most notable women alive ".

The old wildness of the landscape around St. Mary's Loch has not been tamed by the restraining ribbon of the road. This is still, first and foremost, walkers' country, now as when young Thomas Carlyle made one of his walking excursions here with Edward Irving.

"The region was without roads, often without foot-tracks, had no vestige of an inn, so that there was a kind of knight-errantry in threading your way through it; not to mention the romance that naturally lay in its Ettrick and Yarrow, and old melodious songs and traditions. We walked up Meggat Water to beyond the sources, emerged into Yarrow not far above St. Mary's Loch; a charming secluded shepherd country, with excellent shepherd population—nowhere setting up to be picturesque, but everywhere honest, comely, well done-to, peaceable and useful. Nor anywhere without its solidly characteristic features, hills, mountains, clear rushing streams, cosy nooks and homesteads, all of fine rustic type; and presented to you 'in nature', not as in a Drury Lane with stagelights and for a purpose: the vast and yet not savage solitude as an impressive item: long miles from farm to farm, or even from one shepherd cottage to another. No company to you but the rustle of the grass underfoot, the tinkling of the brook, or the voices of innocent primæval things."

The clearest verse-picture—admittedly a water-colour—is perhaps that of St. Mary's Loch itself, sketched by Scott in *Marmion*.

> . . . *nor fen nor sedge,*
> *Pollute the pure lake's crystal edge;*
> *Abrupt and sheer the mountains sink*
> *At once upon the level brink;*
> *And just a trace of silver sand*
> *Marks where the water meets the land.*

I crossed from Yarrow to Ettrick over the mountain road which winds past the loneliest of all the peels, Kirkhope Tower, a sixteenth-century fortalice now, alas, falling into ruin. As the home of the senior sons of the Scotts of Harden, it is generally supposed to have been the place where Auld Wat first brought his bride, the Flower of Yarrow. I then drove up Ettrick, past Tushielaw, almost to the Pen. The tumbled-in Tushielaw Castle was the home of Adam Scott, known in James V's time as King of the Thieves, for which distinction that monarch caused him to be hanged. Then I turned about and drove down the Ettrick valley, in a drizzle of rain which absorbed half the mountains.

Almost everywhere upon which the traveller's eye rests in Ettrick, as in Yarrow, has been the scene of some vivid incident in Border foray, the inspiration of ballad, poem, or song: and it would be pleasant to recall them here. But the process would be interminable.

However, one, in particular—a comparatively modern one—kept singing itself aloud in my head—a song by a member of the distinguished Berwickshire family of Spottiswoode, who married the brother of a Duke of Buccleuch, and so became Lady John Scott:

> When we first rade down Ettrick,
> Our bridles were ringing, our hearts were dancing,
> The waters were singing, the sun was glancing,
> An' blithely our voices rang out thegither,
> As we brushed the dew frae the blooming heather,
> When we first rade down Ettrick.

> When we next rade down Ettrick,
> The day was dying, the wild birds calling,
> The wind was sighing, the leaves were falling,
> An' silent an' weary, but closer thegither,
> We urged our steeds thro' the faded heather,
> When we next rade down Ettrick.

> When I last rade down Ettrick,
> The winds were shifting, the storm was waking,
> The snow was drifting, my heart was breaking,
> For we never again were to ride thegither,
> In sun or storm on the mountain heather,
> When I last rade down Ettrick.

But Selkirkshire does not live in the past, richly-stored though that past be; and its two towns—Selkirk and Galashiels on the Gala Water—are both flourishing centres of Border industry. Since the seventeenth century, and more especially after the peace which the Union of the Crowns brought to the Borders, sheep have flocked the hills, and the towns have developed as centres of woollen manufacture.

Manufacturing in Galashiels, indeed, is said to go as far back as 1622, where there is a mention of it in a charter. The very name of the place is said to derive from *Gala* and *shieling*, the huts of the shepherds. But the present town grew up in the manufacturing spurt of the early eighteenth century.

When Dorothy Wordsworth visited the town with her brother in 1803, she recorded that she:

" Went through a part of the village of Galashiels, pleasantly situated on the banks of the stream; a pretty place it once has been, but a manufactory is established there; and a townish bustle and ugly stone houses are fast taking place of the brown-roofed thatched cottages, of which a great number yet remain, partly overshadowed by trees."

Up until 1829, the chief products from the mills were blankets and cloths made from the home-grown wools, as well as knitting yarns and flannels. But that year a depression forced the industrialists to devise new variants, so they switched over to the manufacture of tartans and tweeds. These things are still made, as well as high quality finished woollen goods. Galashiels also has a few engineering factories, some of which supply and replace the machines used in the weaving industry.

Modern Galashiels straggles. And though the " Braw, braw lads o' Gala Water "—sung, incidentally, to one of the oldest and finest Lowland folk-airs—have as proud a Border tradition as any, little about the town remains to commemorate it. Old Gala House is Galashiel's only stone-and-mortar glory: a huge, rambling mansion, part sixteenth and part seventeenth century, once owned by the Scotts of Gala. Now, one of its rooms is the headquarters of the Galashiels Art Club, who have removed the lath and plaster ceiling and restored the beautiful original painted ceiling which bears the date 1635.

In order to try to stem Border depopulation, a new town is being laid out between Darnick and Galashiels, reaching to the edge of Abbotsford. Forced through by Government planners who, almost simultaneously, agreed to the dismantling of the Edinburgh–Carlisle Border railway, and the ripping up of the track, it seems to stand small prospect of thriving economically. Environmentally, its impact appears certain to be disastrous.

Being the county town, Selkirk wears more of a professional air, though at the foot of the hill upon which it is built; it also has busy mills. But, like all the Border towns, its population is ageing and shrinking as a high proportion of its people emigrate to the already overcrowded central industrial belt of Scotland. In the market place stands a statue of Sir Walter Scott in his robes as sheriff of Selkirkshire, put up in 1839. Another monument, erected in 1859, celebrates the memory of Mungo Park. On the West Port, a tablet commemorates the Old Forest Inn where, in May 1787, Burns stayed during his Border tour. Almost within view of Mungo Park's statue, a plaque, showing the head of the poet in relief, commemorates " J. B. Selkirk ", the pseudonym of a local poet, James B. Brown, whose work achieved more than a local reputation towards the close of the last century.[1] Yet when writing in English, he was Tennysonian; when writing in Scots, Kailyaird. To turn Yarrow into a sentimental kailyaird as he did successfully in " Death in Yarrow " was no small achievement in literary perversity. Much better to remember him as he wrote of a Border burn, his sentimentality for once satisfactorily firmed by the strength of his native patriotism.

> *Ah, Tam! Gie me a Border burn*
> *That canna rin without a turn,*
> *And wi' its bonnie babble fills*
> *The glens amang oor native hills.*
> *How men that ance have ken'd aboot it*
> *Can leeve their efter-lives without it*
> *I canna tell, for day and nicht*
> *It comes unca'd for to my sicht.*
> *I see't this moment, plain as day,*
> *As it comes bickerin' owre the brae,*
> *Atween the clumps o' purple heather*
> *Glistenin' in the summer weather,*
> *Syne divin' in below the grun'*
> *Where, hidden frae the sicht and sun,*
> *It gibbers like a deid man's ghost*
> *That clamours for the licht it's lost,*
> *Till oot again the loupin' limmer,*
> *Comes dancin' doon through shine and shimmer*
> *At heidlang pace, till wi' a jaw*
> *It jumps the rocky waterfa'.*

[1] Andrew Lang (1844-1912) was born in Selkirk in premises which are now the Viewfield Nursing Home. Lang was, of course, a much more versatile and talented man of letters than Brown. " Dear Andrew, with the brindled hair ", as R.L.S. called him, made less of an impact as poet than as historian. But " St. Andrews by the Northern sea " is sure of its place in our literature as well as the poem " Twilight on Tweed ", quoted at the beginning of this chapter.

# CHAPTER VI

# PEEBLESSHIRE

Tweeddale, comprehending the Sheriffdom of Peebles, is so called from the river Tweed, which hath its rise and fountain in this country, near by a mile to the east of the place where the Shire marches and borders with the Stewartry of Annandale, at a place called Tweed's Cross, on the high way, about four miles to the north of Moffat. . . .

From this fountain springeth Tweed, and runneth, for the most part, with a soft yet trotting stream, towards the whole length of the country, in several meanders. . . .

This country is almost every where swelling with hills; which are, for the most part, green, grassy and pleasant, except a ridge of bordering mountains, betwixt Minch-Muir and Henderland, being black, craigie, and of melancholy aspect, with deep and horrid precipices, a wearisome and comfortless piece of way for travellers.

DR. ALEXANDER PENNECUIK OF NEWHALL, 1715.

So wrote the medical laird of Newhall in his *Description of Tweeddale,* one of the earliest topographical accounts to be written about Scotland by a Scotsman. It is a tender account, touched with that love of local hill and vale which is so strong a part of the Border character. "A good sort of man, 'tho' a very bad poet," is how an anonymous contemporary described Pennecuik.[1] His poetry is, indeed, both bad and bawdy; yet he shows a felicitous imagination when he describes the young Tweed as "a soft yet trotting stream".

It rises, as Pennecuik indicates, from a spring at Tweed's Well, high in the hills, and it flows the first thirty-six miles of its course through Peeblesshire. Until it reaches Biggar Water, the Tweed flows parallel to the Clyde, about seven miles apart. Indeed, head-streams from the two rivers rise within three-quarters of a mile of each other, and the Coulter Burn, when in spate, sometimes acts as a living link between them, carrying Tweed salmon into the upper Clyde.

The Tweed and its tributaries give Peeblesshire its character; for the main road and the railway line both follow the river, and Peebles itself is the only place that may with any accuracy be called a town.

---

[1] Who should not be confused with the other contemporary Alexander Pennecuik, also a bad poet, who published alternative versions of several of Allan Ramsay's poems. See note on page 116.

As the Tweed leaves its mountain fastness, flowing past the hamlet of Tweedshaws, it is joined by the first of its many tributaries, Cor Water. Most of the glens in this parish of Tweedsmuir, from where the novelist John Buchan (1875-1940) took his title, have brought down legends with their brown water.

The most interesting of these not improbable tales is carried by the Badlieu Burn. About the year A.D. 1000, a Scots king, Kenneth the Grim, whose name is unknown to historians, left his Queen in his palace at Polmood to hunt in the forest of Caledon. Zeal for the chase overcame discretion, and by nightfall he found himself far from home. So he knocked at the door of a hut at Badlieu, and found himself received by a pretty girl, somewhat unfortunately named Bonnie Bertha of Badlieu.

Kenneth the Grim fell in love with the lady, increased the frequency and lengthened the duration of his hunting expeditions, and in due course had a son by Bertha. Not unnaturally, however, the Queen noticed that her royal consort was taking less interest in her than of yore; so she set out to discover the reason.

Then the King went off to fight the invading Danes. On his way back from the battlefield, where he was the victor, he was met by a messenger who told him that the Queen was dying of a fever. He hurried home to Polmood, to find that she was already dead. So at once he rode off to Badlieu to make Bertha his queen. But when he reached the Badlieu Burn he found the hut in ruins, and the murdered bodies of his mistress and his son inside. His late Queen had had her revenge.

On the left, Old Burn and the burns of Glenbreck and Glenwhappen mell their waters with the swelling Tweed: on the right, the burns Fingland, Hawkshaw and Fruid Water. Three miles up the glen through the Fruid falls, the stump of an old peel is all that remains of one of the earliest homes of the Frasers of Oliver Castle —earliest and most powerful of the feudal barons of Peeblesshire —who owned Tweedsmuir from the thirteenth to the seventeenth centuries. Sir Simon Fraser was captured by the English army at Dunbar in 1296, taken prisoner to London, forced to fight for English Edward in France, and then released with honours, presumably because the English king now regarded him as a safe security risk. But as soon as Sir Simon returned to Scotland, he got in touch with Wallace, fought with him until the end, and suffered an equally barbarous death.

Tweedsmuir Church perpetuates memories of another kind, for round it still stand stones commemorating fallen Covenanters. Up the Talla burn, a Conventicle was held in 1682 which Claverhouse did not discover. It was one of the largest ever convened in the Borders, and is imaginatively described by Scott in *The Heart of Midlothian*. Talla itself, with its feeding tributaries Talla Linn and Gameshope Water, is now a reservoir for Edinburgh. It is here, on either side of the valley of the Meggat, which leads down into Selkirkshire, that the highest of the Border hills stands sentinel: Hart Fell (2651 feet), White Coomb (2695 feet) and Moll's Cleuch Dod (2571 feet) in one cluster; Broad Law (2754 feet), Cramalt Craig (2773 feet) and Dollar Law (2680 feet) in the more easterly mass.

As the Tweed flows on, it is joined by the burns of Kingledores and Stanhope. Kingledores is reputed to have been the site of Burns's Linkumdoddie, where "Willie Wastle dwalt" with his singularly uncomely wife.

Drumelzier lays claim to be the birthplace of an equally improbable character, Merlin Caledonius—there were several Merlins—Druidic prophet, poet and friend of the unsuccessful leader of the Cymric tribe, who was slain in the Battle of Ardderyd, fought in the Forest of Caledon in 573.

If there is some doubt about the flesh-and-blood existence of Willie Wastle and Merlin, there is none at all about the umquhile substantiality of the lusty Tweedies, whose principal stronghold was for long Drumelzier Castle. To disagree with a Tweedie was at one time a certain way of becoming involved in a blood feud. Amongst the most famous private killings in which the Tweedies were involved were the murders of Lord Fleming, David Rizzio and Patrick Veitch.

James Tweedie of Drumelzier decided in 1524 that he wanted to marry Catherine Fraser, the heiress of Fruid. But the Great Chamberlain of Scotland[1] wanted Miss Fraser to marry his son, Malcolm: which she did. Thereupon, James Tweedie led his clansmen against a force of Flemings, as a result of which encounter Lord Fleming was murdered. Tweedie himself was fined, while his associates were exiled. But he failed to pay the fine. James V let him off, provided he agreed to found a Chaplaincy at Biggar, endowed with enough money to pay for a suitable number of Masses on behalf of the murdered laird's soul. Tweedie soon married the widowed Catherine Fleming.

For the part in Rizzio's murder, the Tweedies escaped punishment only because the Government was, at that moment, too occupied with its own affairs to pursue turbulent Border rebels. The Tweedies also escaped direct punishment for the murder of Patrick Veitch, son of the "Deil of Dawyck" (so called because of his remarkable strength), near Neidpath Castle, about the close

[1] A Fleming.

of the sixteenth century. But in the feud which followed, young John Tweedie, tutor of Drumelzier, was murdered by Veitch of Syntoun in the High Street of Edinburgh. Early in the seventeenth century, Veitch of Dawyck killed Tweedie of Drumelzier in a duel by the banks of the Tweed, where they had met by chance. Thereafter, the Tweedies quickly lost their power to the Frasers, and the last Tweedie of Drumelzier ended up a bankrupt in the Tolbooth of Edinburgh. To-day, Drumelzier is a pathetic ruin and none of the land in Tweeddale is owned by a Tweedie.

Biggar Water, which joins the Tweed as it settles on its eastern course, has, as one of its main tributaries, the Broughton Burn. Near the junction, there once stood the home of the Murrays of Broughton. (It was burned in 1773, and the stones were subsequently used in the building of neighbouring farms.) The Murrays succeeded the Tweedies at Stanhope, their most famous representative being John Murray, who became secretary to Prince Charles Edward Stewart; but who, as Mr. Evidence Murray, sullied for ever his reputation by buying his own life at the expense of former Jacobite comrades, most notably Simon Fraser, Lord Lovat.

On the Kilbucho Burn, which flows into Biggar Water from the south, stands Kilbucho Place, a pleasing seventeenth-century L-shaped laird's house built or acquired in 1628 by John Dickson, later Lord Hartree, with whose descendants it still remains.

As the Tweed flows on to meet Lyne Water, it passes Dawyck, on the right, once the home of the Veitches. At Dawyck, the first horse-chestnuts and the first larches to be imported into Scotland were planted in 1650 and 1725 respectively, the chestnuts by the last of the Veitches, the larches by James Nasmyth, botanist and pupil of Linnaeus. Nasmyth also introduced the silver fir to Scotland in 1735.

Across the river lies Stobo, with its splendid nineteenth-century castle by Archibald Elliot and its charming kirk—part of it thirteenth-century Norman—the jougs still hanging in the park, rusty now for want of necks to pillory. Stobo probably gave its name to a local poetic priest, John Reid: the "gude, gentill Stobo", whose death was one of the many catalogued literary demises which perturbed William Dunbar.

Lyne Water rises in the Pentland hills, and flows southwards through West Linton. It passes the ruins of Drochil Castle, built by James Douglas, Earl of Morton, but not occupied by him on account of his trial and execution by the Maiden at Edinburgh Cross, for his part of the murder of Darnley. Nearer the junction with Tweed, Lyne Water passes the site of a Roman camp.

Manor Water, which joins the Tweed just before Peebles, has up its glen the cottage of poor, distorted David Ritchie (1740-1811), the original of Scott's novel *The Black Dwarf*. Scott met Ritchie when he passed through Manor on his way to the Lake District in 1787. (Scott stayed the night at Hallyards, the country seat of Professor Adam Fergusson.) In "The Black Dwarf's Bones", one of the essays in Dr. John Brown's *Horæ Subsecivæ*, the author publishes a description of "Bowed Davie" by Robert Craig, a surgeon at Peebles, who had known many of Ritchie's contemporaries.

"His forehead was very narrow and low, sloping upwards and backwards, something of the hatchet shape; his eyes deep-set, small, and piercing; his nose straight, thin as the end of a cut of cheese, sharp at the point, nearly touching his fearfully projecting chin; and his mouth formed nearly a straight line; his shoulders rather high, his body otherwise the size of ordinary men; his arms were remarkably strong . . . .

His legs beat all power of description; they were bent in every direction, so that Mungo Park, then a surgeon at Peebles, who was called to operate him for a strangulated hernia, said he could compare them to nothing but a pair of corkscrews; but the principal turn they took was from the knee outwards, so that he rested on his inner ankles, and the lower part of his tibias."

A little to the east of the junction of Manor and Tweed stands Neidpath, on the top of a rocky hill on the south bank of the river. It was originally a peel tower owned by the Frasers of Oliver Castle, at one time the earliest and most powerful of the Peeblesshire feudal barons. Mary, the daughter of Wallace's comrade-in-arms, Sir Simon Fraser, married Sir Gilbert Hay, having heired both Oliver and Neidpath Castles. Thomas de Haya, a descendant of theirs who lived at the beginning of the fifteenth century, married a daughter of Lord Gifford of Yester. Sir William Hay of Yester added to the original castle of Neidpath. Charles I made the eighth Lord Yester Earl of Tweeddale. His son, the first Marquis of Tweeddale, wrote one of the earliest love-songs in which the beauties of the Tweed are celebrated.

*When Maggie and me were acquaint,*
*I carried my noddle fu' high,*
*Nae lint'white in a' the gay plain,*
*Nae gowd-spink sae bonnie as she.*

*I whistled, I piped, and I sang;*
*I woo'd, but I cam' nae great speed;*
*Therefore I maun wander abroad,*
*And lay my banes far frae the Tweed.*

Though he " cam nae great speed " at his wooing, the poetic
Marquis indulged in too great a haste in his building operations.
As a result, his family had to sell their estate to the first **Duke of
Queensberry.**

The second Duke of Queensberry became Lord March. He, and
later his son, both lived at Neidpath. The fourth Duke of
Queensberry—the hard-drinking, heavy-gambling. womanizing
" Old Q "—having no heir to think about, stripped Neidpath of
its timber, and so earned Wordsworth's poetic apostrophe:

*Degenerate Douglas! Oh! the unworthy lord!*
*Whom mere despite of heart could so far please,*
*And love of havoc (for with such disease*
*Fame taxes him) that he could send forth word*
*To level with the dust a noble horde,*
*A brotherhood of venerable trees,*
*Leaving an ancient dome and towers like these*
*Beggared and outraged! . . .*

On " Old Q's " death, the Earldom of March passed to the Earl
of Wemyss, who now owns Neidpath.

Further up the glen, relics of pre-history are to be found: a
cup-marked monolith, now on its side, near Bellanridge: a
tumulus known as the " Giant's Grave ", in Glenrath Hope; and
the Ship Stone, under Posso Crags.

Peebles lies at the foot of Eddleston Water. The southbound
road from Edinburgh and Dalkeith threads through the Eddleston valley. About the middle of the fourteenth century, the
lands of Eddleston, then owned by the Bishopric of Glasgow,
were made into a barony, known as the White Barony, while the
lands to the west became the Black Barony, and as such the
territory of the Murrays.

No one is quite certain of the derivation of Peebles. (It
certainly has no more to do with little stones than Dunbarton-
shire's Bearsden ever had to do with bears.) The generally
accepted derivation is from the Welsh *pabell*, a tent. Legend
brings St. Mungo on a visit to a Peebles. The township to
which he came could, indeed, have been little more than a
collection of *pebyll* (to give the old word its plural form) grouped

around a castle. History shows that David II made it a royal burgh in 1367. Its mediæval castle, which has now completely disappeared, was a hunting lodge used by David I, Malcolm IV, William the Lion, Alexander I and Alexander II. Edward I used the castle as a base for less amiable sallies; and Robert the Bruce gave the town a charter. now lost, granting it the right to hold an annual fair.

As that rhyming propagandist John Hardyng relates with relish, the Vice-Admiral of England, Sir Robert Umphraville, raided Peebles in 1367, when he:

> *Brent the town upon their market day,*
> *And mete their cloth with spears and bowis sere*
> *By his bidding without any nay.*

Peebles features not infrequently in early Scots poetry. The poet king James I is supposed to have visited the town more than once, to see the old festival of Beltane (May 1st). He is popularly credited with the authorship of the poems *Peblis to the Play* and *Chrystis Kirk on the Green*, wherein Peebles is also mentioned. The vernacular gusto of these two performances differs so markedly from the courtly strains of *The Kingis Quhair* that some critics, notably W. F. Skeat, have doubted the attribution, preferring James V as temperamentally a more probable author. But the alliterative style of the two poems concerned suggests an earlier date of composition than the period of Sir David Lyndsay: and, as T. F. Henderson pointed out, a similar argument might be used to suggest that Cowper could not possibly have written *John Gilpin*. In any case, both are racy pictures of rural celebration, abounding in vivid portraits of the rustic merry-makers. Thus in *Chrystis Kirk*, the village maiden who perhaps ettled to be loved above her station, is delicately portrayed.

> *Of all thir madynis myld as meid*    [these; meed
>   *Wes nane so gympt as Gillie,*    [slim
> *As ony ross hir rude was reid*    [rose; cheeks
>   *Hir lyre was lyk the lillie*    [skin
> *Fow yellow, yellow wes hir heid,*    [full
>   *Bot scho of lufe wes sillie.*
> *Thocht all hir kin had sworn hir deid,*    [though
>   *Scho wald haif bot sweit Willie*
>     *Allone,*
> *At Chrystis Kirk of the grene.*

> Scho skornit Jok and skraipit at him,        [jibed
> And murgeon'd him with mokkis;        [derided
> He wald haif luvit, scho wald nocht lat him,
> For all his yellow loikkis:
> He chereist hir, scho bad ga chat him,        [hang
> Scho compt him nocht twa clokkis [counted; beetles
> So schamefully his schort goun set him
> His lymmis wes lyk twa rokkis,        [distaffs
> Scho said,
> At Chrystis Kirk of the grene.[1]

From the reign of James III comes another early poetic performance in which Peebles features, "The thrie Tailes of the thrie Priests of Peblis", possibly the work of "gude gentill Stobo". Three genial priests sit down in comfort to enjoy good food and each other's talk.

> In Peblis town sum tyme, as I heard tell,
> The formest day of February befell,
> Thrie Priests went unto collatioun
> Into ane privie place of the said toun,
> Where that thay sat richt soft and unfutesair:
> Thay luifit not na rangald nor repair      [wrangle; hurly-burly
> And gif I sall the suith reckin and say,        [if
> I traist it was upon Sanct Brydis day,
> Where that thay sat full easily and soft,
> With monie loud lauchter upon loft,        [much loud laughter
> And wit ye weil thir thrie thay made gude cheir—
> To them thair was na dainties than too dear—
> With thrie fed capons on a spit with creische [basting on a spit
> With monie uther sindrie divers meis;        [many other kinds of
> And them to serve thay had nocht bot a boy;        [meat
> Fra cumpanie thay keipit them sa coy;
> They luifit nocht with ladry nor with lown        [knave; rogue
> Nor with trumpours to travel through the town,        [tricksters
> But with themself what thay wald tell or crack,
> Umquhyle sadly, umquhyle jangle and jak.  [sometimes sadly;
>                        [sometimes talking about trifles

> Thus sat thir thrie besyde ane felloun fire        [fierce
> While thair capons were rostit limb and lyre.        [skin

---

[1] The eighteenth-century poet, Allan Ramsay, added some supplementary cantos to *Chrystis Kirk*.

*Befoir them was soon set a roundel bricht;* [table top on a trestle
*Ane with ane clean claith fynelie dicht* [laid
*It was ouirset, and on it breid was laid.*
*The eldest then began the grace and said,*
*And blissit the breid with "Benedicete",*
*With "Dominus, Amen" sa mot I thee.*

After they had eaten well and "drunken about a quarte", they
began to tell their tales; kindly, moral stories, such as Friar John's
Tale, in which the son who inherited his father's wealth is shown
as coming soon to ruin, while the son of the poor man prospers
under early adversity. Indeed, the author of the poem gives us
one of our earliest pictures of that figure so revered by the Scots
down the centuries, the Self-Made Man. We are shown first the
poor boy equipped only:

*With hap and half penny, and a lamb's skin;* [chance
*And purelie ran fra toun to toun on feit* [poorly
*And than richt oft wetshod, werie and weit.* [wet

Then we are shown the prosperous man, who ultimately
becomes the owner of a fine ship:

*He sailit owre the sea sa oft and oft*
*Till at the last ane seemly ship he coft,* [bought
*And waxe sa ful of warldis welth and win,*
*His hands he wish in ane silver basin . . .* [washed
*Rich wes his gounis with uther garments gay:*
*For Sunday silk, for ilk day grene and gray.* [every; green
*His wyfe was cumlie cled in scarlet reid,*
*Scho had no doubts of dearth of ail nor breid* [fear

In spite of his priestly calling, Friar John clearly could not
disguise his admiration for this prosperous fellow, whose characteristics differ so little from those of an eighteenth-century tobacco
lord, or a nineteenth-century merchant prince.

But the worthy folk of Peebles, whether they took their leisure
quietly, enjoying good eating and good talking, or more boister-
ously, drinking and dancing at "Peblis to the Play", had their
full share of troubles. In 1545 the town suffered from the great
punitive Border raid of the English army. "Ane grate fyre"
destroyed the rebuilt town even more thoroughly in 1604. Forty-
one years later, a plague swept through Peebles. Scarcely had
survivors recovered from the panic which the spread of the disease

had produced than Montrose arrived in the town, fresh from his defeat at Philiphaugh, but in high—though, as it proved un-justified—hopes of raising support from the Peeblesshire lairds. A division of Cromwell's army stationed itself in the town five years later, while attempting to reduce Neidpath Castle. Their horses were quartered in the Bishop Jocelyn's Parish Church of St. Andrew, built in 1195. (Only the tower and a part of the walls still stand.) Almost a century later, a division of Prince Charles's army passed through Peebles on its way into England.

Modern Peebles, mainly because of its magnificent natural setting, is an oddly attractive little town. Yet its High Street is a jumble of architectural styles, few of them indigenous. Not much of the old town survives. But if little of the stone and mortar of Peebles claims our attention because of its intrinsic worth, some of it has interesting associations. Queensberry Lodging, for instance, where "Old Q" was born in 1725. Now, it is a public building, appropriately named the Chambers's Institute; for the brothers William Chambers (1800-1883) and Robert Chambers (1802-1871) were born in a house in the Biggies-knowe, and William bought the lodging for the town. They achieved a double fame with their *Chambers's Journal* and *Chambers's Encyclopædia*. But Robert's contribution to Scotland's literary lore was by far the more valuable.[1] William was responsible for the somewhat unskilful restoration of St. Andrew's Tower. William ultimately became Lord Provost of Edinburgh, where a street is named after him.

Another Border figure, who made himself an academic name, was Professor John Veitch; he was educated at Peebles Grammar School. Nobody remembers his own poems nowadays, nor his treatises on moral philosophy. But his *History and Poetry of the Scottish Border* is still indispensable to anyone seriously interested in the study of Border balladry.

As the Tweed leaves Peebles, the strip of green fertile fields along its banks widens a little and the river winds towards Inner-leithen. Malcolm IV's son is said to have been drowned in a pool of the river Leithen while out hunting in 1159. When the Prince's body was recovered from the Tweed, it was taken to the church of Innerleithen. So the king granted the church to the monks of Kelso, granting it also the right of sanctuary.

Of all the places which benefited from the invention of Sir Walter Scott, few gained more romantic lustre than Innerleithen. In his novel *St. Ronan's Well*, he associated the spring, hitherto

---

[1] *Traditions of Edinburgh* (1824), *Popular Rhymes of Scotland* (1826) and *Domestic Annals of Scotland* (1856-61) were his most important books.

*Peeblesshire: Manor Valley*

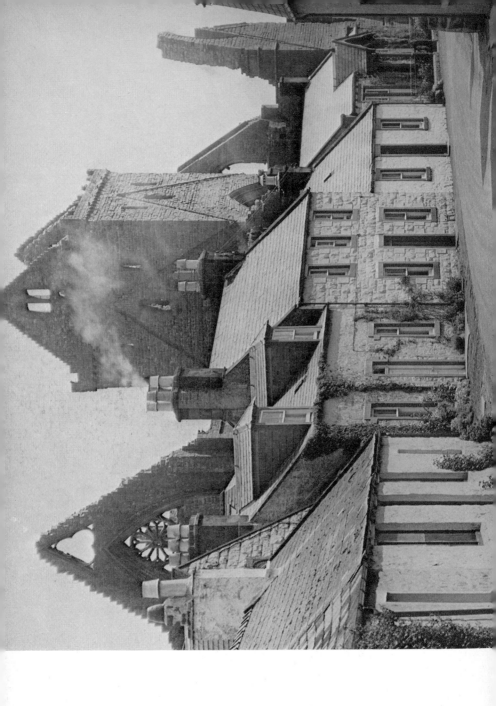

called the " Doo's Well ", with the eighth-century saint, though St. Ronan had no earlier demonstrable connection with the place.[1] The result was that, within a few years of the novel's appearance, Innerleithen had acquired a reputation for the supposed medicinal properties of its waters. In point of fact, however, the lineaments which Scott refashioned for *St. Ronan's Well* were drawn not only from Innerleithen, but from Gilsland in Cumberland—where Scott met his wife, Charlotte Charpentier, or Carpenter—and from Peebles. Indeed, Meg Dodds of Cleikum Inn had a double original: the mistresses of both the Cross Keys in Peebles and the inn at the Moorfoot village of Howgate.

To try to trace the physical starting points of the journeyings of a great imagination is, however amusing, in the long run irrelevant. But Innerleithen naturally made the most of its new-found romanticism. James Hogg played a leading part in organizing the St. Ronan's Games, from 1827 until 1835, getting Scott, Lockhart, Blackwood, " Christopher North " and Henry Glassford Bell to lend their support. The modern counterpart of the Shepherd's junketings is the Cleikum Ceremony and Games.

To-day, Innerleithen earns its livelihood neither by romance nor by games, but through its textile mills first set up in 1788 by Alexander Brodie, a Traquair man who had become a wealthy ironmaster in London.

The ancient house of Traquair stands a little to the south of Innerleithen, on the opposite bank of the Tweed. It is almost certainly one of the oldest inhabited houses in Scotland. It was a home of Scotland's kings from David I to Alexander III; until, in fact, the War of Succession made the Borders too dangerous a place for the Scots royal household to live in in safety. It was from Traquair that, in 1176, William the Lion granted Bishop Jocelyn the charter which resulted in the founding of Glasgow.

Traquair has been in the possession of several Border families. One of its less lucky owners was the musician Rodgers, one of James III's unpopular favourites, who ended his days in 1482 suspended from Lauder Brig at the end of a rope. In 1633, a Stewart owner was made the first Earl of Traquair.

Prudent fellows were these Traquairs. When Montrose sought aid from the Earl after Philiphaugh, Traquair would have nothing to do with him. A century later, another gallant royalist invited a later Earl to march with him to regain the throne of his fathers. Traquair once again turned him away. This time,

[1] The Celtic Cross, now in the Public Library, indicates that the Columban Church must have had an early cell in the district.

*Kirkcudbrightshire: Sweetheart Abbey*

however, if tradition is to be believed, the Earl at least gave a clear indication of the nature of his sympathies. When the Prince passed through the great gates at the end of the avenue, and they were shut behind him, the Earl declared that they would never again be opened until a Stewart ascended the British throne. They have remained closed ever since.

The first Earl of Traquair has had himself made celebrated by an eighteenth-century ballad, as a result of the methods he adopted to make sure he would win a law suit raised against him in the Court of Session.

Finding out that, because of the casting vote of Lord President Durie, the case was likely to go against him, Traquair engaged a Border freebooter, Will Armstrong—a descendant of the famous Johnnie Armstrong—to abduct Durie. Armstrong seized the Lord President on Leith Sands, trussed the judge up behind him and made off as hard as he could ride to the ruined peel of Graeme, near Moffat, in Annandale. Durie's horse was found wandering riderless, so the judge was presumed drowned and his vacant place on the bench was filled with one more sympathetic to Traquair's case. When the suit was finally settled in Traquair's favour, Will Armstrong trussed Durie up again for the return journey, and set him down at exactly the spot where he had lifted him three months before. Durie at first believed that he had been transported by evil spirits, though he later discovered the real nature of his journey.

Fate had a paik in store for Traquair himself, however, for he ended his days a beggar in the streets of Edinburgh, his estate sequestrated after he had been taken prisoner at Preston in 1648, fighting for the royalist cause.

The main part of Traquair House as it now stands dates from the seventeenth century. The rooms in the original house, where Mary Queen of Scots was so discourteously treated by Darnley during their stay in 1566 that their host saw fit to reprove the "lang lad" for his lack of gallantry, are still preserved.

The village of Traquair, which lies further up the Quair valley, is now a peaceful agricultural hamlet. But it has inspired many verses, notably "Lucy's Flittin'", by Will Laidlaw, Scott's amanuensis, and "The Bush aboon Traquair" by a nineteenth-century principal of Glasgow University, John Campbell Shairp. In answer to his own questions:

> *And what saw ye there*
> *At the bush aboon Traquair?*
> *Or what did ye hear that was worth your heed?*

198

He answers:

> *I heard the cushies croon.*
> *Thro' the gowden afternoon,*
> *And the Quair burn singin' doun to the vale o' Tweed.*

As the Tweed sweeps down this vale, it passes through Walker-burn, a village founded in 1854 for the manufacture of woollen goods. Then the noble river flows broadly over the county border, past Elibank and Ashiestiel and Fairnilee, on its way to meet the Ettrick Water.

CHAPTER VII

# DUMFRIESSHIRE

From Drumlanrig, we pursued the course of the Nid (Nith) to
Dumfries, which stands several miles above the place where the river
falls into the sea, and is, after Glasgow, the handsomest town I have
seen in Scotland. The inhabitants, indeed, seem to have proposed
that city as their model; not only in beautifying their town and
regulating its policie; but also in prosecuting their schemes of commerce and manufacture, by which they are grown rich and oppulent.
TOBIAS SMOLLETT, 1766.

WHETHER you see her as she once liked to be called, " The
Queen of the South ", or, as she was perhaps more accurately
dubbed by Burns, " Maggy by the banks o' Nith, a dame wi'
pride eneugh ", Dumfries is indubitably still a pleasant town.
Her former status as a port, which gave rise to the grander title,
was only granted to her out of necessity, for the channel of the
Nith is subject to the " bore " of the Solway, whereby a sudden
rush of water floods up at high tide, leaving exposed wide, shallow
breadths of foreshore during the long hours of ebb. After the
wide-spread establishment of the railway system about the middle
of the nineteenth century, Dumfries's importance as a southern
trading port rapidly diminished.

The county was anciently divided into Nithsdale, Annandale
and Eskdale. Yet Dumfriesshire as a whole is dominated by
Dumfries to a greater extent than most Scottish counties are in-
fluenced by their county towns. One reason for this is the strength
of the ties formed by the erstwhile commercial eminence of
Dumfries—indeed, the town is still eminently commercial, though
not in relation to those larger towns in the central belt with
which it once liked to challenge comparison. Another reason is
that, geographically, Dumfries lies on a flat coastal plain, towards which the dales run down. Dumfries has also been the
scene of some important moments in Scottish history.

Like much of Galloway, of which it was once a part, Dumfriesshire was at one time occupied by the Selgovae; came under
Roman influence; thereafter passed into the kingdom of Strathclyde; shared Galloway's years of rough independence; was conquered by the Scots after the union of the kingdoms by the
Dalriadans and the Pictavians; and achieved more or less its

modern identity under Robert the Bruce, who brought the sheriff-
ship of Nithsdale, the stewartry of Annandale, and the regality of
Eskdale under the jurisdiction of one hereditary sheriff.

Reminders of these phases of the county's story are to be found
in many districts. There are cairns, camps and hill-forts of the
Selgovae in the hills to the south-east. Stone circles have been
found in several parishes; notably in Eskdalemuir, at Wamphray
and at Moffat. The Romans have left evidence of their stay in
the remains of camps or stations at Burnswark, Torwoodmoor,
Warldlaw Hill, Caerlaverock, Overbie and elsewhere, as well as
by the tracks which once formed their connecting roads up
Annandale and westward to Nithsdale. Coins in considerable
quantity and numerous relics of weapons and armour have also
been unearthed.

The famous Ruthwell Cross, one of the major monuments of
Dark Age Europe, comes to us from the early part of the eighth
century. The noble structure on the main faces shows Hellenistic
influence, while the margins contain runic references to the poem
*The Dream of the Rood* nowadays generally ascribed to Cynewulf.
The Cross is preserved in an annexe to the parish church.

Powerful were the nobles who ruled the county at the time
of the wars of succession. There were the Dunegals, who owned
much of Nithsdale; the Maccusvilles, precursors of the Maxwells,
in Caerlaverock; the Comyns at Dalswinton and Duncow; the
Bruces of Lochmaben, in Annandale, with, as their retainers,
Kirkpatricks, Johnstones and Carlyles; while the Soulises, the
Avenels and the Rossedals between them held Eskdale. Many
of these once great Normanized names are now quite unknown.
Of them all, the Bruces alone reached that highest power for
which most of them manœuvred and struggled. The Bruce
castle was at Lochmaben, the runted ruins of which still stand
on a peninsula jutting into the Castle Loch. Protected by four
layers of fosses, which could be flooded with water from the
loch, this home of Robert the Bruce's ancestors was at one time
one of the most powerful fortalices in the Borders. Probably it
was put up early in the thirteenth century, built partly with stone
transported from an earlier stronghold on Castle Hill, across the
loch. It remained the chief residence of the Bruces throughout
the thirteenth century, though later they may have moved to
Annan Castle, which was rebuilt in 1300.

Edward I took possession of Lochmaben Castle in 1298, but
by 1302, Bruce—perhaps because his father, the seventh Earl of
Annandale, lay dying and the son wanted to be sure of inheriting
at least the paternal English estates—was on friendly terms with

the English king. Thus it happened that Bruce, returning from London in 1304, came upon a suspicious-looking traveller hard by the western approaches to his castle. When intercepted, the stranger turned out to be a messenger from the Red Comyn to King Edward, urging Bruce's death or imprisonment to frustrate an alleged plot to seize the Scottish throne: a plot which, some say, Bruce had himself evolved and described to Comyn in confidence. If this story, first put about by John Fordun and Andrew Wyntoun, is correct, then the discovery of Comyn's betrayal is what led Bruce, after beheading the luckless messenger, to seek out Comyn in Dumfries. It seems a likely explanation. On the other hand, those who choose to regard Bruce as a sort of unscrupulous adventurer who made good mainly because the changing winds of self-interest happened to blow also in the right direction for Scotland, prefer to accept the testimony of an English prisoner of war, Sir Thomas Gray. Gray alleges that Bruce sent his two brothers, Thomas and Nigel, to Dalswinton, with an invitation to Comyn to meet him at the Greyfriars Church in Dumfries. At the same time, Bruce charged his brothers to murder Comyn on the journey. According to Gray's account, the two brothers were so well received at Dalswinton that they found it impossible to carry out the second part of their assignment. Consequently, Bruce himself had to do the killing inside the church.

Why the testimony of a captured Englishman who, when writing in 1355 from a dungeon in Edinburgh Castle, had every reason to hate the memory of Bruce, should be regarded as the truth, to the discredit of a man who later proved himself to be a courageous and victorious war-leader, and a wise ruler in the ensuing years of turbulent peace, is hard to understand. But in any case, Bruce and Comyn met in the Greyfriars Church, and had words, presumably about Comyn's treachery to Bruce and subservience to English Edward[1]; words which resulted in Bruce's stabbing Comyn. As he left the church, Bruce met Sir Roger de Kirkpatrick of Closeburn and Sir John de Lindsay, to whom he announced what he had just done: "I must be gone, for I doubt I have slain Comyn," are the words traditionally attributed to him. Kirkpatrick is supposed to have drawn his dagger and hurried into the church, saying: "Then I'll mak siccar." In just under six weeks' time, Bruce was crowned at Scone.

The tenancy of Lochmaben Castle was soon afterwards given by Bruce to his nephew, Randolph, Earl of Moray. It passed to

[1] The historian Fordoun suggests that Bruce believed Comyn had betrayed to Edward a plot to free Scotland of the English yoke, and came from London with the express purpose of settling this score.

Edward III when Edward Balliol gave that monarch Dumfries-shire in part-payment for the English king's assistance in legging him up to a subservient throne. Thereafter, in spite of several Scots attempts to get it back, it remained in English hands until David II recaptured it in 1346. After the battle of Neville's Cross, the castle passed to the Countess of March and her son. During David II's captivity, it again had an English garrison; until 1384, when the Earl of Douglas and Archibald Douglas, Lord of Gallo-way, captured and reduced it, and sent the English scurrying out of Annandale. As a result of this action, the Regent Albany conferred both the castle and the Lordship of Annandale on the Earl of Douglas in 1409.

But the ensuing Douglas tyranny eventually provoked royal counter-moves. Though Douglases successfully defied the King's representatives—the Earl of Orkney, who came down to punish some outrages in the district—James II thereafter himself took over and garrisoned Lochmaben. Five years later, the Douglases were overthrown and turned out of their castles. Lochmaben remained a garrisoned crown stronghold—except for brief periods when, in the course of Border feuding, it fell into the hands of the English—until 1603. Its present state of extreme ruin—so extreme that even the experts cannot with certainty date its stones—is due, more than anything else, to the vandalism of subsequent amateur quarriers. But the ruin still sets the pre-vailing character of Lochmaben village, spread amidst its five lochs, three of which contain a rare fish called the vendace. With so much convenient water around them, it is perhaps not surpris-ing that the villagers of Lochmaben had a high nineteenth-cen-tury reputation as curlers.

Lockerbie, now a bien little town, was at one time the scene of an annual lamb fair, or tryst, and an affair of a very different sort known as the "Lockerbie Lick". The Johnstones—whose country was here around and who owned the ruined tower on a ridge above the village—and the Maxwells fought out the last of the great Border feuds in December 1593 at Dryfe Sands, about two miles from Lockerbie. Though the Johnstones had the smaller force, they not only killed Lord Maxwell himself and about seven hundred of his men, but pursued the fleeing re-mainder to Lockerbie, where the exhausted refugees were slaughtered. The phrase, a "Lockerbie Lick", vividly perpet-uates the unpleasant manner of their death.

The principal town in Annandale, after Annan itself at the mouth of the river, is the upland town of Moffat, which probably derives its name from the Gaelic *magh fada,* a long plain. It was in this little gentle-sloping place that Edward Balliol camped in December 1332, shortly before he and his army marched off to Annan Moor to be routed by the troops of Sir Archibald Douglas. The "Three Stan'in' Stanes" on the Beattock road are traditionally said to mark the site of the battle. Moffat also has Covenanting memories, and was for a night or two in 1678 the field headquarters of Viscount Claverhouse.

Two conflicting views of Moffat hospitality have come down to us. In 1618, John Taylor the Water Poet, setting out on his "Pennyless Pilgrimage", spent his first night on Scottish soil at Moffat, where he found: "good ordinary countrey entertainment; my fame and my lodging was sweet and good, and might have served a farre better man than my selfe, although my selfe have had many times better". An anonymous traveller of 1704 was less impressed. He found Moffat, "a small straggling town among high hills, and is the town of their wells, in summer time people coming here to drink waters; but what sort of people they are, or where they get lodgings, I can't tell, for I did not like their lodgings well enough to go to bed, but got such as I could to refresh me, and so came away". The beds must soon have improved, however, for half a century later, eminent men accustomed to the clarty comforts of Edinburgh visited the town for its waters.

In the later eighteenth century, the waters of Moffat's wells acquired a reputation for their alleged curative properties, and amongst those who came to sample them were John "Douglas" Home, James "Ossian" Macpherson, the blind poetaster, Dr. Blacklock, and Dr. "Jupiter" Carlyle. Home and Macpherson struck up a friendship on the Moffat bowling green, as Carlyle records in his autobiography. The most distinguished visitor, however, was Robert Burns, who composed that noble drinking song "O Willie brew'd a pack o' maut" there in the autumn of 1789. Burns's friend, William Nicol, a master in the High School of Edinburgh, was holidaying at Moffat, when Burns and Allan Masterton, the composer of the excellent original tune, decided to pay him a visit. "We had such a joyous evening", says Burns, that "Mr. Masterton and I agreed, each in our own way, that we should celebrate the business". Thus, casually, was the world's finest drinking song produced.

About five miles north-west of the town, near the source of the Annan, lies the Devil's Beeftub. According to the Laird of Summertrees in Scott's novel, *Redgauntlet,* the place received its name "because the Annandale loons used to put their stolen cattle in there: and it looks as if four hills were laying their heads together to shut out daylight from the dark, hollow space between them. A deep, black, blackguard-looking hole of an abyss it is, and goes straight down from the roadside, as perpendicular as it can do, to be a heathery brae. At the bottom there is a small bit of a brook, that you would think could hardly find its way out from the hills that are so closely jammed around it."

During the '45, a Highlander escaped to safety by wrapping himself in a plaid and rolling down the slope, while the soldiery unsuccessfully peppered him from the roadway. In the killing times, a Covenanter was less fortunate, finding only his grave at the bottom of the hollow.

Most travellers, before they leave Annandale, cross into Hoddam parish to visit Ecclefechan, the birthplace of Thomas Carlyle (1795-1881). When a writer is dubbed a sage, he is usually respected rather than read: and such has been the fate of Carlyle. His heavy Teutonic style does not find many admirers in the twentieth century, and few of his books are even available in modern editions. Yet, in spite of fashion, he was a great man and a writer of unquestioned power and integrity. His birthplace is a two-storey house on the west side of the main street, towards the southern end of the village; an agricultural village, high-placed and whitewashed, which has altered little in its essential features since his day.

Eskdale rises high in the Border country, and does not begin to share the Gallovidian qualities of Nithsdale and the flat coastal strip until it reaches the parish of Langholm, within sight of the Ettrick Pen. Robert Southey summed up the qualities of its northern routes when he passed through the region in 1803. "It has a quiet, sober character, a somewhat scenic melancholy kind of beauty, in accord with autumn, evening and declining life; green hills high enough to assume something of a mountainous sweep and swell; green pastures where man has done little, but where little more seems to be wanting; a clear stream, and about that number of cattle which one might suppose belong to the inhabitants for their own use. . . ." Near the heart of the glen of the White Esk lies one of the most exposed villages of Scotland, Eskdalemuir. White and Black Esk—Esk comes from the Gaelic *uisge*, water—meet in the sinister King's Pool, so-called because a Pictish king is said to have been drowned while attempting to cross its ice-locked surface. Tradition has him buried at the top of the neighbouring Shaw Ring Hill. Hard by, an annual fair used to be held at which the custom of Hand-Fasting was practised. Unmarried couples agreed to pair off together until the next fair, for what was in effect a year's trial marriage.

If the trial proved satisfactory to both parties, regular marriage followed; if not, then both parties presumably tried again. Children resulting from the year's union were regarded as being legitimate, and if the marriage of the parents did not follow, the children went with whichever party found the trial most unsatisfactory, an arrangement which would make our modern divorce court judges and child psychologists shudder. The custom is supposed to have been practised by royalty. Robert III is sometimes said to have been the fruit of Robert II's unsuccessful Hand-Fast with one Elizabeth More, before the king married the daughter of the Earl of Ross. The custom is believed by some to have been of Roman origin, though it was also practised in Scandinavia. Near Raeburnsfoot, a few ramparts and ditches are all that remains of the Roman station of Overbie.

As the Esk flows down towards the Solway, it is joined by several tributaries, most of which flow through picturesque ravines, and past moors and towers rich in ballad traditions. The most famous of all these ballad towers was, of course, Gilnockie, the home of Johnnie Armstrong. It was washed by the Esk on three sides when it stood by the river, about four miles south-east of Langholm. Although not a trace of it now remains—the last stones were pulled down during the nineteenth century to make way for a foot-bridge—and although there are some who claim that the roofless sixteenth-century tower of Hollows (or Hole house) was Johnnie's principal stronghold—the river's name is firmly linked with vanished Gilnockie. For it was from there that the most famous of the Border warriors rode forth to Caerlanrigg to meet his king and his doom. He was, of course, a reiver. He did not unduly molest the cattle belonging to his Scots neighbours; but, like his friends Cockburn of Henderland and Adam Scott of Tushielaw, Johnnie Armstrong was a daring and successful raider against the English. As the English, not unnaturally, repaid his attentions in kind, Johnnie and his friends were thus indirectly responsible for keeping the Borders in a state of fear and uncertainty.

So in 1592 James V decided to put a stop to Border lawlessness once and for all. First, he made sure that the most turbulent of the Border nobles, who might have sided with the reiving lairds, were lured into custody: Bothwell, Home, Maxwell, and the lairds of Ferniehurst, Polwarth and Buccleuch. Then he gave out that he meant to embark on a royal hunt in the Borders. So, as Lindsay of Pitscottie tells us, the king, in company with the Earls of Huntly, Argyll and Atholl, and " many other lordis and gentlemen, to the number of twelve thousand men, assemblit at

Edinburgh, and thairfra went with the kings grace to Meggat-
land, in the quhilk boundis was slaine at that tyme aughteine
scoir or deir ".

Pursuit of the deer conveniently brought the king down Dow
Glen, where he surprised Cockburn of Henderland at his supper.
Without ceremony, the luckless laird was hanged over his own
gate, while his terrified wife fled up the glen. " The Lament for
the Border Widow " commemorates her plight.

> I took his body on my back,
> And whiles I gaed, and whiles I sat;
> I digg'd a grave, and laid him in,
> And happ'd him with the sod sae green.
>
> But think na ye my heart was sair,
> When I laid the moul on his yellow hair?
> O think na ye my heart was wae
> When I turn'd about away to gae?

Next, the king descended on Tushielaw, where Adam Scott
was also soon swinging in the wind. Johnnie Armstrong, however, was altogether a tougher proposition. By means of a
promise of safe conduct, he was persuaded to ride to meet the
king, which he did, accompanied by thirty-six horsemen. Lindsay again tells us the subsequent story.

> "When he entered in befoir the king, he cam, verrie rever-
> entlie, with his forsaid number verrie richly apparrelled, trust-
> ing, that in respect he had cum to the kingis grace willingly
> and voluntarlie, not being tein nor apprehendit be the king,
> he could obtain the more favour, but when the king saw him
> and his men so gorgeous in their apparrell, and so many braw
> men under ane tirrantis [tyrant's] command . . . he turned
> about his face, and bad tak that tirrant out of his sight, saying
> ' Quhat wantis yon knave that a king sould have? ' "

Johnnie thereupon tried to mollify the king, but only raised
the royal ire the more. When at last it was apparent to Johnnie
that the king had trapped him, Johnnie cried:

> To seik het water beneith cauld ice,
> Surely it is a great folie—
> I have asked grace at a graceless face,
> But there is nane for my men and me.

Bitterly Johnnie protested that if he had fled to England the English king would gladly have protected him. This was the final stroke of tactlessness, however, and Johnnie and his men were led out and executed in the name of justice.

But the contemporary balladist took a different view of the proceedings:

> John murder'd was at Carlinrigg,
> And all his gallant companie;
> But Scotland's heart was never sae wae,
> To see sae mony brave men die . . .

Before the Esk flows into Cumberland, it is joined by the Liddel Water. Three miles up the Liddel Water, the cascade of Penton Linns preserves the memory of another of the many pieces of dirty business perpetrated by the sinister Lords de Soulis. One of them, wanting a girl whose cottage lay near the waterfall, set out to seize her by force. De Soulis, however, found himself opposed by her father, whom he promptly struck down. A hue and cry got up, and the fleeing nobleman would likely have been killed but for the appearance on the scene of the Laird of Mangerton, who persuaded the friends of the murdered man to leave off their pursuit, and sheltered de Soulis in the tower of Mangerton until the affair blew over.

That he had been saved by an inferior, however, was more than the arrogant Norman blood of a de Soulis could tolerate. So his lordship invited Mangerton to Hermitage Castle, ostensibly to be rewarded for the favour done to its Warden. Once Mangerton was safely within the walls of Hermitage, de Soulis gratefully stabbed him to death. Mangerton was an Armstrong. This second murder was more than the Armstrongs could abide. So another of the clan, Jock o' the Syde, made it his business to see that the Lord de Soulis died at the end of an Armstrong blade; which, in due course, he did!

The river Nith rises in Ayrshire, and flows the first fifteen miles of its course through that county, passing into Dumfriesshire near the mining village of Sanquhar. Sanquhar owed its initial prosperity to the Drumlanrig Douglases, who became, in 1637, the Dukes of Queensberry, and built Drumlanrig Castle to replace Sanquhar Peel. Sanquhar was the scene of two famous declarations, both of which were originally pinned to the old town cross, which must have been made of wood. In the first, dated June 22nd, 1680, Richard Cameron, founder of the Cameronians, publicly renounced his allegiance to Charles II. In the second, dated 28th May, 1685, the Reverend James Ren-

wick declared against the Government of James II and VII. A
granite obelisk marks the site of the now vanished cross.

Between Sanquhar and Dumfries, the Nith flows down a
luxuriant course, passing through the gorge between the Queensberry Heights, and holms of rich pastoral land. It flows by Friar's
Carse, where Burns's friend Robert Riddel once lived, and past
Ellisland, where the poet farmed.

Dumfries itself, besides providing the stage-setting for the first
act in the drama of Robert the Bruce, provided in nearby Maxwelton House, near the village of Moniaive, the setting for
the song "Annie Laurie". Annie was the youngest daughter of
Sir Robert Laurie, the first Baronet of the Maxwelton family, by
his second wife. Young Annie attracted the attentions of William
Douglas of Fingland, a kinsman of the Queensberry family, and
a Jacobite. They met and dallied on " Maxwelton banks ", and
Douglas declared:

> *Maxwelton banks are bonnie,*
> *Where early fa's the dew,*
> *Where me and Annie Laurie*
> *Made up the promise true;*
> *Made up the promise true,*
> *And ne'er forget will I;*
> *And for bonnie Annie Laurie*
> *I'd lay doun my head and die.*

The ardent poet then goes on to describe his beloved's physical
attributes.

> *She's backit like the peacock,*
> *She's breistit like the swan,*
> *She's jimp about the middle,*
> *Her waist ye weel may span;*
> *Her waist ye weel may span,*
> *And she has a rolling eye;*
> *And for bonnie Annie Laurie*
> *I'd lay doun my head and die.*

No doubt that third last line is evidence of the poet's technical
shortcomings, rather than of any alarming defect about his lady's
vision. Indeed, since Hamilton of Gilbertfield wrote a song about
William Douglas, "Willie was a Wanton Wag", the "rolling
eye" may well have been the poet's own! In any case, he was
never called upon to lay doun his head and die for her. Instead,
he was called to Edinburgh over the head of a Jacobite intrigue;

discovered, and forced to flee to the Continent. Eventually, he married a Galloway girl, Elizabeth Clerk of Glenboig, and had four sons and two daughters. Annie, for her part, married Alexander Fergusson of Craigdarroch. She died in 1761, at the age of 79. The version of the song now so lugubriously sung to a nineteenth-century air, is the work of Lady John Scott, written in 1835, and ultimately published to raise money for the widows and orphans of the Crimean War.[1]

During the eighteenth century, Dumfries produced the poet who celebrated in verse her ancient custom of shooting for James VI's " Siller Gun ", presented for competition by Wapinschawing. He was John Mayne (1759-1836), who, after an apprenticeship as a compositor under the Foulises in Glasgow, spent most of his life as printer and part proprietor of the London newspaper the *Star*. " The Siller Gun " was first published in 1777, and thus appeared three years after Robert Fergusson's death, and almost a decade before Burns's social satires became generally known.

The main interest of the poem lies neither in the description of the seven contesting trades, nor of the weird armoury of guns they employed, but in the vivid picture it presents of a peasant festival; a picture which Burns may have had in mind when describing the congregation at his " Holy Fair ".

*Frae far and near, the country lads,*
*(Their joes ahint them on their yads),*      [mares
*Flocked in to see the show in squads;*
   *And, what was dafter,*
*Their pawkie mithers and their dads*
   *Cam' trotting after.*

*And mony a beau and belle were there,*
*Doited wi' dosing in a chair*
*For, lest they'd, sleeping, spoil their hair,*
   *Or miss the sight,*
*The gowks, like bairns before a fair,*
   *Sat up a' night.*

*Wi' hats as black as ony raven,*
*Fresh as the rose, their beards new shaven,*
*And a' their Sunday's cleeding having*      [clothing
   *Sae trim and gay,*
*Forth cam' our Trades, some orra saving*      [extra
   *To ware that day.*      [spend

---

[1] Maxwelton House has been splendidly restored by the Stenhouse family.

*Hech, sirs! what crowds cam' into town*
*To see them must'ring up and down!*
*Lasses and lads, sunburnt and brown—*
    *Women and weans,*
*Gentle and simple, mingling, crown*
    *The gladsome scene.*

*At first, forenent ilk deacon's hallan*         [inner wall
*His ain brigade was made to fall in;*
*And while the muster-roll was calling,*
    *And joy-bells jowing*         [rocking; tolling
*Het pints, weel spiced, to keep the saul in,*
    *Around were flowing. . . .*

*Broiled kipper, cheese and bread, and ham,*
*Laid the foundation for a dram*
*O' whiskey, gin frae Rotterdam,*
    *Or cherry-brandy,*
*Whilk after, a' was fish that cam'*
    *To Jock or Sandy.*

*O! Weel ken they wha lo'e their chapin,*       [quart
*Drink mak's the auldest swak and strappin',*   [stout
*Gars care forget the ills that happen—*
    *The blate look spruce,*         [backward
*And ev'n the thowless cock their tappin'*     [pithless
    *And craw fu' crouse.*         [boldly

The greatest poet who has been associated with Dumfries is, of course, Robert Burns. Drink, according to his unctuous nine-teenth-century biographers, played no small part in the closing years of his life which Burns spent at Dumfries. Yet modern research has shown beyond doubt that Burns drank no more than his fellows, and that his death was caused by endocarditis brought on by the adult stresses and strains imposed upon his boyhood's frame at the farm of Lochlie. Many of Burns's greatest songs were composed in Dumfries, among them "Scots wha hae", "My luve is like a red, red rose", and "O wert thou in the cauld blast".

The house in which Burns died has been a place of pilgrimage for more than a century and a half now. Among the earliest visitors were Dorothy and William Wordsworth, who arrived in Dumfries in August 1803. After being guided to the then unmarked grave by a local bookseller, Dorothy tells us the Words-worths called at Burns's house:

" Mrs. Burns was gone to spend some time by the sea-shore with her children. We spoke to the servant-maid at the door, who invited us forward, and we sate down in the parlour. The walls were coloured with a blue wash; on one side of the fire was a mahogany desk, opposite to the window a clock, and over the desk a print from the ' Cottar's Saturday Night ', which Burns mentions in one of his letters having received as a present. The house was cleanly and neat in the inside, the stairs of stone, scoured white, the kitchen on the right side of the passage, the parlour on the left. In the room above the parlour, the Poet died. . . ."[1]

[1] Scotland's greatest poet since " the Poet died ", C. M. Grieve (" Hugh MacDiarmid "), was born at Langholm in 1892, where, according to his statement in his autobiography " Lucky Poet ", his father was postman. At the local school, Grieve had the composer F. G. Scott as a master. Thus early was formed the association culminating in a partnership which produced some of the finest songs of this century.

# Chapter VIII

# GALLOWAY

*From the towne of Ayre in Kyle to Galloway,*
*Through Corryct (Carrick) passe unto Nithysdale,*
*Where Dumfryse is a pretye towne alwaye,*
*And plentiful also of all good vytale.*
*For all your army, without any fayle;*
*So that kepying this journey, by my instruccion,*
*That realme ye shall bring into subjeccion.*

JOHN HARDYNG, *circa* 1420.

I

JOHN HARDYNG, whose mathematics we questioned at the beginning of Chapter Three, was a somewhat unskilled forger of documents the object of which was to enable his royal master, Henry V, to "prove" England's claims of superiority over Scotland. At one point in Hardyng's search for material, he made a journey to Scotland, the fruits of which he reaped in his old age, presenting his *Chronicle of John Hardyng in Metre from the first Begynnyng of Englande unto the reigne of Edward the Fourth* to that monarch as a sort of invasion guide. The stanza about Galloway is doubly interesting since it suggests that Hardyng did not, in fact, penetrate further westwards than Dumfries, which was then part of Galloway, while it also shows his consciousness of the need for the subjection of this isolated and for long unruly part of Scotland.

This south-western corner of Scotland was, at the time of the Roman occupation of Britain, occupied by tribes called by Ptolemy in the second century A.D. Novantae and Selgovae. The Novantae probably occupied what is to-day Galloway—the country west of the Nith—and their two towns were Leucopibia, reputedly Whithorn; and Rerigonium, which is generally supposed to have been situated at the Mote of Innermessan, on the east shore of Loch Ryan.

Probably the Novantae were a Gaelic people from Ireland, cut off from the more northerly Gaels by the Britons of Strathclyde. At any rate, the Galloway contingent which fought at the Battle of the Standard in 1138 are referred to as Pictish in a surviving record.

213

Agricola overran Galloway in A.D. 79, but doubtless he had some difficulty in keeping it subdued. There is evidence of Roman occupation in both counties.[1] Once the Roman legions had withdrawn, local kings again held sway until the early seventh century, when the Northumbrian kings of Bernicia brought Galloway under their rule.

It is probably from this Northumbrian period, which perhaps lasted for about two hundred years, that the name of the district derives, *Gall*, in the Gaelic, *a stranger*, relating to the distant rule. According to the Venerable Bede, one of the four bishoprics into which, in his day, Northumbria was divided, had its seat at what was formerly Leucopibia, but which, since St. Ninian had founded his monastery there in 397, had been renamed Candida Casa, "the white house". But, by the end of the eighth century, Anglian power was on the wane, and the Anglian order began to be disrupted by the attack of marauding Vikings.

Until about 1047, when Malcolm Ceannmór ascended the Scottish throne and proceeded to drive out the Norse settlers, Galloway was probably ruled by native lordlings; men whose fierce names may still be found on the faded furthest borders of tradition—Uchtred, Duvenald and—most important of them all—Fergus, who became the first Earl of Galloway in 1138. Some of these leaders seem to have followed Viking example and indulged in piratical excursions of their own.

Malcolm Ceannmór gave Scotland south of the Forth and Clyde to his son, David II, as an earldom. When David became king in 1124, Galloway was thus technically united with Scotland.

But union with Scotland neither made Galloway less unruly, nor the loyalties of the chiefs any more predictable. Fergus married a bastard daughter of Henry I of England, and in 1160, leagued with Somerled, the Norse ruler of Argyll, against Malcolm IV. Malcolm dealt very leniently with the rebellious Lord, for, after defeating him in the last of three battles, the king allowed Fergus to spend the remainder of his days as a canon in Holyrood, provided he resigned his lordship to his sons.

Alas, kingly lenience in mediæval Scotland was more often than not regarded as an opportunity to plot revenge and further treachery. Uchtred and his brother Gilbert followed King William the Lion into England in 1173; but when that careless monarch was caught by a party of English soldiers while he was engaged on a forward reconnaissance near Alnwick Castle, the brothers hurried home to take advantage of their ruler's enforced

[1] Wigtownshire and Kirkcudbrightshire.

absence. They drove west as many as possible of the descendants of the Anglian and the Norse settlers in Galloway, and re-proclaimed its ancient independence; taking the precaution, however, of offering to swear allegiance to the English throne. Uchtred may have had some qualms of conscience about the matter, for he was soon afterwards slain by brother Gilbert at Loch Fergus. On his release from English captivity the following year, William promptly marched into Galloway, and compelled Gilbert to submissiveness.

When Gilbert died in 1185, Uchtred's son Roland succeeded to the lordship, though not before he had put down two claimants, Gilpatrick and Gilcolm. Roland is said to have sworn allegiance to Henry II, as well as to the Scottish king. At any rate, his son Alan, who succeeded him in 1200, assisted King John in his Irish expedition of 1211, and later was one of those who forced Magna Carta upon the reluctant monarch.

There was a revolt when Alan died in 1234. He left three daughters, all married to aliens, but only an illegitimate son Thomas, whose claim the king would not recognize. Thomas thereupon raised the standard of Gallovidian independence, was defeated by Alexander II; fled to Ireland, where he collected an army of kerns for a second attempt; but on landing in the Rhinns and meeting with no support, he surrendered to the king, who surprisingly pardoned him.[1]

On the death of the third of Alan's daughters in 1246, Galloway was divided between the other two brothers-in-law, Roger de Quenci, Earl of Winchester, and John de Balliol; de Quenci held Wigtownshire, Balliol the Stewartry. De Balliol's wife Devorgilla became the mother of that John de Balliol who was for a time King of Scotland.

Meanwhile, Alexander Comyn, Earl of Buchan, married one of de Quenci's daughters, and on the death of his father-in-law, seized the lordship of Western Galloway. Consequently, the Comyns supported Balliol against Bruce in the struggle for the Scottish throne.

Galloway was invaded by Wallace as a punishment for supporting the Comyns and the English. In 1300, it was again invaded, this time by Edward I. The next Scots invasion was by Robert the Bruce in 1307, but on this occasion he was unsuccessful. So the following year, he dispatched his brilliant brother Edward Bruce into Galloway with a sizable army. This time, both native chieftains and English occupiers were defeated. Galloway

---

[1] Two of the Irish chiefs were taken to Edinburgh, where they were torn asunder by horses.

was thereupon conferred upon Edward Bruce as a mark of the king's favour. Edward later became king of Ireland, and died in battle there. His illegitimate son, who was allowed to succeed him in Galloway, also died young, whereupon Galloway reverted to the Scottish crown.

But Galloway was to know little enough of peace, for in 1334 Edward Balliol, John's son, marched into Galloway with Edward III and his army. Because of the young David II's recent defeat and capture at Neville's Cross, Balliol was able not only to retake possession of the family estates but to seize the throne. But Balliol's subsequent raids against Lanarkshire and the Lothians provoked Sir William Douglas to deal finally with him in 1353. Out of gratitude for this action, David II, on his release, granted Kirkcudbrightshire to Sir William's nephew, Archibald the Grim, in 1369. Archibald the Grim, who was the illegitimate son of Sir James Douglas, had already bought Wigtownshire from the impoverished Earl of Wigtown in 1367. He thus became master of all Galloway, and as he had also heired land from his father who fell at Otterburn, one of the most powerful barons in the realm.

The Douglases' stronghold was Threave Castle, built on an island in the Dee. From its water-bound safety they oppressed the neighbourhood, defying even the authority of the king himself. A Douglas captured the sheriff of Galloway, Sir Patrick MacLellan of Bombie, and, on being ordered to return him, according to tradition, beheaded him in Threave, afterwards sending down the body to the waiting king's messengers with an insolent apology that it was "somewhat wanting the heid". Finally, however, Douglas lawlessness became more than even his brother nobles could bear. So in 1543, James the ninth Earl was tried by his peers and stripped of his vast possessions.

Galloway was once again annexed to the crown. But though the big chiefs no longer fought, the little chiefs still squabbled. The worst example of this "neichbour weir" was the feud between Gordon of Lochinver and Sir John Dunbar of Mochrum, the steward of Kirkcudbright. Later, a feud between Gordon of Lochinver—who must have been a singularly quarrelsome man— and MacLellan of Bombie culminated in the murder of Mac- Lellan outside of door of St. Giles, in Edinburgh.

In the days of the Marian struggle, English troops overran the Stewartry of Kirkcudbright in 1547 and in 1570, under Lord Scrope, with assistance from the Earl of Moray, made a punitive sortie against Mary's Gallovidian Catholic supporters.

With such a history of independent struggle behind them, it is hardly surprising that the Gallovidians were amongst the most ardent supporters of the Covenant, and provided the highest number of martyrs for " the Faith ".

It must at least have been an apt Protestant wind which in 1690 blew the ships of William III into Loch Ryan for shelter, whilst he was on his way to defeat the army of James VII and II in Ireland.

Such, then, is the historical background of Galloway's past: a background common to both the Stewartry and to Wigtownshire. Both counties, however, also have topographical aspects and details of history which are not shared.

II

" Romantic Galloway invites you " reads the plaque put out by the Galloway Tourist Association, and prominently displayed throughout the Stewartry and the Shire. It made me reflect, when I first saw it, on the fact that, unlike most declamations of its kind, it really is true; doubly true indeed. For the scenery and the associations of Galloway are indubitably " romantic ", according to the definition of the word offered by my dictionary— *extravagant, wild, fantastic, sentimental* and invitation is necessary since those who " do " Scotland—" Edinburgh, The Trossachs, Loch Lomond, Alloway and Abbotsford, all in three days my dear! "—rarely visit this south-west corner of the country.

However, I ought not to be too censorious; for, until a few years ago when the good people of Stranraer invited me to give a public lecture in their singularly well-equipped library, I, too, had never been in Galloway. That visit, rushed though it was, and undertaken in the snow-filled depth of winter, made me resolve to go back and discover Wigtownshire and Kirkcudbrightshire for myself.

A few years later, to the assistance of my resolve came an unexpected invitation to take part in a broadcast " Country Magazine " programme from Port William. I had to select and introduce a folk-song of the county. The piece of my choice, " The Rover of Loch Ryan ", does not perhaps rank high among the songs of the nation: but at least it has a fine local flavour, and is one of the very few Lowland sea-songs which have been produced. The words were written by an Ayrshire poet, Hew Ainslie, who was born near Dailly in 1792, and who died in America in 1878. The Paisley musician R. A. Smith (1780-1829) composed the music.

*The rover o' Loch Ryan, he's gane*
  *Wi' his merry men sae brave;*
*Their hearts are o' the steel, an' a braver, better keel*
  *Ne'er bowled owre the back o' a wave.*
*It's no' when the loch lies dead in its trough,*
  *When naething disturbs it ava;*
*But the rack an' the ride o' the restless tide*
  *An' the splash o' the grey sea-maw.*

*It's no' when the yawl an' the light skiffs crawl*
  *Owre the breast o' the siller sea,*
*That I look to the west for the bark I lo'e best,*
  *An' the rover that's dear to me;*
*But when that the clud lays its cheek to the flood,*
  *An' the sea lays its shouther to the shore;*
*When the win' sings high an' the sea-whaups screigh,*
  *As they rise frae the deafening roar.*

*It's then that I look thro' the thickening rook,*
  *An' watch by the midnight tide;*
*I ken the wind brings my gallant rover hame,*
  *Frae the sea that he glories to ride. . . .*

As with so many minor Scots eighteenth- and early nineteenth-century poets, the Englishness of that last line dislodges Ainslie from his secure vernacular position—in this case as a weather-observer.  The song lamentably disintegrates as the poet indulges in a hearty swatch of yo-ho-ho blue-jerseyed Jack Tar pastiche, which is better left unquoted.

Loch Ryan's " whitening roar " is not nearly so fierce as the roar of the sea between Ireland and the Rhinns; as the loss of that unlucky vessel the *Princess Victoria* during a storm in January 1953 so dramatically demonstrated.  The stormy impact of the news of her sinking faded slowly from the public mind. Sudden death has become so much part of the paraphernalia of twentieth-century living, that we have come now to accept it. The charred destruction of forty tourists in an aeroplane, or the shattering of the passengers in a ravine-tumbled touring-bus, disturbs our complacency scarcely at all.  Yet a ship-load of steamer-travellers clutching once-safe summer decks and trailing rigging, with a wind, obscene in its noisy power, slowly numbing the strength from the fingers and dropping their chilled bodies into the insatiable maw of the sea, shakes our uneasy complacency. Such a death is not of our age's devising, and is an unpleasant reminder that we have less of permanence and are less masters of the elements than, to be happy, we choose to think.

I drove into Wigtownshire along the coast road, down the shores of Loch Ryan, on a fine June evening. Although Queen Victoria described Loch Ryan, enthusiastically if somewhat mundanely, as being "very fine, the hills and glens lovely, the loch very large and the hills very high and wooded", even under the most favourable weather conditions it has never seemed to me to be an attractive loch. True, its bleakness is not the desolation of infertility—Wigtownshire is sweetly productive—rather the bleakness caused by a lack of marked scenic contrast. Across the water, the mound of the Rhinns raises a long protecting arm, uninteresting at a distance though later exploration proved it to be not so. And neither Cairnryan nor Stranraer are places remarkable for their attractiveness.

Until the beginning of the second world war, Cairnryan was a little village with a sheltered harbour. But during the war, Loch Ryan carried a sea-plane base, and Cairnryan was developed into a major port, concerned mainly with the transport of ammunition. Although the urgency of war forces developments such as these, unfortunately there is no urgency of peace to encourage the removal of disintegrating war-time machinery, and the restoration of the natural amenities.

War remains of an earlier conflict are also in evidence nearby. On a point between Cairnryan and Stranraer, stones may be seen marking the western flank of a fortification known as the Deil's Dyke. It was put up by the Romanized Picts during some early turbulence, and it once extended across the moors to the Solway Firth.

Stranraer owes its importance to the fact that it is the Scottish terminal port for the shortest sea-route linking Britain and Ireland. The older part of the town went up in the latter half of the eighteenth century. It has been badly mutilated by insensitive redevelopment, although the Dutch-capped Town House has been well-restored. At its heart is the still-roofed fifteenth-century Castle of St. John, built by the powerful Kennedy family, and in 1682 the headquarters of Claverhouse during one of his punitive expeditions into Galloway. Another building, also called a castle, stands at the end of the East Pier. It was the home of the arctic explorer Sir John Ross, born at Kirkcolm in 1777. It is still sometimes referred to as the North-West Castle, a "folk-reference" to his voyage in search of the North-West Passage.

I spent a night in Stranraer, and next day drove over to those two peninsulas joined to the rest of the county by a narrow reach of land, and picturesquely called The Rhinns of Galloway. Traditionally, Wigtownshire falls into three divisions. The Rhinns, the Moors and the Machars. The landscape of each division has its own individual quality.

The Rhinns—the name derives from the Gaelic *roinn*, " a promontory "—is a net-work of narrow winding roads. The land is mostly flat, though the hill of Cairnpat gives the promontory a spine. Twenty-eight miles apart, both its rugged tips are capped by lighthouses: at Carsewell Point to the north, and on the Mull of Galloway to the south.

From the earliest days of man's habitation in Scotland, there have been settlements on the Rhinns. Remains of earth tumuli survive on several heads of land. In the porch of the church of Kirkmadrine, preserved from the elements, are two sculptured stones, inscribed in Roman letters to the memory of the fifth-century clerics. These stones must be among the earliest Christian monuments which have come down to us.

Midway down the seaward coast of the Rhinns lies the village of Portpatrick. It is framed in a rocky amphitheatre, and cannot be seen until one is almost upon it. Before the development of Stranraer, Portpatrick was used as the sea-link with Ireland, though it is exposed to a heavy swell from the Atlantic, and was apparently never regarded as a satisfactory place of shelter.

The place derives its name from the patron saint of Ireland, who, according to legend, did not have to depend upon the harbour to make his crossing to and from Scotland, for he straddled the channel at a single stride, leaving the imprint of his arriving foot on a great rock. Another legend tells of the occasion when tribesmen from Glenapp beheaded the saint. After this unhappy business was over, St. Patrick—the accounts are vague—picked up his head, walked with it to Portpatrick, plunged into the sea, and, holding his head between his teeth, swam back to Ireland, where presumably he took steps to have it replaced.

In 1636, however, long after the age of miracles had passed, Sir William Brereton found the crossing highly uncomfortable, even with his head on his shoulders. On July 4th, he arrived at:

" . . . Portpatrick, which is foul winter way over the mossy moors; and there we found only one boat, though yesternight there were fifteen boats here. We hired a boat of about ten ton for five horses of ours, and for five Yorkshiremen and horses. For this we paid £1, and conditioned that no more horses should come aboard, save only two or three of an Irish laird's, who then stayed for a passage, and carried his wife and three horses . . . We shipped our horses two hours before we went aboard. It is a most craggy, filthy passage, and very dangerous for horses to go in and out; a horse may easily be lamed, spoiled and thrust into the sea; and when any horses land here, they are thrown into the sea, and swim out."

In spite of these difficulties of embarkation, a weekly mail ship began to operate from Portpatrick to Donaghadee in 1662. By the middle of the eighteenth century, the trade in horses and in passenger-carrying had so expanded that in 1774 a pier and a lighthouse were built. A much larger artificial harbour was erected in 1821, and two paddle steamers took up the mail service in 1838. But the risks to these bigger vessels proved considerable, and, by the middle of the century, Portpatrick had lost its port to Stranraer. Since then, winter seas have pounded the incompleted harbour to ruin, oversetting and fragmenting the heavy concrete blocks which its designer once was sure promised certain all-seasons shelter. His miscalculation of the power of the Atlantic gales cost the Government of the day five hundred thousand pounds.

Perched on a sea-eaten cliff a mile to the south-east of Portpatrick stand the crumbled ruins of Dunskey Castle. It was built in 1510 by Adair of Kilhilt, on the site of an older castle burned by Sir Alexander McCulloch of Myrtoun in 1489. By the end of the eleventh century, it was ruined and abandoned. It can never have been an important fortalice, but, because of its precarious perch, it is still an interesting spectacle.

Further down the sea-board, in the shallow crook of a sandy bay, the little village of Port Logan—locally Portnessock—crouches behind a raised coastal road. It was once a fishing port, though now it is almost derelict. A local rhyme runs:

*Portnessock is a bonnie place,*
  *It lies beside the sea;*
*If 'twere na far the paikie-dogs,*
  *Portnessoch folk wad dee.*

It is, however, unlikely that either laziness or a shortage of dog-fish contributed materially to the place's decline.

Port Logan produced at least one distinguished son in John McLean, captain of a sailing ship which, on the run from the Antipodes, beat the famous *Cutty Sark* by six weeks. His courage and skill throughout the seven seas earned him the nickname of Hellfire Jack.

Two unusual sights draw tourists to the district. One is a fishpond cut out of the cliffs, where tame cod are still kept. Originally designed as a fish-larder for the M'Douall family, who once owned the estate, the cod that come up to take scraps of food from the fingers of visitors are threatened now with no more serious fate than eye trouble. They are released into the sea at regular intervals, the stock being replaced with newly-trapped fish.

The other attraction is the garden of Logan House. Also in the grounds are the ruins of the Castle of the McDoualls, sentinelled by two stout palm-trees.

From coast to coast, through Kirkmaiden and Drummore, the road down the Rhinns which tapes its white way to St. Medon's Cove, on the Mull of Galloway, confirms the traveller's first impression that he is on an island. The Mull of Galloway, the southernmost point of Scotland, is a rugged head of land crowned by a lighthouse built as long ago as 1828. I reached the Mull on a warm sunny afternoon, and lay on the grass near the cliff-top. A daring sheep nibbled so close to the fringe that I waited for it to slip over the edge. The precariousness of its position brought to my mind the legend of the last three Picts who possessed the secret for making Heather Ale. During a war which had not gone well for the Picts, a Druid tried to buy his safety by revealing the fact that the captured Chief and his sons held the cherished secret. One of the sons thereupon promised to yield up the secret, if his father and brother were first thrown over the cliff, so that they would not hear his treachery. When this was done, the surviving brother suddenly lunged at the Druid, and with the operatic cry " Thus dies the secret " also disappeared over the cliff-edge, sweeping the Druid with him.

My sheep, however, did not fall over the edge: neither, in all probability, did secret-possessing Pict or Druid. It is hard to believe that a twentieth-century brewer could not produce Heather Ale if he wanted to, and harder still to believe that it would be invigorating, or even palatable.

The road which sweeps round the broad curve of Luce Bay, runs through country which, after Ardwell, is singularly flat. The ribbed sand-dunes of Luce Bay are a haunt of sea-birds. At the head of the Bay runs the road which links the narrow reach of land between Loch Ryan and Luce Bay. Castle Kennedy, surrounded by " Dutch style " formal gardens, stands on a peninsula between the White Loch and the Black Loch. It was built in 1607 by the fifth Earl of Cassillis. It passed in 1677 to Sir John Dalrymple, later Viscount Stair, and was accidentally razed by fire in 1716. The second Earl, who became a Field-Marshal and George's II's Commander-in-Chief, occupied his retirement in laying out the gardens. In 1841, the chance discovery in a gardener's cottage of papers containing his plans resulted in the restoration of the grounds in accordance with his original ideas.

A very different setting is that which encompasses Park Place, the great house on a little hill just outside Glenluce, built about 1590 with stones from the nearby abbey. The home of the Hays of Park and one of the finest examples of a sixteenth-century Lowland domestic mansion, it has now been restored for preservation as an ancient monument.

Similar work on the ruins of the Abbey of Glenluce have arrested its further decay. It was founded in 1190 by Roland, Lord of Galloway, and was the cause of a piece of even more than usually dirty business in the sixteenth century. That most violent representative of a family much given to violence, Gilbert, fourth Earl of Cassillis, seeing which way the rumbustious winds of the Reformation were blowing, decided to enrich his purse at the expense of the losing faith. His behaviour at Crossragruel, in Ayrshire, is related elsewhere in this book. At Glenluce, he found a monk skilled in forgery. This monk agreed to reproduce a lease of the Abbey, purporting to be signed by the late last Abbot, in the Earl's favour. With almost mediæval Italian thoroughness, the Earl next hired a thug called Carnochan to murder the monk. This deed safely done, the Earl took possession of his gains, and delivered the murderer to the "lord of pit and gallows", his uncle Bargany, who naturally made sure that Carnochan was promptly hanged. But the Earl did not long enjoy his gains, for in 1587 the lands of Glenluce became vested in the crown, from whom, after various minor vicissitudes, they became part of the temporal barony granted to Sir James Dalrymple.

Michael Scott, the Wizard of Balwearie, paid a visit to Glenluce in the thirteenth century, at a time when the plague was devastating the countryside. Legend credits him with successfully luring the offending plague to a vault of the Abbey, and, with the aid of some local witches, starving it to death. The plague successfully dealt with, it seems he then found that his ladies no longer had enough to do to keep their magic powers occupied. So he set them to spin ropes out of the sands of Luce Bay. The results of their efforts are said to be visible near Ringdoo Point at exceptionally low tides.

Of the Abbey itself, only the Chapter House remains still fairly intact.

Glenluce village, with its sloping main street, is one of the most

charming in all Galloway. It is hard, indeed, to imagine that it
was once occupied by no less a person that the Deil himself.
Fortunately, however, we have as witness Mr. George Sinclair,
Professor of Philosophy at the College of Glasgow who, in 1685,
chronicled the progress of that gentleman's stay in Glenluce in a
work called *Satan's Invisible World Discovered*.

It seems that in the spring of 1655, the Devil saw fit to introduce
himself to one Gilbert Campbell, a weaver to trade, by pulling
the bedclothes off him and his family, cutting up the fabrics in
the house, severing his threads, and finally, repeatedly setting his
house on fire: all of which somewhat inconvenienced the good
Gilbert. Being a true believer, he enlisted the aid of the parish
minister, who forthwith came to the house and began a verbal
wrestling with the invisible Devil, in which encounter both
quoted scripture to confound the other. The Devil, however,
prevailed, and thereafter gave Gilbert so bad a time that he
decided to appeal to higher authority.

"In this sore and sad affliction, Gilbert Campbell resolved
to make his Addresses to the Synod of Presbyters, for Advice
and Counsel what to do . . . namely, whether to forsake the
house or not? The Synod, by their Committy appointed to
meet at Glenluce in February 1656, thought fit that a solemn
Humiliation should be kept through all the Bounds of the
Synod; and among other causes, to request GOD in Behalf of
that afflicted Family; which being done carefully, the event was,
that his troubles grew less till April, and from April to August
he was altogether free."

Alas for the Synod! The "Humiliation" cannot have been
"done carefully" enough. For very soon:

". . . The Devil began with new assaults, and taking the
ready Meat that was in the house, did sometimes hide it in
holes by the doorposts; and at other times did hide it under
the Beds, and sometimes among the Bed-cloaths, and under
the Linnings, and at last, did carry it quite away, till nothing
was left there, save Bread and Water . . . After this, he exer-
cised his malice and cruelty against all persons in the Family,
in wearying them in the Night-time, by striving and moving
thorow the house, so that they had no rest for Noise . . . After
which time the Devil grew yet worse, by roaring, and terrifying
them by casting Stones, by striking them with staves on their

Beds in the Night time. And upon the 18th of September, about Midnight, he cryed out with a loud voice: ' I shall burn the house.' And about 3 or 4 Nights after, he set one of the Beds of fire, which was soon put out, without any prejudice, except the Bed itself."

Fortunately, " by some conjuration or other ", not analysed, the Devil eventually " suffered himself to be put away ". At least we may accept the philosophical author's verdict on the whole affair:

" This weaver has been a very odd man, that endured so long the marvellous disturbances."

About two miles to the north-east, on wild moorland, lie the jagged ruins of Carsecreugh Castle, rebuilt from an older stronghold by Sir James Dalrymple, Viscount Stair (a famous President of the Court of Session), in 1680. In August 1669, Sir James set out for Glenluce Abbey to give his reluctant daughter in marriage to David Dunbar of Baldoon, near Wigtown. The death of the unhappy bride a month after her marriage provided Sir Walter Scott with the material for the plot of *The Bride of Lammermoor*.

Up the valley of the Water of Luce, in a moorland hollow and at the heart of that part of the country known as the Moors, lies the village of New Luce. Lacking a Devil, its only claim on history is that in its church once ministered the Covenanting " prophet " Alexander (" Hoodiecraw ") Peden, whom not a few of a different persuasion from himself very probably regarded as Satanic!

The direct road from Glenluce to Newton Stewart separates the Moors from the Machars. I drove round the coast road, making many detours on the way.

By the village of Mochrum, a road climbs the Moors to where the old Castle of Mochrum once stood among a cluster of Lochs. It was built by the family of Dunbar of Mochrum in the fifteenth century, a family descended from the second son of Patrick, Earl of March.

Port William, where I stayed, is a small place of no great attractiveness: it has a small fishing harbour, the remains of a customs-house which operated against eighteenth-century smugglers, a row of old cottages, and a row of new bungalows fronting the sea. Sir William Maxwell of Monrieth, after whom it was named, founded it about 1770. The hotel at Port William then offered hospitality of a quality which I have rarely found matched elsewhere in Scotland. That being so, it was not until after a leisurely-savoured dinner that I could make myself carry out my planned intention of motoring down the peninsula, through the holiday village of Monrieth, and past the old roofless pre-Reformation church of Kirkmaiden, to Isle of Whithorn.

The accumulated heat of a cloudless day was trembling slowly off the cool grasses: the deep calm water crooked within the protecting arm of the little harbour, sandy-clear except for a few rusty clusters of sea-weed on the bottom; the white, harled buildings sharply-defined in the lingering late-June light—such was my first sight of the Isle of Whithorn, and of the land-linked village of Whithorn beyond. There, I went through the Pend of the roofless, ivy-gripped cathedral. Though it was by now well outwith the limits of his working day, the official guide showed me round, drawing my attention to the architectural points of the buildings, the sculptured armorial bearings, its ancient Runic stone. But I found myself scarcely interested in the facts that he volunteered: that the buildings had been put up in the Gothic First and Second Pointed Styles, and that the twelfth-century Norman doorway, all that survives of the original church, was one of the first of its kind in Scotland. For I was obsessed by my own reflections. Here, in all probability on the same site, had once stood *Candida Casa*, the White House of St. Ninian, son of a chief of the Novantae, and bringer of Christianity to Scotland.

St. Ninian came to Scotland, after studying in Rome and with St. Martin at Tours, about the year 396. He not only set about converting the Picts of Galloway, but he and his followers:

> ". . . marched up the east coast clad in undyed woollen cassocks with pointed hoods, their feet shod with sandals. They tramped along with short stout 'bachalls' or staffs with flat tops like walking-sticks, and they were armed with the gospels and psalters copied by the scribes among them in their little cells at Candida Casa."[1]

In Aberdeenshire and in Northern Ireland St. Ninian taught, so that when the marauding Norsemen, whose strongest creed was the red force of the sword, cut off Candida Casa, the work began there did not perish. Candida Casa became a centre from which many of the Celtic saints went out, and an example upon which other settlements were modelled. Later, when the Celtic Church had been Romanized and monastic contemplation had declined in importance, the ground where St. Ninian and his followers first settled became a place of pilgrimage.

[1] *Celtic Sunrise*: Diana Leatham.

The Angles founded a bishopric of Whithorn in 727, but after only five bishops had filled it, it came to an end. The Priory and Cathedral, whose ruins still survive, were not founded by Fergus, Lord of Galloway, until the reign of David I. Whithorn was then the seat of the bishop of Galloway. At the Reformation, the bishopric of Galloway came third in wealth only to those of St. Andrews and Glasgow, its rental amounting to five thousand six hundred and thirty four pounds Scots. The most famous of the priors of Whithorn was Gavin Dunbar, James V's tutor, who later also became Archbishop of Glasgow and Lord Chancellor of Scotland.

Amongst the roll of famous pilgrims to the shrine of St. Ninian, whose bones are said to rest in the cathedral, are James III's Queen Margaret; James IV, who is reputed to have made an annual pilgrimage; James V; and old Archibald Bell-the-Cat, who died at the Priory in 1514. Candida Casa—Ptolemy's Leucopibia of the Novantae, its name probably deriving from "White House" in Gaelic—suffered the usual Reformation fate, its magnetism as a place of pilgrimage making it doubly obnoxious to the Knoxians.

It is easy to understand that magnetism. Now that the once-arrogant Reformed faiths have mostly sickened into drooling sentimentality, their ruggedness stiffened to mere rigidity; and now that the old religion of St. Ninian has both to appease its narrower followers by manufacturing and adopting new "miracles" as compulsory beliefs, at the same time accepting the fact that others among its members are seeking to compromise it with its deadly enemy Communism: now, then, more than ever, when any belief that is not mere escapism is hard to sustain, the era in which Christianity was once ardent and bright makes wistfully moving contemplation.

Wigtownshire is rich in early Christian relics: amongst others, at Glasserton, where St. Ninian had his cave; and at Kirkmadrine, where there are fifth-century stones showing the Chi-Rho symbol.

On that still-perfect summer evening, I drove up the east coast of the Machars, getting out of my car to look at the worn-down ruins of Cruggleton Castle, supposed to have been built originally by a Norseman, but for long the seat of the Irish McKelies, until, after it had been knocked about by both Edward I and Wallace, it came into the possession of the Agnews. More interesting is the ruined Norman church of Cruggleton, once attached to Whithorn.

Passing through Garlieston, I reached Wigtown at sundown.

As a county town, Wigtown no doubt serves its purpose admirably; but it is too self-consciously Victorian to make much of an impression on a stone-conscious traveller. A town which insists upon having two market crosses seems a little over-anxious to assert its worldly position. The older of these market crosses, put up in 1738, is a neat enough affair; but the preposterous, buttressed monstrosity erected in 1816 to commemorate Waterloo is simply a comic eyesore. Curious, is it not, that military victory so often inspires bad architecture? Neither the stresses of war, nor the exultation of victory can be blamed for the County Buildings, for their cold-blooded mock-Tudor tastelessness dates from 1862, when Britain was at peace.

Wigtown's martyrs lie buried in the graveyard of the old kirk, abandoned in 1853 in favour of its ugly and pretentious new neighbour. The original kirk of the old site went up as long ago as 550, and was rebuilt more than once, certainly in 1730. It is thus not the actual building round which the story of the Wigtown martyrs centred.

In the interest of what was regarded as the general peace, the Government of Charles II decided in 1684 to enforce Abjuration Oaths. Those who would not swear to accept the king and give over Covenanting, together with those who were suspected of Covenanting activity, were dealt with by Justiciary Commissions. Galloway and Ayrshire provided these Commissions with many opportunities for action.

On 13th April, the Justiciary Commission held a court at Wigtown. There is some dispute as to who exactly took part, but general agreement that the Commission probably included Colonel Douglas, Major Winram, the notorious Laird of Lag Sir Robert Grierson and Sheriff David Graham. Four prisoners were arraigned before this body, accused of nonconformity, disorderly behaviour, and absenteeism from church. All were women, Margaret Lauchlison, or McLauchlin, who was past sixty, was well known in the district for her piety. Margaret Wilson, eighteen, and her sister Agnes, thirteen, were the daughters of a local man of small means, who had conformed. Little is known about Margaret Maxwell. She received the lightest sentence. The public hangman flogged her through the streets of Wigtown, then shut her for three days in the " jougs ", all of which she no doubt endured bravely, then betook her aching bones gratefully back into oblivion.

The other three were sentenced to be drowned. Gilbert Wilson thereupon paid down a hundred pounds for the immediate release of Agnes, and rode hastily off to Edinburgh to petition the

*Kirkcudbrightshire: Rutherford's Kirk, Anworth*

Privy Council for the life of his elder daughter. The Council received his petition favourably, and recommended the Secretaries of State to intervene on Margaret's behalf with the king for a remission.

Before news of the remission could be brought back to Wigtown and in spite of the fact that time had been officially allowed for an appeal, the Wigtown officials acted. On the morning of 2nd May, Winram's guardsmen marched down to the shore, where at high tide the Solway runs up the mouth of the Bladnoch. The sixty-three-year-old widow and the girl of eighteen were tied to stakes into the sludge, the older woman farther out.

Their tormentors tried to get Margaret Wilson to repent, first by letting her see the widow drown, then by " dashing her under water ", pulling her up again, and asking her to take the Abjuration Oath and pray for the king. To the latter request she agreed. " Lord, give him repentance, forgiveness and salvation, if it be Thy Holy Will," she is reported to have prayed, provoking Lag to cry out: " Dam'd bitch, we do not count such prayers; tender the oaths to her." But the " sinful oaths " she would not take, and the Solway was left to do its lapping work.

" The sea overflowed them," wrote a sensitive traveller of 1689, " when the stroke of every wave coming on them was as so many repeated deaths."

This was not murder hastily done, but murder coldly planned and put about as justice in the name of the Episcopalian Church.[1] Neither church nor clamouring sect in Scotland has clean hands. In the end, when causes and philosophies have triumphed and been overset, we are left considering " that ultimate entity, the simple human ". It is to the sense of personal humanity in its readers that the tombstone in the kirkyard by the sea speaks in moss-blunted letters:

> Let Earth and Stone still witness beare
> Their lies a virgine martyr here.
> Murthered for owning Christ supreme,
> Head of his church, and no more crime
> But not abjuring presbytery,
> And her not owning prelacy,
> They her condemned, by unjust law;
> Of Heaven nor Hell they stand no awe.

[1] Episcopalian apologists have tried to deny the whole episode by traducing the veracity of its first chronicler, Robert Wodrow. The fullest version of this apologetic verbiage will be found in *History Rescued*, by Mark Napier (in 1870). Wodrow was, of course, an enthusiastic fabricator for the cause of Presbyterianism. But the denials have no greater ring of truth.

*Kirkcudbrightshire: Dundrennan Abbey*

*Within the sea, tyed to a stake*
*She suffered for Christ Jesus' sake.*
*The actors of this cruel crime*
*Was Lag, Strachan, Winram and Grahame.*
*Neither young years nor yet old age*
*Could stop the fury of their rage.*

### III

My introduction to Kirkcudbrightshire was, indeed, a fondness for the work of the Glasgow School painter E. A. Hornel (1864-1933). Not that latterly he often deserted his distant Japanese preoccupations to paint the loveliness around him; but he lived in Kirkcudbright, as many artists have done before and since. Any Scottish county which attracts and spiritually sustains a permanent colony of not undistinguished artists, it seemed to me, must surely possess uncommon qualities.

I motored into the Stewartry through Glenkens, the upper valley of the Ken, and Carsphairn on the Deugh, where I stopped to absorb the view. To the south-west lay the Rhinns of Kells; to the north, half hidden by the trailing lining of the clouds, one of the Stewartry's three Cairnsmores, about which an old piece of geographical jingle still survives.

*There's Cairnsmore of Fleet,*
*And there's Cairnsmore of Dee;*
*But Cairnsmore of Carsphairn*
*Is highest of all three.*

Carsphairn, indeed, introduces the traveller to many of the characteristics of the county: these mountains which rival the Highlands in height if not in bulk; the rolling Lowland scenes; the clean, well-painted villages; and an even larger collection of relics of the struggle of the Covenanters than is to be found in Wigtownshire.

A traveller in Ireland soon discovers that nearly every village and worn-down stump of a hamlet has its martyrs, killed in the "troubles" of the present century. The memory of these men who fought fanatically for their country is usually preserved in over-written, garishly-printed pamphlets. A traveller in Galloway will come quickly upon a similar consciousness of martyrdom. For Galloway, the country of the "wild westland whigs", produced a high proportion of the Covenanters who fought against their Britannic Majesty's refusal to allow them to worship according to their conscience. Their memory is preserved in a less assertive literature: in passionate rhymes which damp and lichen are slowly cooling from mouldering, neglected tombstones.

Dalry, the next village along the road, has more than its share of such traditions, for it was here that the incident took place which led to the Battle of Rullion Green, in the Pentland Hills. On a November morning in 1666, four Covenanters in search of food came down from the hills into Dalry, where they found a group of soldiers threatening to roast alive a farmer who refused to pay his dues to an Episcopalian-minded Government. A fight ensued, a report of which, carried to a conventicle being held at Balmaclellan, stirred so much indignation that the assembled Covenanters at once took up arms, overpowered the local garrison, and marched on Dumfries, from where began the journey to the Pentlands and defeat at the hands of General Tam Dalzell.

Between Carsphairn, Dalry and New Galloway, stand some of the power stations built during the 1930s by the Galloway Water Power Company. Unlike some later water-works which the Hydro Electric Board has constructed in the North of Scotland, the Galloway dams have lost their aggressive utilitarian concrete look, and now seem a natural part of the landscape.

The royal burgh of New Galloway, at the head of Loch Ken, is really little more than a village of one hilly street. But the sight of the wooded loch lying far below and the dazzle of white-wash and gleam of paint from its houses make it oddly attractive. I stayed in it long enough to discover in the grave-yard of the parish church of Kells what is surely the most interesting piece of morturial verse in Scotland. It commemorates a certain John Murray, and was the outcome of a competition organized by the local minister towards the close of the eighteenth century.

> *Ah, John, what changes since I saw thee last;*
> *Thy fishing and thy shooting days are past,*
> *Bagpipes and hautboys thou canst sound no more;*
> *Thy nods, grimaces, winks and pranks are o'er.*
> *Thy harmless, queerish, incoherent talk,*
> *Thy wild vivacity, and trudging walk*
> *Will soon be quite forgot. Thy joys on earth—*
> *A snuff, a glass, riddles and noisy mirth—*
> *Are vanished all. Yet blest, I hope, thou art,*
> *For, in thy station, well thou play'dst thy part.*

John must have been a man of many parts, and the anonymous

guinea-winner preserves for us a vivid picture of the dead man's character. In the same kirkyard lie the remains of the local martyr, Adam McWhan, shot in 1685 for refusing to conform.

Two roads straddle Loch Ken. The road down the west side passes ruined Kenmure Castle, a sixteenth-century L-shaped fortalice, and the seat of the Gordons of Lochinver. This is also the countryside of Samuel Rutherford Crockett (1860-1914), who was born at the farm of Little Duchrae, near Laurieston; a place which:

" . . . lies nestled in green holm crofts. The purple moors ring it half round, north and south. To the eastward pine-woods once stood ranked and ready . . . The loch came after. It lay beneath, at what seemed a Sabbath day's journey from the house of Duchrae, down a wonderful loaning, full of infinite marvels. Beyond a little style there was a group of oak trees, from one of which a swing depended . . . The water-meadows, rich with long deep grass that one could hide in standing erect, bog-myrtle bushes, hazel-nuts, and brambles big as prize gooseberries and black as—well, as our mouths when we had finished eating them. Such a place for nuts! You could get cart-loads and cart-loads of them to break your teeth upon in winter fortnights. You could ferry across a raft laden with them . . . You might play hide-and-seek about the Camp, which (though marked 'probably Roman' in the Survey Map) is no Roman Camp at all, but instead only the last fortification of the Leaders in Galloway—those brave but benighted cottiers and crofters who rose in belated rebellion because the lairds shut them out from their poor moorland pasturages and peat-mosses."

Crockett is Galloway's best-known writer. His fame as a novelist rests on one book, *The Raiders*, a tale for boys. He was in many ways the Kailyairder with the most talent. The perversion of it in the sickly romances which make up most of his output—*The Lilac Sunbonnet; The Banner of Blue; The Stickit Minister's Wooing* and so on—is the more to be deplored. But with all the strength and loveliness of Galloway to fire his heart he spent his gifts brewing verbal sugarally water in his manses, and growing unctuous on the profits.

The road down the east side of Loch Ken goes through Cross-michael to Castle Douglas. Loch Ken, the centre-piece, is a strangely gentle loch, rushes thickening its shore, woodland and rich grasses clustering its banks.

Very different in character is Clatteringshaw Loch, whose power-giving waters high on a shoulder of the Rhinns of Kells must always be stirred by hill winds. I have never seen the tops of these southern mountains free from sweeping mist or driving rain, sometimes sloping visibly downwards catching rays of the clouded sun, like an eighteenth-century painting of an Old Testament judgment. On the day I first came over the narrow climb from New Galloway to Minnigaff, the sun shone warmly on the road—so warmly that I was tempted out of my car to climb the hillock on which stands a granite pencil monument, only to discover that it commemorated one Dr. Alexander Murray, umquhile minister of Urr and Professor of Ancient Languages at the University of Edinburgh when he died in 1813 at the age of 38. As I stood there, doubting the wisdom of erecting monuments of durability to men whose reputations may prove to be made of less lasting stuff, a bedraggled cloud trailed its frayed underside over the monument hill, and in an instant rain as heavy as any I have ever experienced hissed and spat upon the stones, scoring out all vision beyond a yard or two.

A similar change of weather came upon me when, a few months earlier, I drove up to Loch Trool. As I stood beside the huge stone boulder-monument which commemorates the recently-crowned Robert the Bruce's escape from the enclosing forces of England's de Vallance and the bloodhound of John of Lorne in 1307, mist steamed about the hill of Merrick, though Glen Trool itself lay full of sunshine. Imperceptibly the hill mist poured downwards, its greater gravity splashing the cupped sunshine to spill over the opposite rim of the glen. Soon it became difficult even to find the path back to the road; so I abandoned my intention of walking into these steaming hills to find Loch Enoch, and set out instead on a peering, mist-hampered journey over the mountain road into Ayrshire.

On the day of my soaking by the Murray monument, however, I was luckier: for, as I drove down towards Newton Stewart, I came back into the regions of the sun. Bruised and black was the sky around the hills after the battering of the storm: clear the sunshine that played about the blossom-trees hanging over the water of Cree, around which Newton Stewart clusters.

The town takes its name from the second son of the Earl of Galloway, William Stewart, who built some houses and procured for the place a burgh charter from Charles II in 1677. Like so many towns in Ayrshire, Dumfriesshire and Galloway during the eighteenth century, Newton Stewart was at least as interested in illegitimate trade as legitimate. But it was a business man and not a smuggler who tried to rename it. About 1778, Sir William Douglas bought the estate, spent twenty thousand pounds founding a factory for spinning cotton, assisted one Tannahill to establish a carpet factory and put money into the local tannery. He then renamed the place Newton Douglas, and as such, got it a new burgh charter. Unfortunately, however, the cotton-spinning factory did not prosper, and the carpet factory failed. Only the tanning factory, which had been there before, survived. So the inhabitants changed back their town's name to its original form.

Creetown—Creth to the English army of 1300, and afterwards Ferrytown, until 1785, when the burgh bearing the present name was founded—owes its prosperity to its granite quarries. It is a douce town on the Balloch Burn, not particularly remarkable. The Port-an-Ferry of Scott's *Guy Mannering*, it looks out across the sandy fringe of Wigtown Bay. In the early winter of 1954, the Balloch Burn repeatedly overflowed, flooding out the southwest end of the town.

Queen Victoria and Thomas Carlyle are credited with a conversation which has been put into the mouths of other equally pompous persons, and made to refer to different airts. But in its Galloway version, the Queen is said to have asked Carlyle what, in his view, was the finest road in the kingdom; whereupon Carlyle is reputed to have replied: " The coast road from Creetown to Gatehouse-of-Fleet." And when her inquiring Majesty wanted to know what road came next in the sage's favour, the answer she got—and she should have seen it coming to her—was " The coast road from Gatehouse-of-Fleet to Creetown."

I thought of this story as I drove down the east coast of Wigtown Bay and over the first of Carlyle's routes, on a clear July evening. I endorsed his opinion, apocryphal or no. The landscape hereabouts has all the colour of the Hebrides, together with a fuller lushness of vegetation. Sands and rocky caves fill out the tufted coastline; in one of them—at the mouth of the Kirkdale Burn—known as Dirk Hatteraick's Cave, the rock has been " shelved " to make it more suitable for use as a smuggler's store.

Galloway abounds in ruined castles and two of them are passed on the " Carlyle road ". Little is known now about Carsluith, which stands on a promontory overlooking Wigtown Bay, three miles south of Creetown, beyond the fact that it was the birthplace of the last Abbot of Sweetheart Abbey, Gilbert Brown, whose family's arms are preserved on a shield above a doorway in the east wall of the spiral staircase. Three miles further on, perched above the road like a brooding eagle, is Barholm, said to be the original of Scott's Ellangowan, and once to have sheltered John Knox.

The road leans round steeply as it approaches the Fleet. The traveller's eye is attracted across the Fleet estuary by the granite frontage of the eighteenth-century mansion of Cally. Cally House was built in 1763 by Robert Adam for the Murray family and is now a hotel. Gatehouse-of-Fleet is not an old town, since, as its name suggests, it only grew up around the entrance to the mansion. But it is well laid out, and comparatively un-spoiled by Victorian jumblery. At one time, indeed, it seemed to some local optimists to have industrial possibilities. By about 1800 it had four cotton-spinning factories, a wine company, a brewery, a tannery, a number of handloom weavers and, to quote from a guide-book of the time, "workshops of every class of artisan". The Fleet water was deepened and such was local pride that Gatehouse came to consider itself a potential rival to Glasgow. But its isolation—increased when an anti-railway laird forced the station to be set down seven twisting miles behind the town—proved its undoing, and its industries soon declined. To-day, Gatehouse sleeps peacefully, its harbour silted with sand, the old Ship Inn now the Anwoth Hotel.

I spent a night at the Cally Hotel, whose grounds take in the replanted state-owned Cally Forest. It was a strange experience to walk round the still-well-cared-for gardens, enjoy an excellent dinner beneath a finely-decorated ceiling, and then move across to a room of even nobler elegance and find the guests grouped, not about the gracious fire-place, but round a television set in the corner, their attention happily occupied by a tenth-rate American gangster film. Not even environment, it seems, can stimulate a sense of values.

After dinner, I drove down a lushly-winding lane to the ivy-covered ruins of Anwoth Church, where that most imaginative of Covenanting ministers, Samuel Rutherford (1600-61), stood strong for his conscience. His manse was demolished in 1827, the stones being used to build the manse of the present kirk, an operation that nearly led to a strike of the masons, who very properly resented the destruction of so stirring a memorial.

While at Anwoth, Rutherford watched Charles I's manœuvres with apprehension, and, on June 2nd, 1631, reflected his feelings, and those of the Presbyterian faction, in a letter[1] to Marian McNaught.

[1] *Letters of Samuel Rutherford* edited by A. A. Bonar.

" Well-Beloved Sister—My love in Christ remembered, I have received a letter from Edinburgh certainly informing me that the English service . . . and King James' Psalms, are to be imposed upon our kirk; and that the bishops are dealing for a General Assembly. A. R. hath confirmed the news also, and says he spoke with Sir William Alexander, who is come down with his prince's warrant for that effect . . . The great men of the world may make ready the fiery furnace for Zion; but trow ye that they can cause the fire to burn? No. He that made the fire, I trust, shall not say amen to their decreets."

I rejoined the main road and followed it towards Castle Douglas, crossing the Bridge of Dee and leaving the car again, to walk down the river bank that slopes to Threave Castle.

Threave, to my mind, is one of the most impressive castellated ruins in Scotland. Its size, its strength and its position on an island in the middle of a river seem somehow to force the mind to bridge the broken centuries by still arrogantly proclaiming the violent texture of living which characterized the age in which it was built. Its founder, Archibald the Grim, third Earl of Douglas, raised Threave towards the close of the fourteenth century, on the remains of an earlier stronghold of Alan, Lord of Galloway.

Nearly all the Douglas Earls met violent deaths; which inevitably they richly deserved. In 1451, the eighth Earl had more than a thousand armed men disposed about his castle, and it was with such strength behind him that his house defied even the throne. When the ninth and last Earl of this branch of the family was overthrown—he was forced by James II to spend his last years in the Abbey of Lindores, where he died in 1488—Threave became a Royal Keep, remaining so until 1524, when, together with other privileges, it was vested in Robert, Lord Maxwell, for a period of nineteen years. Thereafter, it went to the Lords Nithsdale, one of whom, in 1640, joined the king against the first Covenanters and had the misfortune to lose Threave. Its dismantling was ordered by the Estates, and it became yet another Scottish stone memorial destroyed because of religious squabbling.

From Threave, I drove into Castle Douglas. It takes its name not from the powerful house of Douglas, but from William Douglas, whose power derived not from men but from money. Until 1765, it was a hamlet called Causewayend on the shores of Carlingwark Loch. Marl, much used in the eighteenth century as a fertilizer, was discovered in the bed of the loch, and the mining of it developed the hamlet into the village of Carlingwark. The same Douglas who had earlier tried to rename Newton Stewart acquired Carlingwark by purchase in 1792. He gave it its present name, had it created into a burgh of barony, and established mills which were more successful than those he founded at his Newton Douglas. He was what is commonly called "a self-made man", having been at one time a pedlar in Penninghame. But he had made himself into a merchant prince in the early days of the Virginian trade, and at least had some practical achievement on which to base his pride. Even so, the changing of ancient names seemed to Robert Burns, who visited Castle Douglas while on his Galloway tour, a piece of unnecessary bombast, and the poet bluntly said so in some uncomplimentary lines.

Castle Douglas claims to be the place where that shadowy "smith" McKimm forged Mons Meg, which James II, on equally improbable authority, is said to have used when besieging Threave, in the process of which he successfully blew off the hand of the Fair Maid of Galloway as she sipped a glass of wine in the great hall of the castle. Alas for legend, whose richness of invention is so much greater than reality can ever attain!

Next morning, I set out for Kirkcudbright. Many think it the loveliest town in Galloway, including, presumably, the artists who make it their home. But it has to be seen at full tide for its charms to be evident. The broad expanse of bronze sleech, all too visible at low tide, is never burnished into the gleam which gives the mudflats of Suffolk their sultry fascination.

The town is now dominated by a remarkably ugly concrete milk-powder factory. Once it was more militantly ruled over by the castle which Sir Thomas MacLellan of Bombie built on the site of a former fortalice in 1582, and which is now a majestic red sandstone ruin.

The MacLellans were then a family of great power; which meant, in effect, that they had a considerable capacity for bullying disorderliness. The eighth Earl of Douglas beheaded Sir Patrick MacLellan at Threave in 1452. His lands were forfeited to the crown, and James II offered them to anyone who could deal with a band of Irish gypsies[1] and bring in their leader dead or alive. Young William MacLellan, anxious to regain his patrimony, sought out the gypsy tribe, slew the captain, and with that taste for spectacular messiness which was characteristic of

[1] Called Egyptians because of their fancied descent from the Pharaohs of Egypt; gypsies were numerous along the Borders until the late eighteenth century.

the age, presented the gypsy leader's head to the king on the point of a sword.

Sir William's grandson was created Lord Kirkcudbright in 1633. But the third Lord of Kirkcudbright brought ruin on the family. He resisted Cromwell with such vigour that he impoverished his estate, to say nothing of accounting for the death of most of the male population in the district. So far so good. But the moment Charles II was restored, Lord Kirkcudbright's conscience swung about. He now opposed Episcopalianism, lost his lands, went to prison, and died pointlessly disgraced. Oliver Goldsmith discovered one of his lordship's descendants in charge of a glove-shop in Edinburgh. Though George III restored the family lands, the title became extinct in 1832.

The MacLellan's Castle was often visited by kings, though not all the royal visitors came as invited guests. Among those who were, was Edward I, who stayed for ten days in 1300, Henry VI of England and his Queen, after his defeat at Towton, and James IV. The list of those not invited is headed by James II, who removed the Douglas owners and took possession of the place.

Though Kirkcudbright was also the scene of more than one Covenanting brawl, the history of the town is not aggressively assertive. The real charm of Kirkcudbright lies in its ordinary houses. Its beauty is that of well-ordered stone. Seventeenth-century houses and closes cluster up against more spacious and dignified eighteenth-century dwellings, like Broughton House, once the home of E. A. Hornel, which he bequeathed to the town. Everywhere—or nearly everywhere, for unfortunately there are signs of neglect and ruin in the old corner of the town around the Tolbooth Tower—fresh paint glistens. The artists apparently do not confine their attentions only to their canvases. Kirkcudbright has the appearance of taking some pride in itself. I hope its pride will yet urge it to save those old homes which no one has so far restored.

From Kirkcudbright, I set out for Dundrennan, where the remains of the Cistercian Abbey founded in 1142 by Fergus, Lord of Galloway, sit peacefully in a green fold beneath the village. There was never mob violence here. Dundrennan Abbey might have come to us intact, for it survived the destruction of the Reformation, and became the parish kirk. But unfortunately it was abandoned in 1742, and soon broken up as a quarry. Lord Cockburn's protests in 1839 probably saved it from total destruction. It is now in the safe hands of the Ministry of Works, as also is the Round Tower of Orchardton nearby, the only one of its kind in Galloway and once the somewhat confined seat of a branch of the Maxwell family.

From Dundrennan, I passed quickly through the granite town of Dalbeattie, and came down the coast to Arbigland, where Paul Jones, founder of the American Navy, though persistently called a pirate by British writers, was born in 1747. Another detour off the main road to Southerness Point brought me to the eighteenth-century lighthouse, no longer used but still in an excellent state of preservation.

From Kirkbean, I drove beneath the misty bulk of Criffel, to New Abbey. Here Devorgilla, great-great-granddaughter of David I, third daughter of Alan, Lord of Galloway, and mother of John Balliol, the "toom tabbard" vassal king of Edward I, founded Sweetheart Abbey in 1275 in memory of her husband, calling it "new" to distinguish it from Dundrennan. And here her remains were brought from Barnard Castle in Yorkshire, when she died in 1290, the casket containing the embalmed heart of her husband being laid to rest beside her own body. Gilbert Brown, the last Abbot, imprisoned and banished as a Jesuit, was the original of Scott's *Abbot*. During the seventeenth century and most of the eighteenth, Sweetheart Abbey was used locally as a quarry, until in 1779 an unusually liberal-minded minister founded a fund for its restoration. Not much more than the roofless conventual church, its style late First Pointed, then remained.

From New Abbey, I drove up to Lincluden, which lies across the Nith from Dumfries, and though in Galloway, is now almost within the suburbs of that town. It was founded originally as a nunnery by Uchtred, second son of Fergus, Lord of Galloway, about the middle of the twelfth century. Archibald the Grim expelled the nuns for "insolence" and other unfortunately unspecified "irregularities". He converted the buildings into a collegiate church. Later, Douglases and Maxwells held the rights to it, and finally the Earls of Nithsdale, before it, too, passed into the clean hands of the Ministry of Works.

## CHAPTER IX

## AYRSHIRE

I used to be a great deal at Ayr. It was then filled with the families of gentlemen from the country, from India, and from public service, and was a gay card-playing, dancing, eating and drinking, scandal-loving place. The taste for scandal and guzzling probably remains, but all the rest is gone. The sort of gentry who formed its soul exists no longer. The yellow gentlemen who return now from India take their idleness and their lives to Cheltenham or Bath. The individuals whose station, age, habits, or characters gave respectability to the comfortable country town, are gone and their very families—the scenes of such mirth, beauty, kindness and enjoyment—have entirely disappeared. The fashion of the Ayr world hath passed away.

I went to the point of the pier, along the links, round the edges of the town, and through most of the streets, yesterday, before break-fast. Except Wellington Square, the Court-House, and a few half-country houses, it is all very changed.

LORD COCKBURN, 1842.

ONE of my earliest surviving visual impressions is of a summer garden in Ayr, the scented red roses flashing against the grey stone of the house. I remember the face of the house in which, as a young child, I spent a holiday. Its façade—later, I found that it was part of Ayr's considerable Georgian heritage—imprinted themselves on my imagination, suggesting to me that in some way it must be an important house. In the garden of that house, too, my four-year-old ego played its most considerable drama of assertiveness. The presence of my one-year-old sister, a centre of attraction in her pram, suddenly appeared to me intolerable; so I smote her smartly with a shoe. Neither she nor I suffered any damage in this encounter, however, and, in common with thousands of other Scottish children, we came to know the Ayrshire coastline as a place of pleasant sands and shallow, safe waters.

The county folds round a great bay, on the lower reaches of the Firth of Clyde, tipped at one end by Skelmorlie, and at the other by Glen App, on the shores of Loch Ryan. Set on its side, the outline of the county resembles a graceful fruit-bowl. Less fancifully, it was anciently split into three divisions: in the north Cunninghame: in the middle, Kyle, its northern boundary the River Irvine; in the south, Carrick, separated from Kyle by the River Doon.

More anciently still—in the second century A.D.—Ayrshire

formed the southern part of the territory of the Damnonii. One of their towns, Vandogara, was supposed to have been at Loudon Hill, on the banks of the Irvine. Here, too, the Romans had a camp, which was linked with their administrative nerve-centre at Coria, or Carstairs, by a road.

Vague rumours of battles between the native inhabitants and the Romans, and even between the natives themselves, have come down to us. But we are as uncertain as to the details of their distant encounters as we are about the nature of the Celtic people who occupied the country throughout the Dark Ages, though we learn that Gaelic remained their tongue until the fifteenth century. When the Romans withdrew from Ayrshire, the territory became part of the kingdom of Strathclyde, remaining so until the eighth century, when Kyle and Cunninghame came under the Northumbrian kings. Alpin, a Scots-Irish king, is supposed to have invaded the county in the ninth century, only to meet defeat and death at Dalmellington; while in 1263, King Haco's defeat at the battle of Largs broke for ever the Norse hold on Scotland.

In the Wars of Succession, Edward I invaded Kyle and Carrick and suffered defeats both from Wallace and Bruce, the most significant being that at Loudon Hill. Wallace, though born in Renfrewshire, played some of his most dramatic strokes in Ayrshire, while Robert the Bruce was, of course, the son of the Earl of Carrick, a title his father had acquired by marriage.

In the sixteenth and seventeenth centuries, Ayrshire was a strong centre of the reformed faith—both Wishart and Knox frequently preached within its borders—and, like Galloway, was strong for the Covenant. It therefore remained strong for King George when news of the distant passage southwards of Prince Charlie's army reached its bien lairds' ears.

It has produced a remarkable number of men who have won honour and fame; but by far the most distinguished of them is, of course, Robert Burns. In more modern times, while still nourishing its rich agricultural traditions, it has developed not only its natural holiday attractions, but also a wide range of industries. To many people Ayrshire is, indeed, the "Land of Burns". His work has brought immortality to many of its towns and villages. But to approach Ayrshire, so to speak, through Burns is to do the county itself less than justice. We shall, therefore, make our way through the three ancient divisions of the county, beginning first with Cunninghame.

Skelmorlie, in Ayrshire, is related physically to Wemyss Bay, in Renfrewshire, which lies a little to the north. In 1834, when the Clyde coast was reaching the height of its development, the proprietor of the Georgian Kelly House, John Wallace, had the idea of developing the place as the "Brighton of the Clyde", an idea which neither he nor his son, the local member of Parliament, was ever able to realize. (How rarely places which set out consciously to imitate other places succeed!) When Robert Wallace had to sell Kelly House in 1860, one half became the estate of Castle Wemyss. The other half was bought in 1867 by Dr. James ("Paraffin") Young. It subsequently passed into the hands of the shipping family, the Stephens of Linthouse, who pulled down the Georgian house and erected an ornate affair in keeping with the warmly-glowing but tasteless and pretentious red sandstone houses which line the seafront. This, in its turn, was set on fire by a militant band of suffragettes in 1910. The Montgomery's castle of Skelmorlie still guards the entrance to its wooded glen, as its keep, the oldest part of it, has done since 1502. It has also a fine seventeenth-century addition, and a larger but much less fine Victorian addition.

Largs, along the coast of the expanding Firth, has set itself out since the eighteenth century to be a holiday resort.

One of the earliest reports of the Largs holiday is the recollection of Robert Reid ("Senex"),[1] who stayed at Hely House during the summer of 1782. In these days it was not simply a question of taking a public conveyance. Mrs. Reid, the author's mother, had a horror of "sailing packets and half-decked wherries", so she "hired" James Neilson, with his large covered Paisley caravan, to take us and all our plenishings".

"Matters being thus far arranged, and the day of our departure being fixed, the caravan (which was painted a brilliant blue) arrived at our domicile at the appointed time, and its bottom was quickly filled with feather beds, mattresses, bolsters, pillows and blankets etc, and the other articles of plenishing were stowed away in various parts of the vehicle, as was thought most suitable and convenient. We then all in succession entered this ponderous machine, which put me in mind of Noah and his children entering the ark."

The first eight hours of the journey brought the caravan to Kilbirnie, where they halted at the inn. While his passengers were refreshing themselves, the worthy Mr. Neilson did some inquiring and reconnoitring, as a result of which he came back to inform Mrs. Reid that:

[1] *Glasgow, Past and Present*, by "Senex".

" . . . properly speaking, there was no road at all from Kilbirnie to Largs; that it was just a precipitous descent, over loose stones and rough rocks, and that he would require often to take the bed of some mountain stream in lieu of a path: in short, he was told that if he attempted the journey his caravan would be shattered all to pieces, or capsized on the way . . . Therefore he now most pointedly refused to move a single step farther, saying that he was not going to be answerable for the lives of the children."

Mrs. Reid then discovered that she had left her purse at home. However, being a quick-witted woman, she recollected that a Kilbirnie man owed her husband a bill. So she collected the debt and paid off the canny Mr. Neilson.

"She then hired two strong country carts, with men and horses accustomed to travel over the muir-road, and having loaded the carts with our household plenishings, and placed us all the best way she could on the top of the carts, we proceeded on our journey through the muir. I must confess, after all, that James Neilson was not far wrong in refusing to risk his caravan upon the muir-road, for it was just a track of deep mud-holes, slippery rocks, and loose stones and boulders. In some parts it was very steep, and undoubtedly dangerous; in fact it required the strictest attention of our new carters to keep the carts from being capsized. The country farmers who had occasion to lead peats from this muir at the period in question, used sledges with long trams which are not easily overturned."[1]

After "a good shaking", the family eventually arrived at Hely House. Robert Reid gives us an interesting picture of Largs as it was then.

"There were few Glasgow families that took lodgings in Largs for the season. The lodging-houses were all small, most of them merely single rooms, and none of them self-contained. The inhabitants of Largs had not yet learned how to turn the penny by letting lodgings, and seemed to regard with the utmost indifference any application by our Glasgow folk for furnished apartments; indeed, they appeared to consider it a favour to give up any part of their own houses to strangers. At

[1] I saw two of these sledges being used for the same purpose on the island of Scarba in 1950.

this time there were scarcely any houses in Largs fronting the sea."

Largs's importance in history is as the scene of that decisive battle in which the forces of Alexander III defeated the remnants of King Haco of Norway's army on the plain of Haylie on October 3rd, 1263. Early in the eighteenth century, when ballad-faking was just becoming a popular occupation in cultured Scottish circles, Elizabeth Halket, Lady Wardlaw (1677-1727), mysteriously "discovered" the ancient ballad of *Hardyknute*, which appealed to her contemporaries as an authentic near-contemporary account of the proceedings at Haylie:

*When bows were bent and darts were thrawn,*
*For thrang scarce could they flee;*
*The darts clove arrows as they met,*
*The arrows struck the tree.*
*Lang did they rage and fight fou fierce*
*With little skaith to man,*
*But bloody bloody was the field*
*Ere that lang day was done.*

Forty-one years before Lady Wardlaw was born, Sir Robert Montgomery built an ornamental mausoleum for himself and his wife around the remains of the "courteous knight" Sir Hugh Montgomery, who captured the Percy at the Battle of Otterburn. The Skelmorlie Aisle, as it is called, was probably the north transept of the old church of Largs, and is all that now remains left of it. Three miles north of Largs, Knock Castle stands, well preserved and occupied, though it was built as long ago as 1604. About a mile to the north-east of Knock there once stood Brisbane House, built in 1636. During the second world war, however, it was blown up by Commando troops to give them training in practical destruction!

For many centuries, Largs has held its St. Colm's (Columba's) Fair on the first Tuesday of June after the 12th, the saint's reputed birthday. Robert Reid remembers " the Common of Largs " at " the Fair of St. Colm's, crowded with merry Highland lads and lasses tripping it on the light fantastic toe to the drone of the bagpipes ". He found the Fair " a most entertaining spectacle ".

" There could not have been less than 400 vessels either lying at anchor before the town or drawn up upon the beach. It was a beautiful sight to see the arrival of the numerous

*Kirkcudbrightshire: Galloway country, near Carsphairn*
*Wigtonshire: Priory Pend, Whithorn*

vessels, and the bustle of landing their cargoes. The communications between the lowlands and the highlands being then very troublesome and uncertain, St. Colm's Fair brought vast numbers of Highlanders to the spot, either to buy or to sell . . . The whole common, from the present quay to Noddle Burn, was a condensed mass of Highland Cattle."

By the mid-nineteenth century, however, the boisterousness of the proceedings had become far from saintly; and cattle-dealing had become more centralized. The Fair survives, much gentilified, as a restored attraction for tourists.

Still farther along the coast, Fairlie—to Lord Cockburn in 1842, " the best village of the wealthy in Scotland "—developed during the nineteenth century, from a tiny fishing hamlet into a railhead for the steamers to Millport, on the Greater Cumbrae, and into a successful yacht-building centre. The lands around Kelburne Castle, which stands about a mile to the north, part of it dating from the late sixteenth century, have been in the family of the Boyles, Earls of Glasgow, since the reign of Alexander III. West Kilbride, with its high view over the islands of the Firth, and Seamill, down by the sandy beach, are now mainly residential places and holiday resorts. The roofless fifteenth-century Law Castle, which stands on a hill overlooking West Kilbride, was probably built about 1468 for Thomas, Master of Boyd and later Earl of Arran, when he married James III's sister, Princess Mary.

Ardrossan brings us into industrial Ayrshire. Hereabouts the land was owned by the Montgomeries, Earls of Eglinton. The crumbled remains of Castle Craig, on the headland separating the north and south bays, are said to have been the scene of one of Wallace's early sallies, when he lured the English garrison out by firing a neighbouring hamlet, then ambushed and slew them on their return, throwing their bodies into what was thereafter known as " Wallace's Larder ", until Cromwell demolished the castle, dungeon and all.

The modern town of Ardrossan was largely the creation of the twelfth Earl of Eglinton, who, as Colonel Hugh Montgomerie of Coilsfield, was earlier Burns's friend " Sodger Hugh ". He founded the harbour in 1806. His idea was that since sailing vessels usually had to endure a tedious passage from the Cumbraes to Port Glasgow—after which only the smallest ships could get up-river to Glasgow itself—Ardrossan could be developed as the city's major port, and that port and city should be linked by canal. Both Telford and Rennie were engaged on the initial construction

245

*Ayrshire: Brig o' Doon and Burns Monument, Alloway*
*Renfrewshire: the Cloch lighthouse, on the Clyde*

work, which, if it had followed the original plan, would have made Ardrossan the finest port of the day in Britain. In 1815, however, the money gave out, and the harbour was completed according to less expensive ideas.

Much of the town went up as it had originally been planned, however, and its long right-angled streets along the sea-front are by no means unimpressive, though their good effect is considerably marred by haphazard later developments hemming them in. Ardrossan is now the railhead for Arran, thirteen miles across the Firth; in summer, also for Ireland and the Isle of Man. It earns its living mainly by building and repairing ships, and by refining oil. Yet it still finds some favour as a holiday resort, mainly among Glaswegians.

In Lord Cockburn's day, sea-bathing was its principal attraction. Indeed, it was at Ardrossan, during one of his "Circuit Journeys", that his Lordship had his sensibilities affronted by the spectacle of ladies bathing.

"The ladies' bathing is conducted on the genuine Scotch principle of not being at all ashamed of it, as why should they? Is it not pure? and healthy? and advised by the Doctor? and anything wrong in it? So the ladies emerge, in full day, from their flats, in their bathing dresses, attended by a maid, and a sister or aunt, the maid carrying a small bundle containing a towel and some dry clothes, the friend tittering. The bather crosses the road, and goes to the sea, which is never more than a few yards, or inches, beyond the road's edge. She then enters the water, and shivers or splashes, according to her taste, conversing or laughing or screaming all the while, with her attendant ashore. But it is on coming out that the delicate part of the operation begins, for, as they don't walk home wet, and then dress in their own rooms, they must change their whole raiment before the public. For this purpose the maid holds a portion of the dry vestment over the dripping lady's head, and as the soaked gown descends to the heels, the dry is supposed to descend over the head as fast, so that the principle is, that, between the two, the lady is never seen. Ignorance is sometimes bliss, and it is very wise in the assistants never to tell the patient anything about it. But I wonder how, when they happen to be looking at a fellow-exhibiter, and observe the interest taken from every window, and by all the street, in the proceeding, they can avoid discovering that such feats are seldom performed without revelations, and that a single fold of wet linen adheres too resolutely to the inner surface to require any other revelation. But I never saw bathing performed by ladies in Scotland even with common decency. Why the devil can't they use bathing-machines, or go into retired places, or wall or pale off enclosures?"

Lord Cockburn's views on mid-twentieth-century feminine beach-wear and behaviour would surely make interesting reading.

Stevenston and Saltcoats, which flourish in close association, are both of ancient origin, Saltcoats being established by James V as a hamlet for the production of salt, and Stevenston having been mentioned in a thirteenth-century charter. Saltcoats was expanded by Robert Cunningham in 1686, when he built new salteries, opened up collieries in the hinterland, and gave the place its first harbour. To-day, Saltcoats is rather a dreary little coastal burgh. But its prospect of Arran, and its stretch of sand, give it a holiday attraction to Glaswegians, who throng the narrow, main street during their Fair Fortnight. Stevenston now has a prime place of honour in our civilization, for upon the coastal belt of Ardeer there is an explosive factory. Ardeer is said to have been the first dynamite factory in Britain, having been built by Alfred Nobel towards the end of the nineteenth century.

Irvine was described by the seventeenth-century English traveller Sir William Brereton as being "daintily situate both upon a navigable arm of the sea and in a dainty pleasant level champaign country". "Dainty" is perhaps not the adjective which comes most readily to mind when contemplating modern Irvine. Although Irvine vies with Ayr as the county's oldest burgh, little enough evidence of its antiquity survives. In the High Street still stands the Mercat Cross, restored as a war memorial after nineteenth-century banishment. Burns lodged in the Glasgow Vennel during the few unhappy months in 1781, while he learned the business of flax-dressing. Irvine has one of the oldest Burns Clubs in the world; and fittingly, by far the finest statue of the poet, done by the sculptor-poet Pittendrigh Macgillivray (1856-1938). The old town is now somewhat dominated by Irvine New Town.

Irvine, has had literary sons of her own. The hymn-writer James Montgomery (1771-1854) came into this world in a house in the street now named after him. Montgomery, the son of a Moravian preacher, had a curious career. He became the editor of a Sheffield newspaper, and was imprisoned in York for sedition, his offence being similar to that which so nearly undid Robert Burns: too vocal a sympathy with the cause of the Friends of the People. Fifteen of his hymns are in the hymnary of the

Church of Scotland. While their religious power is no doubt not inconsiderable, their literary power is unfortunately feeble.

Irvine's most famous man of letters is, of course, the novelist John Galt (1779-1839). He was the son of the captain of an East Indiaman. When the future author was four, the family moved to Greenock. Nevertheless, Irvine bore him, and justly claims him as her own.

Galt was a man of many talents and of immense industry. He pioneered a township in Canada, where several other towns are also called after him, and he had large business ambitions. He wrote several indifferent novels, and, under the stimulus of Black-wood, six or seven masterpieces in which he catches the old Scots flavour of Ayrshire life just before it disappeared beneath the oncoming flood of Anglicizing industrialism. In a sense he is thus Burns's prose counterpart: a sort of Scottish Trollope. Yet in spite of the warm vernacular virr of *The Entail* and *Annals of the Parish*, Galt is all too little read in Scotland to-day.

The Relief Church, in the Bridgegait, was the scene of the founding of the sect of the Buchanites in 1783, by Mrs. Elizabeth Buchan and the Reverend Hugh White, one of the church's ministers. These deluded souls claimed for themselves Apocalyptic titles and powers of physical immortality. Ultimately, their claims so roused the people of Irvine to riot that the leaders and their followers were sent out of the town. They moved first to Kilmaurs and then to Dumfriesshire, where they built the village of Crocketford. The natural course of events disproved their remarkable claims.

The hinterland of both Cunninghame and Kyle has been much industrialized. The iron-works of Glengarnock dominate the area triangularized by Kilburnie, Beith and Dalry. Mills also add to the business of the somewhat bleak scene. Dalry, in the valley of the River Rye, preserves many of its old streets and, at its heart, something of the character of the seventeenth- and eighteenth-century small Scottish burgh. In the days of the feudal ties, the " big hoose " was Blair Castle, a most impressive cluster of towers, originally of the fifteenth century but much added to in the seventeenth, and still lived in by the Blair family.

Kilbirnie's " big hoose "—the Place of Kilbirnie—is a ruin. The town itself has been quite despoiled by years of devotion to the causes of cloth and iron. In a mausoleum in St. Breda's Churchyard lies Captain Thomas Crawford of Jordanhill, who led the capture of the Marian stronghold of Dumbarton Castle, and whose evidence of what passed between Mary and Darnley shortly before the blowing up of Kirk o' Field was used at her trial.

Dunlop is best known for its cheese, and because of that loquacious Mrs. Dunlop of Dunlop who was the friend and correspondent of Robert Burns: Stewarton, the Bonnet Town, for its knitwear as much now as for the glengarrys and balmorals which have replaced the old Lowland "Scotch bonnet" in which it specialized. We usually hear this headgear referred to to-day as the "Kilmarnock Bonnet", because the making of hose and bonnets is believed to have originated in Kilmarnock, or "Auld Killie", reference to these activities being made as long ago as 1603. Before that, Kilmarnock was probably a hamlet clustering round a twelfth- or thirteenth-century church, dedicated, no doubt, after a much earlier original, to the Irish saint Marnock or Mernoc, who died in either 634 or 635. Kilmarnock stood out for the Covenant, and in the earlier part of the seventeenth century the Boyds, Earls of Kilmarnock, were on the side of their inferiors. But in 1745 the young Earl of Kilmarnock broke with the Hanoverian feelings of the townsfolk and came out for Prince Charlie, which led to the ruin of his family. Dean Castle, the Boyds' home from the time of Robert the Bruce until 1735, when it was accidentally burned down, has been splendidly restored by Lord Howard de Walden, and presented to the town.

Kilmarnock, while possessing an enormously large crop of eighteenth- and nineteenth-century poets of its own—among them the highly-gifted essayist and laureate of Glasgow, Alexander Smith—has a leading place in the Burns story, since it was from the presses of John Wilson that *Poems Chiefly in the Scottish Dialect* came out. The publication then cost three shillings. Known now as the Kilmarnock Edition, a good copy fetches over two thousand pounds. To-day, Kilmarnock carries the heavy Ayrshire and Galloway traffic through its narrow main street. It makes carpets, water-controlling machinery, locomotives, woollen goods and whisky.

Further up the Irvine valley, Galston flourished once as a mining town, but has declined rapidly since its pits were closed. Newmilns, like its neighbour Darvel, separated by The Cut, is famous for its lace. Darvel was the birthplace of Sir Alexander Fleming (1881-1955), the discoverer of penicillin. Both have Covenanting traditions, as befits places so near to Drumclog, where in 1678 the Covenanters gained one of their rare victories in a skirmish with the troops of Claverhouse.

Kyle is said to have derived its name from a shadowy British local monarch Coel Hen (Old King Coil or Cole), believed traditionally to have been killed in a battle near Coylton. As, however, the whole of the ancient baillerie of Kyle must once have been wooded, a more probable derivation is from the Gaelic *Coille*, a wood. Much of the hinterland of Kyle is now given over to coal-mining. There are pits at, or near, Mauchline, Balloch-myle, and at Old and New Cummock; while at Muirkirk, where Tar Macadam was first made, one of the earliest Scottish iron-works went up in the late eighteenth century. Strange that names so strongly attached to romance and song should now grace coal-pits!

There is little enough pleasure or point in wandering around the desolation which the too-rapid reaving of coal from the earth has wrought on these once pleasant places. Here is name after name familiar to students of Scottish literature: Tarbolton, the scene of Burns's adolescence; Mossgiel; Mauchline, where he set up house with Jean, and where so many of his friends and enemies sleep in the kirkyard; Catrine, where his friend Professor Dugald Stewart had his country seat; and Auchinleck, the seat of the father of Burns's contemporary, James Boswell, and later of his son the luckless Sir Alexander, killed in the second-last duel to be fought in Scotland.

But it is the coastline of Kyle, together with the more immediate landward miles, that attracts most travellers' closest attentions, and justly so. Troon, perhaps from the Cymric *trouwyn*, a nose or promontory, is—in essence at any rate—like Ardrossan, an eighteenth-century creation. The fourth Duke of Portland planned to give " The Trone " a harbour which would help it to develop industrially. But his plans to some extent went awry; for, although shipbuilding goes on at Troon and coal is exported from its harbour, its development was to be along very different lines. It has become not only a holiday resort, but one of the wealthiest dormitories of Glasgow. Troon has many commuters, but, for its size, surprisingly little real communal life.

Prestwick, also a holiday resort, grew up around a church dedicated to St. Nicholas. (The name of the place is said to mean " priest's house ".)

My own memories of Prestwick reach back to early childhood. For many years, we took a house there for a month during the summer. Houses in Prestwick have exotic names. The first of our summer homes was called *Pegu*, the second *Crete*. To my childish mind, *Pegu* suggested clothes pegs, *Crete*, the rubber soles on my father's golfing shoes!

Looking backwards in mid-passage, it is hard to resavour the strange physical pleasure which most of us enjoy on the safe, dry first hinter-level of the beach. Yet I still remember isolated details: the polished flow of sand, dripping smoothly between the fingers: the scrunch of wooden spade on up-turned, pie-moulding tin pail: the remote, salt-scented quiet inside sand houses—dug with impressed parental labour!—from behind whose entrenched walls the impatient sound of the sea took on a muffled, unmenacing quality, like that distant adult life which occasionally hinted at its presence through momentary disturbing revelations. These revelations increased with the years, as the pleasures of the dry sand no longer satisfied, and we moved nearer to the sea.

During our last year at Prestwick, when I was eleven and sailing a model yacht just beyond the fringe of the shallow waves, a green-striped bathing-box with a red roof—similar to those noticed by Lord Cockburn at Ardrossan—was pulled slowly down into the sea by an aged horse. That horse spent each day pulling several of these boxes up and down in turn, and its operations had long since ceased to interest me. But, on this particular journey, it crossed the path of my yacht. As I retrieved the boat from beside the half-submerged wheel, the doors of the box were flung open and a pretty girl splashed out. As she plunged past me, I noticed for the first time that girls were not the same shape as boys.

At one end of the promenade, crouching beneath a sand-doon, stood Connels, a flat-roofed cafe which sold half-penny cones of ice cream. At the other end was the Pavilion, where the Entertainers played in silken pierrot costumes, complete with floppy bobbles. These Entertainers were dreadfully sentimental; I still prickle with embarrassment at the recollection of a monologue supposedly delivered by a father to his son when the boy appears for the first time in a pair of long trousers! But at rainy matinees at least they did encourage the young. When I was six or seven, I made my first appearance before the public in the Pavilion platform, singing a ditty which began " Don't do that to the poor puss cat". It was a highly moral, if not very logical song, the deterrent against anti-feline aggression being the somewhat doubtful supposition that " You might be a pussy-cat yourself some day, so . . . Don't do that etc. ". It won me a consolation bon-bon.

While these delights were summered slowly through, sometimes unfamiliar noises droned above our heads, while Sir Alan Cobham's travelling air-circus was making one of its periodic visits to a grassy field beyond the golf courses. He offered five shilling flights in spidery biplanes. That field has now become Prestwick Airport, the most fog-free landing-place in Britain, though by a crippling lack of feeder services necessarily relegated in status in favour of airports near London. Orangefield House, now destroyed to make way for the present terminal buildings, was once the home of that good friend of Burns, John Samson.

Ayr itself is still a gracious town, with its two Brigs made famous by Burns's poem about them, its striking Wallace Tower in the High Street (built, however, only in 1834, to commemorate the misbelief that the Scottish patriot had once been imprisoned in a previous tower on the same site); its fine early-sixteenth-century house Loudon Hall, recently restored as a civic centre; its many graceful Georgian houses; its broad promenade and beach, looking across to the Arran hills; its "Tam o' Shanter Inn", and its other memories of Burns.

Alloway is, of course, the high altar of Burnsism. Much as I am opposed to the craft of literary hagiology, I admit that it is difficult not to be moved by a first visit to auld clay biggin which, on 25th January, 1759, was Burns's birthplace. In spite of the fresh paint and the museum cleanliness which now prevails, it is not difficult to imagine the smoky, steaming cattle-breathed-on atmosphere which must have unhealthily warmed the cramped little rooms when William and Agnes Burnes were producing and bringing up their family there. No other great poet's birthplace awakens this sense of peasant immediacy.

Nearby stands the Auld Kirk where William Burnes is buried, and which was the setting of the folk-tale that inspired "Tam o' Shanter". In elegant contrast—really a memorial to Burns's Augustan aspirations rather than to his sturdy peasant achievement—stands the Burns Monument of David Hamilton, built in 1820, a Corinthian cyclostyle with an elaborate cupola similar to the Burns Monument on Edinburgh's Calton Hill.

The banks and braes of Bonnie Doon—rising out of lonely Loch Doon, whose islanded Balliol's Castle, scene of the death of King Alpin of Dalriada in 741, was rebuilt on the shore before its original base was submerged when a hydro-electric dam raised the level of the water—separate Kyle from Carrick.

At drearily-frequent intervals, the thought of Scotland's greatest poet inspires well-meaning Scotsmen to behave absurdly. Some of them try to write plays about the Bard (though, like Mary Queen of Scots and Bonnie Prince Charlie, Burns has hitherto proved a certain ingredient for dramatic disaster; with Burns as a part of the recipe a play falls flat in the oven of its creator's imagination): others have trumpeted abroad the notion that

Scotland ought to have a National Theatre to honour the plays
that Burns himself never had time to write.

A few years ago, when a Holiday Camp was opened beneath
the Heads of Ayr, I was invited to attend a performance of a
"folk opera" called *Robert Burns*. I wrote for a British daily
newspaper, and for the *Scots Review*. As that excellent journal
has died the premature death of almost all little reviews, and
as my critique attacks the practice of Burns hagiology rather than
merely one more bad play about the poet, I include it here almost
in its original form.

"When I pulled back my bedroom curtains that morning, it
was raining. Living in the West of Scotland, I have by now
steeled myself in the philosophy that one must never let rain
interfere with one's activities. Even so, it was not without a
pang of disappointment that I backed my car out of its garage,
and set off on the road to Ayr. As I threaded my way through
the backstreets of Glasgow, the rain ceased. But the skies were
almost as grey as the broad road which carried my car on swish-
ing wheels towards the land of Scotland's National Bard. Either
because patriotism rides easily in my veins, or because I had
gulped my breakfast, I was conscious of a sense of occasion.

I was on my way to the opening performance of XYZ's
*Robert Burns*, described in the advertisements as a 'folk
opera'.

Over my lunch in the newly-painted, tree-shrouded hotel at
Monckton, I meditated on the spectacle which might unfold
itself in the 'Brig o' Doon' Theatre, at a holiday camp. Since
I am a poet, I naturally take more than a common interest in
Burns, as I do in the other great Scottish Makars. But the rain
came on again during lunch, and when I let in the clutch and
eased off slowly down the drive, the smell of the dripping trees
was thick and oppressive. I was never the one to be daunted by
ill-founded superstitions, so I dismissed the notion that this
might be an omen, and resolutely continued my course to Ayr.

Once across the new brig, I took counsel. 'Where,' I asked
a benign-looking yokel, 'is the Brig o' Doon Theatre?' He
wrinkled his face for a moment, then ventured. 'Ay, it'll no
be faur frae Brig o' Doon, I'm thinkan.' Then revelation
broke upon him. 'Jist keep the way ye're goan an ye canna
miss it.' I followed his advice until the car began to climb
between the fields on the far side of Ayr. The rain thickened,
and a mist crept up from the beaches. I had almost decided
to turn back and seek out a policeman, when suddenly a huge

building loomed out of the foul weather. It was yellow and rectangular in shape. When I moved nearer I found it to be salvation. For a notice board informed me that a narrow road down the side led to the holiday camp. Slowly I slid the car down the hill, under an ancient flimsy-looking railway-bridge, and round a sharp corner. There, before me, lay the goal of my endeavours!

I had scarcely time to drink in this vision of architectural novelty which stretched down to the sea before a beliveried attendant inquired my business. I told him that I had come to write about *Robert Burns* for a leading Scottish newspaper. He grew most deferential, and told me to park the car wherever I liked, because the camp had only opened two hours before, and two-thirds of official Ayr were enjoying the kindly hospitality following the opening ceremony. I thanked him warmly, took his advice, and set out on a tour of inspection. The buildings in their bright colours gleamed through the rain. Water ran down the shining roofs in runnels. I looked at the shops, at the huge inquiry office with its desks marked 'Ration Books', 'Visitors' Mail', 'Inquire here about anything', and so forth. I wandered into the 'Games Room' where young people were playing table tennis on about twenty tables, and thirty odd dart boards hung round the walls. I peered into the 'Quiet Lounge' where older people were reclining in armchairs restfully decorated in red, yellow, blue, green and cream. I crossed over to the ballroom, quite the largest I have ever seen, and marvelled at its red and blue strip lighting, its gilded gargoyles glaring over the floor, and its plastic crests of the Scottish clans punctuating the mirrored walls.

It was at this point that I had my first encounter with an attendant proper. The man at the entrance might, after all, have been found outside any palatial city picture palace. But not the attendants proper. They were dressed in kilts, and to cover their upper parts, they wore red blazers with a crest embroidered in black upon the pocket. They were suave, polite, helpful. I spoke to about half-a-dozen of them, and was hard put to it to preserve an unruffled countenance when their accents betrayed their places of origin—Lancashire, Yorkshire, London and its environs. As the sixth of these gentlemen directed me to the 'Brig o' Doon Theatre' (the other half of the building which housed the dance-hall) I reflected on how excellent it would be for the Scottish National Party if similar camps were started all over Scotland. Within a few years, thousands of kilted Englishmen would feel in duty bound to pay their half-crown and support the cause which provided them with a living.

But flippancy abandoned me as soon as I entered the theatre. Managers, sub-managers, and sub-sub-managers stood around, interspersed with programme girls dressed in red, and seat-finding girls dressed in black. An entirely new and original portrait of the Bard, quite unlike any previous portrait, graced the entrance hall. I followed the attendant into an auditorium. I accepted the brochure thrust into my hands by a smiling red girl, and followed my black girl to the front of the theatre. On the way down the passage, three sub-managers and a manager most courteously wished me well. When I arrived at our destination—the fourth row—I was overjoyed to see that I had been placed amongst those whom a prominent Socialist politician once charmingly described as 'the nobs and snobs'. The front four rows of chairs were painted dark brown, the colour presumably conveying some rich distinction from their paler yellow brethren.

I was, however, the first arrival. The back of the theatre began to fill up, but when the appointed hour of starting came, I was still the only occupant of rows 1 to 4. I noted my pro-gramme. I admired the photos of Mr. XYZ, and Mr. ABC, Hon. Pres. of the Burns Federation. I read Mr. ABC's welcome to Mr. DEF on 'coming to this sacred corner of Ayrshire'. I read that 'with conscientious care . . . the author, Mr. XYZ, has written a libretto which will appeal to all who take Burns seriously'. Still no sign of the nobs and snobs. I entered into conversation with one of the red girls, who remembered seeing a list somewhere of the guests who were 'nearly all titled or important people.'

Then there was a scuffling at the back. The Lords and Ladies, Magistrates and Bailies, had arrived. I was reminded of Army days, when the arrival of the officers used to cause a similar sort of commotion at battalion shows.

At last, however, everyone was settled, and the curtains rose.

Burns was standing by his plough, gazing heavenwards, whilst his spirit muse Coila sang lustily, though rather shrilly, into his ear. After expressing some touching sentiments anent his future genius, she removed her crown of silver paper and placed it on the poet's head. Burns smiled awkwardly, the curtain fell, and the audience applauded.

The next scene showed us Tam o' Shanter's Inn. Farmers, shepherds, and townsfolk were merrymaking. Curiously enough, all their stories inevitably led into a Burns song. Where no music exists already, as in the case of the refined version of 'Holy Willie's Prayer'—no 'lawless leg' could be permitted here!—Mr. XYZ obligingly remedied Burns's oversight. To keep the fun going, bewhiskered and bewhiskyed figures, amply draped in tartan, told twentieth-century music-hall 'coamic' stories. Burns could hardly have known them, of course, but that is no reason why his stage re-creation should not have had that pleasure.

By a curious coincidence, it was Burns's birthday. So Soutar Johnnie sang 'There was a lad was born in Kyle'. Suddenly Burns remembered that the sheriff was after him. Sure enough, somebody looked out of the window, and at that very moment the sheriff's officer appeared on the threshold: so Burns hid in a cellar, whilst the officer of the law was disrespectfully bundled back into that oblivion from which he had made such a startlingly sudden descent. The Bard then reappeared to lead the company in 'Scots Wha hae', verse two with index fingers pointed quiveringly at the audience, verse three with all the cast on their knees.

Not even the old Scots calendar equated Hallowe'en and 25th January. By a further coincidence, however, this happened to be the night that Tam o' Shanter visited Kirk Alloway. Burns learned of the ride by intuition, for while it was in progress, he was able to recite his poem to his cronies as a sort of running commentary. Some shapely young women in tights and some others in sarks floated aimlessly about a stage bathed in lurid orange and red light, and the curtain fell.

I have often wondered just how Burns proposed to his Highland Mary. Imagine my intense gratification when I discovered that he declared his passion, between songs, in the glorious Technicolor English of Hollywood's screen lovers. Imagine the thrill of delight which raced through my system when I discovered that Highland Mary answered, between songs, 'Robert, I love you,' with a perfect Morningside accent.

The scene entitled 'Hallowe'en' proved to be much the same as that entitled 'Tam o' Shanter's Inn', except that Burns now heard some more music-hall jokes, and was treated to the sight of a twentieth-century military piper in full dress leading in a haggis, followed by a twentieth-century beach-pavilion glamour-boy highlander. The Bard raised his eyebrows a little, and it was no doubt this surprising sight which caused him to misquote his own grace. By a further coincidence, a messenger from Edinburgh's Dr. Blacklock arrived just as the meal was ending, thus conveniently preventing the poet from embarking for the West Indies.

After an interval of ten minutes, we next found Burns in Edinburgh, singing and reciting so much that it was small wonder the literati grew tired of him. Even the audience grew tired of him. I was therefore relieved when another curtain preluded the death scene.

Jean Armour made her first appearance as her husband lay dying. We had been given delicate hints about her naughty goings-on, of course. Quite obviously such a woman could hardly be permitted to darken such a theatre. It seems that Burns's death was not even a happy one, for his shrill-voiced Muse, Coila, again appeared, together with a vision of his deceased Edinburgh patron, the Earl of Glencairn. Highland Mary and their child also joined the ghastly throng. Words of mine are inadequate to convey the final climax, so I must quote from the official programme—' The phantom clasps his hand, to lead him to the Land of the Leal . . . he passes over in the highest ecstasy'.

With tears in my eyes, I broke through the tumultuous applause and struggled round to my car.

As I drifted back to Glasgow, I thought of the future building on the edges of the Holiday Camp, its roof gleaming far out over the Clyde. I thought of the poetry-loving millions who would flock beneath its portals to witness Mr. XYZ's masterpiece of imagination. I thought of the Scotch Comics whose jests about drink and wives and mothers-in-law would echo round its stucco walls, and carry the almost unknown memory of Robert Burns over every continent in the world. I thought of my vast, presumptuous impertinence in ever supposing for a moment that a poet's works are all the monument he needs. My heart flushed with gratitude towards Mr. DEF, Mr. XYZ and Mr. ABC as I trod lightly on the accelerator, and passed over Fenwick Moor in a state of the highest ecstasy! "

The Burns cult, which periodically gives rise to absurdities such as this, is hard to explain or analyse. Its devotees make a kind of annual pagan religious festival out of the celebration of his memory. They use his poems as a quasi-biblical source-book for inaccurately remembered quotations, which they apply to illustrate platitudinous moralizing on the virtues of universal brotherhood, temperance and peace.

No other artist, before or since, has had his reputation turned into a Federation. No other artist has been metamorphosed into a widely-accepted legend so entirely at the expense of his work. Yet, ultimately, all that really matters about Burns is his poetry.

Burns caught and fixed that old, agrarian Scotland which had persisted almost since the Middle Ages, just as it was beginning to disintegrate before the forces of industrialism.[1] From the local squabbles which form the subject matter of so many of his satires, he drew inferences of universal significance. His international reputation rests largely on his ability to express the daily commonplace in such a way that it assumes the force and unquestioned validity of a proverb. It is his wisdom and his sentiment that have been carried over into more than twenty tongues, not the subtle texture of his verse.

To many Scots, he is a symbol of the values which make up their country's story, though not a compelling enough symbol to make them want to preserve the " guid Scots tongue " in which he wrote his best poems. When a man becomes a symbol and a legend, he at once attracts the attentions of politicians, bores and charlatans. So Robert Burns the poet, but for whose work the Scots literary tradition would have dried up early in the nineteenth century, remains neglected, his work only in our own day considered worth a definitive edition, while Robert Burns the symbol and the legend provides a convenient key for cheap publicity-mongers, over-sexed novelists and under-sexed orators to hang out their puny egos for periodic display. The Burns cult has become an undignified racket, a disgraceful disfigurement on the memory of a great poet, and a pathetic testimony to the vulgar impotence of contemporary Scotland.

Out past the Heads of Ayr lies the little fishing village of Dunure, its crags crowned by the jagged ruins of its castle. This was the home of the locally powerful Kennedy family, Earls of Cassillis, from the fourteenth century, and the scene of a disgusting piece of joukery-poukery in 1570. The fourth Earl coveted the lands of Crossraguel Abbey, of which one Allan Stewart had been made Commendator at the Reformation. Since Stewart refused to give up his property voluntarily, Kennedy had him seized and brought to the Black Vault at Dunure, where the unfortunate man was stripped, basted and roasted until eventually he signed away his lands. So powerful were the Kennedys that an appeal to the law merely resulted in a mild rebuke to the offending Earl, who was thereafter bound to keep the peace with Stewart. The Earl at least gave his victim a pension.

[1] See the present author's *Burns: the Man: his Work: the Legend.*

Crossraguel itself, a Cluniac monastery founded by Duncan, Earl of Carrick, in 1244 as a subordinate house of Paisley, lies on the Maybole-Girvan road. A magnificent example of the latest phase in Scottish Gothic, there survives the still-extensive remains of the church, cloistral buildings, outer court, castellated gate-house, and the abbot's house and tower. The monks of Crossraguel once minted their own pennies and farthings, which are highly valued by collectors.

In Maybole itself there are the remains of a fifteenth-century church, built by the Kennedys of Dunure for a college established by them in 1373. In 1561 the disputatious John Knox had a famous debate with the cleric Quentin Kennedy in the provost's house, now unfortunately " improved " out of existence.

The Earls of Cassillis were also responsible for Maybole Castle, built early in the seventeenth century (and still in the hands of the chief of the Kennedys, the Marquis of Ailsa and Earl of Cassillis), and also for Cassillis House, a noble seventeenth-century building gathered round a fourteenth-century tower standing high above the River Doon, about five miles from Maybole. It also is still in the hands of the family.

Until 1945, when the Marquis of Ailsa presented it to the National Trust for Scotland, his principal seat was Culzean Castle, built in 1777 on a basaltic cliff above Culzean Bay, by Robert Adam, in place of the " pretty pleasant-seated house or castle which looks full upon the main sea " built in the late sixteenth century by an earlier Earl's younger son, and visited by Sir William Brereton. In the face of the cliff are a number of caverns—the Coves of Culzean—probably once used by smugglers, but peopled by legend with supernatural occupants.

Girvan stands in Bruce country. It is also a popular holiday resort, and the nearest land-link with Ailsa Craig. Fishing boats are built there, and fishing boats still operate from its harbour. Ballantrae is known throughout the world because of Stevenson's novel *The Master of Ballantrae*; but alas! for romance. Stevenson's scene is really set in Borgue, in Kirkcudbrightshire, the author merely substituting the name of Ballantrae because of its more euphonic properties. Its native river—the Stinchar—inspired a substitution in reverse: for Burns changed the first line of his song, " Beyond yon hill where Lugar flows " from " Beyond yon hill where Stinchar flows ", because he felt that the Ballantrae river's name was insufficiently poetical!

By the fort of Knockdolian—from the Gaelic *cnoc dall*, " the hill to mislead ", evidently so-called because in bad weather preradar sailors sometimes mistook it for Ailsa Craig—lies Colmonell, with its two castles, its nineteenth-century " big hoose ", and an old church around which are several Covenanter's graves, among them that of Mathew McIlwraith, prototype of Scott's Muckle-wrath in *Old Mortality*.

Ayrshire meets Wigtown across the shores of Loch Ryan, down the sweeping descent of Glen App.

# CHAPTER X

# LANARKSHIRE

*Would God I might but live*
*To see my native soil,*
*Twice happy is my happy wish*
*To end this endless toil.*
*Yet still would I record*
*The pleasant banks of Clyde,*
*Where orchards, castles, towns and woods*
*Are planted side by side;*
*And chiefly Lanark, thou,*
*Thy country's lowest lamp,*
*In which the bruised body now*
*Did first receive the stamp.*
    WILLIAM LITHGOW, *circa* 1640.

So wrote a son of Lanark, Scotland's earliest traveller-author, as he stood alone one night " in a creek of the Grecian Archipelago, dreading the attack of Turkish galliots", towards the close of a life of wandering which had taken him across Europe, the Levant and North Africa, lost him his ears, and earned him the undignified sobriquet, " Lugless Will ". Though his lines may not, as Neil Munro observes, be " the pure gold of poetry", yet they are " eloquent of the true *maladie du pays* which always makes the exiled Scot a poet of sorts ". Much of Lithgow's Lanark has been changed out of all recognition by the fierce industrial expansion of the nineteenth century. But there are still " orchards, castles, towns and woods" planted " side by side", and long stretches of the banks of Clyde which are undeniably pleasant.

Coal bings; grimly industrial towns wearing a little weary, now that the raw material which brought them into being is running thin beneath the soil; foundry flames flapping against the damp night air, casting a muffled glow over the sprawling environs of Glasgow: these are the images which first come to mind when twentieth-century Lanarkshire is envisaged. Yet the picture is incomplete, the nineteenth-century-flavoured image of industry is a one-sided thing. Up the sheltered valley of the Clyde, fruit-blossom tassels in the light breezes of early summer, and boughs hang heavy with plums and pears and apples in the fullness of autumn. Higher still, the rolling uplands, where the Clyde has its source, lean against those gentle hills which form the bastions of Borderland.

Since 1893, Glasgow, once a part of Lanarkshire, has been an "islanded" county city, with the Lord Provost as its Lord Lieutenant. Even with Glasgow's million and a half inhabitants subtracted from the total, Lanarkshire still remains the most populous county in Scotland.

The singularly featureless twentieth-century road which links Glasgow and Edinburgh drives straight through the Lanarkshire Black Country, although it contrives to by-pass most of its towns and villages. At Newhouse, the Glasgow-Edinburgh road meets the county's main traversing highway. To the left, grouped thickly along and back from the Clyde, lie Uddingston, Motherwell and Wishaw; to the right Airdrie and Coatbridge.

It has been said, with reasonable justification, that one family turned what was described towards the close of the eighteenth century as "an immense garden" into a Black Country. The founder of that family was Alexander Baird, who was born near Coatbridge in 1765, a poor farmer's son. Young Alexander soon gave up farming in favour of coal and ironstone mining—iron ore had been discovered near Coatbridge almost a century earlier and had already been developed by David Mushet, who, in 1830, set going at Gartsherrie the first round blast furnace in Scotland. Baird had eight sons, all of whom were reputed to have become millionaires. The Bairds became the principal ironmasters in Scotland. Alexander Baird lies buried in the churchyard of Old Monkland—so-called because the land once belonged to the monks of Newbattle Abbey. (Indeed, Coatbridge has taken as its motto the Benedictines' "Laborare et orare" and worked the figure of a Franciscan friar into the burgh crest.) A near neighbour of the worthy ironmaster's is Janet Hamilton (1795-1873), the daughter of a cobbler in Langloan—now part of Coatbridge—and a local self-taught poetess. She had an embarrassing turn for poetic piety—alas, how rarely poetry and piety mix!—and in a lengthy effusion called "The Sunday Rail", satirized the running of the first Sunday trains on the North British Railway. Unfortunately, in the hands of the unskilful, satire often assumes the characteristic of a boomerang. Miss Hamilton was unskilful; what was meant to be scathing condemnation, now seems merely a pleasing animated period picture.

*Now range up the carriages, feed up the fires!*
*To the rail, to the rail, now the pent-up desires*
*Of the pale toiling million find gracious reply,*
*On the pinions of steam they shall fly, they shall fly,*

*The beauties of nature and art to explore,*
*To ramble the woodlands and roam by the shore.*
*The city spark here with his smart smirking lass,*
*All peg-topped and crinolined, squat on the grass.*

*While with quips and with cranks and soft-wreathed smiles,*
*Each nymph with her swain the dull Sabbath beguiles.*
*Here mater and pater familias will come*
*With their rollicking brood from their close city home.*
*How they scramble and scream, how they scamper and run,*
*While pa and mamma are enjoying the fun!*
*And the urchins bawl out, "Oh, how funny and jolly,*
*Dear ma, it is thus to keep Sabbath-day holy."*

*Now for pipe and cigar and the snug pocket-flask,*
*What's the rail on a Sunday without them, we ask?*
*What the sweet-scented heather and rich clover-blooms*
*To the breath of the weed as it smoulders and fumes?*
*So in courting and sporting, in drinking and smoking,*
*Walking and talking, in laughter and joking,*
*They while the dull hours of the Sabbath away.*
*What a Sabbath it is! Who is Lord of the day?*

Airdrie—*aird airigh*, the hill pasture—made itself over to industry before iron-making began in Coatbridge, for in the eighteenth century, Airdrie had a thriving weaving community. She preserves the bell from Glasgow's mediæval University—rashly torn down during the 1880's—in the tower of New Monkland church, as well as the tradition that the battlefield of Aerderyth, where in the year 577 King Aidan of Dalriada was defeated by the King of Strathclyde, lay somewhere near the present burgh.

The towns of Motherwell and Wishaw, however, do not even trouble to make historic pretensions. Yet the seventeenth-century Dalzell House, once the home of the Hamiltons of Dalzell but now in civic ownership, survives to remind us of the time when the countryside was so lovely as to make the itinerant William Cobbett opine that, if he had to live in Scotland, he would live here. (Admittedly, a carefully qualified verdict!) Nearby, too, stands Jerviston, now, alas, unoccupied and entering into its decline, but once the home of the Baillies of Jerviston.

Motherwell itself is the steel-making centre of the Black Country. Originally a quiet country shrine to the Virgin Mary, the town flushed rapidly into being in the fever of mid-nineteenth-century industrial expansion. First, it had iron works in 1849; then the Dalzell Steelworks in 1871. To house the workers in these new concerns, hastily-erected tenements were built, hectic rashes over the fair face of the countryside. They must have been drab when they were built. Now, flaking and dowdy, coated with grime, and ringed round with the sprawls of successive lairs of unco-ordinated industrial development, the drabness has increased ten-fold. To be in Motherwell and Wishaw beneath a wet grey sky is to feel the full force of the degrading human tragedy brought about by the industrial revolution. Of course, the thing had its glory too: in the proud craftsmanship of the Clyde's shipbuilders; in Glasgow-built locomotives threading the values of European civilization across distant continents; and in bridges, taming the intransigent rivers. But there is nothing left of the glory about Motherwell and Wishaw to-day.

On my last visit, it was with a rather selfish feeling of relief that I climbed up to Cambusnethan, on a ridge above the Clyde, to look at the Manse where, in 1794, John Gibson Lockhart was born. Between the years of his boyhood and his death at Abbotsford in 1854, the face of his native countryside had changed almost beyond recognition.

Two places on the western fringe of the Black Country draw many of these visitors who come to Scotland with preconceived notions about her: Bothwell and Blantyre. Bothwell is a shrine of the romanticists: Blantyre a place of pilgrimage for those who value the Scot most as a pioneer in foreign lands.

Bothwell made several appearances in Scottish history: the earliest of them stand commemorated in the proud, noble ruin of Bothwell Castle, which looms high above the edge of the Clyde a little to the north-west of the town. When the castle was first built—perhaps by the builder of the French Château de Coucy, who was the brother of Alexander II's queen—for Walter Oliphant, Sheriff of Lothian, during Alexander's reign, it was regarded as the most impressive fortalice in Scotland. As such, it was used as a base for the operations of successive invading English armies during the Wars of Independence, when it frequently changed hands. Bruce had the castle stripped, and Edward III set part of the donjon up again. But the main reconstruction was carried out after it had passed by marriage to the Douglas earl, Archibald the Grim. The Douglases kept possession of Bothwell until James II brought about the downfall of their too-powerful house. It was held thereafter for short periods by, amongst others, the English Earl of Pembroke and a son of Chancellor Crichton, before James IV gave it to Patrick

Hepburn, Earl of Bothwell. The Hepburns occupied Bothwell Castle for only four years, after which they exchanged it for the fifth Earl of Angus's lands of Liddesdale and Hermitage. So Bothwell Castle came back to the Douglases, whose restless ambition stands reflected in their many additions and embellishments to the place.

A later Douglas knocked down the north-east tower, and used the stones to build himself an eighteenth-century mansion. It was in this house, demolished during the present century, that Scott wrote his ballad " Young Lochinvar ".

The mansion was still comparatively new when Dorothy Wordsworth visited Bothwell Castle, in company with her brother and Coleridge, during the Autumn of 1803. She recorded her impressions in her *Journal*.

" The castle stands nobly overlooking the Clyde.[1] When we came up to it, I was hurt to see that flower borders had taken the place of the natural overgrowings of the ruin, the scattered stones and wild plants. It is a large and grand pile of red freestone, harmonizing perfectly with the rocks of the river, from which, no doubt, it has been hewn. When I was a little accustomed to the unnaturalness of a modern garden, I could not help admiring the excessive beauty and luxuriance of some of the plants, particularly the purple-flowered clematis, and a broad leaved creeping plant without flowers, which scrambled up the castle wall along with the ivy, and spread its vine-like branches so lavishly that it seemed to be in its natural situation, and one could not help thinking that, though not self-planted among the ruins of this country, it must somewhere have its native abode in such places."

Dorothy Wordsworth eventually decided that the justification of the modern garden was the nearness of the new house to the old castle, the new house at that time being occupied by Archibald Stewart, Lord Douglas, the leading figure in the Douglas Cause which so set eighteenth-century tongues a-wagging. She had:

" . . . then only to regret that the castle and the house were so near to each other; and it was impossible not to regret it; for the ruin presides in state over the river, far from city or town, as if it might have had a peculiar privilege to preserve its memorials of past ages and maintain its own character and independence for centuries to come."

[1] Now, it also overlooks pit bings.

To-day, the Ministry of Works preserves the castle's character, but now it lies almost within sight of both city and town, though the " new " house is gone.  Across the river, it looks down on the remains of Blantyre Priory.

In the village of Bothwell itself, the much restored kirk contains a few fragments of the old collegiate church of St. Bride, where David, Duke of Rothesay, married Marjorie Douglas two years before he was starved to death by his uncle at Falkland Castle.

It was at the Manse of Bothwell that a once-famous poetess, Joanna Baillie (1762-1851), was born.  In her lifetime, she enjoyed the friendship of Byron and Scott, who called her in *Marmion* the " bold Enchantress " whose strains might make the swans of Avon think " their own Shakespeare lived again "!  On the strength of her twenty-seven plays, she built up for herself a considerable literary reputation, particularly on account of her " Plays of the Passions ".  Probably her rather pallid, dramatic verse appealed to Scott because in her plays she evinced a similar interest to his own in a romanticized " chivalrous " past, while in her other poems she showed herself the nearest he ever had to a metrical disciple.  But although some of her plays were staged, with indifferent success, she wrote quite deliberately in the so-called English Senecan tradition, which the Countess of Pembroke had made popular in the England of Queen Elizabeth. Poetic plays designed for reading rather than acting had some vogue until the close of the nineteenth century.  The whole conception of unactable plays, however, implies a fundamental contradiction of artistic principles.  Like the rest of their kind, Joanna Baillie's plays, along with her pious " Metrical Legends ", are now quite forgotten, though we still remember some of her versions of old songs like " Saw Ye Johnnie Comin'? "

South-east from Bothwellhaugh, whose umquhile laird, James Hamilton, murdered the Regent Moray at Linlithgow, Bothwell Brig spans the Clyde.  Though it was added to in 1826, when the gateway that guarded its crown was removed, the Brig is still substantially the same as that round which two Covenanting skirmishes took place.  In the affair of 1650, a force roughly equal to about a couple of battalions of infantry, led by Colonel Gibby Kerr, repulsed a much larger force of Cromwell's, and captured his General Lambert.  But the famous battle of Bothwell Brig was fought on Sunday, June 22nd, 1679, just twenty days after a gang of Covenanters had murdered Archbishop Sharp on Magus Muir, near St. Andrews.  Hackston of Rathillet, one of the principal murderers, had a contingent of about four thousand

Covenanters with him when they encountered a force of Royalists under Monmouth.

But the Covenanters were over-confident as a result of their recent victory over Claverhouse at Drumclog, and, as always, torn by the dissensions of bickering ministers who thought arguments on points of doctrine of more importance than military common sense. Rathillet fortified the gatehouse on the bridge, and for a time held it successfully. Meanwhile, his superior commander was devoting his attentions, not to winning the battle, but to the erection of a gallows on which to hang the anticipated royalist prisoners. The defending force had thus to retire in confusion, four hundred being killed and twelve thousand being taken prisoner during the withdrawal and the subsequent royalist pursuit.

Blantyre gives its name to the remains of a Priory, founded by Alexander II, almost opposite Bothwell Castle, which moved Dorothy Wordsworth to exclaim that nothing could be " more beautiful than the little remnants of this holy place ", to a parish, and to the villages of High and Low Blantyre. Low Blantyre was built in 1780 by the Glasgow merchant prince David Dale. There was originally a cotton mill, and a row of " single end " tenements, Shuttle Row, in one of which the missionary and explorer David Livingstone was born in 1813. Before his African servants found his dead, dysentery-racked body, kneeling beside his bed in prayer on the banks of the Molamo, on 1st May 1873,[1] he had not only done much to solve the problems of African hydrography, but by his horrifying reports of the cruelties of the slave trade still conducted in the interior by the Arabs and the Portuguese, he helped to bring about a stirring of the British public conscience; this, in turn, resulted in local rulers being brought under political pressure, which led to the eventual abandonment of the slave trade in Africa.

The mill in Blantyre where Livingstone worked as a boy has long since been abandoned. By 1925, his birthplace was a derelict slum, about to be pulled down. But a public appeal was launched, and a substantial sum was gathered, part of it raised by Sunday School pupils of the Church of Scotland. The place was then laid out by Sir Frank Mears as a Livingstone Memorial, housing many relics of the explorer's African journeys, as well as a series of eight sculpted scenes by C. d'O Pilkington Jackson, depicting some of the moral qualities conspicuous in Livingstone's character.

---

[1] The date of his death is disputed, as he died in the night. I follow the views of J. McNair in his book *Livingstone's Travels*, 1954.

Bothwell Brig leads across the Clyde to Hamilton, said to derive from a thirteenth-century owner of the lands, Walter Fitz-Gilbert, called Hamilton; the place from which Scotland's premier Duke takes his title, and which is now also the home of the Cameronians—fittingly enough, since there are Covenanting martyrs buried beneath their usual passionate doggerel within the town's bounds. Unfortunately, Hamilton has suffered severely from the improving urges of successive generations of civic fathers, and even more severely from nineteenth-century undermining, which has provided a completely unanswerable excuse for the blowing up of two of the most interesting buildings in the county. In the old town, between Cadzow Street, Muir Street and the Castle, many crow-step gabled seventeenth- and eighteenth-century houses have been torn out to make way for newer buildings. The ogee-capped Tolbooth, built during the reign of Charles I, became so seriously cracked that it could not even be under-pinned, and had to be blown up in 1954. The octagonal church, built in 1732 by William Adam, still stands near Cadzow Street; before it the twelfth-century Netherton Cross transported from the Mote Hill, in the Low Park, where once there was a Celtic settlement. It was hereabouts that King Rhydderich of Strathclyde is supposed to have had his residence: here, too, that his Queen unwisely parted with the ring she received from her husband to an over-ardent knight. One day, the King came upon Queen Languoreth's lover asleep by the river, and was horrified to find the ring on his finger. Without waking the warrior—he must have been an uncommonly heavy sleeper—the king removed the ring, and threw it into the Clyde. Then he challenged his adulterous lady to produce the ring, under threat of unpleasant consequences characteristic of the times. In repentant despair, the Queen turned to Mungo, who ordered a fishing-line to be cast into the Clyde. A salmon took the hook. When the fish was cut open, it was found to have swallowed the ring. Mungo thereupon restored the ring to the Queen; the royal couple lived, according to the best traditions, happily ever after, and this Lanarkshire incident became perpetuated pictorially in Glasgow's coat-of-arms.

But in the Haughs, which lie about the Clyde and contain Hamilton race course, " Glasgow's Epsom ", once stood what was probably the largest palace ever to be built in Scotland. Hamilton Palace grew up about 1591 around an older tower, and was substantially added to between 1705 and 1717. When the English poet Thomas Gray saw it in 1764, he thought it a " great ill-contained mass ", a verdict endorsed by Dorothy Wordsworth in 1803 when she saw it as "a huge building without grandeur, a heavy lumpish mass".

Alexander, the tenth Duke, completed the rebuilding in 1822, adding a Corinthian touch to its hugeness. He married the daughter of Beckford of Fonthill, the eccentric and wealthy author of the Gothic horror-comic novel *Vathek*, and so heired the Fonthill library and art treasures—probably the finest ever to be assembled privately in these islands. In 1882, however, the whole collection was sold by auction, fetching almost four hundred thousand pounds! The Palace was vacated by its owners early in the present century, and by 1927 had suffered so severely from the uneven subsidence of its heavy bulk that it was impossible to do anything other than destroy it.

But one memorial of Duke Alexander's splendid eccentricity still remains. In 1852, he commissioned the architect David Bryce to build a mausoleum to house a sarcophagus which had been brought from Memphis. Four years later, the extraordinary edifice was complete. It cost more than a hundred and fifty thousand pounds. The floor alone—a wheel mosaic containing almost all the known varieties of marble, many of them rare—absorbed a large part of that sum. The sonorous echo effect was not, of course, intended—until very recent years, architects were quite unable to estimate acoustical effect in relation to their art—and made the place useless as a chapel, though until their bodies were removed to a local cemetery, the mausoleum did perform its silent function of housing the remains of several departed Dukes.

Now it stands alone, surrounded by Cadzow Forest, whose huge oaks are a remnant of the Caledonian Forest, and among whose trees still roam white cattle traditionally (though, let us admit, improbably) descended from the "quhit bullis" noticed there by Hector Boece almost five hundred years ago.

As the Clyde flows down through the High Parks, it is joined by the chasmed River Avon. On the edge of a cliff above the Avon, the donjon tower of Cadzow Castle stands out. It was to this Hamilton stronghold that Mary Queen of Scots came after her escape from Loch Leven, on her way to the Battle of Langside. Barncluith, also on the Avon, was built in 1583 by John Hamilton, whose family later became the Lords Belhaven. Claverhouse is supposed to have spent the night before the Battle of Bothwell Brig at Barncluith.

From Hamilton, up the valley to Lanark, lie the rich orchards of the Clyde. May is the time to enjoy the fruit-growing countryside, whose image William Lithgow carried in his heart, at its most spectacular: for then the leaves are green with that intense brightness which dulls before the dog-days, and the blossom sits lightly on the branches; so lightly that the slightest frost can blight it, and doom the boughs that should have bent with heavy fruit to an unstraining barrenness.

In May, too, the Lowland sky is most often cloudless, and sunshine gleams and shimmers on the glass tops of the tomato-houses, sloped as if in prayer, as many of the growers must often be too, so brittle is the promise of plenty, and so slight and so fatally sudden the night breathing of late frost.

Into this orchard-land stretch of the Clyde flows the Nethan, joining the greater water at the peaceful village of Crossford. Up the Nethan valley lies Craignethan Castle, where Scott once thought of making his home, and which he immortalized as Tillietudlem.

In front of the hill on which Lanark stands, the Clyde, swollen by the Douglas Water, tumbles over its three falls. Bonnington, the upper fall, surges over a drop of thirty feet into a deep and narrow chasm, where it boils and presses along the half mile which separates it from Corra Linn, the middle fall. Corra Linn moved the eighteenth-century poet John Wilson to try to tame its force within the rigid banks of his Augustan couplets.

> *Where ancient Corehouse hangs above the stream,*
> *And far beneath the tumbling surges gleam,*
> *Engulphed in crags the fretting river raves,*
> *Chafed into foam resound his tortured waves.*
> *With giddy heads we view the dreadful deep,*
> *And cattle snort and tremble at the steep,*
> *Where down at once the foaming waters pour,*
> *And tottering rocks repel the deafening roar,*
> *Viewed from below, it seems from heaven they fell;*
> *Seen from above, they seem to sink to hell;*
> *But when the deluge pours from every hill,*
> *And Clyde's wide bed ten thousand torrents fill,*
> *His rage the murmuring mountain streams augment,*
> *Redoubled rage in rocks so closely pent.*
> *Then shattered woods, with ragged roots uptorn,*
> *And herds and harvests down the waves are borne.*
> *Huge stones heaved upward through the boiling deep,*
> *And rocks enormous thundering down the steep,*
> *In swift descent, fixed rocks encountering, roar,*
> *Crash as from slings discharged and shake the shore.*

Yet, in spite of Wilson's eloquence, the prevailing impact which Corra Linn makes is not so much of sound as of sight.

From out of the deep Bonnington there rises that dank, thin steam which is the thunder of falling water made visible, dizzying the senses with the breath-oppressive smell of ungovernable power. It is an awesome pleasure which Bonnington inspires. Not so Corra Linn: for though its waters fall nearly ninety feet, there is no sheer drop: no visual reminder of the ceaseless pull of gravity, but a series of cascades which, if looked up at from beneath, present a spectacle of sprawling, shimmering disintegration which makes the earth on either side tremble in a kind of continual vague unease.

Two miles further down, the waters of the Clyde are convulsed again, this time over Stonebyres, the broadest of the falls. The Wordsworths thought it the first of the three. Dorothy recorded:

"We saw it from the top of the bank of the river at a little distance. It has not the imposing majesty of Corra Linn; but it has the advantage of being left to itself, a grand solitude in the heart of a populous country."

Overlooking Corra Linn, a little to the north-west, stands the village of New Lanark, another of David Dale's experimental cotton-spinning villages. Here, for a short time, Dale worked in partnership with Richard Arkwright, the inventor of the "Spinning Jenny". When they fell out—allegedly over the hanging of the bell on the belfry of the church in the main street—Robert Owen took over New Lanark and made it famous as the setting of an early experiment in practical socialism.

The poet Southey, who had himself once held idealistic principles similar to Owen's, visited New Lanark in 1819. Owen arranged a children's dancing demonstration for Southey's benefit, and showed him over the mill. But Southey, by then something of a reactionary, saw in the system of benevolent autocracy which Owen had set up a situation which made him feel uncomfortable.

"Owen in reality deceives himself. He is part-owner and sole director of a large establishment, differing more in accidents than in essence from a plantation: the persons under him happen to be white, and are at liberty by law to quit his service, but while they remain in it they are as much under his absolute management as so many negro-slaves. His humour, his vanity, his kindliness of nature (all these have their share) lead him to make these *human machines* as he calls them (and too literally believes them to be) as happy as he can, and to make a display of their happiness. And he jumps at once to the monstrous conclusion that because he can do this with 2210 persons, who are totally dependent on him—all mankind might be governed with the same facility . . . Owen reasons from his cotton mills to the whole empire. He keeps out of sight from others, and perhaps from himself, that his system, instead of aiming at perfect freedom, can only be kept in play by absolute power. Indeed, he never looks beyond one of his own ideal square villages, to the rules and proportions of which he would square the whole human race . . . Yet I admire the man, and like him too. And the Yahoos who are bred in our manufacturing towns, and under the administration of our Poor Laws are so much worse than the Chinese breed which he proposes to raise, that I should be glad to see his regulations adopted . . . for a colony of paupers."

Unwittingly, the reactionary Southey betrays the real reason for the objections which Owen's fellow mill-owners raised to his methods; for they implied an eventual end to the delicious condescension of bestowing charity; of conscience-salving " good works ", and of the " dear Poor " attitude so firm a bulwark of the nineteenth-century social . economic structure. Yet Owen was responsible for some early measures of factory reform: for first applying the principle in Scotland that "labour is the source of all wealth": and for founding, in his "Association of All Classes of All Nations", a body whose international aspirations had to wait for more than a century before their necessity was even realized. He severed his connection with New Lanark in 1829, and spent most of the last thirty years of his life in America.

Lanark lies up the face of a steep slope, most spectacularly approached from Hyndford Bridge, which carries the main road over the Clyde. Although Hamilton has attracted away some of the county offices and far outdoes it in size and economic importance, Lanark remains the county town and a place of considerable importance in Scotland's story. Even though it may not have been the Colania of Ptolemy, there was a royal castle in Lanark in the twelfth century. At the foot of the main street stands a gigantic statue of William Wallace, given to the town in 1882 by the sculptor, Robert Forrest. (Its grotesque proportions make it easy to accept the popular notion that Forrest was self-taught!) This commemorates the tradition of the murder of Wallace's wife, Marian Bradfute, by the English Earl of Clydesdale and Sheriff of Ayr, William de Hazelrig, in May 1297. The part of the story which relates to Wallace's wife is, to say the least of it, regarded with suspicion by most historians: but that history-writing knight of Northumberland, Sir Thomas Grey, alleged that his father was one of the Lanark garrison upon which William Wallace and his followers so ruthlessly fell. Thereafter, Wallace is said to have hidden in a cave below Castle Qua, in the chasm of Cartland Crags, high above the banks of the Clyde's least aggressively named tributary, the Mouse.

Castlegate—once an eminence fortified by the Romans—and Bloomgate preserve the old street names, if not the spellings. At the lower end of the town the ruins of the second Church of St. Kentigern reach out their First Pointed style red sandstone arches from the thirteenth century. (The first church on the site was built a century earlier by David I for the monks of Dryburgh.) It survived the Reformation, but not the "killing times". By 1657 it was part-ruinous, and by 1777 finally abandoned as a place of worship in favour of the parish church behind the Wallace statue.

In the graveyard of St. Kentigern's lie some of Lanark's Coven-anting martyrs, the traveller William Lithgow (whose grave is unmarked and unknown) and the original of Stevenson's Weir of Hermiston, the brutal eighteenth-century judge Lord Brax-field, whose seat, Braxfield, lay on the outskirts of New Lanark, and was, ironically enough, for a time the home of Robert Owen.

To the West of Lanark lies moorland, and six hundred feet above sea-level the village of Strathhaven, still presided over by its ruined castle of Avondale. Over a burn, at the centre of the village, a curious old bridge still arches its back. It was at Strathhaven that the Scots comedian Sir Harry Lauder built his last home, *Lauder Ha'*, where he died.

East out of Lanark lies Carstairs, thought, on the evidence of both Roman and earlier remains, to have been the capital of the Damnonii tribe in the second century A.D. Carstairs is a railway junction, but Carluke—anciently Kirkstyle[1] —is at the junction of the road to the Black Country, the road to the south and the road to Lanarkshire's delightful Pentland villages of Dunsyre, Dolphinton, Newbigging and Carnwarth, where James IV's annual race for a pair of red hose, first competed for in 1500, is still run. Mauldslie Castle, in Carluke parish, built by Robert Adam in 1793 for the fifth Earl of Hyndford, stands in what was once a royal hunting-ground.

South of Lanark, the land rises as the county drives its wedge

[1] Carluke Church was known as the Forest Kirk.

into Peeblesshire and Dumfriesshire, a wedge ultimately blunted by the Lowther Hills. Tinto rules over this upper world: Tinto which, because it dominates a wideness of moorland, seems small from afar, yet is in reality large and impressive.

> *How small a thing is Tinto hill*
> *At twenty miles remove!*
> *It could be folded bright and still,*
> *Within your hand, my love.*
>
> *It could recline, imparadised,*
> *In either of your eyes,*
> *Or with the blue vein keep a tryst*
> *That on your white breast lies.*
>
> *But did we walk by Tinto's side*
> *Or climb its heath and stone,*
> *Such sleights of eye could not abide*
> *Under its thunder throne.*

So wrote that gentle visionary William Jeffrey (1896-1946), who so often sang of Scotland's high places.

Other aspects of Tinto have been commemorated in verse:

> *On Tintock Tap there is a mist,*
> *And in the mist there is a kist,*
> *And in the kist there is a caup,*
> *And in the caup there is a draup.*
> *Tak up the caup; drink aff the draup,*
> *And set the caup on Tintock Tap.*

The meaning of that rhyme, if it ever had any, is lost in what are usually conveniently described as "the mists of antiquity". They relate directly to a cup-shaped boulder on the summit known as "Wallace's Thumb-Mark"; indirectly to the Devil's fire-rites of Beltane, thought once to have been observed there, since Tintock derives from the Gaelic *teinteach*, "place of fire".

Another rhyme credits Tinto with fire-raising powers of a different sort: the fires of love.

> *Be a lassie ne'er so black,*
> *Gin she hae the penny siller*
> *Set her upon Tinto's tap*
> *The wind will blaw a man till her*

Lest Tinto should suddenly be over-run with hopeful virgins, it is only proper to add that one version of the old rhyme contains an additional, qualifying couplet:

> But gin she want the penny-siller,
> There'll ne'er a ane be even'd till her.

To the north of Tinto, the road runs past Culter Fell through Biggar and into Peeblesshire. Biggar, with its broad main street, is a place of bustle on market day. Dr. John Brown (1810-1882), the essayist, whose *Rab and his Friends* will no doubt make delightful period reading to later generations, was a native of Biggar. C. M. Grieve ("Hugh MacDiarmid") chose it for his home during his later years. Biggar was once Fleming territory, as the ruins of Boghall Castle remind us. Grose's *Antiquities of Scotland* shows that what remains would have been stronger but for local quarriers. Before its downfall in the seventeenth century, it had housed Edward II, Queen Mary—who found there Mary Fleming, one of her four Marys—and the Regent Moray. Its Cromwellian defenders held it against Charles II when he passed through Biggar on his way to Worcester. And it was one of the last places to be visited by Sir Walter Scott who, in company with Lockhart, came to it a month before his death.

It was also a Fleming—Malcolm, the third Lord—who founded the last collegiate church in Scotland, the Church of St. Mary. Put up in 1545, well preserved and lovingly restored, it is now one of the finest pre-Reformation churches in Scotland.

The Clyde meanders round the south of Tinto; past Lamington, where the arch of a Norman church survives; and Roberton. Further up the narrowing river lie Abington, Crawford and Elvanfoot, pastoral villages all. Near Elvanfoot, the Clyde rises on Clyde Law, in spite of the fact that Neil Munro once tried to stop it up with the cork from a bottle of hock, and that there are some who, flouting the old couplet

> Annan, Tweed and Clyde
> Rise a' out o' ae hill-side,

maintain that the real source of the river is on Gadd Hill in Dumfriesshire.

Leadhills, a bleak village among the barren heights, has been known for its lead mines certainly since the thirteenth century, if not from Roman times. They have been worked sporadically down the centuries. The poet Allan Ramsay (1686-1758) was the son of a superintendent of the mines when they were the property of the Earl of Hopetoun, and it is typical of his worldly-wise muse that when he apostrophized the charms of the " Lass of Patie's Mill ", he offered her, not the love that lasts " till a' the seas gang dry ", but a prospect somewhat more staple.

> O had I all the wealth
>      Hopetoun's high mountains fill,
> Insur'd lang life and health,
>      And pleasure at my will;
> I'd promise and fulfill,
>      That none but bonny she,
> The lass of Patie's mill,
>      Shou'd share the same wi' me.

Winding citywards by a slightly devious route when last I explored Lanarkshire, I went to Crawfordjohn. This barony was once violently possessed by the picaresque character Sir James Hamilton of Fynnart, amiably known as " the Bastard of Arran ". When not taking part in official battles, he organized raids, risings and murders on his own account. Finally, even his abilities as an architect could not deter James V from executing him. Boghouse, little of which now remains, was built by that same monarch for one of his mistresses, Katherine Carmichael. Nearby Gilkerscleugh, a charming vernacular seventeenth-century laird's house, was a Hamilton home throughout the seventeenth and eighteenth centuries.

Douglas, which stands on Douglas Water (from the Gaelic *dubh ghlas* " black water "), is one of the most famous glens in Scotland, for out of it originally came all the branches of the Douglas family. There, after he had killed off the English garrison, Bruce's comrade-in-arms " the guid Sir James " built a new fortalice so difficult of access that it became known as Castle Dangerous, giving Scott the title and the theme of one of his last novels. A fire destroyed it in 1758, whereupon the only Douglas ever to be a Duke commissioned Robert Adam to build a mansion greater in dimensions than that which the same architect had just finished at Inverary for the Duke of Argyll. The only wing of the Douglas mansion to be constructed was pulled down in 1937.

Late in life this Douglas married his cousin, Margaret Douglas, who had to force her coachman to cross the swollen Douglas Water at pistol point to get to her wedding. But the marriage was fruitless.

Not so, however, the marriage of the Duke's sister to one Colonel Sir John Stewart, in her 48th year. When she gave birth to twins in Paris, at the age of 50, the event occasioned not only surprise among the gossips, but allegations in some quarters that the children were not the issue of her body, but changelings brought on the scene to ensure the Douglas succession. The Duke, however, accepted them as genuine. On the Duke's death, the elder of the twins, Archibald Stewart, only succeeded to the estate after a five-year legal wrangle with the Duke of Hamilton, the nearest male heir. The affair engendered much heat, became known as the Douglas Cause, and went the length of the House of Lords before it was finally settled in Stewart's favour. Prim Henry (" Man of Feeling ") Mackenzie recorded that:

" On its ultimate decision, the mob of Edinburgh broke out into violent outrage, and broke the windows of most of the judges who had been of the majority in the Court of Session who decided against Douglas, whose decision was reversed by the House of Lords. They were particularly violent against President Dundas, and some of them followed the sedan chair in which he was going to Court the morning after the intelligence of the final decision arrived, with threatenings and abuse.

James Boswell, who was one of the counsel for Douglas, was a particularly active partisan of the Douglas party, joining in the huzzas of the mob for the victory which they had gained. In the theatre, where they had the tragedy of *Douglas* acted for several nights, Mr. Boswell, whose spirits were elevated and his zeal inflamed by wine, headed a Douglas party of the audience and joined in very extravagant demonstrations of their triumph. They would hardly suffer Glenavon to speak a word of his part, so that the play might be said to be performed without the character of Glenavon. The poor actor who played the part, when hissed and hooted, begged to know in what he had given them displeasure. They did not allege any offence, but they would not suffer an enemy of Douglas to appear even in the fiction of the drama."

It was in the now much-reduced and over-restored thirteenth-century kirk of St. Bride that the earlier Douglases were buried, and where an old sword, said to be that of the " good Sir James ", is still preserved in a case.

Lesmahagow stands equivocally on the edge of both Black Country and fruit country. Named after the sixth-century St.

Machute, Lesmahagow is famous as the birthplace in 1830 of Alexander Muir, who wrote the words and composed the air of the national anthem of Canada, where his parents emigrated when he was a boy; and as the scene of the discovery of a bronze-age vessel, the Lesmahagow Flagon, now preserved in Glasgow's Hunterian Museum.

I thought of this curious vessel, which time and the action of the burn in which it lay over the centuries has distorted, as I drove back towards Glasgow; for it is now a symbolic reminder of the close association of county and town down the ages, without which neither would have achieved their present power, position and eminence.

# Chapter XI

# RENFREWSHIRE

After having passed through Nieuwark [Newark] that is on the side of the gulf of Dunbriton, which lay on my left hand, to enter into a country surrounded almost on all sides by mountains, I descended into some very agreeable valleys. . . . From thence I followed a small river where the country grew a little better, to go to Paslet (Paisley) on a river forded by a large bridge abutting to the castle, where there is a very spacious garden enclosed by thick walls of hewn stone. It was once a rich abbey. . . . Those who go from Krinock [Greenock] to Glasgow, pass from Kemakoom [Kilmacolm] to Reinfreu, but the way is full of marshes, difficult to pass over, and where there is a boat that does not work on Sundays.

JOREVIN DE ROCHEFORD, 1661.

M o s t of the modern county of Renfrewshire was inhabited about the beginning of the Christian era by the Goidelic Dumnonians, or Damnonii. In the east, there was a settlement of the Maeatae, from whose name the Mearns is somewhat fancifully said to derive. Thereafter the Romans occupied the county, having a fort at Oakshawhead, with outposts at Woodside and on Castlehead. Recently an additional station of the wall of Antoninus has been discovered on the Renfrewshire side of the Clyde, obviously designed to prevent the defences being turned by an attack from the river.

Renfrewshire's first major mark on history, however, goes back to 1141, when David I returned to Scotland after helping the Empress Maud, his niece and the mother of the boy Henry II of England, against Stephen. The Scots king brought back in his train Walter Fitz Alan, a knight of Breton descent. It is highly probable that Walter suggested some means of controlling the native Celtic nobles. Whatever his service, he was rewarded by the king with lands amounting to almost the whole of Renfrewshire, then called Strathgryfe and apparently regarded as part of Lanarkshire.

Walter also became the first Steward of Scotland. He proceeded to feudalize his land. In 1164, he beat off an attack by Somerled, Lord of the Isles (during which that savage Gael was killed and—according to tradition, supported by Thomas Pennant, who, in 1172, saw the " mount or tumulus, with a foss round the base "—buried in a field near the Knock). Four years later,

Walter brought monks of the order of Clugny from Wenlock in Shropshire, where his brother was sheriff, to found a monastery. Under the next three Stewards, Walter's monastery by the White Cart increased in wealth and influence, and around it grew the future town of Paisley.

During the Wars of Succession, Renfrewshire, because it lay a little off the main westerly routes linking south and north, did not suffer unduly at the hands of the English, though the army of Edward II crossed its borders in 1310. But because it was the seat of the Stewards and the birthplace of William Wallace, the county was nevertheless closely involved in the long struggle.

Wallace was born at Elderslie about the year 1270. He was probably the first son of Sir Malcolm Wallace of Elderslie and Auchenbothie. About his early years little is known. He may have been educated at the monastery of Paisley, or he may have studied at Dunipace and Dundee, in which places his uncle was successively a priest. His first blow for Scotland is said to have been the slaughter of a young Englishman, Selby, son of the Governor of Dundee, who challenged Wallace's right to freeman's dress. The subsequent sentence of outlawry against Wallace confirmed him in his course. Around him he gathered a band of patriots, among them the Steward, Sir Andrew de Moray, Sir David de Graham and the Bishop of Glasgow. They attacked first the English justiciar at Scone, then followed this up by burning the Barns of Ayr, an English barracks, by way of avenging the murder of Wallace's uncle, Sir Reginald Crawford.

These events moved English Edward to send up an army to deal with the troublesome patriots. At Irvine, most of Wallace's titled friends hastily made submission to England. But Wallace himself retired north, and at the head of a Scots army was soon besieging Dundee. Edward now sent up a larger English force under Surrey and Cressingham. When Wallace heard of the arrival of the English army in Scotland, he marched rapidly to Stirling and took up his position around the Abbey Craig. On September 11th, 1297, he suddenly descended upon the English from two sides while they were trying to cross the Forth, and routed them. When news of this defeat reached Edward, he was in Flanders. The situation in Scotland now assumed prior importance. So, in July the following year, he himself led an army into Scotland, coming upon the Scots near Falkirk. The Scots nobles, always individualists, chose this highly inconvenient moment to quarrel, and some of them deserted Wallace's colours in a huff. The battle was a bitter one, but it ended in an English victory. Wallace thereafter resigned his office as Guardian of

Scotland in disgust, and resorted to his earlier practice of organizing anti-English raiding parties.

By the winter of 1301-4, Edward had received the submission of almost every Scottish noble. His terms of clemency expressly excluded Wallace from pardon. Indeed, to the more pliable nobles, Edward probably made it plain that if they wanted to work their passage towards full forgiveness, Wallace must be delivered up. At Robroyston, now a part of Glasgow, the patriot was betrayed by Sir John Menteith—forever stigmatized in balladry as the "faus Menteith"—on August 5th, 1305. On the 23rd of August, Wallace was tried in London. He denied having been a traitor, insisting that he had never been a subject of the King of England. On the day of his inevitable sentence, he was butchered with sadistic cruelty.

Within a year of Wallace's death, Bruce—who had originally vacillated in his loyalty—was crowned King of Scotland. Walter, the sixth Steward, was his ardent supporter, and married his daughter Marjorie. When Robert the Bruce was succeeded by his son David II, a brave enough man, but a weak and foolish king, the Steward at first stood loyally by the great King's son. But loyalty to foolishness is not easy to sustain. By 1371, when David II died, the Steward and his sons were all in prison. Released on David's death, the Steward ascended the Scottish throne as Robert II. Renfrewshire's laird was now King of Scotland. Probably in 1404, his successor, Robert III (1390-1406), separated the barony of Renfrew from the county of Lanark, and made it a separate shire.

The town of Renfrew had early assumed prime importance in the county, becoming a royal burgh during the reign of David I, though a charter was not obtained until 1396. Renfrew had its royal castle, and probably a certain amount of trade in mediæval times; but thereafter Paisley, with its Abbey, quickly drew ahead of Renfrew. Rivalry between the two places sometimes led to feuds.

Paisley Priory, to which the Shropshire monks moved in 1163, was not raised to the status of Abbey until 1219. The original building was destroyed by the English in 1307, during the Wars of Succession, and not rebuilt until the fifteenth century. Abbot Thomas Tervas (1445-59) did much to restore the Abbey. "The body of the kirk fra the bucht stair up he biggit, and put on the ruf and theekit it with sclats, and riggit it with stane, and biggit ane great porcioun of the steple. . . ." Further reconstruction was carried out by a son of Shaw of Sauchie, Abbot George Shaw (1472-99). Unfortunately, the fifteenth-century tower was not built on the soundest of principles, and soon collapsed. So, too, did the new tower built by the last Abbot of Paisley, John Hamilton, the destruction thus accidentally begun being accelerated by followers of that fanatical reformer the Earl of Glencairn, who seized the place in 1544 and again in 1559, when they set fire to it.

Hamilton had by this time left Paisley, having become Archbishop of St. Andrews. After his deposition from the Scottish primacy he had been allowed to retain the Abbey of Paisley in trust for his nephew, Lord Claud Hamilton. It was the elder Hamilton who, at Langside, vainly urged Mary Queen of Scots not to trust to the mercies of Elizabeth of England, and who was finally captured in Dumbarton Castle when it was taken by Crawford of Jordanhill. After having been hanged and quartered, his remains were interred somewhere in the precincts of the Abbey. He was a curious mixture of cunning and ability, a typical example of the powerful political prelate of the early sixteenth century. Though he became the leading churchman in Scotland, he had six illegitimate children by the widowed Lady Stenhouse, daughter of the third Lord Semple.

Meanwhile, the Abbey, of which Lord Claud Hamilton was commendator, had been created into a temporal lordship, and in 1587 Lord Claud became Lord Paisley. But the Abbey passed by purchase from his grandson and heir, first to the Earl of Angus, then to the Earl of Dundonald. In 1764, Dundonald sold it to the Earl of Abercorn, whose family proceeded to feu out the gardens and precincts. Since the setting up of a public committee in 1897 to protect the Abbey and its environs, the main buildings, which pressed in upon it, have been removed.

The present nave is thought to be largely the work of Abbot Thomas Tervas. A pillar in the south aisle carries the Cathcart arms as a memorial to Sir Alan Cathcart's safe return from Spain, bearing the Bruce's heart. Since the Reformation, four restorations have been carried out on Paisley Abbey; in 1788, 1859-62, 1898-1907 and 1919-28. The first restoration merely consisted of the re-roofing of the nave. The newly-appointed minister in 1859 recorded that when he came to the Abbey, the place " was like a charnel house. The burial-ground outside reached above the sill of the windows. The floor was earthen, and you were afraid if you stirred your foot you would rake up some old bones that lay uncomfortably near the surface ".

The architects employed to carry out the most recent restoration were MacGregor Chalmers and Sir Robert Lorimer. They reconstructed the choir, which had been completely destroyed by the collapse of Abbot Hamilton's tower. The Chapel of Youth, re-consecrated in 1936, was originally put up in 1459 to the honour of Paisley's patron saint, St. Mirren, a sixth-century Celtic missionary from Bangor, who set up his cell in the Seed hill district, by the River Cart.

Many illustrious men and women famous in Scotland's story, lie buried in Paisley Abbey: all the High Stewards of Scotland, except the last of them, Robert II, who is buried at Scone; the unlucky and unhappy Robert III; Robert the Bruce's daughter Marjorie, mother of Robert II, who, killed by a fall from her horse while out hunting, had her son taken from her by Cæsarean operation; and John, last Lord of the Isles. When Queen Victoria visited the Abbey in 1888, she caused a slab to be raised over the then unlettered grave of Robert III.

The persecution of the Catholics kept the Knoxians busily occupied for a decade or so after the Reformation. When the supply of Catholics began to run short, the persecution of women alleged to be witches took the place of the older sport. Under an Act of Parliament passed in 1563, witchcraft, sorcery and necromancy became punishable by death. But it was not until the seventeenth century—until Renfrewshire had shared the trials of the "killing times" with its neighbouring counties—that the pursuit of witches became really enthusiastic.

One of the earliest of the Renfrewshire magic-dabblers to face a Presbytery was a man named Dougall. He was accused, among other things, of teaching John Hunter "how to mak his neighbour's corn go back by sowing soor milk amang it at Beltane", and for providing a recipe for the curing of fits which was frowned upon by the medicos of the time.

"Tak pairings fra the nails of the person subject to the fits, some hairs fra his eyebrows, and ithers fra the croon of his heid; hap them in a clout with ane halfpenny, and syne place the parcel in ane certain place—when found, the fits well leive the sufferer, and be transferit to the finder of the said parcel."

The most famous of the Renfrewshire witch-cases was, however, that of Christian Shaw, daughter of the laird of Bargarran, in the parish of Erskine. This young lady suddenly became subject to fits, during which she disgorged "a considerable quantity of hair, folded up straw, unclean hay, wild fowl feathers, with divers kinds of bones of fowls and others, together with a number of coal cinders, burning hot candle grease, gravel stones, etc." In due course, the remarkable Miss Shaw denounced Elizabeth

Anderson and John and James Lindsay as being mainly responsible for her affliction. These people and seventeen other suspects were in due course apprehended. Before the trial, the ministers preached to the judges on the text, "Thou shalt not suffer a witch to live", while the jurors were warned by the prosecuting counsel that if they brought in any other verdict than guilty "they would be accursory to all the blasphemies, apostasies, murders, listures and seductions wherof these enemies of heaven and earth should hereafter be guilty". Naturally the worthy jurors, fearing that their own turn for persecution might come next, were unwilling to risk receiving the burden of so much uncommitted guilt. So they brought in the verdict the ministers desired. On June 9th, 1697, waited on to the last by the ubiquitous ministers, six of the victims were hanged on the Gallow Green in Paisley, and then burnt. The seventh committed suicide in prison.

Miss Shaw ultimately recovered from her fits, and lived to become Mrs. Miller, wife of a Kilmaurs clergyman, who predeceased her. During her widowhood, Mrs. Miller smuggled a twelve-bobbin twisting reel from Holland, then the leading cloth-producing country in Europe, out of which she evolved an apparatus which wove the once-celebrated "Bargarran Thread". She thus became the founder of Paisley's staple industry.

The lie of the land has largely governed Renfrewshire's development since the eighteenth century. Paisley stands strategically at the back of the county's thin coastal strip, and on the edge of the boggy Renfrewshire moors. Since Mrs. Miller produced the first Paisley thread, the Coats and Clark families have developed it until, long since combined, they have made the name of Paisley synonymous with thread throughout the world.

Inevitably, Paisley became an early centre of hand-loom weaving. During the first half of the nineteenth century, the town established a reputation for its silken shawls. Paisley shawls were copies of Kashmir shawls, first introduced into Britain after Napoleon's invasion of Egypt. Similar shawls were, of course, made also in England and in France. But the Paisley weavers lavished their traditional craftsmanship upon them, and until the more sophisticated Paris fashions of the 1870's drove them out of fashion, a Paisley shawl was a part of every Scots bride's trousseau.

Apart from the Abbey, little of Old Paisley has survived. But the town has produced three men of letters, two of whom have won places of permanence in Scottish literature. Robert Tannahill (1774-1810) was born in a weaver's cottage in Castle Street, now marked by a plaque, and at the age of twelve and a half was apprenticed to the weaving trade. But he ettled to be a poet. Modelling his own work on the then contemporary work of Burns, he achieved a certain amount of popular success with his poems and songs. So well known did one of them become that a late nineteenth-century school inspector, on asking a small child who Jesse was, received what was to him the surprising answer: " Please, sir, the flower o' Dunblane."

> The sun has gane down o'er the lofty Ben Lomond,
>    And left the red clouds to preside o'er the scene,
> While lanely I stray, in the calm simmer gloamin',
>    To muse on sweet Jessie, the flower o' Dunblane.
> How sweet is the brier wi' its saft faulding blossom,
>    And sweet is the birk, wi' its mantle o' green;
> Yet sweeter, and fairer, and dear to this bosom,
>    Is lovely young Jessie, the flower o' Dunblane.

Some of Tannahill's verses were set to music by the Paisley organist and minor composer, R. A. Smith (1780-1829). Tannahill's talents, however, were strictly limited, and his health never very good. A meeting with the ebullient and more richly-endowed James Hogg during March 1810 seems to have resulted in the lesser poet becoming acutely aware of his inferiority. Early in the morning of May 17th, Tannahill rose from his bed, hurried out into the night, and drowned himself in the Candren Burn.

The other Paisley man of letters, John Wilson (1785-1854), was born in the High Street. He won early fame as a poet for his artificially elegant " Isle of Palms"; and fame of a wider kind when he was appointed to the Chair of Moral Philosophy at Edinburgh University with no greater qualification than his ability to persuade many men of influence, including Scott, to vote in his favour. As " Christopher North", he played a colourful part in Edinburgh's *Modern Athens* phase, some of his brilliance surviving, slightly tarnished, in his *Noctes Ambrosiannae.*

Not far from Tannahill's statue, on the Abbey Green, stands the statue of Alexander Wilson (1766-1813). Like Tannahill a weaver, Wilson used his rhyming gifts to satirize the weavers' employers, and ultimately found himself in prison for one of his lampoons. On his release, he tried to live by peddling his poems. Half-starved and bitter, he emigrated to America, where he peddled, taught in a school, met the naturalist William Bertram, and made himself into the foremost American ornithologist of his day. Before he died, he had engraved and coloured the plates of most of what became the standard nineteenth-century work on bird life in America, *American Ornithology.*

Renfrew (*rhyn*, ancient Welsh for a point, and *frwd*, current), like Paisley, is now joined to Glasgow. The Knock, where Marjorie Bruce died and King Robert "Bleareye" was "cuttet out of his mother's womb", is surrounded by houses. The ancient Cockles Loan is quite built over. Renfrew reminds most people now that it is the home of many of the world's queer ships (for Lobnitz of Renfrew specialize in vessels designed to perform unusual functions): and the air terminal on which centres Scotland's internal services and the London link.

The road along the coast passes behind Erskine House, so-called because the lands of Erskine parish were once owned by the family who became Earls of Mar. The present house was built in 1828 by Sir Robert Smirke, the designer of the British Museum. Erskine House forms the centre-piece of extensive outbuildings making up the Princess Louise Hospital for Limbless Soldiers. It faces across the Clyde, opposite Bowling, not far from the elegant Erskine Bridge.

Bishopton earns its living through its ordnance works and the Inchinnan tyre factory. Dargarvel, south of the village, was a Maxwell home, dating from 1584. To the south-west, the imitation "old" castle of Formakin was the twentieth-century work of Sir Robert Lorimer, built to satisfy the whim of a Glasgow stockbroker but unfortunately never finished.

The coast road leads down the southern shore of the Firth of Clyde, through the steeply-sloping village of Langbank, to Port Glasgow and Greenock. Both have ancient histories, though fifteenth-century Newark Castle, preserved as an ancient monument in the midst of a press of Port Glasgow shipyards, is almost the only sign of antiquity. It, too, was a Maxwell stronghold.

Up from Greenock, a steep road climbs the Renfrewshire moors. From the brae above the town, the view over the opening Firth is one of the finest in all Scotland. To the north, the peaks of Argyll rise abruptly out of the blue water, their fringes specked with the villas of the coastal townships—what a narrow divide between Highlands and Lowlands the Clyde must once have seemed to the folk of the south bank, ever fearful of Highland raiding-parties! To the west lies Arran, and beyond, the open sea; to the east, the dreich brown moors. High on the top of this moorland stands Kilmacolm. It takes its name from the Gaelic *Cille ma Coluim*, the Cell of Columba. Modern Kilmacolm, however, is no centre of austerity. The parish church has ancient foundations, though the present structure dates only from 1833. The residential arms of the place are made up of prosperous houses, spaciously set out over the hillside. One of them, Windy-hills, was built by Scotland's most famous architect, Charles Rennie Mackintosh (1868-1928), whose only major Scottish monument is the Glasgow School of Art. As with so many Scots in so many walks of life, Mackintosh's forward-seeing greatness was less appreciated in his own country than abroad.

In Duchal Castle, now only a few worn stumps on a peninsula formed by the meeting of Green Water and Blacketty Water—tributaries of the Gryfe—James IV's mistress Margaret Boyd bore him a son who became Archbishop of St. Andrews at the remark-able age of twelve, and who, before dying at Flodden with his father, founded St. Leonard's College. Further up the Gryfe water, Bridge of Weir earns its living by tanning. The Orphan Homes of William Quarrier (1828-1871), a Greenock-born man who built up a prosperous boot and shoe business in Glasgow, lie just outside the village.

Houston, between Kilmacolm and Paisley, is one of the rela-tively few villages in Scotland which still have their Mercat Cross. Effigies of the fifteenth-century laird, Sir John of Houston, and his lady are preserved in the Victorian church. One wing of the late nineteenth-century Houston House is a survival of a seven-teenth-century mansion which an eighteenth-century Macrae owner heired. He pulled down the rest of his property, intending to rebuild it, but, before he could complete the work, got himself involved in an Edinburgh duel, killed his rival, and had to spend the last twenty years of his life in exile. The character of Houston village is currently threatened with envelopment in a " new town ", an obliterating fate which the inhabitants do not regard with much favour.

On one of the two main roads which traverse the moors of Renfrewshire and lead into Ayrshire, the village of Neilston stands in the Loch Libo Gap. Even from the foothills north of the Clyde, the flat-topped Pad of Neilston is a characteristic landmark. One of the most interesting of Scotland's poets, John Davidson (1857-1909), was born at Barrhead, a son of the Free Kirk minister. After teaching in Greenock for a few years, Davidson went south to join the writers and artists who contributed to John Lane's Yellow Book. Although Davidson, in order to earn a meagre living, had to write too much, and write it too quickly, for the quality of his poetry to be sustained, there is enough of merit in his best work to make it certain that eventually a greater meed of fame will be bestowed on his reputation. In his poem " Thirty

Bob a Week ", he anticipated Kipling, without touching the level of tastelessness which the great imperialist author explored so thoroughly in verse:

> *I couldn't touch a stop and turn a screw,*
> *And set the blooming world a-work for me,*
> *Like such as cut their teeth—I hope, like you—*
> *On the handle of a skeleton gold key;*
> *I cut mine on a leek, which I eat it every week:*
> *I'm a clerk at thirty bob as you can see.*
>
> *But I don't allow it's luck and all a toss;*
> *There's no such thing as being starred and crossed;*
> *It's just the power of some to be a boss,.*
> *And the bally power of others to be bossed:*
> *I face the music, sir; you bet I ain't a cur;*
> *Strike me lucky if I don't believe I'm lost!*
>
> *For like a mole I journey in the dark,*
> *A-travelling along the underground*
> *From my Pillar'd Halls and broad Suburban Park,*
> *To come the daily dull official round;*
> *And home again at night with my pipe all alight,*
> *A-scheming how to count ten bob a pound.*
>
> *And it's often very cold and wet,*
> *And my missis stitches towels for a hunks;*
> *And the Pillar'd Halls is half of it to let—*
> *Three rooms about the size of travelling trunks.*
> *And we cough, my wife and I, to dislocate a sigh,*
> *When the noisy little kids are in their bunks.*
>
> *But you never hear her do a growl or whine,*
> *For she's made of flint and roses, very odd;*
> *And I've got to cut my meaning rather fine,*
> *Or I'd blubber, for I'm made of greens and sod:*
> *So p'r'aps we are in Hell for all that I can tell,*
> *And lost and damn'd and served up hot to God.*

Davidson's use of imagery, and his preoccupation with the intellectual content of his work, foreshadowed poetic developments in the between-the-wars period. He became a scientific materialist, denounced the idea of a benevolent God in his two verse plays, *Mammon and his Message* and *The Triumph of*

288

*Mammon,* and drowned himself in a terrible anger when he fancied (wrongly) that he had developed cancer.

Davidson left a curious will, which forbade anyone to write his biography, and prohibited the issue of a selected volume of his best work. Both prohibitions have been violated. Since his output was enormous, and about three-quarters of it around or below his mean average, the good quarter has been dragged with the rest into oblivion. Yet has any other poet so nobly commemorated courage in the face of disillusion as did Davidson in the Epilogue of "The Testament of John Davidson"?

> *My feet are heavy now, but on I go,*
> *My head erect beneath the tragic years.*
> *The way is steep, but I would have it so;*
> *And dusty, but I lay the dust with tears,*
> *Though none can see me weep: alone I climb*
> *The rugged path that leads me out of time—*
> *Out of time and out of all,*
> *Singing yet in sun and rain,*
> *"Heel and toe from dawn to dusk,*
> *Round the world and home again."*

> *Farewell the hope that mocked farewell despair*
> *That went before me still and made the pace.*
> *The earth is full of graves, and mine was there*
> *Before my life began, my resting-place;*
> *And I shall find it out and with the dead*
> *Lie down for ever, all my sayings said—*
> *Deeds all done and songs all sung,*
> *While others chant in sun and rain,*
> *"Heel and toe from dawn to dusk,*
> *Round the world and home again."*

The second main road through Renfrewshire, linking Glasgow and the south, traverses the district of Mearns. Mearns probably derives from the Gaelic *maigh eorna,* a plain of barley, and would originally be the name of a farm, the Scots term for which was "toun". When, during the thirteenth century, another farm was built on the same plain it became the New Toun. Newton Mearns is now a twentieth-century residential suburb of Glasgow. But the Kirk of Mearns dates from the eighteenth century, while ruined Mearns Castle, a Maxwell stronghold, goes back to 1449.

At a minor road junction on the Glasgow-Kilmarnock road an obelisk commemorates Robert Pollok, a secession minister who

piously traced out "The Course of Time" in verse, and published
the result in 1827. Though to-day its didactic blank verse is all
but unreadable, it had a tremendous success in mid-Victorian
times, and ran through numerous editions. This, too, in
spite of the fact that, in Book VIII of the poem, the poet thus
describes critics:

> . . . some, but few
> Were worthy men, and earned renown which had
> Immortal roots; but most were weak and vile.
> And, as a cloudy swarm of summer flies,
> With angry hum and slender lance, beset
> The sides of some huge animal, so did
> They buzz about the illustrious man, and fain,
> With his immortal honour, down the stream
> Of Fame would have descended: but alas!
> The hand of Time drove them away. They were,
> Indeed, a simple race of men, who had
> One only art, which taught them still to say,
> Whate'er was done might have been better done;
> And with this art, not ill to learn, they made
> A shift to live. . .

Although the moorland village of Eaglesham, on a by-road
further east, was built only a century and a half ago, it was from
the start a planned village, its planner the twelfth Earl of
Eglinton. Once it was a weaving village.[1] Now, many of its
cottages have been converted into modern homes. It is one of
the finest Conservation Areas in Lowland Scotland, its one-time
"big hoose", Polnoon Lodge, admirably restored by the former
Renfrew County Council.

[1] Like Kilbarchan, where the National Trust for Scotland has preserved
not only the two-hundred-year-old kirkless steeple containing a bronze effigy of
the sixteenth-century piper Habbie Simpson, celebrated by the poet Robert
Semphill of Beltrees, but also one of the old weavers' cottages.

# L'ENVOI

*Your holiday was of a rarer mood,*
*A dedication loftier than mine;*
*But yet I swear my holiday was good:*
*I went to Glasgow just for auld lang syne.*
    JOHN DAVIDSON (*Fleet Street Eclogues*, 1893).

THE fringes of Glasgow trail over into Renfrewshire; and so my Lowland circuit is complete.   Like Davidson's Fleet Street journalist, Sandy, I come back to Glasgow for auld lang syne; not, however, on holiday, but because it is the city of my birth. Glasgow, with her Victorian splendours, her negative fervours, her bastard lingos, her social schizophrenia, her obstinate, violent mindlessness: Glasgow, to whom, however much I may revile her, I know that I belong.   For the heart is firmly rooted in the place of its first consciousness: and, in this troubled age that has drained away the assurance and the certainty which enabled Glasgow to make herself what she is, it does not do to be too critical of positive values, wherever they may be found, however slight their ultimate significance.   For, to quote Davidson again, " It cannot be said too often that there is no greater illusion than disillusion."

In the Introduction to *The Lowlands of Scotland: Glasgow and the North*, I explained that the urge to make this double-volumed journey of personal re-discovery through Scottish time and space, came upon me in London during the war.   Then and there that same impulse impelled me to write a poem, " The Exiled Heart ". Although it has been fairly widely anthologized and is not free of blemishes the exuberance of youth might overlook though maturer judgment must view with a less partial eye, I quote it by way of leave-taking, because a kindly critic one opined that it expressed an emotion of wide significance in a localized context. That seems to be a proper way to end a book of this sort; and I am sure I could not fashion the same thing again with the plain tools of prose, however hard I tried.

*Two purple pigeons circle a London square*
*as darkness blurs and smudges the shadowless light*
*of a winter evening.   I pause on the pavement and stare*
*at the restless flutter of wings as they gather flight,*
*like rustling silk, and move out to meet the night.*

And my restless thoughts migrate to a Northern city—
fat pigeons stalking the dirty, cobbled quays,
where a sluggish river carries the cold self-pity
of those for whom life has never flowed with ease,
from a granite bridge to the grey Atlantic seas:

The bristling, rough-haired texture of Scottish manners;
the jostled clatter of airless shopping streets
where lumbering tramcars squeal as they turn sharp corners
the boosy smell from lounging pubs that cheats
the penniless drunkards' thirst with its stale deceits:

where my heart first jigged to the harsh and steady sorrow
of those for whom mostly the world is seldom glad;
who are dogged by the flat-heeled footpads steps of to-morrow;
for whom hope is a dangerous drug, an expensive fad
of the cushioned rich, or the young and lovesick mad:

where chattering women in tea-rooms, swaddled with furs,
pass knife-edged gossip like cakes, and another's skirt
is unstitched with sharp words, and delicate, ladylike slurs
are slashed on the not-quite-nice or the over-smart,
till their cigarette smoke is a hazy prickled hurt.

I remember Glasgow, where sordid and trivial breed
from the same indifferent father; his children side
with the mother whose sour breasts taught them first to feed
on her hot, caressing hates that sear and divide,
or swell the itched, distorting bladder of pride.

Yet my casual smile is the tossed-down, beggar's penny
the goaded heart throws out in vain to procure
the comfortable forgetfulness of the many
who lie in content's soft arms, and are safe and sure
in the fabled Grecian wanderers' lotus-lure:

who forget the sullen glare of the wet, grey skies,
and the lashing Northern wind that flicks the skin
where hum-drum proverty's dull and listless eyes
are pressed to the window, hearing the friendly din
of the party, watching the lights and the laughter within.

But oh, I cannot forget!  So I wait, and wonder:
how long will the thinly-dividing window hold?

# L'ENVOI

How long will the dancing drown the terrible anger
of those, the unwanted, who peddle their grief in the cold,
wrapped in their own despair's thick and unkindly fold?

Yet evil is no pattern of places
varied, like terraces from town to town.
A city's charms and individual graces
are but the sculptor's bleak and basic stone,
the photographic face without a frown.

The wound is in this bewildered generation,
unfriended, lost within the Freudian wood,
its compass-point no longer veneration
of that lost God who rewarded the simple and good,
vivid and real, now, only in childhood.

For we, the children of this uncertain age,
breathing its huge disasters and sad airs,
have seen that our warm, humanitarian rage
is impotent to soothe war's animal fears,
and cannot quell the lonely exile's tears. . . .

So the heart, like a wounded seabird, hungers home
to muffled memories on fainter-beating wings
which once soared over history's clouded foam,
to that first shore where each new hero flings
his careful stone, that fades in slow, concentric rings.

# BIBLIOGRAPHICAL NOTE

THIS list is intended purely and simply as a guide to further reading. It does not contain all the books to which the author made reference during the writing of his own books.

County histories are not included. Most of these are now at least fifty years old, and are unreliable and out of date. The basic facts are to be found in F. H. Groome's *Ordnance Gazetteer of Scotland*, which, however, is also more than half a century old. It is more than high time that an up-to-date version of this most valuable work was issued.

V. GORDON CHILDE. *The Pre-History of Scotland.*

V. GORDON CHILDE. *Scotland Before the Scots.*

R. G. COLLINGWOOD AND J. N. L. MYRES. *Roman Britain and the English Settlements.*

SIR GEORGE MACDONALD. *The Roman Wall in Scotland.*

O. G. S. CRAWFORD. *The Topography of Roman Scotland.*

W. F. SKENE. *Celtic Scotland.*

W. DOUGLAS SIMPSON. *The Celtic Church in Scotland.*

DIANA LEATHAM. *Celtic Sunrise.*

COSMO INNES. *Scotland in the Middle Ages.*

W. MACKAY MACKENZIE. *The Medieval Castle in Scotland.*

AGNES MURE MACKENZIE. *Scottish Pageant.*

P. HUME BROWN. *Early Travellers in Scotland.*

EDWIN MUIR. *John Knox.*

STEFAN ZWEIG. *Mary Queen of Scots.*

R. GORE-BROWN. *Lord Bothwell.*

JOHN BUCHAN. *Montrose.*

C. V. WEDGEWOOD. *Montrose.*

A. AND H. TAYLER. *Graham of Claverhouse.*

J. MACKINNON. *The Union of England and Scotland.*

W. C. MACKENZIE. *Andrew Fletcher of Saltoun.*

A. AND H. TAYLER. *1715: The Story of the Rising.*

C. S. TERRY. *The 'Forty-Five.*

ANDREW LANG. *Prince Charles Edward.*

SIR COMPTON MACKENZIE. *Prince Charlie.*

HAROLD W. THOMPSON. *A Scottish Man of Feeling.*

HANS HECHT. *Robert Burns.*

MAURICE LINDSAY. *Robert Burns: The Man; His Work; The Legend.*

J. G. LOCKHART. *Life of Scott.*

JOHN BUCHAN. *Sir Walter Scott.*

UNA POPE-HENESSY. *Scott.*

ELSIE SWANN. *Christopher North.*

JENNIE W. ABERDEIN. *John Galt.*

ALEXANDER CARLYLE. *Autobiography.*

LORD COCKBURN. *Memorials of His Time.*

J. P. MUIRHEAD. *James Watt.*

E. GRANT. *Memoirs of a Highland Lady.*

J. G. FYFE. *Scottish Diaries and Memoirs* (2 vols.).

C. S. TERRY. *The Scottish Parliament 1603-1707.*

R. S. RAIT. *Parliaments of Scotland.*

I. F. GRANT. *The Economic History of Scotland.*

H. GREY GRAHAM. *Social Life in Scotland in the Eighteenth Century.*

MARION LOCHHEAD. *The Scots Household in the Eighteenth Century.*

TOM JOHNSTON. *A History of the Working Classes in Scotland.*

ANDREW LANG. *History of Scotland.*

AGNES MURE MACKENZIE. *History of Scotland.*

COLIN WALKINSHAW. *The Scots Tragedy.*

# BIBLIOGRAPHY

A. DEWAR GIBB. *Scottish Empire.*

SIR JOHN STIRLING MAXWELL. *Shrines and Homes of Scotland.*

McGIBBON AND ROSS. *Castellated and Domestic Architecture of Scotland.*

NEIL MUNRO. *The Brave Days.*

JOHN TONGE. *The Arts in Scotland.*

HENRY FARMER. *A History of Scottish Music.*

IAN FINLAY. *Art in Scotland.*

J. M. REID (editor). *Some Scottish Arts: An Outline.*

AGNES MURE MACKENZIE. *An Historical Survey of Scottish Literature.*

T. F. HENDERSON. *Scottish Vernacular History.*

J. H. MILLER. *A Literary History of Scotland.*

JOHN SPIERS. *The Scots Literary Tradition.*

MAURICE LINDSAY. *The Scottish Renaissance.*

JAMES KINSLEY (editor). *Scottish Poetry: A Critical Survey.*

J. A. BOWIE. *The Future of Scotland.*

J. A. A. PORTEOUS. *The Wealth of Scotland.*

C. A. OAKLEY. *Scottish Industry To-day.*

C. M. GRIEVE ("HUGH MACDIARMID"). *The Golden Treasury of Scottish Poetry.*

MAURICE LINDSAY. *Modern Scottish Poetry: An Anthology of the Scottish Renaissance, 1920-1945.*

G. F. MAINE (editor). *A Book of Scotland.*

# INDEX